"[Margaret Jacobs] has taken the study of these nineteenth and early twentieth century institutionalizing policies in a rewarding new direction. . . . I highly recommend this book to anyone who is interested in indigenous studies, women's studies, and the history of intercultural relations in colonizing situations like the American West."
—*Journal of Arizona History*

"Jacobs gives us a fascinating window into a range of white women reformers and their networks in both sites and shows the commonality of their attitudes toward indigenous women."
—*Pacific Historical Review*

"Jacobs' focus on the role of white women, and specifically the function of maternalism, generates important insights into the interrelationship between race and gender in the creation of the modern white nation. Attention to the specificities of colonial regimes in the different locations of Australia and the American West—revealing the uncanny similarities as well as significant differences—can only enhance our critical understanding."
—*International Journal of Critical Indigenous Studies*

# A GENERATION REMOVED

PUBLICATION SUPPORTED BY

Jewish Federation of Greater Hartford

# A Generation Removed

The Fostering and Adoption of
Indigenous Children in the Postwar World

MARGARET D. JACOBS

University of Nebraska Press | Lincoln and London

Library of Congress Cataloging-in-Publication Data

Jacobs, Margaret D., 1963–
A generation removed: the fostering and adoption of indigenous children in the postwar world / Margaret D. Jacobs.
pages   cm
Summary: "Examination of the post-WWII international phenomenon of governments legally taking indigenous children away from their primary families and placing them with adoptive parents in the U.S., Canada, and Australia"— Provided by publisher.
Includes bibliographical references and index.
ISBN 978-0-8032-5536-4 (hardback: alk. paper)
ISBN 978-0-8032-7656-7 (epub)
ISBN 978-0-8032-7657-4 (mobi)
ISBN 978-0-8032-7658-1 (pdf)
1. Interracial adoption—History. 2. Interethnic adoption—History. 3. Foster children—History. 4. Indigenous children—History. I. Title.
HV875.6.J33 2014
362.734089'97—dc23
2014011395

Set in Huronia Latin Pro by Renni Johnson.
Designed by A. Shahan.

*To Tom*

# CONTENTS

# ILLUSTRATIONS

## TABLE

## ACKNOWLEDGMENTS

This book would not have been possible without the institutional support of the University of Nebraska–Lincoln. I am deeply grateful for the strong backing the university has given me to pursue this project. The American Council of Learned Societies provided me with a much-needed fellowship for 2012–13 to finish the research and writing of this book. Thank you, ACLS, for the gift of time.

I appreciate the many archivists who assisted me at the University of Minnesota Special Collections and Princeton University Library. Thank you, too, to the staff at the National Archives and Records Administration in Washington DC, who helped my research assistant Teresa Houser; and the staff at the National Indian Law Library of the Native American Rights Fund, who were so helpful to my research assistant Kellie Buford. I am grateful to the current staff of the Association on American Indian Affairs (AAIA), especially Lisa Wyzlic, who generously allowed my graduate student Rebecca Wingo to rummage through their old photographs. Thank you, too, to the AAIA for allowing me to use the photographs in this book. In Canada, my kudos to archivists at the Saskatchewan Archives Board and the Archives of Manitoba, and in Australia, thank you to the librarians at the State Library of Victoria and at the Australian Institute for Aboriginal and Torres Strait Islander Studies.

I am grateful to the many scholars I have met on two continents and in three countries while researching this book. Thank you to Julie Davis and Matt Garrett for sharing your unpublished work with me. Thank you, too, to Amy Lonetree for many stimulating intellectual conversations on the topic. My gratitude as well to Pam Sharpe, who convened the workshop "Investigating the Long History of Child Welfare and Adoption: Global,

Historical, and Comparative Perspectives," bringing together a dynamic group of scholars from the United Kingdom, Sweden, Canada, the United States, and Australia in Hobart, Tasmania, in February 2011. Thank you to another group of scholars who came together at the Berkshire Conference on the History of Women at the University of Massachusetts, Amherst, in June, 2011: Laura Briggs, Karen Dubinsky, Shurlee Swain, Denise Cuthbert and Marian Quartly (in absentia), Erica Newman, Allyson Stevenson, and Katrina Jagodinsky.

Thanks especially to Erica Newman for hosting me in grand style in Dunedin, New Zealand, in February and March 2013. I learned so much from Erica, Paerau Warbrick, and other generous scholars at Te Tumu, the School of Maori, Pacific, and Indigenous Studies at the University of Otago. Thank you as well to Tony Ballantyne, Angela Wanhalla, Barbara Brookes, and Judith Collard in the Department of History and to the archivists at the Hocken Library who assisted me with my research. My research on Maori fostering and adoption did not make it into this book but informed my conclusions.

In Saskatoon, my sincere thanks to Allyson Stevenson, who helped guide me to useful sources. Thanks, too, for our many fruitful conversations and good laughs. My gratitude as well to Jim Miller, for sharing his broad knowledge of Canadian Indigenous history and for hosting me at the University of Saskatchewan. I was grateful for the opportunity to meet Jackie Maurice at the Native American and Indigenous Studies Association conference in 2013 and to attend the special event she hosted one evening to start a new healing center for Indigenous people in Saskatoon. Finally, in Saskatoon, I was deeply moved by meeting Robert Doucette, president of the Métis Society of Saskatchewan, and talking with his mother Rita Doucette, who endured incalculable grief at the hands of provincial authorities. I am deeply grateful for their willingness to talk with me in Saskatoon on a rainy morning and to allow me to include their story here. In Winnipeg, my thanks to Adele Perry for her warm hospitality and to dinner companions Jarvis Robin Brownlie and Sherry Farrell Racette. Thanks, too, to Mary Jane McCallum for keeping me up well past my bedtime in a long conversation about our mutual interests. My gratitude as well to Andrew Woolford for inviting me to the Colonial Genocide and Indigenous North America workshop at the University of Manitoba in

September 2012 and for his incisive scholarship on Canadian residential schools and American Indian boarding schools.

In Australia, many thanks to Denise Cuthbert for providing me with a desk away from home at RMIT University in Melbourne in March 2013; to the women's history group at the University of Melbourne; to Kat Ellinghaus, Shurlee Swain, Karen Balcom, Bain Attwood, and Lorenzo Veracini for great conversations about our mutual interests; and to Lynette Russell, whose scholarship, personal writing, and friendship has been a source of inspiration and support. Thank you to Lynette for putting me in touch with Diane Singh, another remarkable advocate for stolen Aboriginal children, who generously shared with me her memories and many sources related to Mollie Dyer, her foster mother. Diane also helped me link up with John Dommett of Connecting Home, who updated me on the latest developments concerning the Stolen Generations in Australia.

This book has been a departure for me in that I was often writing about people who are still alive. It has been an unanticipated pleasure to meet many of these people. I owe a great debt to Steven Unger, one-time staff member of the Association on American Indian Affairs, who met with me on an East Coast visit when I was beginning this project in earnest. Steve put me in touch with Mary Lou Byler, with whom I enjoyed a phone conversation about her work and that of her husband William "Bill" Byler with the AAIA. Steve also connected me with Evelyn Blanchard and Bert Hirsch, a former attorney with the AAIA. My extensive interviews with each of them proved invaluable. I will never forget my four-hour lunch with Evelyn in Taos. Evelyn, in turn, put me in touch with other Indian women activists, including Ada Deer, the Menominee activist and social worker. I have been teaching about Ada's activism in my women's history classes for years, so it was a particular delight to speak with her in person. Like a giddy teenager reluctant to wash her hand after shaking hands with a pop star, I intend never erasing Ada's messages from my cell phone.

I have talked more informally with many other remarkable advocates for Indian child welfare, including Walter Echo Hawk, Marc Tilden, and David Gover of the Native American Rights Fund; Robbie McEwen of Nebraska Appleseed; and Judi gaiashkibos, the dynamic executive director of the Nebraska Commission on Indian Affairs. Thanks to these individuals for taking time away from their important work to teach me.

It seems, too, that nearly everyone I tell about my project has a personal connection to it of one kind or another. My thanks go to the many people—adoptees, adoptive families, and birth families—who have shared their personal stories with me. In many cases they have wished to remain anonymous. Their perspectives have deeply informed this book even though they may not agree with all my conclusions.

I have been blessed with several remarkable graduate student research assistants as I have worked on this book. Many thanks to Kellie Buford, Mikal Brotnov Eckstrom, Teresa Houser, and Susana Geliga, all with their own gifts. A special thank you to Rebecca Wingo (and her sister Ellen), who helped me find photographs at the last hour. Thank you, too, to my colleagues Tim Borstelmann, who oriented me to the post–World War II era; Will Thomas, who is always up for a talk about research and writing; and Dawne Curry and Katrina Jagodinsky, who read parts of the book and offered many helpful suggestions.

I am fortunate to publish this book with the University of Nebraska Press and to have the guidance of Matt Bokovoy, their Indigenous Studies acquisitions editor, whose incisive comments and careful editing have made this a much better book.

The book has been enriched as well through the insights of two close friends, Chantal Kalisa and Isabel Velázquez. Thank you for listening as I thought aloud about this book. Finally, I thank Tom, Cody, and Riley, who have taught me the most about what it means to care and be cared for.

# A NOTE ON TERMS

There is no ideal term or agreed upon terminology for the original inhabitants of North America and Australia. I have used tribal nation designations in their original languages when possible. I use American Indian and Native American interchangeably when making more general references for the United States. I refer to Aboriginal people in Australia. Canada's Indian Act created four categories of people with Indigenous ancestry: treaty Indians, non-treaty Indians, Métis, and Inuit. I describe these in detail in chapter 6. I refer to people of Indigenous heritage in Canada as First Nations and Métis or simply Indigenous. When making broad global references to the first inhabitants of these three modern nations, I use the term Indigenous people.

Historically, many settlers referred to groups of American Indians as "tribes." This term often connoted primitiveness, so many American Indian groups have preferred to call themselves "nations" to designate their sovereign status. They point out that the United States negotiated treaties with them as one nation to another. The status of Indian groups in relation to the U.S. government is complicated. I sometimes use the term *nation*, or *group*, but I also use the word *tribe*. I want to reclaim the term as a valuable way to designate the hundreds of unique cultural groupings of Indigenous people, all of whom have distinct languages and religions that deserve recognition and respect.

I use the term *white* to refer to descendants of Europeans living in the United States, Canada, and Australia. I fully realize that this is an invented racial term and concept that settlers created to distinguish themselves from Indigenous people and some other immigrants. Whiteness conferred great privileges, including entitlement to land, authority to govern, and full citizenship. I sometimes refer to non-Indian, non-Aboriginal, or non-Indigenous people when I wish to include more than just whites.

I use the names Bureau of Indian Affairs or BIA throughout the manuscript. The United States government set up this agency in 1824 and originally called it the Office of Indian Affairs. Many of its employees referred to it as the "Bureau." In 1947 it formally became the BIA. For clarity, I simply call it the BIA for all time periods.

# ABBREVIATIONS

| | |
|---|---|
| AACP | American Academy of Child Psychiatry |
| AAIA | Association on American Indian Affairs |
| AAL | Australian Aborigines' League |
| ACCA | Aboriginal Child Care Agency (Australia) |
| ACPA | Aboriginal Child Placement Agency (Australia) |
| ADC | Aid to Dependent Children (United States) |
| AFSC | American Friends Service Committee |
| AICCA | Aboriginal and Islander Child Care Agency (Australia) |
| AICPDP | American Indian Child Placement Development Program |
| AIM | Adopt Indian Métis program (Saskatchewan, Canada) |
| AIM | American Indian Movement (United States) |
| ARENA | Adoption Resource Exchange of North America |
| AWB | Aborigines Welfare Board (New South Wales, Australia) |
| BIA | Bureau of Indian Affairs (United States) |
| CAR | Council for Aboriginal Rights (Australia) |
| CAS | Children's Aid Society (Canada) |
| CWLA | Child Welfare League of America |
| DAA | Department of Aboriginal Affairs (Australia) |
| DIA | Department of Indian Affairs (Canada) |
| FSI | Federation of Saskatchewan Indians |
| FSIN | Federation of Saskatchewan Indian Nations |
| GAO | General Accounting Office (United States) |
| HEW | Department of Health, Education, and Welfare (United States) |
| IAP | Indian Adoption Project (United States) |
| ICWA | Indian Child Welfare Act (United States) |
| IEC | Indian and Eskimo Association (Canada) |
| IHS | Indian Health Service (United States) |
| ISPP | Indian Student Placement Program (United States) |

LDS     Church of Jesus Christ of Latter Day Saints
NAIWA  North American Indian Women's Association
NCAI   National Congress of American Indians
NSW    New South Wales
OEO     Office of Economic Opportunity (United States)
PL-280  Public Law 83–280 (United States)
REACH  Resources for Adoption of Children (Saskatchewan, Canada)
SNAICC  Secretariat of National Aboriginal and Islander Child Care (Australia)
SNWM  Saskatchewan Native Women's Movement
TRC     Truth and Reconciliation Commission
VACCA  Victorian Aboriginal Child Care Agency (Victoria, Australia)
VISTA   Volunteers in Service to America

Little did I know when I traveled to Minneapolis in May 2009 to attend the Native American and Indigenous Studies Association Conference that my life would take an unplanned turn. I had come to participate in a panel about the history of American Indian boarding schools, Canadian Indian residential schools, and Homes for Australian Aboriginal children. When I began my presentation, I noticed in the audience an older man with silver hair and thick bangs. I caught my breath. He was Simon Ortiz, the Acoma Pueblo writer. I had read much of his poetry, and I used to attend his readings when I lived in New Mexico. I had never met him in person; nor did I share his Native American ancestry. But I had long felt a particular connection to him. Both he and my Uncle Stanley had been patients at Fort Lyon Veterans Hospital near Las Animas, Colorado. I remember the long car ride there as a child with my mother and grandmother, the scenery getting bleaker and bleaker as we sped farther east out onto the plains from the Rocky Mountains.

Ortiz wrote *from Sand Creek* based on his stint at Fort Lyon. It had been the staging post from which Colonel John Chivington and the Colorado Territory Militia had carried out a massacre of up to 163 Cheyennes and Arapahoes at their peaceful encampment on Sand Creek, just about forty miles away. Two-thirds of the victims were women and children. Ortiz's book of poems linked the 1864 massacre to the struggles he and other Native American veterans experienced in the hospital and its surrounding community a hundred years later. Even though I grew up in Colorado, I never learned of this massacre until after I moved away.

These thoughts gusted through my mind as I prepared to deliver my presentation. What was this esteemed writer doing here at my panel? And what would he think of my paper? I took a deep breath and plunged into my presentation. After my co-panelists delivered their papers, Ortiz immediately lifted his hand. We called on him first. He said, "I've published nineteen books, and yet I've never written about my boarding school experience. Why is it that we American Indians have not come to terms with this?" Other Indigenous members of the audience piped up. We all puzzled over why both Australia and Canada had launched inquiries into and delivered formal apologies for their nations' forced removal of Indigenous children but the United States had not.

When I attended this conference, I thought I was done writing about Indigenous child removal. I had recently published *White Mother to a Dark Race: Settler Colonialism, Maternalism, and the Removal of Indigenous Children in the American West and Australia, 1880–1940.* I had collected material on Indigenous child welfare in the late twentieth century, but I hadn't had room for it in *White Mother*. I carefully filed this material away for some later day or for some other future researcher. I thought instead I would start research about something less troubling. I had spent the summer of 2008 in an Australian winter to start a new comparative project on Indigenous dance. That would be the perfect antidote, I thought, to studying the trauma of child removal.

Simon Ortiz's question and the conversation that followed, however—which I described in my journal as "powerful, rich, and moving"—reminded me that there was so much more to the story. For weeks and months after the conference, I felt haunted by the discussion Simon Ortiz had conjured up. The subject seized me and refused to let go, and it gradually elbowed my dance project out of the way. One day I reorganized my study. I put all my dance files in a box and shoved the heavy carton into a corner. I arranged all my Indigenous child welfare books and files in a prominent place on my shelves. This book had begun.

# INTRODUCTION

Matt and Melanie Capobianco appeared on the popular daytime television talk show *Dr. Phil* on October 18, 2012, to bring their case to the public. The white middle-class South Carolina couple had sought to adopt a newborn, Veronica, with the consent of her unwed mother in 2009. Authorities served notice of the adoption to Veronica's father, Dusten Brown, four months later, less than a week before he was to be deployed for military service in Iraq. He petitioned to gain custody of his daughter. After almost two years of legal wrangling, the family court ruled and the South Carolina Supreme Court affirmed that Veronica belonged with her father, and she had moved to Oklahoma to live with Brown in January 2011. The reason? Dusten Brown is a member of the Cherokee nation, and the provisions of the 1978 Indian Child Welfare Act (ICWA) require that where possible Indian children should grow up in Indian families. Dr. Phil, his guests, and audience members expressed outrage at the awarding of custody of Veronica to her father and deep sympathy for the adoptive couple on live television that day in 2012. The Capobiancos and their supporters argued that ICWA is a racist law that undermines the best interests of children like Veronica.[1]

The U.S. Supreme Court agreed to review the case, known as *Adoptive Couple v. Baby Girl*, in early 2013, and they ruled in favor of the Capobiancos in a 5-4 decision in June that year. They remanded the decision to the South Carolina Supreme Court to reconsider the proper placement of Veronica. The court soon required that Brown return Veronica to the Capobiancos. Brown fought the order for several months but finally and reluctantly gave up his daughter to the South Carolina couple in September 2013.[2] Dr. Phil, his guests, and his audience were surely elated at the outcome. They had belittled the biological father who wanted to raise his daughter. They had castigated the tribe who wished this little girl to grow up as a citizen of their nation. Dr. Phil had created a compelling television show by demonizing Dusten Brown and the Cherokees and casting the Capobiancos as innocent victims of an outdated piece of legislation. But had he done justice to the story?

Media coverage of the controversial case failed to reveal the full back story of ICWA, an act meant to redress the long history of forcible child removal that American Indian families had suffered for generations. Many Indian families who lost their children suffered trauma equal to that of the Capobiancos, but their stories have rarely garnered much public attention. Consider the story of Rosebud Sioux mother Bernadine Brokenleg, who had married Bernard Butts, a white machinist, in California. Brokenleg soon bore a daughter, Tiffany, but the marriage was troubled. According to some reports, Butts beat his wife and had not yet terminated an earlier marriage. Brokenleg annulled her marriage to Butts when Tiffany was just eighteen months old and returned to South Dakota to live on the Rosebud Reservation in 1972. When Tiffany was three years old, Brokenleg allowed her former husband and his parents to take her daughter for what she thought was a brief vacation. Instead the Butts grandparents absconded with Tiffany to Kermit, Texas, and refused to return the child to her mother. Brokenleg visited Tiffany in Texas several times between 1973 and 1975, while working as a secretary, teacher's aide, and part-time tutor of college students in South Dakota. She spoke with Tiffany regularly on the phone, sent money for her support, and consistently insisted that she wanted Tiffany back.[3]

The Butts grandparents filed a petition in Winkler County District Court in Texas in 1975 to gain full custody of Tiffany and terminate Brokenleg's parental rights. The judge ruled in favor of the Buttses, declaring that Brokenleg had left Tiffany in the possession of her paternal grandparents "without expressing an intent to return" and "at no time provided adequate support" for Tiffany while she lived in Texas. He awarded full custody of Tiffany to the Butts grandparents and then terminated Brokenleg's parental rights altogether, asserting that "it would be detrimental and would endanger the physical and emotional well-being" of Tiffany to "return her to her mother's custody to be reared on the Indian Reservation."[4]

Brokenleg appealed the case to the Texas Court of Civil Appeals in 1977 with the help of an Indian advocacy organization, the Association on American Indian Affairs (AAIA), and its Indian family defense lawyer, Bertram Hirsch. Hirsch argued that his client was a fit parent who should have her child restored to her custody. Tribal officials and a psychiatrist testified that Brokenleg was a competent and caring mother who nurtured her child in a healthy and happy environment. The judge, however, focused on economic factors. He contrasted Brokenleg's meager earnings—a salary of $2.30 an hour as a teacher's aide plus $200 per month as a tutor—to the Butts's combined income of $2,000 per month. He noted that in Texas, "Tiffany has her own bedroom. She is doing well in school and attends church regularly. She is well-fed and clothed and receives good medical attention when needed." The judge claimed that although Brokenleg "testified that she had adequate housing for her daughter on the Reservation, [the Buttses] said the house was dirty and without adequate bathroom facilities which resulted in the need for an outhouse, and that when Tiffany was bathed, the dogs were in and out of the water." "Undoubtedly," the judge ruled, "the evidence shows greater stability in the home of the grandparents."[5] Citing precedent, the judge concluded that "a parent-child relationship may be terminated even though there is no proof or finding of unfitness on the part of the parent," when it is "in the best interest of the child." He refused to go this far, however, and queried, "does the fact that the [grandparents] have a more stable home . . . mean [Tiffany] should have all relationships with her mother terminated?" He left standing the earlier decision that Tiffany should live with her grandparents but overturned the termination of Brokenleg's parental rights.[6]

Outside Indian circles, Brokenleg's case gained little public attention, let alone the kind of sympathy the Capobiancos garnered. The AAIA publicized Brokenleg's case in their newsletter, *Indian Family Defense*, and *People* magazine covered the story in a brief article in 1979 shortly after Hirsch sought to appeal Brokenleg's case to the U.S. Supreme Court. While waiting to find out if the high court would consider her case, Brokenleg told a reporter, "The rest of my life depends on this decision. . . . The worst now is the waiting and the emptiness of being without your own child." Brokenleg despaired, too, that Tiffany was "losing what she is. . . . You have to live your Indianness to respect it." Unlike the Capobiancos, Brokenleg did not get her day in court or on daytime television. The Supreme Court declined to hear her case, and Tiffany stayed with her grandparents until she came of age. Then, according to Hirsch, she immediately returned to live with her mother on the Rosebud Reservation.[7]

Brokenleg's experience was not exceptional among American Indian women in the 1960s and 1970s. Many faced social workers and judges who believed their families to be inadequate and their communities to be unfit places to raise a child. Thousands suffered the loss of their children through one means or another. And American Indian children like Tiffany experienced removal from their families at rates far higher than other American children in the second half of the twentieth century. The per capita foster care rate for Indian children in 1976 in Brokenleg's home state of South Dakota was *twenty-two times* higher than for non-Indian children. The AAIA estimated that *between 25 and 35 percent* of Indian children had been separated from their families.[8] This was nothing less than an Indian child welfare crisis. State authorities institutionalized some of these children, but they promoted the fostering and adoption of thousands more in non-Indian homes. The breakup of Indian families and loss of children became an all-too-familiar and, indeed, defining feature of modern Indian life. As Marla Jean Big Boy (Oglala Lakota), an attorney, explained on a radio program recently, "This was just part of every native family's history."[9] Yet few non-Indian Americans were aware of this phenomenon then or know anything about it today.

Explanations for this Indian child welfare crisis diverged sharply. Government authorities and social workers asserted that Indian families and communities exhibited such a degree of social dysfunction that it was necessary to apprehend large numbers of Indian children in order to protect them from neglect and a grim future. These officials claimed they were making necessary interventions to uphold "the best interests of the child." Many Indigenous critics claimed, by contrast, that social workers and court officials were using ethnocentric and middle-class criteria to remove Indian children unnecessarily from their families and communities. They charged officials with committing "cultural genocide." Activists, social workers, psychologists, sociologists, and legal scholars became polarized over the issue in the 1960s and 70s, and today the issue still generates fierce controversy on blogs, talk radio, newspapers, and television shows like *Dr. Phil.*

The Baby Veronica case made national headlines and sparked a much-needed public debate on the issue for a brief time. But other 2013 Supreme Court rulings eclipsed the case. The high court overturned the Defense of Marriage Act and key provisions of the 1965 Voting Rights Act in the same session, and these dramatic rulings captured the majority of media attention. As Americans debated the diverging implications of these rulings for gay equality and African American rights, the story of Veronica receded from the headlines. Only Indian media continued to offer comprehensive coverage of the case.[10] Yet the Baby Veronica case, and the history of the Indian child welfare crisis behind it, is every bit as relevant to equality and rights for all Americans as the other two landmark rulings.

The story of this crisis is not just an American Indian story either, but a profoundly American one. For every Indian family who lost a child to foster care or adoption, another non-Indian American family gained a son or daughter, a brother or sister. The Bureau of Indian Affairs (BIA) and state government agencies enlisted thousands of American families in their plan to end Indian dependence on government assistance, to solve the so-called Indian problem. Many non-Indians came to believe that the best way to help impoverished Indian communities was to take care of their children through separating them from their families and bringing them up in middle-class households. They regarded the fostering and adoption of Indian children as a supreme act of compassionate benevolence that would herald a new age of reconciliation between American Indians and descendants of those who had colonized them. As one woman put it in an anti-ICWA letter to Congress in 1977, "Surely the type of white parents who are glad to adopt an Indian child are the type who would have the child's best interests at heart. Furthermore, I think [adoption] is an encouraging effort towards unifying Indians and whites. Much of this individual assistance is going to be necessary to raise children of Indian heritage to be leaders of their own people."[11] Such sentiments cast white families in the dual roles of valiant rescuers of benighted Indian children and harbingers of racial harmony. American Indian families and communities saw it differently. They experienced heartbreak and trauma and deeply mourned the loss of their children. They saw state intervention into their families and the placement of their children in non-Indian families as one of the most egregious violations of their rights. Their campaign to reclaim the care of Indian children undermined the image of good-hearted American families and led to the uncomfortable question: Have white Americans been complicit in an unjust practice? The history of the Indian child welfare crisis is inescapably an American story—but a paradoxical one with competing narrators, tangled plot lines, and a cast of complex characters. The moral of this story depends on who is telling the story.

This history of Indian child removal, fostering, and adoption is not just an American story but also a chapter in a larger global and transnational epic. Indigenous people in Canada and Australia endured similar histories of child removal and faced parallel child welfare crises in the post–World War II era. These phenomena have become major public issues in those nations, however. Indigenous activism supported by legal advocacy and historical scholarship eventually led to introspective national dialogues on Indigenous child removal in Canada and Australia. Government authorities in both countries committed resources to investigate Indigenous charges of wrongdoing, which led in Australia to the National Inquiry into the Separation of Aboriginal and Torres Strait Islander Children from their Families, in the 1990s, and in Canada to the Indian Residential School Settlement Agreement and the Truth and Reconciliation Commission, in the first two decades of the twenty-first century. Prime ministers in both nations issued formal apologies in 2008 to Indigenous peoples for past policies that involved the removal of their children. The governments of Canada and Australia still violate the rights of Indigenous peoples, but both nations have generated a crucial public debate about their histories as settler colonial nations and the rights and role of Indigenous minorities in modern industrial liberal democracies.[12]

The United States, on the other hand, has never had the kind of painful, though productive, public discussion that has taken place in Canada and Australia. Imagine if Dr. Phil devoted air time to the experiences of Bernadine Brokenleg and other Indian families who endured the greatest indignity of all—the loss of their children. Listening to the stories of Indian families in the 1960s and 1970s would compel Americans to grapple with the U.S. government's role as a settler colonial power and to examine the legacies of its colonialism. Americans would confront the persistent injustices that still bedevil Indian communities and ponder the place of modern Indian nations within the borders of the United States. Through this historical reckoning, we might move toward a genuine reconciliation based on a recognition of past wrongs and a respect for Indian peoples' rights.

# PROLOGUE

The widespread removal of Indian children by government authorities and their frequent adoption in white families grew out of a particular historical moment after World War II. Yet this phenomenon also had many earlier precedents. American Indians, as a group of colonized peoples, had endured heightened levels of intervention into their families since at least the late nineteenth century.

From around 1880 up to the 1930s, lawmakers and social reformers had devised an elaborate system of boarding schools to which they removed thousands of Indian children for at least a portion of their childhood. Many Indian families resisted the removal of their children, especially after disease, malnutrition, and unsanitary conditions took the lives of large numbers of boarding school pupils. Government authorities often turned to withholding rations or military force to wrest children away from their families. The schools brutalized not only families but often the children in their care as well. They sought to strip the children of their earlier associations through military-style regimens, uniforms, Christianization, instruction in English, and work details. Authorities instructed children for only half of each day; children carried out manual labor for the rest of the day, sometimes for the school and at other times for local white families.[1] Canada's and Australia's Indigenous children had suffered from similar removal and institutionalization in the decades before World War II. Canada had in fact modeled its Indian residential schools on the U.S. boarding schools.[2]

Paradoxically, the boarding school scheme had originated among a group of humanitarian Americans who were appalled at violent policies toward Indian peoples. The U.S. military and territorial, state, and local militias as well as vigilante groups of white settlers committed a series of massacres against Indian peoples throughout the nineteenth century, such as the attack at Sand Creek in 1864 that Simon Ortiz immortalized.[3] These massacres particularly targeted non-combatants, as in the Marias Massacre of 1870, when the U.S. Army killed 173 Blackfeet or Piegans in Montana Territory, the vast majority women and children.[4] Massacre leaders often justified their attacks by claiming to be acting in self-defense or as retribution for crimes committed by Indians. California militiamen exterminated 240 Yuki Indians on the Eel River in 1859 in retaliation for the killing of one prized stallion (and by some accounts three cows) owned by a local white settler.[5]

Many Americans were horrified by these extermination campaigns against Indian peoples. In 1881 white middle-class reformer Helen Hunt Jackson compiled copious documentation of such atrocities in *A Century of Dishonor*.[6] She and other influential reformers with the Women's National Indian Association and the Indian Rights Association shamed the American government into moving from a military strategy of conquering Indian tribes and containing them on reservations to a domestic policy of assimilation. Officials and reformers claimed that the boarding schools offered a humanitarian alternative to military conquest that rescued children from hardship and provided them with an education.

But the new policy of assimilation had more in common with the military policies of the past than reformers were willing to admit. Both outright violence and benevolent paternalism served the settler colonial goals of the United States: the complete transfer of all land from its original occupants to the new settler population. Many colonial ventures, such as those of the Dutch in Indonesia or the British in India, centered on extracting natural resources through mobilizing the labor of local people. Europeans remained a small, albeit powerful, minority in such colonies. Settler colonies such as the United States, Canada, and Australia, by contrast, rested on European settlers becoming a demographic majority through "a logic of elimination" aimed at the Indigenous population.[7] It is easy to see how this logic played out in the nineteenth-century American West as the U.S. military, state and territorial militias, and local vigilante groups took up arms against Indigenous peoples. Many settlers and state agents, in their quest for land, turned to the physical extermination of Indigenous peoples who stood in their way.

It is less obvious how the new ethos of humanitarianism and benevolence, as enacted in the boarding school policy, extended the logic of elimination. The policy was more subtle, but it had devastating effects on Indian families and communities. By removing children and reeducating them in the schools, authorities still sought to eliminate Indigenous peoples—but now through cultural assimilation. They primarily designed the schools to sever the cords that connected Indian children to their families, tribes, and lands. If Indigenous people assimilated into American society, they would no longer exist as a distinctive group that could lay claim to land and contest the legitimacy of settler authorities.

The institutionalization of Indigenous children caused undue trauma within families and threatened the very existence of Indigenous communities. The viability of Indigenous cultures depended on rearing new generations of children who understood, were invested in, and carried on their groups' practices and knowledge. Authorities took children at the very time they would have been socialized into their clans' religious ceremonies and cultural practices, so Indigenous communities found it difficult to sustain their languages and knowledge systems. Generations of removed children often never learned the skills of caring for children that had been developed over centuries within their communities. Nor, as inmates in institutions, did they truly learn mainstream American methods of parenting either.[8] These multi-generational histories of child removal left a painful legacy for American Indians and provided precedents for renewed government intervention into Indian families.

For Indigenous peoples, however, family remained an important bulwark against state intervention. No matter the official government policy, many Indigenous families sought to follow their customary ways of raising children. Their distinctive style of caregiving functioned in part as an act of cultural preservation and resistance to assimilation. Indigenous communities defined family broadly and designated many caregivers beyond the biological mother and father, particularly grandparents. In many matrilineal Indigenous cultures, a mother's brother played the fatherly role to his nephews and nieces, and a child might consider all his or her maternal aunts as mothers. Women took primary responsibility for the care of children. In contrast to many societies, Indigenous communities highly valued women's caregiving, and motherhood endowed women with social and cultural authority in the entire community.[9]

Active resistance to child removal arose from some unexpected places in the twentieth century. Some boarding school students gained the tools to strike at the ideological edifice on which authorities had built the schools. Gertrude Bonnin, or Zitkala-Ša, a Nakota or Yankton Sioux, exposed the harshness of child removal and institutionalization in a serialized memoir in the *Atlantic Monthly* in 1900.[10] Bonnin and others established the Society of American Indians in 1911 to advocate for Indian rights and a greater say in policymaking, but the group often divided over assimilation policy.[11]

Many non-Indian Americans had become enamored with Native American cultures in the 1920s, and some of them launched a campaign with American Indians to challenge government assimilation policies. Reformer John Collier became particularly active and effective in exposing the corruption and cruelty that had become endemic to much Indian policy. As a result of his critique, the government commissioned a formal investigation from the Brookings Institution. It sent out a team of ten experts led by Lewis Meriam to survey and report on conditions. The group published their findings in *The Problem of Indian Administration*, often called the Meriam Report, in 1928. This document reserved some of its harshest criticisms for the boarding schools. The survey team deemed the schools' "provisions for the care of the Indian children" as "grossly inadequate" and condemned school officials' use of cruel discipline and punishment. Meriam and the other authors also lambasted the ways in which the schools separated children from their families, pointing out that child removal "largely disintegrates the family and interferes with developing normal family life."[12]

During the Great Depression and World War II Indian people found a respite from the unrelenting intervention of the BIA in their families. President Franklin Roosevelt had appointed the upstart John Collier to serve as the commissioner of Indian Affairs. Through the Indian Reorganization Act of 1934, Collier and the BIA enabled tribes to exercise limited self-determination, and he sought to open more day schools while shuttering some of the boarding schools. Many of Collier's policies were paternalistic and short-sighted, but his administration offered Indian people spaces to maneuver, and he envisioned a nation in which Indian people could still exist as Indians on their own terms.[13] Indigenous people in Canada and

Australia had some non-Indigenous allies in the same time period, but they never achieved the types of government reform that occurred under Collier's administration in the United States.

Government support for limited Indian self-determination in the 1930s and during World War II came to an abrupt end in 1945 as Congress finally cut funding for key aspects of the Indian New Deal and achieved John Collier's ouster. The so-called Indian problem seemed alive and well to government administrators. The war had not lifted most Indian people out of the poverty of the Great Depression, as it had done for so many other Americans. The horrors of war and the atrocities of the Holocaust led to international concern with human rights and a new era of liberal humanitarianism. Indian families seemed to be out of step with the dawning age of affluence and in need of new liberal benevolence. The federal government returned to an assimilative mode and turned its attention once again to Indian families, but now it devised a new strategy.

# A GENERATION REMOVED

# PART ONE

# Taking Care of American Indian Children

Recently, when I was at my annual check-up, my health care provider asked me about what I was writing. I told her about my research, and she disclosed that in her work at a low-income clinic, she meets Indian families all the time who face the loss of their children. But what can be done, she asked me, when alcoholism rates on reservations in Nebraska are over 90 percent? This shocking number didn't sound right to me, but I didn't have any hard data on hand about American Indian rates of alcohol use and abuse.

Later I looked up the latest research. My provider and most Americans might be surprised to learn that overall, American Indians drink *less* than other Americans and are actually more likely to abstain altogether. And rates of heavy alcohol use among Indians are comparable to those of white Americans. According to the report, *2010 National Survey on Drug Use and Health*, only 36.6 percent of American Indians or Alaska Natives had used alcohol in the past month, compared with 56.7 percent of whites. The report characterized 17.9 percent of American Indians as binge alcohol users and 6.9 percent as heavy alcohol users. Among whites, 16.3 percent were binge alcohol users, and 7.7 percent were heavy alcohol users. (The Americans with the highest rates of alcohol abuse are college students; 42.2 percent were binge drinkers, and 15.6 percent were heavy drinkers.)[1] Despite such statistics, however, the public perception persists that Indian communities suffer from rampant alcohol abuse.

Media reports have shaped and reinforced the notion that American Indian families and communities are hopelessly dysfunctional as a result of out-of-control alcoholism. In ABC's broadcast of "A Hidden America: Children of the Plains" in October 2011, journalist Diane Sawyer toured the Pine Ridge Reservation in South Dakota and detailed alcohol abuse, dilapidated and overcrowded housing, high suicide rates, unwed teen pregnancy, and unemployment.[2] This is virtually all that non-Indians learn about Indian people. Little wonder, then, that my health care provider and many other Americans believe that Indian communities are beyond hope.

I have visited quite a few reservations and other Indian communities over the years: the Tolowa ranchería in northern California, Zuni Pueblo and Taos Pueblo, and the Wind River, Navajo, Hopi, Mescalero Apache, and Omaha reservations. And in Lincoln, Nebraska, I've gone to the Lincoln Indian Center on occasion. From what I have seen and taken part in, life seems to be proceeding in Indian communities in the same mundane ways that it does in other places that I have lived and visited. Friends and family get together and share meals, community members gather for ceremonies, governing councils deliberate, children attend school and play sports, teachers instruct children. Indian communities assuredly have more than their share of hardship, tragedy and controversy, but they also provide spaces where Indian families can sustain their distinctive languages and cultures.

Most Americans have never witnessed or shared in the everyday life of Indian people, nor have they been exposed to the rich ceremonial culture that persists among Indians. Few have had the opportunity to visit Indian communities, whether an urban Indian center or a remote reservation. Instead they rely on media to give them a picture of Indian life, and this picture is usually grim. For most Americans, the glass of modern Indian life is empty of all but pain, suffering, and misery. But what if we saw it as half full? Admittedly, we would see sorrow and hardship—but also pulsing life, joy, and beauty.

# CHAPTER 1

# The Bureaucracy of Caring for Indian Children

Adam Fortunate Eagle was five years old when his father died, leaving eight young children without his financial support during the Great Depression. Adam's mother sent the six oldest children, including Adam, from their home on the Red Lake Indian Reservation in Minnesota to Pipestone Indian Boarding School in the southwestern part of the state. She later married a Sisseton-Wahpeton man from the Lake Traverse Reservation and moved to South Dakota. Adam came home nearly every summer to Red Lake, where he and his siblings stayed with various Chippewa relatives until his teen years, when he went to live with his mother, by now living in Oregon. Adam later discovered that many other children at Pipestone had similar experiences; one or more parents had died, desperate financial hardship haunted their families, and sometimes a rupture had occurred in family relationships.[1]

Pipestone was but one of dozens of boarding schools that the Bureau of Indian Affairs had originally set up in the late nineteenth or early twentieth century to solve the so-called Indian problem through assimilation. Their champions posited that by intervening in Indian family life and removing Indian children to institutions, the government could transform Indian dependents into self-sufficient members of American society. Thousands of Indian children up to the 1930s experienced removal—often coercive—from their families and communities and endured institutionalization in one of the dozens of boarding schools for at least a portion of their childhood.[2]

The boarding schools failed miserably in their goal of ending the "Indian problem." Instead the schools triggered many unforeseen consequences. For one, Indian families like that of Adam Fortunate Eagle had come to use boarding schools as a means to supplement the family care of children. Some indigent families sent their children to the schools to make sure they received adequate meals, shelter, and clothing. By the mid-twentieth century the BIA believed the boarding schools had become just one more aspect of the government's largesse that sustained rather than ended Indian dependence.

The federal government readily sought to shed its responsibility for the care of Indian children like Adam by the early 1950s, and many states seized the chance to have greater control over the affairs of Indian people within their borders. The BIA closed Pipestone Boarding School in 1953, and the state of Minnesota took over child welfare services for Indian children. By 1957 the state was providing assistance to 1,919 Indian children. The Minnesota Indian population accounted for just 0.5 percent of the total state population, but Indian children made up 9.2 percent of the caseload of child welfare services. Of these cases, just under half still lived with their parents, while the state had placed the other children in foster homes or institutions.[3]

The question of who should care for Indian children, how they should do so, and more importantly, who should *pay* for this care, remained a murky and contested jurisdictional issue. The state of Minnesota found itself in a quandary. Suddenly they needed to fund services to Indian children that had been borne by the federal government through the BIA's boarding schools or its Social Services program. The BIA contracted with the state of Minnesota to provide child welfare services for Indian children, but state legislators asked Congress and the Department of Interior to appropriate more funds to the state to provide "a necessary and valuable service to Indian children in need."[4] From the 1950s on, state and federal bureaucrats wrangled over who should bear the cost for Indian children who came under state care.

The BIA devised a solution in 1958 that appealed to both federal cost cutters and cash-strapped state agencies: the Indian Adoption Project. This project promoted the placement of Indian children in non-Indian adoptive families; it looked to the ultimate private sector to take over the expense of raising Indian children and assimilating them once and for all. Reducing the costs of care for Indian children served as their priority, but BIA and state bureaucrats justified the Indian Adoption Project as a caring program that would rescue supposedly forgotten Indian children and find them permanent homes.

Disturbingly, most bureaucrats by the late 1950s rarely imagined a solution to the care of Indian children that involved strengthening Indian families and keeping Indian children within their homes. Most government officials deemed Indian families inherently and irreparably unfit, and so they ignored the proposition of funding preventative and rehabilitative services to Indian families. Ultimately they regarded this path as too costly and out of step with the overarching policy goals of the period: to terminate Indian tribes and de-Indigenize Indian people. Policymakers now used new terms and strategies, but the primary settler colonial goal of eliminating American Indian people remained unchanged. Indian children and Indian families suffered as a result.

By all socioeconomic indicators, Indians in the post–World War II era endured the most extreme hardship of any American minority. They had the highest rates of unemployment and suicide and the lowest incomes and life expectancies. The infant mortality rate, a sensitive indicator of overall socioeconomic status, was nearly three times as high among Indians as in the general population in 1957. In some regions the rate was much higher: Arizona and New Mexico had the highest infant Indian death rates: 127 and 121 per 1,000 live births, compared to 28 for the United States overall. For Indian infants 28 days to one year old, the death rate was almost six times as high as for the general population.[5] These dire economic conditions on reservations led many Indian families to depend on public assistance. From the vantage point of federal authorities and legislators, little had changed since the late nineteenth century; Indian people were still hopelessly reliant on government programs. The "Indian problem," as defined by non-Indian bureaucrats, was alive and well.

Many such government officials lay the blame at the feet of commissioner of Indian Affairs John Collier, believing that his halting steps toward Indian self-determination in the 1930s and 1940s and his support for the persistence of Indian languages and cultures had kept Indians back. They insisted that what was needed instead was an aggressive drive toward assimilation. These legislators and administrators gained ascendancy after World War II, and they shaped a new federal policy that called for a termination of Indians' unique tribal status vis-à-vis the federal government, the increased relocation of Indians to urban areas as a means to promote their employment, and the transfer of some responsibilities for Indian affairs to the states. The new orientation toward the care of Indian children emerged as both a consequence and a manifestation of these new government policies.

Congress officially legislated their intent to terminate Indian tribal status in 1953 with House Concurrent Resolution 108. The bill called for the termination over the next few years of five specific tribes—the Klamaths, Flatheads, Menominees, Pottawatomies, and the Turtle Mountain Chippewas—and all tribes in California, Florida, New York, and Texas. Senator Arthur V. Watkins of Utah was the primary proponent of termination. He claimed that it would free Indians from their status as government wards and that it was as revolutionary as the Emancipation Proclamation. As historian Paul Rosier points out, "the discourse of termination was that of the Cold War—the avowed goal was to 'liberate' the enslaved peoples of the world, who, according to American cold warriors, included Indians 'confined' in 'concentration camps' or 'socialistic environments.'" The bill ended federal supervision and dissolved federal control over thirteen tribes.[6]

Congress enacted several other bills to eliminate additional tribes following this resolution's passage. In all, of about two hundred tribes that were officially recognized in the 1950s, Congress slated 109 for termination. Legislators left it to the BIA to carry out termination, which sometimes took up to seven years. Officials stipulated that tribes designated for termination had to dispose of all tribal properties, either through organizing into a corporation for continued management under a trustee of their choice or through selling all properties and assets with proceeds to be distributed among tribal members.[7]

Termination proved an unmitigated disaster from the point of view of both tribes and the federal government. As scholar Charles Wilkinson describes it, "every terminated tribe floundered. Members of the smaller tribes . . . got a few hundred dollars apiece for their sold-off land and migrated to the cities or lived in shantytowns near their former reservations." Termination did not free Indians or promote their self-sufficiency; instead, Wilkinson notes, most terminated Indians "found themselves poorer, bereft of health care, and suffering a painful psychological loss of community, homeland, and self-identity." Bureaucrats quietly discarded the policy by the late 1960s, and the government formally abandoned it in the 1970s. The shortsighted and hastily enacted policy, however, had already had devastating consequences for Indian people.[8]

Alongside termination, the government proposed moving Indians from rural reservations and communities to urban centers. The BIA's Operation Relocation, begun in 1952 and extended through the early 1960s, mounted a major public relations campaign to encourage Indians to leave their reservations, move to urban areas, and ostensibly acquire job training and regular employment. The BIA footed the moving bill, paid the relocated families' first month's rent, and promised vocational education. Lured by visions of full employment and greater opportunity, more than thirty-five thousand Indians relocated to urban areas through the BIA's program, and many others moved on their own. In 1950 just 20 percent of American Indians lived in urban areas, but by 1980, 55 percent did. Major destinations included Los Angeles, San Francisco, Denver, Albuquerque, Phoenix, Minneapolis, and Chicago.[9] BIA bureaucrats touted relocation as a means of integrating Indians into American life, but financial concerns underwrote this policy. Once Indians had been relocated to an urban area for a defined period, usually six months, they ceased to be wards of the federal government. If they required public assistance, the states and local municipalities would then bear the cost.[10]

In addition to termination and relocation, Congress passed Public Law 83–280 (commonly known as Public Law 280 or PL-280) in 1953, which transferred some jurisdiction over Indian affairs from the federal government to some states. Congress initially reassigned criminal and some civil jurisdiction over tribal lands to California, Minnesota (except the Red Lake Chippewa Reservation), Nebraska, Oregon (excluding the Warm Springs Reservation), Wisconsin, and Alaska (upon statehood) and later allowed other states to gain partial jurisdiction over Indian tribes in their states. Arizona, Florida, Idaho, Iowa, Montana, Nevada, Utah, North Dakota, South Dakota, and Washington all later became PL-280 states.[11]

Tribal officials had neither requested nor consented to this transfer of responsibilities, and they were overwhelmingly opposed to it. Nevertheless, Congress imposed PL-280 on Indian communities to "relieve federal

financial obligations and to address perceived 'lawlessness' on reservations."
Congress amended the act in 1968 to require tribal consent, but this provision did not apply retroactively.[12] Ironically, PL-280 actually led to increased lawlessness on reservations, since it defunded tribal justice systems. PL-280 did not just affect the resolution of disputes on reservation lands; now states were to assume the same responsibility for education, welfare, and the health care of needy Indians as they did for needy non-Indians, but without being given additional federal funds to carry out these services. Ultimately tribes in PL-280 states were at a decided disadvantage compared with other tribes; they suffered from lower levels of federal support and an absence of compensating state support.[13] PL-280 thus increased the power of state welfare agencies over Indian people at the same time as it clouded the jurisdictional responsibility for and authority over Indian people.

As Congress slated tribe after tribe for termination in the 1950s, the BIA discovered a need for new welfare services for Indians. The BIA had been administering a form of welfare since the late nineteenth century through its distribution of rations on reservations. Missionaries, field matrons, and then public health nurses, almost all of them white women, had also been carrying out welfare work in Indian communities. In 1931 the BIA began to hire social workers, a relatively new profession that attracted large numbers of white women, and it organized a separate Welfare Branch in 1941. In 1944 it converted its rations program into monthly cash payments for needy families who were "ineligible for assistance under any other county, state, or Federal welfare program."[14]

The BIA's Welfare Branch took on increased importance in the termination era. In 1946 it had just two employees in its national office and twenty-three social workers in the field, but by 1955 it supported a staff of five in the national office plus sixty-three field social work positions. The branch also created eight "area social worker" positions in the early 1950s. Its budget expanded from $488,910 in 1946 to $3,413,405 in 1955, a sevenfold increase in less than a decade.[15] In 1955 the Welfare Branch became a separate entity in the BIA that coordinated with the branches of Education, Health, Relocation, Law and Order, and Tribal Affairs and was responsible to the assistant commissioner for community services.[16]

Administrators tasked the Welfare Branch with providing transitional support as the BIA terminated tribes and relocated individuals to cities.

The BIA established an additional social worker position for the Klamath tribe in 1955, for example, as they embarked on what the chief of the Welfare Branch called their "readjustment program."[17] The branch held a conference later that same year to clarify their objectives and goals and make a plan of action, and one administrator suggested that "a statement of our overall objectives should include plans for administering social services so that termination will be taking place 365 days a year; that termination should be considered to be a constructive and beneficial program and that the thought of termination services should not be a program of denial."[18] Paradoxically then, just at a time when the BIA was phasing out its trust responsibilities for Indian tribes, its bureaucracy was growing immensely more complex. And through social workers, the Welfare Branch had become a key manager of Indian peoples, especially in regard to child welfare.

The branch's senior staff of five surely must have been the most multicultural team working in all of the United States in the 1950s. A chief of welfare, first Robert Beasley and then Charles Rovin, headed the branch, and an administrative assistant supported it. Three women formed the core of the branch: Aleta Brownlee, Lucile Ahnawake Hastings, and Vinita Lewis. Brownlee, a white woman, had pursued a distinguished international career in child welfare before taking up her post as child welfare consultant with the BIA in 1952. In 1945 she had worked with the United Nations Relief and Rehabilitation Administration (UNRRA) as a welfare specialist on the Yugoslavian Mission. Later that year she transferred to Vienna and became the director of child welfare in Austria. She worked with displaced children both with UNRRA and its successor, the International Refugee Organization, until 1950. Brownlee held her position as child welfare consultant with the BIA for eight years until she retired in 1960.[19]

Lucile Ahnawake Hastings, who sometimes served as acting chief of the Welfare Branch in addition to her job as general welfare consultant, was a Cherokee woman who had attended Vassar College and the University of Chicago, where she obtained a masters in social work. She was the daughter of William Wirt Hastings, a Cherokee man who became a member of Congress from Oklahoma.[20] Vinita Lewis, an African American woman, pursued her undergraduate training in social service administration at the University of Chicago (like Hastings) and earned a masters in social work at the New York School of Social Work at Columbia University. Lewis started working for the federal government in 1936. She worked as a member of the International Refugee Organization (like Brownlee), in the U.S. zone of Germany after World War II. In 1953 she took up her position with the BIA as "Welfare Specialist on Social Administration of Laws Pertaining to Indian Children with Special Reference to Guardianships and Adoptions." After Congress passed termination legislation, the BIA thought it important to create this position with the "responsibility for policy governing conservation of minors' funds and resources."[21] These three women implemented key aspects of termination policy within Indian communities in the 1950s.

The BIA charged its Welfare Branch with closing down the boarding schools and transferring the responsibility for the education and care of Indian children to states. BIA officials had once championed the schools as the solution to the Indian problem, but now they realized that the institutions had failed miserably in their primary goals of assimilation and building economic independence among Indian people. Instead, indigent Indian families, like that of Adam Fortunate Eagle, often used the schools as an economic support system. Legislators and BIA authorities were dismayed by these developments, claiming that Indian parents now "looked upon the boarding school as a right, and . . . found the care of their children by the school to have economic advantages."[22]

Administrators, too, believed that the schools had "become a repository for children who have no parents or whose parents have abandoned them." Brownlee claimed in 1958 that sixteen of the BIA's boarding schools and four of its dorms "carry a large responsibility for the care of dependent and neglected children." She asserted that "many of the children were born out of wedlock and were first given by the mother to the maternal grandmother who when they reached school age turned them over to 'Uncle Sam' and permanent residence in a boarding school. Some of the children were abandoned by their mothers immediately after birth and lived in hospitals until they were old enough to attend school."[23] Brownlee and other administrators by the late 1950s criticized Indian families, and particularly Indian women, for using the boarding schools as a safety net. What had been the BIA's preferred means of removing Indian children and supposedly assimilating them into American society had become an expensive anachronism that seemed to be causing more problems than it was solving. To rectify the situation, the BIA closed all its boarding schools in PL-280 states in the 1950s, and terminated tribes lost all eligibility for BIA educational assistance. The Welfare Branch conducted annual reviews of thousands of Indian children still enrolled in the boarding schools in an effort to transfer their care to their families and their education to their states' public school systems.

Administrators found it difficult, however, to phase out the boarding schools totally, and they remained a fixture of Indian life for thousands of Indian children in the post–World War II era. Boarding schools actually expanded in this era for Navajo and Alaska Native children. Congress considered it too expensive to provide schools within their communities, so these children were forced to enroll at distant boarding schools or to attend public schools while living in BIA dormitories far from their home communities. Thousands of Indian children lived in such dormitories in Arizona, New Mexico, Oklahoma, and Utah.[24] As late as 1974, 35,000 Indian children still attended boarding schools. On the Navajo Reservation, 90 percent of the K–12 Indian population—some 20,000 children—were still in boarding schools.[25] These were not just older children. In 1968 the BIA Welfare Branch compiled statistics showing that 8,608 children *under the age of nine* were enrolled in sixty-two boarding schools.[26]

It is true that the boarding schools were a profound source of problems for Indian people, but not because they were an economic or social crutch, as most officials complained. Although the government rarely acknowledged it, generations of child removal and institutional upbringing had damaged Indian families. Officials removed children at a crucial time in their upbringing, such that they missed out not only on an education in their cultures and languages but also on learning the proper way to raise children within extended family networks. Instead, the boarding school regimes exposed children to brutal corporal punishment, harsh military-style discipline, and, often, sexual abuse. Even in the best of circumstances, boarding school matrons and teachers could give students only limited attention and affection. And in some cases, higher authorities chastised the most loving and nurturing of teachers for coddling the children.[27]

Boarding schools were indeed a poor substitute for family upbringing within their communities.

The desire of Indian peoples to keep their families intact and the mandate of the BIA Welfare Branch to close most of the boarding schools converged for a brief period in the 1950s. When first charged with closing the boarding schools, the BIA's Welfare Branch concerned itself with preventing family "breakdown" and "disintegration," and it took steps to strengthen Indian family supports as it de-enrolled many Indian children from the boarding schools.[28] As the BIA child welfare consultants engaged in this effort, Brownlee admitted: "I am getting more and more frightened about moving large numbers of children out of our schools *successfully* and no other way will do."[29] Initially, Brownlee and her team wanted to make sure that Indian children would thrive in public schools and have the necessary resources within their own families and communities. In many cases BIA social workers made this possible through providing simple economic supports, such as "arrangements for free lunches, changes in bus routes," and "the provision of clothing and other school necessities." In other cases social workers arranged more extensive support. "Some children were enabled to remain with their families," they reported, "through provision of aid to dependent children or other assistance, and others to live with relatives."[30] BIA social workers also sought to provide education and counseling. Brownlee reported in 1955 that their services included "improving the quality of family life by helping parents and children in their relationships with each other."[31]

Even into the 1960s Clare Jerdone (née Golden), Brownlee's replacement in the Welfare Branch, supported the strengthening of Indian families. She noted, "It is likely that the availability of the boarding school has delayed the development of alternative services that would be better suited to the needs of some children." Further, "services that help children and families in their own homes (except for financial assistance) are largely undeveloped on the reservations," she pointed out. "Rather than an alternative, such services should be primary," she believed. "Availability of such services would mean that some children would not have to be separated from their own parents," she advised, "that is if the caseworkers had sufficient time to provide counseling and other supportive services."[32] Seven years later Jerdone again recommended that "an attack at the basic cause for enrollment [in boarding schools] on social criteria should be considered, namely services to strengthen families so that some children wouldn't have to leave home." She asserted that "one effect of such services would be to enrichen [sic] whole families and thus not drive deeper the wedge of children having such experiences and their parents not sharing them."[33] Thus there was a strong constituency within the BIA's Welfare Branch that advocated for keeping Indian children in their families.

Termination policy mandated, however, that the Welfare Branch eventually transfer Indian child welfare services to state social service agencies. In 1952, for example, the BIA's welfare program in California ended when county departments of public welfare "assumed full responsibility for providing any needed social services to Indian residents whether living on or off a reservation," including child welfare services to Indian children within their own homes and to those in foster homes. The BIA optimistically asserted, "California Indians will now receive needed social services on the same basis as other citizens of the State."[34] States were now to take over the BIA's child welfare duties, and it remained to be seen whether state welfare workers would share the concern with strengthening Indian families that Brownlee and her team had championed in the mid-1950s.

Most states resisted the federal mandate to take over the care of Indian children, claiming that they had no legal jurisdiction over Indian children living on a reservation and therefore no financial responsibility to provide services to them.[35] Initially only California and Florida had "accepted responsibility for financing in full any needed welfare services to Indians without a Federal subsidy." States with large Indian populations began requesting federal subsidies to provide child welfare services. They argued that Indians did not pay state taxes on their land and that there was a greater need for social services to Indian people, which put an unfair financial burden on the state.[36]

Nevada provides a telling example. HR 3239, the Nevada Readjustment Bill, required that five years after its enactment, the federal trust relationship toward the Nevada "colony," as they so aptly referred to Indian communities there, would be terminated. At that point "members of the colony shall not be entitled to any of the services performed by the United States for Indians because of their status as Indians." But the BIA's Welfare Branch looked with despair on the situation. Its director pointed out in

1955 that unemployment among Indians was severe, and "the State Welfare program provides only old age assistance and aid to the blind with a skeleton child welfare setup. It has no aid to dependent children program." In fact, he pointed out, "Through the years bills to establish aid to dependent children have been defeated, among other reasons because of the contemplated large burden of Indian dependency."[37] Attempts to transfer BIA responsibilities for Indian child welfare to the states deeply disadvantaged Indian people. As state authorities squabbled with the federal government over who should bear the cost for services to Indians, struggling Indian families could not count on the same level of assistance as non-Indian families.

Other states sought to resolve the issue by negotiating contracts with the BIA. Authorities in Minnesota argued that they were saving the federal government money. The cost of supporting an Indian child in the Pipestone Boarding School had been about $750 per year per child, they calculated, whereas the cost of funding an Indian child in foster care was just $468.63 in 1956.[38] The BIA awarded a contract to Minnesota and several other states for providing foster care and other social services for children.[39]

State bureaucrats rarely made the same efforts to keep Indian families together as the BIA Welfare Branch had done in the 1950s. Instead they increasingly regarded foster care and adoption into non-Indian families as the best solution for dependent Indian children. The Minnesota Department of Public Welfare's story of "Chuck" shows how state bureaucrats were redefining what was best for Indian children in the 1950s. When Chuck was born to his Indian mother, her husband insisted that the child was not his. The family situation became so strained, according to the department, that Chuck's mother asked the county welfare board to find a good home for her child. "Had Chuck been born several years earlier," department officials wrote, "his mother, *following what had been the long tradition of her people,* undoubtedly would have wanted Chuck to grow up in an Indian school." Willfully ignorant of the origins of the boarding schools just a few generations before, department officials obscured their coercive aims and turned them into an Indian "tradition." Moreover, now they critiqued Indian boarding schools. If Chuck had been placed in an Indian boarding school, welfare authorities asserted, he "would have grown up with no experience in family living and no family to turn to in those moments when all of us . . . need to belong to someone." Institutional placement for children had long been out of favor for non-Indian children; now welfare workers argued that a home placement was better for Indian children like Chuck, too.[40]

Interestingly, though, the county welfare board never sought to place Chuck with extended family members, as the BIA Welfare Branch might have done. Instead it initially placed Chuck with a non-Indian foster family and then, supposedly with the consent of Chuck's mother, in a permanent adoptive home.[41] While foster care was cheaper than institutionalization, state officials imagined the adoption of Indian children in state care as the ultimate solution to their budgetary concerns. The BIA Welfare Branch's concern with strengthening and preserving Indian families faded quickly as states took over Indian child welfare services.

The BIA's Welfare Branch had not considered adoption as a serious option for dependent Indian children throughout most of the 1950s. In 1955, in a list of twelve services they offered to children, the branch listed "arranging adoptions" as number 9, and "providing guidance, and when necessary, care for young unmarried mothers and their children" as number 11.[42] Within just a few years of generating this list, however, the branch had become enthusiastic about adoption. Looking back on her tenure from 1960, Brownlee reflected that in 1952 her office had focused on dependent, delinquent, abandoned, or neglected children in boarding schools. Now, she noted, the emphasis was on "finding a more suitable form of care," and she observed that "much more is done than to provide foster care—our emphasis now is on court action and adoption."[43]

What prompted the BIA's Welfare Branch to move to court action and adoption? Intense public interest in the adoption of Indian children may have been one factor. Hundreds of would-be adopters wrote to the BIA requesting help in adopting an Indian child. For example, Mrs. Ira Mikesell of Monticello, Indiana, asked, "Is it possible for you to help us find a small boy of Indian parentage, or perhaps of mixed blood, for us to adopt?" She explained their interest: "My husband and I both have some Indian blood in our veins and we think an Indian child or one who is part Indian would just suit us to a tee."[44] J. R. Bryant of Atlanta was quite specific in his request; he wanted an Indian boy, two years old, and a girl aged one, from a reservation in Wyoming or Oklahoma (though Indians did not live on reservations in Oklahoma). He added that he "Would like to go And Pick Out a Couple."[45] In the 1950s the BIA simply referred these letter writers to state departments of social welfare. After receiving hundreds of these requests, perhaps it occurred to them that adoption would help to resolve their perceived problem.

Still, the BIA was cautious about the legal issues involved in promoting the adoption of Indian children in the mid-1950s. At their 1955 conference, they noted, "We need clear material on adoptions and do not think that we can participate in the adoption process without more knowledge of the legal status of the tribal courts. We are concerned with such questions as 'Do states accept the adoption decree of tribal courts?' 'How do we advise families to proceed with adoptions?'" After learning that South Dakota state courts would not recognize tribal adoptions, one administrator declared that it was vital to find out where jurisdiction lay.[46] Thus the BIA Welfare Branch imagined that adoption could only take place in contexts in which tribal courts no longer held jurisdiction; that would mean PL-280 states and among tribes that had been terminated.

Within just a few years, however, the BIA decided to make adoption the centerpiece of its child welfare efforts. In 1958, for the first time, the Annual Report of the Bureau of Indian Affairs mentioned "planning for adoption" as part of the BIA's Welfare Program, and in September that year Brownlee contracted with the Child Welfare League of America (CWLA), a highly regarded umbrella organization of private and public child placement agencies, "to set up a [three-year] pilot adoption project involving the placement of approximately fifty Indian infant children from a few reservations throughout the country." The Indian Adoption Project (IAP) stipulated that these children were "to be placed primarily in non-Indian adoptive homes through specialized agencies in the eastern area." It included a study and evaluation of these placements "by a qualified social scientist," David Fanshel, and "the development of a permanent inter-state plan for the placement of Indian children requiring adoption." The CWLA hired former white BIA worker Arnold Lyslo to head the IAP from 1959 to 1967.[47] Lyslo had attended the University of Minnesota and been active in the Lutheran Student Association in the 1940s. In the 1950s he worked as the area child welfare worker in the BIA's

Portland office. In 1958 he left the BIA to work on a special project of the CWLA to survey foster care programs in different states.[48]

Here was the ultimate solution to the Indian problem, from the point of view of government bureaucrats. Children would have no contact with their Indian tribal communities or with peer groups within the boarding schools, and they would grow up in middle-class homes. Thus, officials believed, Indian children would be truly assimilated into mainstream American culture. And because adoptive families would bear the cost of raising the children, neither the federal government nor the states would have to fund their care. The chief of the BIA's Welfare Branch justified the IAP to his supervisor in 1958 by noting, "This could in future years reduce the expenditures of the Bureau for foster home care since we are now paying for care for a number of children for whom adoption should be possible."[49] The promotion of Indian adoption thus served both the assimilationist and bureaucratic imperatives of the termination era and provided an early model for the privatization of government services.

Administrators carefully calculated the cost savings of adoption. Fanshel, who conducted a study of almost one hundred Indian adoptions through the IAP, admitted:

> There is another matter which is not usually mentioned in evaluating adoptions. From the perspective of society at large, the adoption of children who are destined to spend all of their childhood years in foster care or in Indian boarding schools provides a substantial financial saving. . . . The savings per child would . . . come close to $100,000. For a group the size of our study population, the savings would be approximately ten million dollars over an eighteen-year period. If one were to apply the approach of cost-benefit analysis to the adoption phenomenon, such data would be seen as highly significant.[50]

Lyslo, too, championed adoption as a means of saving the taxpayer money. He asserted that "many children who might have been firmly established in secure homes at an early age through adoption, have been passed from family to family on a reservation or have spent years at public expense in federal boarding schools or in foster care." In the cruelest irony, Lyslo added that these children "have never had the security of family life to promote their development and assure their future," implying that Indian families who sent their children to the schools were unfit.[51] No BIA authority took responsibility for the policy of child removal and institutionalization in Indian boarding schools that had been so detrimental to Indian families. Instead, officials deflected blame to rest upon Indian families themselves.

The IAP placed 395 Indian children in adoptive homes for its duration. Arizona, South Dakota, and Wisconsin "supplied" the largest numbers of Indian children: 112, 104, and 48, respectively. Adoptive families from northeastern, mid-Atlantic, and midwestern states accounted for the largest numbers of placements, with families from New York (74), Illinois (48), Missouri (39), Indiana (34), Pennsylvania (33), and Massachusetts (31).[52] The CWLA incorporated the IAP into a new project in 1968, the Adoption Resource Exchange of North America (ARENA) for "hard-to-place" or "special needs" children, and it placed several hundred more Indian children up for adoption, primarily with non-Indian families, until the Indian Child Welfare Act of 1978.[53] The IAP and ARENA probably placed no more than a thousand Indian children for adoption, but their influence far exceeded these modest numbers. Lyslo worked assiduously with state social service departments and private agencies to increase the supply of Indian children at the same time as he engaged in extensive public relations efforts to promote interest in adoption among non-Indian families.

The CWLA gave Lyslo wide latitude in carrying out this project. The job description enabled him to define the "purpose and plan of project" as well as the "operation and problems to be investigated" and stipulated that he would work "extensively and significantly through agencies, stimulating participation, integrating and evaluating both interim and terminal results of their activities."[54] As a result Lyslo was able to conduct his project without the constraints of other standards the CWLA developed and disseminated to its member agencies in the 1950s and 1960s.

Lyslo presented his efforts as merely responding to a self-evident need. In reality, to succeed, he had two tasks: to cultivate the demand among adoptive white families for Indian children and to boost the supply of adoptable Indian children. Lyslo spent a great deal of time on each endeavor. Chapter 2 focuses on how he helped to shape the growing interest in and "demand" for Indian children among white families. Here, I examine how Lyslo sought to make more Indian children adoptable. His efforts involved convincing private placement agencies to participate in the IAP, working with state-run welfare agencies to identify adoptable Indian children, promoting in-state as well as interstate adoptions, working to change state laws and practices that were obstacles to the adoptive placement of Indian children, and locating and providing services to the "unmarried Indian mother."

First Lyslo worked to get private adoption placement agencies and public state agencies on board. Joseph Reid, head of the CWLA and Lyslo's supervisor, declared in a 1959 memo to all CWLA member organizations,

> We do know . . . that there are Indian children, legally free for adoption and considered adoptable, who are living in foster family care and children's institutions throughout the country because there are no adoptive homes for them. Some of these children are the direct responsibility of the BIA and are supervised by Indian Bureau social workers on the reservation, while other children, living off the reservations, are the responsibility of the respective state welfare department. The BIA has expressed an interest in making permanent adoptive plans for those children needing this type of care, and would be willing to provide transportation and escort service for any child involved.[55]

This task proved relatively easy. With the clout of the highly regarded CWLA, fifty agencies throughout the country willingly partnered with the IAP to place Indian children, most notably the Illinois Department of Children and Family Services, Louise Wise Services in New York, Children's Bureau of Delaware, Missouri Division of Welfare, Spence-Chapin Adoption Service in New York, and Children's Bureau of Indianapolis.[56] Some private agencies had already been involved in the placement of Indian children before the advent of the IAP. The Boys and Girls Aid Society of Oregon, for example, placed 132 American Indian children for adoption between 1944 and 1977.[57]

Next the IAP sought to identify and even increase the numbers of adoptable Indian children. The BIA sent inquiries to all of its reservation social workers in 1960, "asking the approximate number of children currently in care who might be available for adoption . . . . [and] interviewed state departments of public welfare in the Indian states." According to

Lyslo, "the reports received from these workers presented conclusive evidence that there were many children badly needing adoptive placement who were now free *or who could be made free for adoption* if adoptive resources were available."[58] Through the IAP, the BIA shifted away from taking rehabilitative steps to reunite Indian children with their families toward making Indian children free for adoption.

Once aware of the numbers of "adoptable" Indian children, the IAP set out to facilitate in-state adoptions. Lyslo wrote in 1960, "Equally important [to the interstate placement of children] . . . will be the stimulation and encouragement afforded those social agencies currently responsible for the planning for Indian children, to develop new and intensive programs for their adoption within their own states."[59] The intrepid IAP director regularly traveled across the United States to drum up support for in-state adoptions of Indian children.[60] He boasted that adoptions of Indian children had increased in all states where the IAP had operated, noting that in Alaska, Montana, and Arizona, in-state Indian adoptions had doubled between 1960 and 1963.[61]

Lyslo's crusade appears to have accelerated trends toward increased adoption that were already taking place in the states. The IAP queried 102 state and private agencies in 1965 and found that 66 agencies had placed 696 Indian children for adoption in 1965, not including the 49 Indian children placed through IAP. Welfare workers had placed 584 of these children with white families.[62] Lyslo claimed that he referred well over five thousand prospective adoptive families for Indian children to state agencies, and he quoted one BIA agent in Aberdeen, South Dakota, as writing, "'I think you and the Project have been given insufficient credit i[n] the stimulation that has been given the local state and private agencies in Indian country to expand and develop their own adoption activities for Indian children. Here in South Dakota these activities have expanded to such an extent that we no longer consider the Indian infant a hard-to-place child.'"[63] The IAP's influence extended well beyond its own relatively small mission.

As the project progressed, Lyslo encountered and sought to overcome some significant barriers to the interstate adoption of Indian children. He complained of adoption laws in some states that "have prevented the adoption of Indian children, or [caused] considerable delay in referral to the Project due to efforts to make them free for adoption." Lyslo bragged that "the League, through the Indian Adoption Project, has been instrumental in helping some states change their adoption laws. Wyoming was one such state. Through participation in the Project, agencies in several states discovered that their adoption law was obsolete and not conducive to the interstate placement of children. Ways have been found in most states to place these children, however, mainly by special interagency agreements."[64] Lyslo and the IAP, in their zeal to promote Indian adoption, exerted considerable authority on state and interstate adoption practices.

Adoption proponents lamented that the wheels of bureaucracy moved too slowly, and the IAP sought to speed up the adoption processing of Indian children. CWLA director Reid noted the problems with state departments of public welfare "that are not set up adequately to process these adoptions, which admittedly are more difficult to accomplish because another agency and state is involved." The CWLA committed to "trying to do everything that we can to solve this problem, including asking the BIA Area Social Workers to work with the welfare departments to assist them in processing these adoptions."[65] Both the federal government and the CWLA were willing to muster considerable resources to promote Indian adoption.

They were also willing to challenge fledgling tribal jurisdiction that frustrated their ambitions. "When a state court does not have jurisdiction of Indian children residing on a reservation," Lyslo wrote, "these children frequently are not relinquished for adoption."[66] Lyslo and Reid were particularly dismayed by the "dispute over civil jurisdiction of Indians having residence on reservations in North Dakota," which "prevents many Indian children from that state from being adopted." Here, they lamented that 146 Indian children in foster care were "considered to be adoptable," but "the courts refused to take action [to place them for adoption] on the grounds that they did not have jurisdiction."[67] In line with termination efforts to undermine tribal sovereignty, Lyslo challenged tribal court jurisdiction.

He sought to smooth the way for Indian adoptions by bringing more tribes under state jurisdiction in regard to child welfare. He asserted that "tribal courts should be encouraged to request civil [state] courts to handle all civil matters relating to the Indian child."[68] Beyond simple voluntary encouragement, Lyslo lobbied for establishing "uniform civil laws in all states whereby Indian children living on reservations would come under the same jurisdiction as all other children in the state."[69] Lyslo often intervened in such disputes. He visited Red Lake Indian Reservation in Minnesota in 1963, where "because the attitude of the Beltrami County Courts is one of lack of jurisdiction of Red Lake Indians living on the reservation, *children have been deprived of adoption opportunities.*" Lyslo claims to have convinced BIA social workers and tribal leaders at Red Lake to be included in the IAP as well as the Minnesota State Department of Public Welfare.[70] Through the free rein he enjoyed as the IAP's director, Lyslo sought to make Indian children more readily available for adoption through a number of bureaucratic maneuvers: decreasing tribal jurisdiction over child welfare, increasing state control over Indian children, and easing any legal obstacles to the free circulation of these children on the adoption market.

All these bureaucratic efforts would be for naught, however, if BIA and state social workers could not convince Indian mothers to give up their infants at birth. Authorities had shown little concern with children born to unmarried Indian mothers in the 1950s. Suddenly the specter of "the Indian unmarried mother" appeared with increasing frequency in BIA and social service agency reports by 1960. Officials claimed, with no statistical evidence, that Indian unwed motherhood had increased and had become a problem. Lyslo contended that "reports by health, education, and social work personnel on the reservation indicate that the figure [of out-of-wedlock births] is high," although he admitted that "the figure . . . has never been accurately determined."[71]

Indian communities, however, saw little problem with unwed motherhood and readily accepted children born out of wedlock into extended kin networks. Lyslo even admitted that "illegitimacy among Indian peoples is frequently acceptable."[72] Stella Hostbjor, a BIA social worker on the Sisseton Indian Agency in Sisseton, South Dakota, similarly acknowledged that "we never hear a disparaging tone or term used in speaking of the [illegitimate] child," and "we do not sense that most members of the tribe see a lack of a father person as a big problem for the child." Many Indians would not have even considered these births illegitimate. Hostbjor noted that in 1960, while the local hospital recorded one third of Sisseton-Wahpeton Indian hospital births as illegitimate, many of the mothers were members of Indian custom marriages, marriages recognized by the tribe but not the state.[73]

In Indian communities it was common and desirable for extended family members, especially grandparents, to take in and raise their kin. Hostbjor noted, "the old kinship system has not completely disappeared," and therefore if an Indian woman did have a child that she could not care for, "there is often a willingness on the part of grandparents or other relatives to take the child."[74] In actuality, then, unwed Indian mothers and their families rarely saw a need to place their infants up for adoption. As Hostbjor explained, "The readiness of relatives to accept the child makes it easy for the unmarried mother to keep the child herself or give it to a relative, usually her mother."[75]

Given the strong extended family support for Indian children, why then did the BIA and the CWLA decide to promote adoption? Hostbjor herself acknowledged, "There might be some question about the need for adoptive homes for Indian children." Authorities justified their program in two main ways. They claimed that Indian women should be given the choice to put their children up for adoption. Hostbjor contended, "We find that not all Indian unmarried mothers want to keep their children or are able to care for them."[76] Lyslo lamented the lack of counseling services to Indian women that would encourage them to put their babies up for adoption. "Services to Indian unmarried mothers have been extremely limited," he explained, and therefore "very few unmarried mothers are ever given any choice but to keep their children."[77] Just as Congress characterized the termination of tribes in the liberal Cold War language of liberation, so, too, did Lyslo and other Indian adoption advocates couch the increased pressures on young Indian women to place their babies for adoption as a broadening of opportunity and choice. Undoubtedly, some young Indian women did want to give their babies up for adoption. However, as we shall see in chapter 3, social workers often used coercion and subterfuge to gain the "consent" of many other Indian women to adoption. Officials also believed that Indian family models that relied on extended kin networks to care for children were inappropriate. Lyslo mentioned the "poor quality of [Indian] foster family care provided for children referred to the Indian Adoption Project," noting that "the foster parent may have been an aged grandmother."[78] What Indian families regarded as normal and, in fact, ideal for childraising, Lyslo deemed substandard.

Instead authorities believed that in order to become properly assimilated, Indian people had to assume nuclear family models, a staple of Cold War America. Brownlee asserted that "considerable effort on the part of social workers and Indians themselves" was needed to put into effect the "following principles commonly regarded as desirable in family life in the United States:

1. The father works and supports his family to the best of his ability.
2. The mother cares for her home and her children, keeping them clean, well fed, properly clothed, and happy.
3. Both parents maintain for themselves and establish for the family standards of morality.
4. The parents are concerned for the education and the future of their children.[79]

Social workers such as Hostbjor steeped themselves in the psychosocial brew of the day and believed that "many [Indian] children [who] grow up without a father person or have a stepfather or a succession of stepfathers . . . do not have a wholesome family pattern to follow, and normal psycho-sexual development may be impossible."[80] This was a time when popular cultural outlets and trained experts alike lionized the consumerist middle-class nuclear family with the male as breadwinner and the female as keeper of the home. They even imagined this ideal family as a bulwark against communism. Social workers and government agents, by contrast, regarded the extended Indian family as an aberration.[81] Many officials believed that Indian family arrangements were holding Indians back from assimilation and social and economic mobility in American society.

Lyslo and other social workers did not believe that extended family members should care for Indian children, so they promoted more adoption services for unmarried Indian mothers. Lyslo asserted that "for [only] a small percentage of the[ir] children, a plan can be developed on the reservation for their care; . . . for the majority, resources outside the reservation must be found."[82] He assumed that it was desirable and nearly inevitable for unwed Indian mothers to give up their children for adoption. "An interesting research project," he wrote, "could be developed with Indian unmarried mothers who keep their children to see what happens to the child in later years."[83] This suggestion implies that the relinquishment of Indian children by unmarried Indian mothers should be the norm and ideal rather than the exception.

The IAP thus promoted increased intervention into the lives of unwed mothers. Ideally, Lyslo envisioned, young Indian women would move to maternity homes far from their families and tribal communities. There the influence of extended family members, who often would have welcomed children into the fold, would be minimized. In some states, like North Dakota, Lyslo complained that there appeared "to be no aggressive approach on the part of the Bureau [of Indian Affairs] or other agencies in the state to reach these unmarried [Indian] mothers. Unless a girl goes to an agency herself, it is unlikely that she will receive service in planning for herself or her child."[84] Lyslo encouraged authorities in such states to make more concerted efforts to identify these Indian women and refer them to off-reservation maternity homes.

Lyslo targeted vulnerable tribes that he expected to provide increased numbers of children available for adoption. He met with state welfare authorities in Colorado in 1963 and noted that "there was some discussion of the agency's services to the Southern Ute Tribe, and the agency was encouraged to work more closely with this group of Indians, since they appear to be in a very real period of cultural transition and will need to be more aware of all services provided through the state. It is thought that some of the unmarried mothers of this tribe may be releasing their children for adoption within the near future, a new phenomenon for the tribe."[85] Lyslo's language and approach is chilling. The BIA had terminated many of its services to the Southern Utes, thus ushering in a "period of cultural transition." The tribe created many of its own programs to replace those of the BIA, but Lyslo clearly did not expect them to succeed. He recommends that state authorities circle like vultures over the Southern Utes, waiting for them to fail. Then they can swoop in with "services" that will give Indian women a choice to "release" their children for adoption.[86]

Lyslo wanted to increase such services not just to reservation women but also to urban Indian unmarried mothers. In his 1968 report he mentioned that "the increasing number of Indians moving into the [Los Angeles] area for employment reasons has increased the need for a network of social services for them. Indian unmarried mothers are now being referred to social agencies by the workers of the Bureau of Indian Affairs and Indian organizations. . . . The Indian Adoption Project has encouraged the development of these services."[87] The IAP targeted "the Indian unmarried mother," whether on the reservation or in urban areas.

Lyslo claimed that by 1968 the IAP had become more successful in convincing Indian unmarried mothers to give up their children for adoption. "Increased social services have been made available to Indian unmarried mothers to enable them to make a satisfactory plan for themselves and their children," Lyslo contended. He noted with satisfaction, "Many unmarried mothers prefer to live in maternity homes awaiting the birth of their children, rather than stay with their own families or relatives on a reservation." Lyslo concluded at the end of his tenure as the IAP's director, "As adoption opportunities have become increasingly available, unmarried mothers have been more willing to release their children for adoption, knowing that adoption may afford the child greater opportunity for a better life."[88] Hence Lyslo presented the IAP as an unmitigated success in its efforts to increase the numbers of Indian unmarried mothers willing to give their children up for adoption.

In reality Lyslo and other social services workers had created and magnified a problem that scarcely existed before. Indian families did not stigmatize unmarried mothers and readily incorporated their children into extended kin networks. They did not have a need for adoptive homes outside their Indian communities. For government officials, however, unmarried Indian motherhood *was* a problem. To them it both reflected and exacerbated the Indian problem of persistent dependence on the federal government. By dealing with the problem early—at the very birth of an Indian child—authorities believed they would literally nip it in the bud. Under Lyslo's influence, BIA and state social workers zealously promoted a new ethos for "the unmarried Indian mother." Now authorities strived to convince Indian women to give birth in maternity homes far from their communities. There social workers would convince them of the wisdom of giving up their children. They would tell the young women that it would be better for their children to be raised in a nuclear family with all the trappings of middle-class life.

The IAP may have stimulated the increased removal of older Indian children as well as newborns. Most adoptive families preferred to adopt infants, but authorities also increasingly removed from their homes other young Indian children who were later "made available for adoption." BIA and state social workers "have reported that because of this new interest shown in the Indian child and his adoptability," according to Lyslo, "action has been taken more promptly to remove Indian children from neglect situations."[89] Lyslo claimed in 1960 that Margaret Lampe, adoption consultant for South Dakota's State Department of Public Welfare, reported that since the advent of the IAP, the number of Indian children referred to the welfare department for services "had increased tenfold."[90] Lyslo justified this as protecting and rescuing Indian children, but many Indian families regarded such intervention as unwarranted. The definition and interpretation of neglect became a highly contested notion. Indian people, as I explore in chapters 3 and 4, charged that social workers regarded children living with extended family members, in poor housing, or without modern sanitation as grounds for removal.

Authorities made strenuous efforts to increase the supply of adoptable Indian children, but they expended little or no energy to prevent the breakup of or to reunite struggling Indian families, as they once had in the 1950s. The logic of bureaucratic care, honed over nearly a century of implementing federal Indian policy, came to focus on Indian child removal and the interests of adoptive families. The IAP promised interested adoptive families that they could generate Indian children to be adopted. Reid explained that "in the event the BIA did not have an Indian child suitable to meet the needs of an interested family, we are sure that arrangements could be worked out with a few of the state welfare departments to find an appropriate child."[91] In the casual rhetoric of the IAP, administrators spoke as if it is was perfectly natural that Indian children should be readily available for adoption.

Lyslo's fanatical efforts to stimulate Indian adoption were at odds with other standard child welfare practice of the 1950s and 1960s. The CWLA asserted in a 1953 report, under "Concepts basic to all child welfare programs," that *"Parents have the right and the responsibility for the care, nurture, and guidance of their children."* Furthermore, the report stated, "In providing care and protection to the child the community has an obligation to recognize fully and to safeguard parental rights. No administrative child welfare agency, public or private, can remove children from their own homes without the parents' consent. Only the Judicial authority can take away parental rights."[92] The CWLA constantly reiterated this notion: "No parent or legal guardian may be deprived of his child without due process of law."[93] The CWLA's standards prioritized the rights of the birth parents and family.

Lyslo and the IAP routinely violated these standards when it came to Indian families. He wrote in 1963, "Indian placements have provoked critical discussion between agencies as to how best to effect the placement of a child on an interstate basis. Gradually we have come up with some common procedures which are usually acceptable to all agencies. *This means protection of not only the child but of the adoptive family.*"[94] Notably, Lyslo identified only the child and the adoptive family, not the birth parents or family, as in need of protection. Lyslo implicitly positioned the Indian family as beyond notice and unworthy of consideration. He and other social workers routinely invoked the "unmarried Indian mother" but only in the abstract. The concerns, perspectives, and rights of Indian women and families are eerily absent in IAP documents.

The CWLA championed special preventive services for families experiencing difficulties so as to prevent child neglect or abuse and the need to remove a child from home, but many social workers failed to offer such aid to struggling Indian families. The CWLA's 1958 manual "Social Work Practice in Child Welfare" mentions "services designed to supplement care which parents can give: a homemaker service; day care for children; and friendly service such as Big Brothers or Big Sisters." The homemaker service was a particularly popular option to provide help "that will enable the child to receive adequate care in the home when, for example, the mother is absent, ill, incapacitated, or needs aid in developing improved standards of homemaking and child care."[95] Yet social workers did not utilize these standard approaches in the practice that developed around Indian children. They rarely promoted preventive services for Indian families. Lyslo did mention in his 1968 report that "improved counseling services to Indian families are needed to better enable parents to provide a wholesome environment for their children," but this was buried on page 9 of the report.[96] Lyslo's efforts centered on making Indian children available for adoption, not on strengthening and providing resources to struggling Indian families.

This divergence in social work practice toward Indian people derived to a great degree from the policy initiative of the time to terminate Indian tribes. Brownlee epitomized the terminationist mindset in 1958 when she proclaimed that the American Indian "needs to shake himself free of 'the Great White Father.' If he is to live proudly in today's world he must adapt to the dominant culture while retaining vestiges of his own culture which are useful or pleasant."[97] Brownlee did not elaborate on what aspects of Indian culture she found useful or pleasant or who should judge them so.

Cost cutting and termination lay at the heart of the IAP, but bureaucrats were rarely so crass as to pronounce this publicly. Instead Lyslo and other pro-adoption advocates presented their efforts as expressions of genuine care for Indian children. Lyslo claimed that "as the League engages in this project, it is believed that it can be involved more deeply in basic problems in the care of Indian children and can help improve the general conditions among Indians."[98] It is hard to tell if Lyslo was being disingenuous or if he was simply blind to the ways in which his program undermined Indian families and their desire to care for their own children. Perhaps like so many benevolent "friends of the Indian" before him, he was just utterly convinced that he knew what was best for Indian people.

From an American Indian point of view it seemed inconceivable that the widespread removal of Indian children from a community could possibly "improve the general conditions among Indians." Instead it looked like a well-coordinated effort to prevent Indian people from reproducing their families and communities and maintaining their traditions and cultures. Many Indian people felt like Lee Cook of Red Lake, Minnesota, who declared at the 1974 U.S. Senate subcommittee hearings on Indian child welfare, "I think that the BIA and the state welfare workers have been carrying on like at Auschwitz."[99] Cook and many other Indians believed that through promoting adoption, the BIA and state governments were following the settler colonial logic of elimination. The U.S. government had a long history of dispossessing Indian people of their land and undermining their sovereignty. The promotion of Indian adoption represented yet another assault on Native societies.

Brownlee, Lyslo, Reid, and other bureaucrats represented their adoption advocacy as merely a response to a problem within Indian country and as a gesture of sincere caring, but they actually appear to have invented a problem that they then sought to resolve through increased intervention in Indian families. Through contracting with the CWLA to carry out the IAP, the BIA fervently promoted the continued removal of Indian children from their families and communities, but this time to white families instead of to institutions. This project depended, however, not just on making Indian children available for adoption but also on making Indian children desirable as adoptees among white families. The liberal climate of Cold War America proved to be an amenable environment for promoting Indian adoption.

I assumed that most non-Indians would know little and care less about this topic when I began this project. Yet I have found that many people I meet have a direct or indirect connection with Indian adoption. I discussed my research with a prospective graduate student, and she became very animated. Her brother is an adopted Indian. Two university colleagues similarly grew up in families with adopted Indian siblings. One of them put me in touch with her mother, and we began an email correspondence.

Dana, as I will call her, told me about the myriad reasons they decided to adopt an Indian child. She and her husband had already lost one pregnancy, and after another child was born two months prematurely they were told it wasn't safe to have another pregnancy. Media reports and the couple's religious faith also influenced them. As Dana put it, "There were often stories in the newspaper and other media lamenting the fact that homes could not be found for mixed race children. Our strong Christian faith had a role in this decision. At that point, we knew we didn't care about skin color, and learned that the [adoption agency] placed children of many colors."

Dana and her family adopted a baby girl, whom I will call Jane, through an agency in a midwestern city. Agency officials told them that Jane's mother was from the Rosebud Reservation and her father was Mexican. They also told Dana that the mother had requested a white family for the child. Looking back on it now, Dana does not fully trust what she was told. "I'm not sure that any of these facts are completely true," she writes. Her neighbors had adopted an Indian boy, and social workers had told them he was Sioux but later found out he was from a southwestern tribe. Agency personnel also misled Dana about other information about the birth mother. "Feeling sorry for the young girl who had to give her child up for adoption," Dana explains, "I asked what her plans were for the future and was told she would return to college. Later we learned that the girl was only 16 and had not finished high school."

The adoption went well during Jane's early childhood and elementary school years. Dana writes that "Our daughter was a happy loving child until about 6th grade." Then "her problems became more and more severe with puberty" and after trying several options, "she was committed to an adolescent mental health unit . . . for most of 8th grade." After Jane was released, Dana took her to a nearby city for weekly counseling sessions, "which kept things under semi-control until she graduated" from high school. Psychiatrists diagnosed Jane as suffering from "fetal alcohol effect" and later with bipolar disorder.

In high school, Jane stole her parents' car and in a separate incident was arrested for armed robbery. For a year, she was in a treatment facility that seemed to help her, but after her release, she "continued to spiral downhill." As an adult, Jane "could not hold a job and was thrown out of every place she tried to live." She married, had two children, and then divorced. Jane's children lived with Dana for a while, but Jane eventually lost custody of them. They were placed in foster care and later adopted by their foster family. Dana and her husband maintain a very close relationship with their grandchildren and their adoptive family. Jane, too, now on medication for her bipolar disorder, has reconnected with her children. She calls Dana almost every day.

I sensed that Dana struggles to make sense of her family's experience. Jane's mental illness complicated the family's problems. "Things may have gone better for all of us had she not been bipolar," Dana surmises. On the other hand, their neighbors also had "big problems" with their adopted Indian son "because of alcoholism." In his case, a local Indian man "took th[e] boy under his wing and became a mentor to him," and "he straightened up."

I asked Dana if she was aware of ICWA and what she thought about it. She replied, "Based on what I know now from personal experience and the experiences of others we knew, I now think keeping the Indian children with their tribes is probably best for the children even though they would not have the advantages that a middle-class white family could offer." And yet, she adds in another email, "I think our daughter would also tell you that her adoption was a positive experience—because we stuck by her through all the misery when we could have easily walked away." She concludes, "She's our child forever, despite the problems."

Dana's complex view mirrors that of many adoptive families I've learned about while researching this book. Adoption rarely seemed to live up to the ideal promoted by Arnold Lyslo. Adoptees often experienced great difficulties at adolescence as they sought to come to grips with their Indian identities, and adoptive families struggled to help their children through this tumultuous time. Adopters often empathize with the Indian families who lost children at the same time as they care deeply for the children they brought into their homes. Like Dana, many adopters are full of equal parts sorrow and joy.

# CHAPTER 2

# Caring about Indian Children in a Liberal Age

Helen and Carl Doss were a devout white Methodist couple who were unable to have children. They sought to adopt a baby in the 1940s. They found there were not many children available, and one social worker called the Dosses "financially unstable." Eventually a social worker assigned them a blue-eyed little boy, Donny. They tried to adopt another similar child but again faced obstacles. So they told agencies they would be willing to adopt a child of any racial background. Social workers were reluctant to place a dark-skinned child with white parents, however. One told the Dosses that "crossing racial lines is against all our *principles* of good social-work practice." The Dosses insisted that "a surplus of homes existed for the fair and perfect child, while nobody wanted those of mixed or minority race." They finally persuaded agencies to let them adopt eleven children of "minority" or mixed racial background.[1]

The "family nobody wanted," as Helen Doss titled the book she wrote about her adoptive family, included two American Indian children—a Cheyenne-Blackfoot baby named Gregory, and Richard, identified as Canadian Chippewa and Blackfoot and Scottish-American—whom the Dosses adopted when the children were seven months and nine years old, respectively.[2] The Dosses also fostered several Indian children. When Helen Doss approached an adoption agency in northern California, no children were available for adoption, but "two little Indian children . . . needed a boarding home immediately." Cousins Toby and Rose-Marie came to the Dosses for a weekend visit. "Although red tape kept them as county wards at present," Helen learned, "they might in the near future be legally free for permanent adoption. In the meantime, they needed a home which would care for them." The Dosses also fostered for a summer an eleven-year-old

Fig. 1. Helen and Carl Doss and their first five adoptive children (clockwise from top): Donny, Laurie, Ted, Susan, and Rita, ca. 1949. From Helen Grigsby Doss, "We Adopt an International Family," *Christian Advocate* (July 7, 1949): 4.

Indian boy named Little Beaver, who was not yet "free" to be adopted, but social workers hoped to complete legal action to "put him in the adoptable category."[3] Before the advent of the Indian Adoption Project, it was not as easy to adopt Indian children, the Dosses found. Yet they persisted; they were likely one of the first non-Indian American couples to foster and adopt Indian children in the post–World War II era.[4]

The Dosses were unusual in their desire to create a multiracial adoptive family in the 1940s and 1950s, but they set a precedent for thousands of other white American families in the 1960s and 1970s. Many of these families found that the supply of what Helen Doss called "fair and perfect" babies could not keep up with the demand for their adoption. Many, too, were moved to adopt across racial lines by their religious principles or their commitment to a color-blind society. The Dosses embodied a new liberal ethos of the postwar era; they "believed that all races were basically alike underneath. . . . Differences were there, . . . but [they] didn't feel that such differences were important." Carl and Helen's liberal racial ideas derived from their progressive Christian background. Carl declared to a neighbor that "the whole idea of Christianity is radical. . . . And the whole idea of democracy is radical. Think how really radical it is to say that all men are created equal, and that all men are brothers—and that the individual is important!"[5]

The collective conscience of Americans toward American Indians awakened in the 1950s and 1960s, an era of heightened liberalism in American society. The nation as a whole flourished economically after World War II, but it became apparent through news reports, government studies, and church chronicles that American Indians had not shared in the bounty. For many Americans, this represented a source of national shame and an urgent social issue. They cared about American Indians and wanted to do something.

Church authorities and liberal writers posed several solutions to the persistence of Indian poverty and inequality. Some, especially in the 1950s, critiqued the reigning government policy of termination and relocation and blamed poverty on past and present government policies as well as unscrupulous non-Indians who bilked Indian peoples out of their economic resources. Other concerned Americans sought to extend welcome and support to relocating Indians in urban communities. Still other Americans, imbued with Helen Doss's belief that "nobody wanted [children] of mixed or minority race," increasingly sought to extend their care to Indian children through adoption as a means to make recompense for past injustices.

This trend also came about in part through the strenuous efforts of the Indian Adoption Project (IAP), which worked as assiduously to cultivate the demand for Indian children as it had labored to make them available for adoption. The IAP created several stock figures: the forgotten Indian child, the unmarried Indian mother, the deadbeat Indian father, and the deviant Indian family. As IAP director Arnold Lyslo and others promoted adoption as a solution to the so-called Indian problem, other liberal political and economic solutions to the "Indian plight" that had flourished in the 1950s receded. Thus instead of working with American Indians to define and address the roots of their problems, many liberal Americans turned to the "rescue" of individual Indian children. As in the past, then, many compassionate white Americans unwittingly supported and participated in a devastating government policy and practice—the removal of Indian children from their families and communities.

Most Americans had little direct contact with American Indians in the postwar era. They gained knowledge about American Indians indirectly through popular culture, news reporting, government studies, and church-related publications and campaigns. Many scholars have focused on representations of Indians in films in this era, finding that they consigned Indian men to two major categories—the bloodthirsty savage or the noble red man. They reduced Indian women to two equally stereotyped images: the Indian princess who facilitates colonization through her alignment with white male colonizers or the "sexualized maiden." Nearly all depictions of Indians in the movies took place in the nineteenth century, leaving viewers with the notion that Indians had truly vanished.[6]

Yet it was not just movies that shaped public opinion about American Indians. Many church leaders were well aware of the persistence of American Indians; they labored to educate their congregations about contemporary American Indian issues and to prick their collective conscience. Representations of Indians in church publications undoubtedly exerted a significant influence on non-Indian Americans. Americans flocked to religious institutions at an unprecedented rate in the postwar era, in part as a result of the uncertainties of the nuclear age and the Cold War. By 1960, 65 percent of Americans held membership in a church or synagogue, the highest percentage at any time in the country's history, and 96 percent of Americans identified with a specific religious group.[7] Many American religious groups concentrated on opposing Godless communism as part of the Cold War, while other liberal Christians grappled with race problems and social justice issues, including what they so often referred to as the "plight" of American Indians.[8]

Whether reporting for secular or religious publications, nearly every writer about Indians in this era produced what I call a plight narrative. They amassed a litany of grim statistics on the poor economic and social conditions that afflicted most Indian reservations and urban communities. A series of articles on the "plight of the Navajos," an economic crisis brought on by decline in wage income, drought, and three harsh winters, filled American newspapers and magazines in the late 1940s.[9] *The Chris-*

*tian Century's* coverage of American Indians in the 1950s focused almost exclusively on their poverty and economic deprivation. The magazine highlighted the Turtle Mountain reservation in North Dakota in 1955 to inform its readers of "what Indian poverty means." If all the assets of the tribe were divided equally among the group's 8,928 members, the magazine reported, each would have just a little bit over thirty-seven dollars.[10] Other news articles reported high rates of infant mortality, low life expectancy, and devastating unemployment rates.

It is inescapable that Indian communities suffered material hardship and grievous inequalities compared to the rest of American society in the postwar era, yet this did not encompass the entirety of Indian experience in this era or any other. Many non-Indian writers in the 1920s and 1930s had focused not just on the economic deprivation of Indian societies but also on facets of Indian cultural life that they deemed exotic, wondrous, and commendable. Oliver La Farge had published *Laughing Boy* in 1929 to critical acclaim and a Pulitzer Prize. The novel chronicles the life of a Navajo man and "contrasts the material squalor of Navajo life with the culture's overarching goal of achieving beauty and harmony."[11] Many of these writers romanticized aspects of Indian culture and sometimes sought to freeze Indian societies in an idealized past, but they also presented multidimensional images of Indian cultures.[12] The late 1920s and 1930s, too, saw the publication of several novels and memoirs by American Indian authors conveying the complexity of contemporary Indian life, including John Joseph Mathews's *Sundown* and *Wah'kon-tah: The Osage and The White Man's Road* (a Book-of-the-Month Club selection in 1929), D'Arcy McNickle's *The Surrounded*, and Luther Standing Bear's *Land of the Spotted Eagle*. Many non-Indian editors also collaborated with native authors to produce "as-told-to" autobiographies, including John Neihardt's *Black Elk Speaks*. Tellingly, though published in 1932, *Black Elk Speaks* would not gain a significant following until the 1960s.[13]

Writers of the late 1940s and 1950s narrowed the scope of perspectives on Indian societies and peoples. Scholar Mary Ann Weston asserts that a style of "hard news" reporting in the 1950s led to the accretion of stereotypical images of "the degraded Indian," an image of Indians as "desolate, poverty-stricken people." Weston explains that "stories conveying the degraded Indian image tended to describe . . . what Indians lacked *vis-à-*

*vis* white society without mentioning the strengths of Native American cultures. Usually the deficiencies were in material comfort, health care, and education."[14] These writers reduced Indianness to a series of socioeconomic statistics and thereby helped to create a ubiquitous set of images of American Indians that would inadvertently contribute to Indian child removal in the 1960s and 1970s.

Writers differed in their assessment of *why* Indians were so poor and what should be done about it. Some Christian commentators put forth analyses and solutions from an earlier era. Muriel Day, the executive director of the Methodist organization Woman's Division of Christian Service, echoed maternalist women reformers of the nineteenth century when she declared that "the problem of paganism" kept the Navajos down and insisted that "Christian character is the greatest need of the Navajo today." She offered "the rudiments of good housekeeping and happy home-building" as an antidote to Navajo problems. Many Christian commentators believed, too, that termination of Indian peoples was key to their advancement. Day seconded the opinion of the superintendent of the Navajo Methodist Mission School, who asserted that "any plan aimed toward betterment of conditions among the Navajos should be considered incomplete unless it provides for the release of the Navajos from wardship."[15] Like legislators in Congress, these writers portrayed termination as a "release" from a subservient, dependent status.

A competing strain of Christian liberalism spread in the 1940s and 1950s, however, that analyzed the Indian problem more radically and was sharply critical of government policy.[16] Harold Fey epitomized this progressive Christianity. Fey had graduated from Yale Divinity School in 1927 and become an ordained minister in the Disciples of Christ. He worked as the executive director of the Fellowship of Reconciliation, a Christian pacifist organization, from 1935 to 1940. From 1940 until 1964 he served as a correspondent, field editor, executive editor, and then editor-in-chief of the *Christian Century*, a nondenominational Protestant weekly.[17] Fey published a series of articles on American Indians in 1956 that became part of an educational campaign for the National Council of Churches in 1957. In 1959 he published *Indians and Other Americans: Two Ways of Life Meet* with D'Arcy McNickle (Salish Kootenai), a prominent Indian New Dealer and founding member of the National Congress of American Indians.[18]

Writers such as Fey focused on poverty as the true root of American Indian problems, including the problems of struggling Indian families. "When the minimum is lacking, as it is in far too many Indian tribes," Fey pointed out, "personal, family and social demoralization sets in. Conditions that crush the individual, disrupt family life and breed delinquency among the young . . . are common."[19] Unlike more conservative Christians such as Muriel Day, who tended to believe that Indian family deficiencies led to poverty, Fey held the opposite view.

Progressive Christians believed that the persistence of Indian poverty in the age of affluence represented a stain on the American nation and Christianity. Fey and others emphasized a sense of obligation to American Indians that was both a Christian calling and an American responsibility, especially in regard to America's role in the world. Fey compared the persistence of Indian poverty with that in "underdeveloped lands." He queried his readers: "With American prosperity at unprecedented heights, we are rightly concerned to help the world's exiles and the people of underdeveloped lands attain a higher level of life. Should we not be equally ready to help hundreds of thousands of American citizens whose poverty condemns them to live in rural and urban slums, without adequate food, housing or even clothing? . . . Should we not be equally aware that life expectancy of Indians in America is in many places less than half that of a white person?"[20] Liberal Christian rhetoric about American Indians invoked familiar associations in the Cold War era.

Progressive Christian writers like Fey charged the government with exacerbating Indian poverty. The BIA had failed to promote adequate economic development and to safeguard natural resources on Indian reservations, they charged. Fey wrote a scathing exposé on the lack of water on the Pima reservation in Arizona. He traveled to the home of World War II hero Ira Hayes (one of the marines who raised the flag on Iwo Jima) while Hayes's relatives were at his funeral at Arlington National Cemetery in Washington DC. Fey was appalled to find that the Hayes home on the Pima reservation "presented a picture of dust and desolation, since no water was available for irrigation. A few miles away [off the reservation] water runs in the irrigation ditches and the desert produces cotton, barley, wheat and alfalfa, to say nothing of citrus fruit." Fey discovered that non-Indians had settled upstream from the Pimas, had taken their water, and had successfully lobbied Congress to prevent the Pimas from irrigating with water that rightfully belonged to them.[21] Fey sought to educate his fellow Christians about such ongoing injustice and challenged them to speak out against it.

Progressive Christian writers believed that both the church and the federal government in the postwar era had fallen short in their dealings with Indians. Fey asserted forcefully in one of his editorials: "Honesty requires us to admit that we have largely bungled our relations with the original inhabitants of this continent and their descendants." He called upon Christian Americans to exercise "justice and mercy" toward the Indian minority. "No question of human relations involves our spiritual integrity more deeply than this one," he declared. "At no point does the relation between the 'white' and 'colored' races more clearly pose the issue of social justice.... The means to correct ancient and recurring wrongs are at hand. It is possible for us to make our actions more nearly consistent with our Christian professions."[22] Fey urged his fellow Christians to face up to their role in injustices that the American government had visited upon American Indians.

Progressive Christians emphasized that rather than dispensing charity to Indians, caring Christians should use the political system to seek justice for them. Fey noted that it might be easier for churchwomen in Phoenix to hold a cake-social to raise money for an Indian boy or girl to go to school, but if the Pima Indians got all the water to which they were entitled, "they can and will earn a good living and be able to educate their own children." Fey declared that "Indians prefer justice to charity," and he supported empowering Indian peoples with the means to support themselves economically.[23]

Fey and many other progressive Christians regarded postwar government Indian policy as profoundly undemocratic, as reflected in House Concurrent Resolution 108, Public Law 280, and other termination bills, for it failed to consult with Indian tribes or require their consent.[24] Fey wrote in one of his "eyewitness" articles, "Nobody can convince the Indians that I met that [Public Law 587, terminating the Klamath Indian tribe] honorably fulfills the pledges our government has made in solemn treaties and agreements." Fey concluded that the termination bill for the Klamaths represented a "very serious injustice."[25] Progressive Christians favored greater Indian control over their own affairs and recommended that the termination process be slowed or halted altogether.

Fey did not embrace Indian self-determination wholeheartedly, however. He harbored reservations about the viability of Indian cultures and believed that ultimately Indians would and should become integrated into American culture. He distinguished his position from that of John Collier and other like-minded Americans of the 1930s, noting that in recent years "some officials have taken the view that one religion is as good as another, and that the Indian should be encouraged to return to his ancient beliefs as an essential element in his retention of Indian culture." Fey asserted instead that "this sentimentalism is no service to the Indian." He regarded American Indian religions as inferior to Christianity, as "animism, which was what would be expected of a people at their stage of development." Fey and other progressive Christians above all sought to "build a new tribe or society," and the church, to Fey, "cannot rest until this community of the redeemed includes all tribes, all nations, all races, dwelling together in amity on the whole earth." Fey was fond of suggesting that Indians should retain what was good in their own culture, which he did not elaborate on, but be open to adopting the good in western culture—namely Protestant Christianity.[26] He never completely abandoned a paternalistic attitude toward Indian people.

Many radical and progressive Christians were moved by such reporting on the "plight" of Indians. They favored the forging of direct personal relationships with Indians as a means of alleviating their hardships. As the government's Operation Relocation program went into effect, churches took a leadership role in welcoming Indian families and easing their transition into city life.[27] The United Church Committee on Indian Work in Minneapolis and St. Paul ministered to urban Indian families. "In their effort to adjust themselves to urban life," the Reverend David Clark, reported, "Indian people have encountered innumerable problems, spiritual, moral and material which they have often been unable to resolve because of inadequate preparation and resources on their part." To "concern itself with a Christian solution of these problems," the United Church Committee brought together representatives from various Protestant evangelical denominations and church-related agencies. The group assisted Indian migrants to the city to "find a church home in the congregation of their choice, and to help them in the solution of their social and material problems by relating them to the proper agencies already existing in the community."[28]

Other liberal church-based groups took a somewhat different approach; they joined *with* Indian people in providing these services. The American Friends Service Committee (AFSC), a Quaker group, sponsored the Los Angeles Indian center in the 1950s. The AFSC's 1952–53 brochure about the Indian center made clear that while sponsored by the AFSC and funded by "contributions by the public," the center was "a self-help project under the responsible guidance of Indian people." "A Council made up of 20 Indians and 4 Quakers plan and carry out an active program," the brochure explained, and "four full-time employees, 3 of whom have Indian blood, work under the Council's direction."[29] The AFSC was concerned with how to "close the gap of misunderstanding" between Indians and non-Indians, and they sponsored a Southwest American Indian Program in the 1950s. This program offered volunteer summer work camps for non-Indian college-age youth to "work side-by-side" with Indians on "vital Indian community projects." The AFSC also organized two-week summertime visits by Navajo and Hopi children with non-Indian families in California as a means to "close the gap we have allowed to grow between us" and to cultivate a "two-way development of understanding and continuing relationships."[30]

The AFSC defined their objective in Indian work overall as "a satisfying and integrated life for each individual attainable on reservation and off." Their approach rested on the belief that the "lives of non-Indians and Indians alike are enriched by an increased understanding and application of the values inherent in each of our differing cultures."[31] Such a view was at odds with the terminationist mindset that Indian cultures held little of value and that assimilation into the dominant culture represented the only viable fate for Indian peoples. The AFSC's attitude of working *with* rather than *for* Indian people and its activism in the 1950s represent perhaps the most forward-thinking approach of all the Christian groups, one that eschewed paternalism and aligned with the emerging Indian self-determination movement.

Many churches became quite critical of the BIA relocation program as a result of their work to help relocated Indian families. The Association on American Indian Affairs report on the relocation program mentions that "the churches in the Relocation cities, like the Indian centers but not as acrimoniously, began to question the reasons underlying the Program and the conditions to which Indians were being relocated." The BIA then began to regard the churches as "benevolent troublemakers."[32] Thus many liberal Protestant churches in the early to mid-1950s represented a strong voice of opposition to the government's termination and relocation policies.

Other churches, however, developed programs that supported terminationist goals more than the aspirations of most Indians. In 1947 the Church of Jesus Christ Latter Day Saints (LDS), or Mormon Church, developed an extensive outreach program to American Indians—primarily Navajos—that paralleled the government's efforts. LDS theology regarded American Indians as Lamanites: "lost Israelites descended from the mythical Laman who traveled to the Americas with his family around 600 BC." Lamanite wickedness had led God to curse them through marking them with a dark skin. Historian Matthew Garrett explains, "Mormons . . . believed that Lamanites could overcome this stigma through industrious and moral behavior." The 1830 *Book of Mormon* prophesied an eventual Lamanite redemption through the guidance of white-skinned Mormons.[33] The LDS Church sought to put into practice this fundamental religious tenet in the post–World War II era.

The LDS Indian Student Placement Program (ISPP) operated a foster care program from 1947 to 2000 that had much in common with the BIA's Indian Adoption Project. It placed an estimated 30,000 to 50,000 Navajos and some other Indian children with LDS families for at least nine months of each year while the children attended local schools in Mormon communities. The program fulfilled Mormon goals but also met the needs of some Navajo families who lacked educational opportunities within their own communities.[34] Unlike the AFSC, however, the LDS church did not imagine a future for distinctive Indian communities and cultures. ISPP leader Elder Kimball asserted in 1962, "I firmly believe that tomorrow there will be no reservations," and "I believe that integration into our economy and community life is essential and I look forward to the day."[35] The BIA's Indian Adoption Project was not dissimilar from the LDS Indian Student Placement Program. Both programs had the similar goal of changing Indian culture and assimilating Indian people through the removal of children from their families and their placement in non-Indian families.

The IAP arose within and drew strength from this climate of religious responsibility toward and liberal concern with Indians. IAP director Arnold Lyslo worked to cultivate demand for Indian adoptees by exploiting liberal Americans' desires to reach across racial boundaries and undo legacies of colonial mistrust to form genuine relationships with American Indians. At the same time, Lyslo eschewed and downplayed other aspects of the liberal viewpoint—its indictment of termination and analysis of economic underdevelopment within Indian communities. Instead Lyslo and his allies invoked longstanding images of the unfit Indian family as the basis of Indian poverty, and they promoted intervention in the Indian family and child removal as the means to resolve the chronic "Indian problem." Due in part to Lyslo's concentrated publicity campaign, liberal Americans became drawn to the adoption solution over other more radical alternatives. In this way the IAP deflected liberal Americans from finding common cause with Indian communities to effect true social and economic justice.

Lyslo portrayed the IAP as simply responding to public interest in adopting Indian children, but he actually worked tirelessly to produce a demand for adoptable Indian children. A good deal of Lyslo's work, and later that of the ARENA director and associate director, centered on public relations. Lyslo published a number of articles in *Child Welfare*, a journal primarily for social workers, to encourage them to inform prospective adoptive parents of the availability of Indian children.[36] He was successful, too, in getting national mainstream coverage of his program, including an article in *Good Housekeeping*.[37] As a result of the publicity he generated, Lyslo reported that he received twelve hundred inquiries regarding the adoption of Indian children in 1967.[38] In the 1970s ARENA published its own newsletter with pictures of Indian children who were available for adoption, as for example, "Arlene and Darlene, twins, age 12 yrs.," who were "dress alikes, but not look-alikes." "These Thlingit [sic] Indian girls live in the Great Land (Alaska)," the ad continued, "but would welcome living in any state that could offer them parents."[39] By 1972 the ARENA director's job description included "work[ing] with reporters and writers of newspapers and magazines on articles and publicity about ARENA and adoption" and participating in "TV and radio programs in relation to adoption and ARENA." The program gained publicity in *Reader's Digest, Newsweek, McCall's,* and *Redbook.*[40]

Lyslo particularly realized the value of working with churches in his work to stimulate demand for Indian adoptees. He noted in 1960 that due to a yearlong, nationwide study of American Indians, conducted by the National Council of Protestant Churches in the late 1950s, "many inquiries were made concerning the general welfare of the Indian child, including his availability for adoption."[41] Lyslo carefully cultivated relationships with a variety of church groups. He attended a three-day conference on services to Indians sponsored by the National Council of the Episcopalian Church in Kansas City, Missouri, in 1962. He published or placed articles about the IAP and its need for adoptive families in *Catholic Charities,* the *Lutheran Standard,* and the *Lutheran Witness* and coordinated with Lutheran and Catholic social service bodies in many states.[42] Some religious groups created their own adoption programs for Indian children as a result of Lyslo's efforts. Lutheran Social Services of South Dakota started its own Special Child Placement Project in 1965 and placed 305 Indian children in 240 white families up to 1976.[43] Hence Lyslo capitalized on and channeled the interest of churches in Indian affairs.

Lyslo and the ARENA directors produced particular sentiments regarding Indian children that both harked back to an earlier era and reflected the liberalism of their time. The IAP's benevolent rhetoric of saving Indian children echoed common refrains from the turn-of-the-twentieth-century assimilation era. Joseph Reid, the executive director of the CWLA, explained the genesis of the IAP as originating from concern "for the numbers of homeless Indian children living on reservations who were being deprived of homes of their own because Indian families were unable to absorb these children through adoption."[44] Reid's statement resuscitated the narrative of the suffering Indian child who must be saved by humanitarian non-Indians at the same time as it obliquely revived earlier images of unfit Indian families.[45]

Reid, Lyslo, and other BIA and state welfare officials repurposed this earlier benevolent rhetoric to fit the postwar liberal era and its new colorblind racial ideology. Postwar American liberalism, as Carol Horton writes, "featured a strong, principled stand against racial discrimination" in addition to a continued value on individual rights and liberties, a new commitment to the expansion of the New Deal welfare state, and Keynesian economic policies that promoted economic growth through consumption.[46] This new opposition to racial discrimination included the development of what historian Peggy Pascoe has labeled "colorblindness": "the powerfully persuasive belief that the eradication of racism depends on the deliberate non-recognition of race." Liberals who championed colorblindness in the late 1950s and 1960s viewed it as the "celebrated end of racism," but Pascoe considers it a "racial ideology of its own."[47] IAP rhetoric about Indian families epitomized this new ideology. Adoption supporters contended that Indian children suffered from racial discrimination because they had "been deprived of adoption opportunities" available to other children. A color-blind approach to Indian children rested on the belief that they should have the same access to child welfare services as other American children. Paradoxically, this led to differential attitudes toward and treatment of Indian children.

The discourse and practice of the IAP and the CWLA did not transcend racial categories and hierarchies but actually reified them. The CWLA's programs for "hard-to-place" children reinforced whiteness as normative and non-whiteness as problematic and even pathological. CWLA spokespersons routinely contrasted "blue-ribbon" (blond, blue-eyed) babies with hard-to-place children, those with "special needs—older children, . . . the physically handicapped and children of racial minorities or racial mixtures." Such children were "handicapped by color," one reporter wrote.[48] Another reporter promoted ARENA's "ability to cross lines of 50 states and 10 provinces and escape regional prejudices," and then noted that "ARENA does not restrict its activities to hard-to-place cases. Occasionally, when a community has *more normal, healthy, easy-to-place children* than it does family applicants, ARENA goes to work with agencies in areas where families are waiting for children."[49] Such rhetoric conveyed that white children were normal and in high demand while non-white children were aberrant and undesirable.

Helen Doss's chosen title for her book, *The Family Nobody Wanted*, made similar intimations. She revealed this position more explicitly when she told social workers that "a surplus of homes existed for the fair and perfect child, while nobody wanted those of mixed or minority race."[50]

Though she was a proponent of colorblindness, Doss's juxtaposition of the "fair and perfect child" with the child of mixed or minority race that "nobody wanted," served to fortify rather than break down racial barriers.

This color-blind approach to Indian child welfare upheld racial ideologies in other ways, too. Adoption proponents, in accordance with liberalism's veneration of individual rights, envisioned the individual Indian child as the victim of racism, not the Indian family or tribal community. Lyslo sought to stimulate the conscience of his liberal white audience by positioning Indian children as "forgotten."[51] "During the past decade," Lyslo wrote, "there have been many programs designed to promote the adoption of all children—the handicapped child, the child in the older age group, children of other racial groups both within the United States and from foreign lands. But the Indian child has remained the 'forgotten child,' left unloved and uncared for on the reservation, without a home or parents he can call his own."[52] Lyslo and other policymakers and welfare workers claimed that Indian children were denied racial equality, not because their communities still suffered from colonial policies on the part of the U.S. government that had deepened poverty and inequality, but because they lacked the opportunity to be adopted.[53]

This liberal approach to Indian child welfare not only evaded the differential treatment that Indian people suffered on the basis of race and colonialism. It also laid much of the blame for Indian children's plight on their own families. Lyslo's characterization of the Indian child as "unloved and uncared for" —in the passive voice—scripted Indian parents and families as shadowy offstage figures who had neglected their children and now had little role to play in the liberal drama of rescuing the Indian child. Lurking beneath the new language of colorblindness was a decidedly color-aware notion of Indian adults that relied on timeworn racial stereotypes. Lyslo's use of the singular "forgotten child," to stand in for all Indian children, had the effect of denigrating *all* Indian families as unloving and uncaring and positioning *all* Indian children as in potential need of removal to a new home with new parents. Thus the IAP extended a hand of assistance to Indian children while at the same time virtually slapping down their families with the other hand. Lyslo's rhetorical moves represent what sociologist Eduardo Bonilla-Silva calls "color-blind racism," which "disallow[s] the open expression of racial views" but enables "whites [to] develop . . . a concealed way of voicing them."[54] White authorities rarely made overt comments about Indians as unfit parents, but their characterizations of the "forgotten Indian child" implicitly condemned Indian families. The discourse of Indian adoption thus evaded structural issues about why Indian communities were impoverished and historical questions about why Indian families struggled.

The IAP and many social workers created a corollary to "the forgotten Indian child" in the figure of the "Indian unmarried mother," whom authorities manufactured as an unfit parent. One IAP form listed "unmarried motherhood" as the top social problem—*above* alcoholism, gross neglect of family, criminal record, and mental illness—that social workers should be concerned with in possibly placing an Indian child for adoption.[55] Social scientist David Fanshel, in his longitudinal study of ninety-seven adoptive families from the IAP, pathologized Indian women who gave birth out of wedlock by creating an "index of the biological mother's disability" based on "summating the conditions reported in the referral summaries." Fanshel divided the birth mothers into three types: (1) "conditions where the mothers appeared *least* impaired," (2) "mothers showing problems somewhat more serious," and (3) "very severe cases of personal disorganization."[56] Fanshel started from the assumption that having a child out of wedlock was a sign of psychological problems and proceeded from there to link single Indian motherhood with a host of other pathologies.

Welfare authorities in this era applied some of the same psychological analysis to unwed Indian mothers that they did to white women who bore children out of wedlock. As one social worker put it, "The fact that a woman in violation of the moral code becomes pregnant outside of marriage often means that either her conscience and judgment are not sufficient to control her impulses, or that there is a compelling unhealthy urge to bear a child regardless of the consequences to herself or the child. Certainly, it is true, therefore, that such an unmarried pregnancy is usually symptomatic [of some underlying mental problem]." The social worker added, "To keep an infant born of such unhealthy or casual relationship is usually even more extreme behavior."[57] Social worker Stella Hostbjor applied this prevalent view to Indian women, asserting that "most of the Indian unmarried mothers we have known have had emotional problems which played a part in their illegitimate pregnancies, and that their behavior served a purpose for them."[58] Hostbjor and many other social workers adhered to the psychological theory of the day in their belief that illegitimacy among women demonstrated some inherent mental instability.

Unwed Indian mothers, however, experienced a qualitatively different public attitude than white women who had children out of wedlock. Indian motherhood became virtually synonymous with unwed pregnancy in the eyes of non-Indians. Many outside observers did not regard Indian custom marriages as legitimate. Reid asserted, for example, "There are no formal marriages or divorces among the Southern Ute Indians; the children follow their mother in marital breakups."[59] These views led to commonplace assumptions that by definition an Indian mother was unwed and therefore psychologically unstable and unfit. Thus the gender ideals and sexual norms of the era that proscribed out-of-wedlock pregnancy became particularly racialized in the case of Indian women. This contributed to a climate that made the removal of Indian children much more likely, all in the name of providing the same benefits and services to Indians as to non-Indians.

The image of the deadbeat Indian father who failed to play his manly role as economic provider also featured as a constant of bureaucratic rhetoric. Ben Reifel, the part Lakota director of the Aberdeen Area for the BIA in the 1950s, claimed that "habituation to hard work in order to earn a living has not been part of the Indian way of life, especially for the men." Aleta Brownlee, child welfare consultant to the BIA in the 1950s, similarly indicted the Indian father as "disinclined to get a job or go to where he can get a job to support his family."[60] If the unmarried Indian mother was failing to live up to Cold War era domestic ideals, the supposedly deadbeat Indian father was similarly evading his proper role in the nuclear family.

IAP publicists also portrayed Indian families as deviant because children had multiple caregivers within their extended families. Hostbjor disapproved of Indian families in which children "frequently pass back and forth between mother and grandmother or some other relative."[61] Lyslo contended that "from the experience of the BIA, many of these children are left to run loose on the reservation without proper care or supervision, and no permanent plan is made for them."[62] Here again, through his use of the passive voice, Lyslo implicates an offstage Indian mother who is neglecting her maternal duties. American social norms exalted the middle-class nuclear family and the containment of women's sexuality within it in this era, so such comments conveyed a critique of both Indian gender and sexual norms and Indian childrearing.[63] Further, Lyslo's mention of the need for a "permanent plan" suggests a deeper concern. Discourse about the alleged impermanency, and thus illegitimacy, of Indian family life reflected longstanding settler colonial narratives about Indians. British settlers in early America frequently disparaged the lack of permanent settlements among Indian tribes and justified European takeover of Indian lands on this basis. The post–World War II concern with permanency reflected government agents' desires to resolve the so-called Indian problem for all time. They sought a "permanent" solution: termination.

Social welfare authorities created a composite of Indian life through the accretion of these stereotypical images of the forgotten Indian child, the unmarried Indian mother, the deadbeat Indian father, and the deviant Indian family. This composite then underwrote their support for Indian adoption. Mary Davis, the supervisor of the Family Service Department of the Children's Bureau of Delaware, an agency that worked with the IAP, summed up this narrative:

> The impressions I have of the reservation Indian are gleaned largely from my cursory survey of two reservations, and from social material sent to us about the families of children in our care. Since most children placed for adoption were born out of wedlock, perhaps it is also true that my knowledge is gathered from families with a degree of social pathology. Within these limits, I have formed a few rather clear impressions of the Indian on the reservation. I have the sense that for many Indians living on a reservation, there is a dead-end quality and a humdrumness to their existence which transcends any ability or wish to accomplish or achieve. The soporific quality to life on a reservation must have some bearing on the fact that, among the families of our children, heavy drinking seems to be the rule rather than the exception.[64]

Davis completes the stereotypical composite with her inclusion of "heavy drinking" as a dominant feature of Indian life. Scholar Mary Ann Weston notes the fixation with stories of drunken Indians in news coverage of Native Americans in the twentieth century. She cites a brief wire service

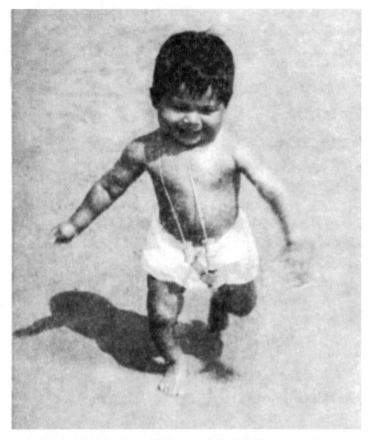

Fig. 2. "Dead end—or a chance?" From Arnold Lyslo, "The Indian Adoption Project: An Appeal to Catholic Agencies to Participate," *Catholic Charities Review* 48, no. 5 (May 1964): 13.

story from Oklahoma, carried in papers all over the country, about an exposition there that drew over two thousand Indians. The article focused on the arrests of fourteen people for drunkenness. Weston explains that the article "could not help but reinforce the image of degraded Indians as alcohol abusers. . . . If there was an Indian gathering, the number of arrests for drunkenness was automatically newsworthy."[65] Alcohol abuse did plague Indian communities, as well as middle-class American suburbs, but it became a defining feature of Indian dysfunction.

Adoption supporters increasingly conveyed these characterizations of Indian family life with single images and a minimum of text. Lyslo included in an article he wrote for *Catholic Charities* a photograph of an Indian toddler happily frolicking on a stretch of sand, captioned, "Dead end—or a chance?" The caption encapsulated this dual characterization of Indian pathology and the benevolence of adoption.[66] Such narratives became ubiquitous among most non-Indian Americans in the late 1950s and 1960s.

This new narrative about Indian life and experience displaced the 1950s progressive Christian explanation of Indian problems. No longer was it government policy or economic underdevelopment that caused the persistence of Indian poverty and dire economic prospects; it was the pathological Indian family.[67] This account found support and resonance within the increasingly popular field of social science in the postwar era. The roots of this social science orientation toward American Indians owed much to the Indian New Deal, when John Collier readily employed anthropologists as consultants on Indian policy.[68] Earlier anthropologists had focused on recovering traditional cultures, their approaches sometimes derogatorily referred to as salvage ethnography. These new social scientists focused on contemporary Indian cultures and nearly always characterized them as experiencing cultural breakdown, disintegration, and disorganization.[69] Many of these studies incorporated trendy new psychological approaches and focused primarily on children and family life.

The Committee on Human Development at the University of Chicago and the BIA initiated one such project in 1941 that gives the flavor of such studies. The project resulted in the publication of "five integrative studies of Indian personality," four of them in the late 1940s on the Pine Ridge Sioux, Hopis, Navajos, and Papagos, and one on the Zunis in 1966. The Pine Ridge Sioux study, Gordon MacGregor's *Warriors without Weapons*, involved ten case studies and the intensive examination of 166 children.[70]

The first part of MacGregor's book reveals an Indian community that is maintaining many of its traditional family structures and methods of childrearing to provide children with a safe and secure upbringing. Mac-Gregor described in one early chapter the persistence of the traditional *tiyospaye*, ten to twenty families living together as a band, despite the rise of the nuclear family as an outcome of government policies in the assimilation era.[71] He mentioned the ubiquity of extended families and the lack of a stigma against premarital sex or unwed pregnancy. He demonstrated, too, the continued use of traditional Dakota childrearing methods that emphasized the child as an individual with responsibility for his or her own actions from an early age. MacGregor reported that as a result of these extended family relationships and child-rearing methods, family appeared in Dakota children's stories as "a haven and a source of pleasure."[72]

MacGregor decided, however, that Dakota children were troubled. He subjected the 166 children to a battery of psychological tests—IQ, Emotional Response, Moral Ideology, and Thematic Apperception—and concluded that the children regarded the world "beyond the family or circle of relatives" as hostile. He contended that "Dakota child personality seems crippled and negative, as if it rejected life." Of the ten case studies he featured, he claimed that half of the children were maladjusted, a favorite phrase of psychologists in this era. MacGregor attributed this to "the unfriendly environment, which offers so little opportunity or satisfaction, retards the growth of personality and prevents it from becoming positive, rich, and mature." He concluded that the "modern Indian way of life is one of emptiness."[73] MacGregor failed to analyze the historical factors and ongoing structural inequalities that contributed to the hostile, "unfriendly environment" the children inhabited outside their families.

MacGregor also downplayed his own findings and dismissed the extended family as a source of strength for these children, many of whom endured the alienation of boarding school. Instead MacGregor overwhelmingly conveyed dysfunction among Pine Ridge families. He utilized social science terms of his day to raise an alarm about increasing "sexual delinquency," which he linked to "general social disorganization." He disapprovingly noted that many children were living with relatives other than their nuclear families, even though this was a longstanding practice. "The frequency with which children are now voluntarily living away from their parents' home without disapproval by the adults," he writes, "may be looked upon as symptomatic of cultural breakdown."[74] MacGregor attributed the problems in Pine Ridge families in part to changes in gender roles. He noted that mothers now occupied the center of the present-day Sioux family and that the father's role had been minimized due to the disappearance of men's former occupations, including cattle ranching. The Sioux had traditionally been a male-centered culture, he asserted, but men's roles had been reduced while the position of women in family and community had risen. As a result, he claimed that women had become critical of men's behavior and that hostility had erupted between the sexes.[75]

If MacGregor's analysis seems somewhat familiar, it is because he makes many of the same points that another social scientist cum politician would make in a famous document from the 1960s: "The Negro Family: The Case for National Action," a report released in March 1965 by President Lyndon B. Johnson's assistant secretary of labor, Daniel Patrick Moynihan. Moynihan argued that "the family structure of lower class Negroes is highly unstable, and in many urban centers is approaching complete breakdown." He noted that "nearly a quarter of urban Negro marriages are dissolved," that "almost one-fourth of Negro families are headed by females," and that "the breakdown of the Negro family has led to a startling increase in welfare dependency." Calling the Negro family a "tangle of pathology," Moynihan claimed that "in essence, the Negro community has been forced into a matriarchal structure which, because it is too out of line with the rest of the American society, seriously retards the progress of the group as a whole, and imposes a crushing burden on the Negro male and, in consequence, on a great many Negro women as well."[76] The Moynihan Report, as it came to be known, blamed poverty in African American communities on family structure, unwed motherhood, and a so-called black matriarchy.

A year later another sociologist, Oscar Lewis, published his influential article "The Culture of Poverty," based on his research into poor Puerto Rican families in San Juan and New York City. Lewis coined the phrase "culture of poverty" as a "label for a specific conceptual model that describes . . . a subculture of Western society with its own structure and rationale, a way of life handed on from generation to generation along family lines."[77] Lewis argued that many social traits that had been attributed to particular racial or ethnic groups were actually traits of the culture of poverty. Echoing both Moynihan and MacGregor, Lewis claimed that in the culture of poverty, "With the instability of consensual marriage the family tends to be mother-centered and tied more closely to the mother's extended family. The female head of the house is given to authoritarian rule."[78] These liberal social scientists explained away social inequalities by denigrating American Indian, African American, and Puerto Rican families and especially women.

Social workers readily applied such social science studies to Indians. "As one would expect," social worker Stella Hostbjor wrote, "there is [among Indians] the social disorganization of a group in the process of cultural change. Symptoms include poverty, dependency, marginal standards of living, family breakdown including illegitimacy, child neglect, alcoholism, delinquency and crime."[79] These representations did not merely lead to stereotyping and prejudice against Indians. They became the basis for social workers removing Indian children from their families and judges placing them with non-Indian families.

With this new narrative about Indians, Lyslo and other welfare workers presented adoption as a benevolent act of caring for Indian children. As David Fanshel put it in his study of IAP adopted children, "When one contrasts the relative security of their lives with the horrendous growing up experiences endured by their mothers—well documented in the summaries Arnold Lyslo received from agencies referring the children, one has to take the position that adoption has saved many of these children from lives of utter ruination."[80] Similarly, Mary Davis of the Children's Bureau of Delaware wrote, "After almost two years of experience in the project, I look back and sometimes think, 'Oh, but it's so infinitesimal in the light of the need.' But then I take another look, and think of what life would have held for [the children they had placed] if we had not helped them on their way to a new start." Davis concluded, "When there is a job to be done and we can help with it, is it right to turn our head in the other direction? Isn't this what the American people have been doing in relation to the American Indian for the last hundred years? This is a good and a growing project, and I am glad to be part of it."[81] Revealingly, both Fanshel and Davis regarded a failure to remove Indian children from their families and communities as an immoral act, as a refusal to care.

Adoption advocates characterized adoption as a means of rectifying past injustices. As Davis explained, "I believe all Americans feel a certain sense of guilt about our country's treatment of the Indian, and so [the Children's Bureau of Delaware was] glad of the chance to do something concrete to offset our nebulous sense of shame."[82] IAP advocates encouraged non-Indians to become agents of racial integration, and many well-meaning liberal families took up the charge. During the Senate subcommittee hearings on the Indian Child Welfare Act, for example, one white woman submitted a statement in support of continued adoptions, concluding, "We *cannot* point with pride to the results of government policies during the past 150 years; in fact we should be ashamed of the way Indians have been treated. It seems to me that this present-day trend towards person-to-person assistance should be encouraged, not frustrated."[83] Thus it was not that non-Indian Americans did not care about Indians. Many Americans did care deeply about the ongoing injustices faced by Native peoples. However, bureaucratic authorities—who were primarily concerned with cutting costs and meeting the policy goal of termination—carefully channeled this caring toward their solution: removal and adoption of Indian children.

Lyslo's efforts to cultivate white sentiment in favor of the adoption of Indian children proved wildly successful. Initially, interest in adoption was fairly modest. Lyslo reported that he received only six to ten letters each month in 1960, two years after the IAP began, from non-Indian families wanting to adopt Indian children.[84] The popularity of Indian children as adoptees grew dramatically over the next decade. By 1968 Clare Jerdone of the BIA's Welfare Branch stated that there were an "excess of approved adoption homes for Indian children over available Indian children."[85] ARENA noted in 1971 that "the number of families interested in adopting these children has mushroomed." They had registered four hundred families who wished to adopt Indian children, but the supply, except for older Indian children, had not kept up with the demand.[86] ARENA asserted in its newsletter in 1969, "Undoubtedly, many of you are aware how popular the Indian child is. He is no longer a child who is hard-to-place unless there are other factors such as his age, a physical or emotional handicap, or the fact that he is a member of a sibling group from which he cannot be separated." ARENA credited the IAP's publicity with generating "much of the interest in adopting the Indian child."[87]

This success resulted in part from the decline in the numbers of so-called blue-ribbon babies to adopt. Fanshel estimates that only one in five adoptive parents he studied set out to adopt an Indian child, and another researcher similarly found that only two of the twelve couples she studied had intended to adopt an Indian child.[88] Fewer white infants were available for adoption as birth control options became more readily available, abortion became legal in the 1970s, and the stigma attached to unwed motherhood declined. The waiting list for blue-ribbon babies was long at many agencies, and many social workers refused to place children with older couples.[89] One adoptive father told Fanshel, "We learned there was an enormous waiting list for the Protestant, Caucasian children who were available for adoption. It was at this point that we became aware of the fact that our best possibility would be to consider a child of mixed racial background or a Caucasian child who was physically handicapped. . . . When the caseworker suggested the possibility of an American Indian child, we were both immediately enthusiastic."[90] Thus pragmatic considerations among adoptive families meshed with a culture that evoked sentiment for Indian children and encouraged their adoption.

The IAP's and ARENA's success also resulted from changing adoption practices. The CWLA had initially supported racial matching in placing children for adoption, but in the 1960s they championed a new colorblind approach. Members of the CWLA's Ad Hoc Committee on Race in Child Welfare at a meeting in May 1965 discussed "activities to promote provision of services on the basis of a child's *need* [original underlined] (regardless of his race)."[91] By 1968 the CWLA left out all mention of race as a determining factor in placing a child for adoption and asserted, "It should not be assumed that difficulties will necessarily arise if adoptive parents and children are of different racial origin. . . . In most communities there are families who have the capacity to adopt a child whose racial background is different from their own. Such couples should be encouraged to consider such a child."[92] In short, the CWLA sought to enact a color-blind policy in regard to the placement of children for adoption.

Adoption practices to some extent reflected the new liberal racial climate and to some extent helped to create it. Progressive families like the Dosses pushed social workers to transcend racial boundaries and helped to raise support for transracial adoption. Helen Doss originally published an article about her adoptive family in the August 1949 *Reader's Digest*; *Life* featured the family in 1951; and a national NBC radio show named them "Christmas family of the year" that same year. Doss's *The Family Nobody Wanted* went through twenty-four printings and was translated into seven languages before going out of print in 1984; and then it was reprinted again in 2001. *McCall's* serialized the book in 1954, and both the Sears People's Choice Book Club and Scholastic Books sold it. The book was also made into two film versions, including a 1975 TV film. Doss estimates that the book sold 500,000 copies; it became required reading in many schools. Published four months before the *Brown v. Board of Education* Supreme Court decision, this story of a multiracial family "opened important cultural fault lines" and gave readers "a white woman's personal view of race and family in America."[93] The book effectively underwrote the new rhetoric of color-blind liberalism.

Some of the rise in interest in Indian adoption can be attributed to religious motivations. Of Fanshel's ninety-seven families, about 70 percent were Protestant, 10 percent were Catholic, and 12 percent were Jewish. Only one family indicated they had "no religion." Fanshel described many adoptive couples whose "deep sense of religiosity" affected their decision to adopt an Indian child. One adoptive father noted about himself, "It may be that I was motivated to some extent by my religious and social beliefs. I do belong to a church that preaches love for all regardless of race. Further, my mother was a kind of missionary among Indians and maybe some of this rubbed off on me."[94] Many families wanted to adopt Indian children as a means of putting their religious principles into practice.

Fanshel's data also reflect strong liberal interest in adopting Indian children, although he downplayed it. He developed an index of adoptive parents' "liberal vs. conservative political orientation," which revealed that 57.8 percent of the ninety-seven adoptive mothers and 54 percent of fathers described themselves as somewhat or very liberal or radical. The Jewish mothers in his study were significantly more liberal than other mothers.[95] When asked whether they were concerned with discrimination against minority groups, a whopping 92.7 percent of mothers and 88 percent of fathers answered that they were somewhat or very concerned.[96] Fanshel compared parents who adopted Indian children with those who adopted white children and found that the IAP families showed more tolerance for differences in others as well as a belief that discrimination is evil.[97] Fanshel often noted a combined liberal sense of social justice and strong religious bent.

Many adoptive families readily understood and explained their decision to adopt Indian children by referring to the ubiquitous imagery of "forgotten" Indian children. One mother in Fanshel's study claimed, "We could have taken any child. However I was aware that *we were doing more for a child when we were adopting an Indian child.* Little has been done for the American Indian and it's about time something more was done." Another adoptive mother declared, "One of the biggest appeals to us was the fact that *these were children who other people did not want as easily,* whereas, we never really cared what children looked like because we just wanted children."[98] Adoptive families accepted the IAP's notions that Indian families were not taking proper care of their children.

Many adoptive parents of Indian children professed an allegiance to colorblindness; they declared that "race doesn't matter." Racial considerations actually figured quite intensively in their motivations and decisions, however. In Catherine Roherty's 1968 study of twelve Wisconsin white families who adopted Indian children, she asked if the adopters would consider adopting a child of mixed race. Some responded affirmatively but stipulated "must not look Indian"; "must be at least half white"; or must be "as light as possible."[99] Most of the adoptive parents in Fanshel's study would not consider or had major reservations about adopting a child of mixed Negro-white parentage but were drawn to the idea of adopting American Indian children.[100] One father told Fanshel, "We had not applied for an Indian child but when they asked us, we readily indicated our willingness. I suddenly got very taken with the notion of adopting a full-blooded American Indian—there was something that moved me about the idea." One mother was initially "quite upset" about adopting "Billy," but "as time went on, Billy's being Indian became very exciting to me. It opened up new areas of interest for us even though we had not gone out looking for this aspect of adoption."[101] Far from being a gesture of colorblindness, the adoption of Indian children involved particular racial calculations and preferences.

It may have been difficult for an individual to change government policy or improve the economic prospects of Indian communities, but adopting an apparently "forgotten" Indian child could serve as a statement of caring about American Indians. An adoptive father told Fanshel,

We had applied for an Oriental child. After the caseworker talked with us about the Indian Adoption Project, we promptly decided to apply for an American Indian child. We have always been very moved by the story of the plight of the Indian and we gave up the idea of adopting a child from abroad on the basis of 'Let's solve our own problem first.' We feel that the American Indian owns the country by right and he has been pushed around and never given a break. In accepting the child, we feel we have done a little bit for the American Indian.[102]

Many adoptive parents shared this father's view that the adoption of an Indian child represented a genuine act of reconciliation toward America's most benighted people.

The heightened concern with Indians among Christians and liberals in the 1950s and 1960s dovetailed with changing federal policies and state practices. Churches urged their followers to address the dismal socioeconomic circumstances of Indian communities, rural and urban. For a brief time, committed Christians sternly criticized the government's termination policy and supported radical solutions aimed at protecting Indian resources, spurring economic development, and even at times calling for Indian self-determination. Through the IAP, however, a new narrative emerged that subtly blamed Indian social and economic woes on incorrigibly deviant Indian families, among whom unmarried Indian mothers were giving birth to and then neglecting "forgotten" Indian children. This new discourse on Indians resonated with other popular social science literature of the period, including the Moynihan Report and Oscar Lewis's "Culture of Poverty" article. As these views gained strength, the radical analyses of liberals in the 1950s receded, and liberal non-Indians increasingly supported the rescue of individual Indian children rather than a more collective struggle for justice. Thus what may have been genuine acts of caring for and about Indian children among white adoptive couples became perverted by the IAP and other pro-Indian adoption groups as means to terminate Indian peoples. Most Americans then, as now, had no idea how devastating the practice of adoption could be for Indian communities, especially Indian women.

PART TWO

# The Indian Child Welfare Crisis in Indian Country

I met "John" at an academic conference. He is one of the most inquisitive academics I have ever encountered. He read all the conference papers carefully in advance and found the most incisive—and often infuriating—questions to ask each presenter. He picked out the flaws in each presenter's arguments and the weaknesses in our evidence.

He is not in my field of history but has done much research about mental health in Indian communities. He has become my go-to reference whenever I have a question in this area. I know he will be able to point me in the right direction.

I asked him one day if there is much recent scholarship on the long-term psychological impact of Indian adoptions. He shared a few articles and dissertations with me, then casually mentioned that by the way, he was adopted. I wanted to know more about his perspective, so we arranged to have a phone conversation.

He told me that a white couple, an attorney and a homemaker, adopted him when he was six months old. They separated when he was five. His family did not live far from Indian communities and wanted him to be aware of his heritage as he grew up. His father, in fact, had worked on an Indian reservation for a while and made sure that John was enrolled in his tribe. His family adopted another Indian boy, too, and John danced in powwows when he was young.

For a time John hoped to become a minister, then after a period of enlistment, he entered one of the nation's military academies. Soon he was studying at an Ivy League university. And today he works as a professor at one of the top public universities in the United States, is happily married, and has three small children. All did not go as well for his adopted brother, who has struggled with alcohol addiction and has had recurrent trouble with the law.

While in college, John found an opportunity to identify his birth family. One spring break when he was in his early twenties, he made a trip to visit his tribe's reservation and met his family. Describing that visit as "completely overwhelming," John learned that his father had once struggled with alcohol but had sobered up and become an activist. He characterized some other members of his family as "a mess."

John tells me he is grateful that he was raised by his adoptive mother and believes that if he hadn't been adopted, he might have shared the fate of too many of his reservation relatives: lost, broken, wounded, or dead before their time. Still, after that first visit, he calls his reservation home, and he has found other relatives whose resilience, he says, is "remarkable." Since then he has become a full-fledged member of his Indian family.

# CHAPTER 3

# Losing Children

David and Louisa Rendon, a White Earth Chippewa couple from Minnesota, had moved to Texas for David's employment in the oil fields in the 1970s. Twenty-four-year-old Louisa had suffered several stillbirths, so the couple was overjoyed when she delivered a premature but healthy baby boy, Jason, in a Texas hospital in April 1974. But the Rendons' elation was shortlived. While the baby was still in the hospital, the Texas Welfare Department obtained a court order giving the state temporary custody of Jason on the grounds that Louisa Rendon "had personal habits which keep her outside the home," and that she "was not prepared for such child," because she had not yet bought a crib or diapers. The Welfare Department also deemed the child to be in a potentially dangerous situation because Mr. Rendon, a migrant worker, "is gone from the home for periods of time." For months the Rendons tried to regain custody of Jason. Finally in January 1975, with the help of the Association on American Indian Affairs attorney Bertram Hirsch, the couple had their day in the Menard County District Court. Hirsch pointed out the unprecedented nature of removing an infant who had not yet even gone home with his parents, on the basis that this couple "would *probably* neglect this child." He also noted how unfair it was to expect the Rendons to have purchased items for the baby already, since he was born prematurely, and to fault David Rendon for engaging in migrant labor. The judge decided in the Rendons' favor, but according to Hirsch, the judge told him during a court recess, "I'm going to give this child back to the Rendons but I'm not going to do it for another thirty days. In thirty days from now they can have this child back." Then the judge astonished Hirsch further when he added, "I don't care what they do with this child; they can barbecue the child, for all I care."[1] The Rendons' harrowing experience was but one of thousands of such scenarios that played out among Indian families across the United States from the 1950s to the 1970s as state authorities took over Indian child welfare services. Yet their stories are largely unknown.

The reports and articles crafted by Indian Adoption Project director Arnold Lyslo and other pro-adoption advocates had rendered Indian families like the Rendons faceless and voiceless, assumed guilty of neglect, abandonment, or abuse. The notion that Indian parents were unfit to raise their own children had become so ingrained within American society that a state welfare department like that in Texas could convince a court to remove a newborn child, despite no evidence of any neglect or abuse on the part of his parents. Many state welfare authorities and courts had become indifferent to the legal rights of Indian families and even downright punitive, as the Rendons' experience illustrates. The judge's arbitrary decision to wait thirty days to return Jason to his parents and his callous comment reveals that he did not regard the Rendons as deserving of the same respect and access to due process as other Americans.

Indian families experienced such disregard at the same time as the field of social work was developing professional standards emphasizing that newborns should only be given up for adoption with the full and informed consent of the mother, that all efforts should be made to prevent the breakup of families, and that children should only be removed as a last resort and for reasons of documented neglect and abuse. Social workers did not apply these same standards to Indian people, despite the noble rhetoric of colorblindness. The experiences of Indian families who lost children reveal that racial and class discrimination as well as prevailing gender norms led social workers to intervene frequently in Indian family life and to remove children. The ubiquitous and reductive narratives regarding Indians in the post–World War II era had devastating consequences for Indian families as social workers and judges often based their decisions to remove Indian children on the stock character of the "forgotten child" as well as his or her allegedly irresponsible parents and aberrant extended family.

Many non-Indian Americans had come to regard the separation of Indian children from their own families as such a commonsense notion that they did not question its effect on Indian caregivers, let alone Indian communities. Social scientist Catherine Roherty, for example, conducted interviews with twelve adoptive families in Wisconsin and concluded that her "findings . . . are sufficient to encourage the enthusiastic continuance of the practice of placing Indian children with Caucasian couples."[2] Roherty reached this conclusion without interviewing Indian parents, extended family members, or community members from whom the children had been taken.

Yet we cannot fully understand the gravity of the fostering and adoption of Indian children outside their communities without recovering the traumatizing experiences of Indian families who lost children. Undoubtedly, some Indian caregivers voluntarily relinquished their children, and social workers removed some children for good cause. BIA and state authorities engaged in untold instances of unwarranted intervention, however, such as that experienced by the Rendons. These Indian families offer a very different story of the Indian child welfare crisis than that of Arnold Lyslo and his associates.

BIA and state authorities claimed that Indian women were gladly relinquishing their babies for adoption once new social services became available to them. Lyslo blithely reported in 1964 that "Indian unmarried mothers are making much more use of maternity home services today than they did five years ago, and with the assurance that good families are interested in adopting Indian children, the unmarried mother is more likely to release her child for adoption."[3] Certainly there were some Indian women who chose to place their children for adoption. Deborah Juarez, a Blackfeet woman who grew up on the Puyallup Reservation in Washington, was just fifteen years old when she was raped and became pregnant. With the help of older Indian women when she was seven months pregnant, she made the decision to relinquish the child. Juarez echoed what many other frustrated young Indian women felt; she asserted in a radio interview that she did not want to raise her child under the circumstances of her family: on welfare and in poverty. Even in such cases of voluntary relinquishment, it is apparent that many young Indian women's choices were extremely constricted. Juarez, a former social worker and now an attorney, believes that if the Indian Child Welfare Act had been in place when she had her son, many of her relatives would gladly have raised him.[4]

Fig. 3. Cheryl Spider DeCoteau of the Sisseton-Wahpeton Sioux nation in Lake Traverse, South Dakota, giving testimony to the 1974 congressional hearings on Indian child welfare. Courtesy and permission of the Association on American Indian Affairs.

Many Indian women experienced intense pressure from social workers and other authorities to put their newborn infants up for adoption. Cheryl Spider DeCoteau, of the Sisseton-Wahpeton tribe in South Dakota, testified to a U.S. Senate subcommittee in 1974 that one of her children had been removed while staying with a babysitter. While DeCoteau was pregnant with another child, she recounted, a male social worker "kept coming over to the house . . . every week. . . . and they kept talking to me and asking if I would give him up for adoption and said that it would be best. They kept coming and coming and finally when I did have him, [the social worker] came to the hospital. After I came home with the baby, [the social worker] come over to the house. He asked me if I would give him up for adoption and I said no." The social worker persisted; he made weekly visits to DeCoteau's home. Finally the social worker demanded that DeCoteau come to his office to sign some papers. "When they took me in the office there, the social worker went and called another lady in to watch the baby in the next room until I got done," DeCoteau recalled. "I was kind of sick then . . . and I didn't know what I was signing." The social worker refused to return her now four-month-old son, Bobby, as soon as she signed the papers.[5]

Like DeCoteau, many Indian mothers who did sign consent forms claimed that they were not aware that the form they had signed made their child available for adoption or terminated their parental rights. This may sound disingenuous, but at least one copy of a consent form that I have found does not clearly state its intent. Titled "Authorization for Discharge of Infant Child to Person Other than Parent and Related Matters," the form, according to a memo for social workers, was "intended for use in cases where a newborn infant is being surrendered by a parent for adoption." Yet the form is misleading in that it does not explicitly state that the parent is giving the child up for adoption or terminating parental rights. Officials did recommend that "whenever possible, arrangements be made to have one of the parents make the actual delivery [into state care] even though the form has been signed."[6] From the testimony of many Indian women, this rarely occurred. Social workers coaxed or bullied Indian mothers in many cases, without the presence of relatives or the father of the child, into signing such a form and relinquishing their children. State authorities may have been complying with the letter of the law regarding consent, but they clearly engaged in coercion and subterfuge.

Some social workers have confirmed what many Indian women claimed to have experienced. Renee Samson Flood, a social worker in southeastern South Dakota from 1980 to 1987, routinely witnessed the intimidation used against young Indian mothers. She describes one day when she went to a local hospital with another social worker. A young Lakota mother had just given birth and was holding her sleeping baby boy wrapped in a blanket. The social worker barged into her hospital room and pelted her with questions: "Are you having trouble finding a place to stay? . . . . How will you raise your child without money? . . . What kind of life can you provide for him on the reservation?" The social worker told the young woman that if she really loved her baby boy, she would give him a chance in life by allowing him to be adopted by one of a long list of couples who could give him more opportunities in life. "Tears ran down [the young mother's] cheeks and dripped from her chin," Flood remembered. Flood became upset and went out into the hall. "It seemed like hours before the social worker finally came out carrying the signed papers and the tiny

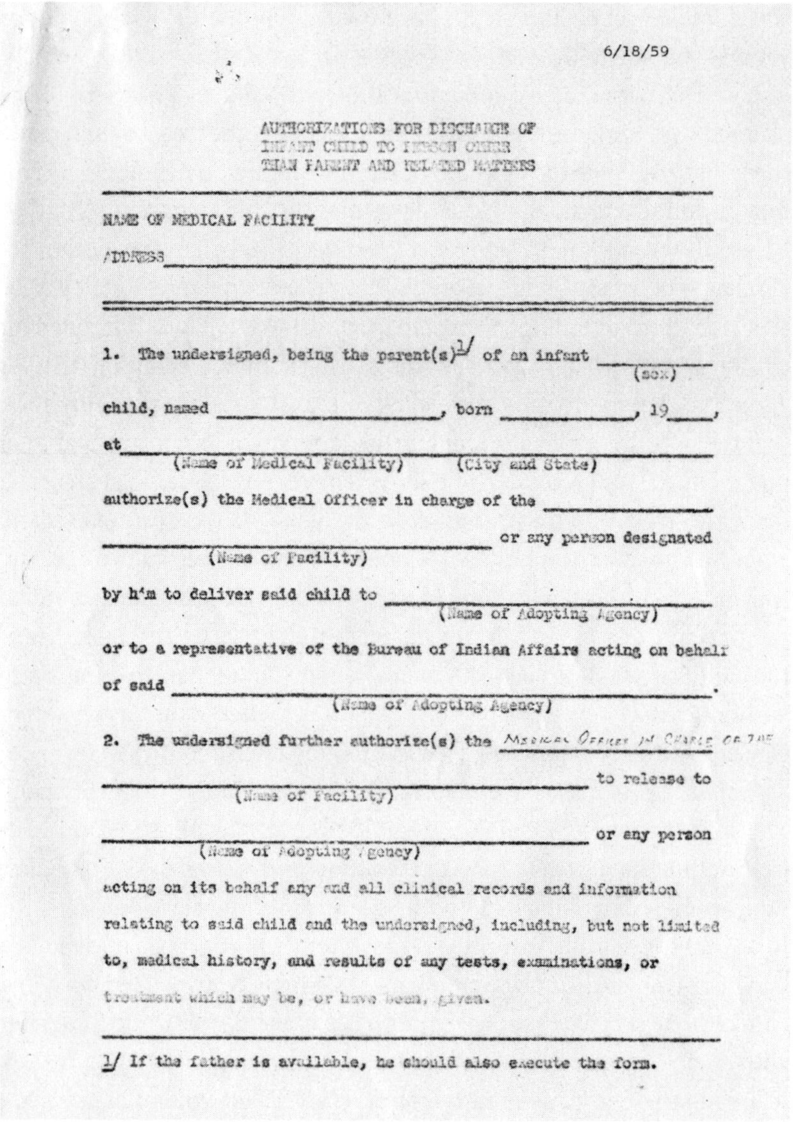

AUTHORIZATION FOR DISCHARGE OF
INFANT CHILD TO PERSON OTHER
THAN PARENT AND RELATED MATTERS

NAME OF MEDICAL FACILITY_____

ADDRESS_____

1. The undersigned, being the parent(s)[1] of an infant _____
(sex)

child, named _____, born _____, 19____,

at_____
(Name of Medical Facility)        (City and State)

authorize(s) the Medical Officer in charge of the _____

_____ or any person designated
(Name of Facility)

by him to deliver said child to _____
(Name of Adopting Agency)

or to a representative of the Bureau of Indian Affairs acting on behalf

of said _____
(Name of Adopting Agency)

2. The undersigned further authorize(s) the *Medical Officer in Charge of the*

_____ to release to
(Name of Facility)

_____ or any person
(Name of Adopting Agency)

acting on its behalf any and all clinical records and information

relating to said child and the undersigned, including, but not limited

to, medical history, and results of any tests, examinations, or

treatment which may be, or have been, given.

[1] If the father is available, he should also execute the form.

Fig. 4. "Authorization for Discharge of Infant Child to Person Other Than Parent and Related Matters," 1959. Courtesy and permission of the Association on American Indian Affairs records, 1851–2010, Public Policy Papers, Department of Rare Books and Manuscripts, Princeton University Library, Princeton, New Jersey.

3. The undersigned also authorize(s) _ANY MEDICAL OFFICER IN CHARGE_
(Name of Facility)

to provide any examination, medical care, treatment or surgery for said
child upon the request or with the consent of any person in whose care
the child has been placed, or if no such person be available, at the
request of a representative of the Bureau of Indian Affairs responsible
for providing for the care of the child.

The undersigned (has, have) read the above (the above has been read
and explained to the undersigned2/ by _____

_____ )
(Street Number, City, State)

and this consent is voluntarily executed on the _____ day of

_____, 19____.

Signature of Mother3/ _____

_____

Address _____

City and State _____

Witness:

_____        _____
                                  (Address)

2/ If parent is illiterate, signature should be made by mark as follows:
                        Her
                     Mary X Doe
                        Mark
                         . also execute the discharge form
3/ If father is available, he should sign immediately below the mother's
   signature.

baby," Flood recalled. The other social worker scolded Flood for leaving the room and confided to a nurse that the young mother "did the right thing." The nurse responded, "They usually do . . . . Once they realize their children have no future if they keep them." Flood thought all the young Lakota mother needed was "the right supportive services" or perhaps just a bus ticket home. As Flood and the social worker drove away from the hospital to the foster home, "the worker talked incessantly of the negative aspects of reservation life," a disquisition that Flood, who was married to a Yankton Sioux, described as "ten minutes of bigoted generalizations about Indians. 'They never go to college. Their houses are filthy. They all drink. They dress in rags and never bathe. They all get government checks every month.'"[7] Clearly this social worker had imbibed the popular perceptions that adoption advocates and social scientists had helped to create over several decades. Not all social workers behaved this way, and it is important not to stereotype social workers in the same fashion that this social worker stereotyped Indians. Unfortunately, however, many Indian women did suffer the kind of unrelenting intimidation from social workers described by DeCoteau and Flood.

Indian women's experiences were not unique in this period. Social workers also sought to compel young white middle-class unwed mothers to put their babies up for adoption in the 1950s and 1960s. Ann Fessler estimates that between 1945 and 1973, unwed mothers relinquished one and a half million babies for non-family adoptions due to such pressure.[8] Yet Indian women faced more intense scrutiny and intimidation to give up their babies because of stereotypes of Indian women as unfit mothers, the notion that nearly all Indian mothers were unwed, and popular perceptions of dysfunctional Indian family life. Moreover, the consequence of removing Indian infants from their mothers not only violated the individual rights of women, as it did with so many white unwed mothers, but also undermined the viability of Indian tribes and violated their rights to exist as a group.

It was not just young unwed Indian mothers who endured such experiences; many married Indian women did as well. Lyslo gave the impression that most Indian adoptees came from unwed teen mothers. According to Fanshel's study of nearly one hundred children who were put up for adoption through the IAP, however, only 28.1 percent of birth mothers were aged fifteen to nineteen. The median age of birth mothers was twenty-four years old, the same age as Louisa Rendon.[9] The majority of these birth mothers were married or in committed relationships according to Indian customs. Fanshel noted that only 46.8 percent of the birth mothers were single, never married.[10] Thus unlike American women more generally, Indian women, whether they were unmarried or not, commonly faced harassment to relinquish their children for adoption.

We will never know how many of these Indian women actually wished to place their children for adoption. This question misses a significant point, however. To Indian people, children did not belong only to their mothers or to their nuclear families but were also members of extended families, clans, and tribes. Thus the decision to place a child outside the tribe affected and rested not just with the birth mother or father but with many others as well. Such a conception seems unfathomable to members of the dominant American culture who prize individual choice above collective rights. Yet if we imagine what it would mean to remove children en masse from other distinctive minorities— Jews, Mormons, or the Amish—we may gain some understanding of Indian points of view. Furthermore, because they assert a sovereign status, tribes object to the removal of their children much as other nations such as Guatemala have reacted to the widespread adoption of children from their country.[11]

Indian families lost children in other ways, too. Many caregivers felt compelled to relinquish children because of the health problems that so disproportionately affected Indian people. Both the birth mother and father in one family contracted tuberculosis and agreed to have their child put in a foster home. Later an IAP couple adopted the child.[12] The parents in another family approached an agency to have their unborn child placed for adoption because "the mother said she was unable to care for an infant due to the presence in her home of an older child who was sick and required constant care."[13] Sadly, the greater prevalence of serious illnesses and disabilities and the lower life expectancies among Indian people often undermined family life and made "voluntary" child relinquishment virtually the only option.

Other Indian families lost older children because state authorities charged them with neglect. This was warranted at times. A Minnesota

Child Welfare Services report from 1957 alleges that the biological parents of "Joe" neglected their seven children. One night while his parents were out, Joe thought his siblings were too cold. He started a fire in the stove but it went out of control. Four of his brothers and sisters perished in the fire, and authorities removed Joe to a center for disturbed children, then to multiple foster homes.[14] Clearly there were some Indian parents who were not adequately taking care of or were endangering their children, leading to disastrous consequences like that experienced by Joe and his siblings. However, as explored in the following chapter, many Indian social workers, tribal leaders, and community activists believed that Indian people possessed the skills to address these problems adequately without resort to widespread fostering and adoption of children in non-Indian families.

In many other instances, it appears that authorities removed Indian children on claims of neglect but without just cause. Many of these cases came to the attention of the AAIA in the early to mid-1970s, and it developed a legal program to defend Indian families. AAIA staff members learned, for example, that the Whatcom County Juvenile Bureau and Whatcom County Department of Public Welfare in Washington state prepared dependency and neglect proceedings against a Lummi mother and her four children, based in large part "on deficiencies in the mother's apartment resulting from the landlord's failure to make repairs."[15] In another case "a Michigan county welfare department removed six Ottawa children from their parents on the grounds that their home lacked indoor plumbing." An AAIA attorney wryly noted, "If such grounds are allowed to stand, approximately one out of every two reservation Indian families would be disqualified from raising children."[16]

These cases raise the question of just what constituted neglect. What standards should be used to evaluate whether children should be removed from their birth mothers, biological parents, or other caretakers? And are these standards objective and universal or do they inevitably reflect social norms and ideals that are particular to a class, culture, and era? Throughout the course of the 1950s and 1960s the Child Welfare League of America drafted a series of standards designed to rationalize social work practice in regard to child welfare. A 1960 booklet regarding "Standards for Child Protective Service" noted:

It is presumed that physical, emotional and intellectual growth and welfare are being jeopardized [by parents or caregivers] when ... the child is:

malnourished, ill-clad, dirty, without proper shelter or sleeping
    arrangements
without supervision, unattended
ill and lacking essential medical care
denied normal experiences that produce feelings of being loved,
    wanted, secure and worthy (emotional neglect)
failing to attend school regularly
exploited, overworked
physically abused
emotionally disturbed, due to continuous friction in home, marital
    discord, mentally ill parents
exposed to unwholesome and demoralizing circumstances.[17]

Some of these standards—"proper . . . sleeping arrangements," for example—betray a class and culture bias premised on the belief that children should not share beds or sleep in the same room with their parents. This standard would mean that millions of children worldwide—then and now—would be considered neglected.

Furthermore, American Indians suffered from high rates of unemployment and ill health and often lacked access to indoor plumbing, adequate housing, and health care, so many of these standards—"malnourished, ill-clad, dirty, without proper shelter" and "ill and lacking essential medical care"—made them particularly vulnerable to child removal. Clearly these standards regarded poverty rather than verified parental neglect or abuse to be grounds for removing children. This was an era of relative affluence, when the post–World War II economic boom had lifted the economic prospects of millions of Americans, and many child welfare workers associated the persistence of Indian poverty with moral and cultural failing.

Many Indian families also fell into a particularly galling catch-22. They often lacked the social service benefits that would have alleviated such material deprivation. Some states denied indigent Indian people the same benefits and services available to other poor residents—and then removed their children due to their low socioeconomic status. The state of South Dakota became notorious for such practices. George Keller, superintendent of the Rosebud Agency, wrote in frustration to the state's Department of Social Services in 1976 about several cases in which the state was refusing to serve Indian people. In perhaps the most egregious example, an Indian mother applied for Aid to Dependent Children (ADC), federally administered assistance that was funneled through the states, on October 8, 1976, but within a week, state authorities charged her with neglect and placed her child in foster care. When questioned as to why South Dakota had not provided any social services to the mother before removing her child, the state denied that they had any responsibility to provide social services to the mother "on the basis that the mother was not approved for ADC payment." The state denied the mother's application for ADC on November 3, 1976, "on the basis that she no longer had the child in her care."[18] Thus an Indian mother applied for benefits that would have made it easier for her to care for her child, but before she could be approved for benefits, state authorities removed her child and then denied her benefits because she no longer had a child to support!

Other states similarly sought to evade their responsibilities to Indian residents, especially when tribes questioned whether state courts held jurisdiction in child welfare cases. After tribes in North Dakota challenged the high rates of Indian child removal, the state attorney general ruled that state and county government lacked jurisdiction on reservations. He then made it impossible for tribes to obtain funds available from the state that were administered through the Aid to Families with Dependent Children foster care program. Thomas Smithson, an attorney with the Native American Rights Fund, explained to Hirsch in 1972 that "North Dakota is attempting to use its lack of jurisdiction of civil and criminal causes of action as a basis for the refusal to provide services to Indian people to which other persons in the state are entitled." Smithson remarked, "I would guess that such a position is a self-serving attempt by the state to avoid responsibilities which appear to me to be dictated under the state-wide requirement of the Social Security Act." In short, he asserted, it was "a jurisdictional dodge."[19]

Indian families who moved to cities as part of the government's relocation program similarly faced this "jurisdictional dodge" at the same time as they experienced a lack of extended family support and heightened scrutiny from child welfare authorities. The BIA's relocation program had promised better economic opportunities and employment for Indians who migrated to urban areas, but many Indians found instead that they had traded reservation poverty for urban impoverishment. Chronic unemployment and underemployment caused many urban Indians to turn to social service agencies for help, but relocated Indians faced policies that barred them from receiving public welfare assistance in urban areas until they had met a residency requirement. Many relocated Indians told a team of researchers that "City Relocation Offices cut off their financial help before relocated Indians have resided in a city long enough to qualify for community welfare aid."[20] Moreover, when urban Indians sought aid at state and county agencies, social workers often responded by removing their children rather than extending necessary financial support. Psychiatrist Joseph Westermeyer compiled a list of cases in Minnesota in which Indian families at a time of crisis voluntarily sought help from a state agency for welfare assistance because of insufficient funds for food and shelter. In his study of eight such families, Westermeyer found that the state agencies summarily removed the children in each case and placed them in white foster homes without providing meaningful social services to keep the family together.[21] Westermeyer explained that "Indian people have to go to these nonhelpful helpers, or kind of involuntary helpers, because there is no place else to go."[22] As Indians struggled to gain an economic footing in urban areas, authorities targeted their family structures, and not their economic hardship, for reform.

This bureaucratic maneuvering meant that struggling Indian families did not have access to the same pool of funds and social services that other state residents did, which exacerbated their poverty and economic deprivation, which in turn increased their vulnerability to child removal. Persistent structural inequities between Indians and other Americans conditioned the options available to Indian families. What Indian people needed was not the color-blind "opportunity" of adoption for their children but concrete action to remedy the glaring disparities they faced in income, employment, life expectancy, and health care.

What of the other standards promoted by the CWLA as a basis for removing a child? Some Indian children "fail[ed] to attend school regularly" because many Indian communities—especially on the Navajo reservation—lacked public schools and had to bus children long distances for them to attend school. Other standards warranting removal of children—"without supervision, unattended," "denied normal experiences that produce feelings of being loved, wanted, secure and worthy," and "exposed to unwholesome and demoralizing circumstances"—left much discretion to social workers.

Social workers often seemed to remove children based on vague and subjective criteria. Fanshel's data on birth mothers reveal that actual neglect or abuse played little role in the removal of Indian children. He included a chart with the "frequency of selected disability conditions of biological mothers of adoptees (identified in case histories)":

| | REPORTED | NOT REPORTED |
|---|---|---|
| Drinking problem or alcoholism | 39 | 59 |
| Mental illness | 3 | 95 |
| History of incarceration | 16 | 82 |
| Physical health problem | 18 | 80 |
| Personality disorder | 41 | 57 |
| Neglect of children | 18 | 80 |
| Abandonment of children | 5 | 93 |
| Abuse of children | 1 | 97 |
| Severe neglect or mistreatment by own family | 11 | 87 |
| Other problem | 43 | 57[23] |

This chart reveals that the *actual* neglect or abandonment of children—the purported basis for removing a child in social work practice—was relatively rare. Neglect was reported in less than 20 percent of cases and abandonment in only about 5 percent of cases. Abuse was extremely rare, reported in only one case. The chart suggests instead that social workers were basing their decisions to remove Indian children on ill-defined criteria such as "drinking problem" or "personality disorder."

Notions about proper female behavior based on predominant postwar gender ideologies also figured into the decisions of social workers to remove Indian children. Postwar ideals called for containment of women's sexuality within marriage, so authorities were particularly concerned with unwed mothers. For the adoptees he studied, Fanshel compiled statistics on the "number of children born out-of-wedlock to [their] biological mothers." He noted that only 10.4 percent of the women had no children born out of wedlock. (Given that more than half the women in his survey were married, this suggests that many had married since bearing a child.)[24] Fanshel and many social workers deemed these women's sexual behavior "maladjusted." In reality, though not always legally married, many of these Indian women were in long-term relationships. Fanshel divided up the married mothers into several categories that reflect his disapproval of Indian custom marriage as well as divorce and remarriage; he noted Indian birth mothers who were in legal single marriages (37.3), common law marriages (5.3), second marriages (8.5), or third marriages (2.1).[25] Fanshel also categorized the nature of the relationship between biological parents. Fanshel deemed 41.2 percent of the relationships "fleeting, casual," 21.7 percent somewhat sustained, and 36.1 percent long-term.[26] Birth parents were engaged in viable relationships in the majority of cases (57.8 percent), but Fanshel's categorization subtly condemned the sexual habits of Indian women who defied the postwar sexual ideal of monogamous marriage.

Authorities regarded other aspects of Indian women's lives as unconventional with respect to gender as well. Fanshel's study reveals that Indian birth mothers were likely to be working women, but unlike many middle-class wives, they were not earning extra income to buy new consumer goods. Fanshel found instead that they labored outside the home to support their families by holding menial service positions such as waitresses, housekeepers, and dishwashers in restaurants and cafés. Indian women's work outside the home was common in part because if they were married, their husbands' income was unlikely to be adequate to support the entire family.[27] Social workers believed that working outside the home was incompatible with proper motherhood. In fact they rarely placed adoptive children in families where mothers were working.[28] Consciously or not, then, social workers assumed a correlation between nonconformity to gender roles and unfit motherhood.

The preferred family arrangements of Indian people also put them at risk for child removal. Social workers and court authorities often deemed Indian children neglected and improperly supervised if they stayed regularly with caretakers other than their biological parents. This bias conflicted with Indian notions of proper care, as grandparents, aunts, and uncles often served as important caregivers for Indian children. Nearly all of the eight Indian leaders who attended a small symposium on the traditional upbringing of Indian children in 1972 had been raised in whole or in part by grandmothers and attributed their success in life to this fact. As Kiowa Allen Quetone asserted, "Being raised by our grandparents couldn't have been a happier time. Having this contact with them meant a great deal." The leaders explained to their non-Indian sponsors that in their cultures, "The grandmother plays a very important role in teaching and forming the values of children and in trying to rear them in accordance with tribal and family standards."[29]

It was often grandparents who battled to gain custody of their grand-children against social workers who deemed extended family members unfit to care for young Indian relatives. In one such case, six Indian chil-dren had been removed from a young couple I will call the Elks, who had moved from a North Dakota reservation to Portland, Oregon, in 1973. The Elks, like many relocated Indians, could not find work and faced hous-ing discrimination. They got discouraged and started drinking with other Indians. The five oldest children were found wandering Portland streets, three naked and with sores and bruises. Their parents were not at home and the house was disorderly. A court removed the Elk children, claim-ing their parents were chronic alcoholics.[30] The state removed the chil-dren for true neglect, but the ensuing events in the case reveal the bias against Indian extended families.

The children's grandparents from the North Dakota reservation asked to adopt them. The children's grandfather asserted, "We want to adopt the children because they are our blood relations. We believe that when trouble is faced by the parents, the grandparents take over responsibility of the grandchildren. That is the Indian way of doing things." Yet the State of Oregon turned down the elder Elk's plea, reasoning that "it would be unhealthy to place the children with their grandparents because their par-ents could then visit them." Instead the state placed four of the children with a family in California and two with a family in Washington. The Elk grandparents were not allowed to see the children.[31] Social work prac-tice rested on a notion of permanent separation of children from parents who had been deemed negligent; thus social workers regarded extended family placements as anathema. This common belief clashed with Indian notions of adoption, which resemble current concepts of open adoption, where adopted children are informed of their backgrounds and even kept in frequent contact with their biological families.

Authorities regarded nuclear families, even among strangers, as preferable to extended family arrangements. The CWLA insisted that "the biological family of father, mother, and their children constitutes the most natural means of providing family life for children, and should for that reason be fostered and preserved whenever possible."[32] This statement seems to respect the rights of a child's birth family, but its normalization, even deification, of the *nuclear* family meant that many Indian families, who relied on extended family kinship arrangements, would come up short in the minds of social workers. The IAP's ideal plan for the placement of an Indian child stipulated that the "child has two parents either through marriage of the mother or through adoption, and is assured a reasonably normal homelife offering love, security, and opportunity for a good life."[33] Marriage and a nuclear family model, in the minds of social workers, constituted a prerequisite for a "reasonably normal homelife." Most social workers remained bound to this particular model of family and unable to see that Indian extended kin models represented an equally viable alternative.

Even those child welfare authorities who evinced more respect for Indian cultures often held an inherent bias against extended family care. Beatrice Garrett, a social worker who conducted a review of the foster family care program on the Devils Lake Sioux Indian Reservation for the Children's Bureau in 1969, was sympathetic to and presented a fairly positive picture of Indian foster families at Devils Lake. Despite dire poverty and unemployment, she noted, "The foster parents in accordance with their cultural values [of] sharing were warm, accepting of the children and the agency and concerned about being good foster parent[s]. The emotional climate was good, the children seemed wanted and cared for." Children attended school regularly and were "receiving physical care which was average or better for the community." The foster parents accepted the "rights of natural parents and relatives to visit." This specialist from the Children's Bureau, however, was critical because more than 60 percent of foster fathers and mothers were older than fifty-eight years of age. "These foster parents are more like grandparents and although foster children should not be removed, because of the age of the foster parents alone, it is true that foster children should not be placed for long-range care with foster parents where there is too great a disparity in age. *Children need normal role models* and disparity in age adds to generation gap problems."[34] Most social workers, even well-meaning ones, regarded normative Indian family relationships as abnormal and as grounds for removing children.

The very nature of social work standards stacked the deck against Indian families. If malnourishment, poor health, substandard housing, and general impoverishment could be grounds for removing a child, many Indian families found themselves under increased scrutiny from public authorities. When social workers added criteria with an inherent bias against nontraditional gender roles, nonconformist sexual practices, and extended family arrangements, it could only increase the odds that social workers would find Indian families unfit to raise their own children.

Bernadine Brokenleg's battle to regain custody of her daughter Tiffany, as explored in the introduction, encapsulates how middle-class bias, racial stereotyping, and disapproval of working women and single mothers could undermine an Indian woman's claim on her own child. No one questioned whether Brokenleg loved and cared for her daughter, and no one openly accused her of neglect. The case hinged instead on the ability to provide a middle-class lifestyle in a two-parent family. The Buttses, her ex-husband's parents, in seeking custody of Tiffany, made reference to Brokenleg's lack of indoor plumbing and accused her of having a dirty and unsanitary home, suggesting that she was not fulfilling her proper role as a mother. The Butts grandparents argued that Tiffany was better off growing up in their affluent nuclear family. Both courts agreed. Ironically, whereas courts found Indian grandparents like the Elks unfit to care for their grandchildren, they were willing to let white middle-class grandparents have custody of an Indian child.

The Brokenleg case shows where the logic embedded in the Indian Adoption Project led. If Indian mothers and families could not care for their children to a middle-class standard, wasn't it "in the best interest" of these children to be raised by those who could provide them with all the trappings of a middle-class life? It might be regretful that Indian families lived without indoor plumbing and had difficulty making ends meet, but wasn't that just a result of their dysfunction and the "culture of poverty?" Why should Indian children suffer when there were non-Indian families who wanted to care for them? Many non-Indian Americans believed that through removing Indian children from their families, they could save these children. Indian adults, by contrast, seemed beyond redemption and incorrigibly dysfunctional.[35] Thus the government should not dedicate resources to promoting economic development and self-determination on reservations and in urban Indian communities, this line of thinking went, but should instead continue to channel its funds into making Indian children available for adoption.

Some Indian families lost children not through state intervention but through religious programs. The Mormons, or the Church of Jesus Christ of Latter Day Saints, through their Indian Student Placement Program, placed up to fifty thousand American Indian children with Mormon foster families for nine months of each year, ostensibly for educational purposes, from 1947 to 2000. The program often tried to limit contact between Indian children and their families. A social worker with the program wrote to Navajo parents in December 1969 regarding the impending holiday, "Many of you may be thinking of visiting your child and his foster family sometime during the Holidays," he wrote. "I hope you will not do this. Most of the time it is not good for you or your child. It makes you both homesick and your child must adjust again after you leave." The LDS program required that the child be with his or her foster family on Christmas day. Furthermore, the social worker informed the parents, "As you know, *no* student is allowed to go home for any reason during the school year and children should not be kept away from their foster families for more than a few hours and definitely not overnight."[36] Many critics of the program believed that this approach was damaging to Indian children and their families. Martin Topper, a psychologist who conducted several studies of Navajo students who had been on placement, considered it a "harsh psychological experience over which . . . Indians, adults and children alike, have no control." Indian students in the program, he asserted, did not have an opportunity to develop a positive Indian self-image during adolescence, which often resulted in "serious behavioral and psychological problems."[37]

The program also seems to have led to the removal of many Navajo children "from the reservation without proper authority." The *Navajo Times* warned Navajo parents in 1964 never to sign papers that they did not understand, especially in regard to the care or custody of a child. "Too often children are placed in the care of a person who leaves the reservation taking the child with them and later perhaps giving the child to still another person," the newspaper reported. "Children are being taken across state lines without legal authority, making it difficult for the parent to regain custody." The issue arose again in 1966, when "the Tribal Welfare committee . . . met with many missionaries to stress that children who come to their attention in need of care should not be given to any person other than a relative and that a request for assistance in planning for the child should be made to the BIA. In the past, many children have been taken or given away informally and all too often the placements have proven to be unsuccessful."[38]

The ISPP was ostensibly just a temporary foster care program, but it may have increased adoptions of Navajo children off the reservation because it was run by the LDS Social Service Program, which also oversaw adoptions by Mormon families of Navajo and other Indian children. Perry Allen of the Navajo Tribal Court asserted in 1975 that most adoptions of Navajo children by non-Navajo families occurred through the LDS Social Service Program.[39]

Critics of the program believed that Mormons were exploiting Navajo disadvantage, especially in regard to education, to fulfill their own religious aims. The Navajo were particularly susceptible to the program because educational opportunities were so limited on the reservation. One insider working in the mental health field in San Juan County in southeastern Utah hand-wrote a thirteen-page letter to Hirsch at the AAIA explaining the dire educational situation on parts of the Navajo Reservation. No high schools existed on the Utah portion of the reservation, so Indian parents had five less than ideal options: they could send children to Blanding High School in Utah, a trip that was up to eighty miles one way; they could send their children to group homes licensed by LDS Family Services in Blanding, where couples who operated the homes receive $125 per month per child; they could send children to a BIA-operated boarding school; they could allow their children to be placed with Mormon families through the ISPP; or they could simply keep their children out of school (which only a small number did).[40] What Navajo families needed, but federal authorities failed to provide, were day schools within their own communities so that children could remain at home without long daily commutes to and from school.

Many Indian families took advantage of the LDS program to gain better opportunities for their children, but the ISPP, like the IAP, rested on an individualist notion of rescuing and redeeming the Indian child from what its founders believed was a backward and even wicked life. Indian critics of the program called for Indian-run education and efforts to strengthen and preserve Indian families rather than removing Indian children.[41]

Some Indian children experienced removal from their families neither by governmental authorities nor by religious organizations but through the actions of individual visitors on Indian land, some of whom were liberal idealists connected with the Volunteers in Service to America (VISTA) program. Dubbed a domestic Peace Corps, VISTA was a Great Society program of the 1960s designed to place young Americans in poor communities to aid in anti-poverty efforts. Many VISTA volunteers worked on reservations or in urban Indian communities, and many were sympathetic to Indians who lost children to the child welfare system. In Wausau, Wisconsin, for example, volunteer Yvette Hall worked to raise funds for the Milwaukee Indian Center's efforts to address the Indian child welfare crisis.[42]

Other VISTA volunteers, however, shared in the commonly held view of Indian families as dysfunctional and actually participated in the removal of Indian children. While serving as a VISTA volunteer on the Crow reservation in 1971, Lynn Tibble became enamored with two children: Ross Half, aged two, and Sharon Walks, aged six. Tibble said she hired Ruby Half, aged seventeen, as a Neighborhood Youth Corps worker and that Ruby brought her baby Ross to work with her. Tibble claims that Half left her son for two weeks with Tibble and eventually signed papers giving Ross to her. "It took three tries to get her to a notary, but I finally got it done," Tibble asserted. Tibble claimed that when she took Sharon home from the library, the child's mother was not at home—only her grandmother. Accusing Sharon's mother of being an alcoholic, Tibble claimed that Sharon's grandmother gave her permission to keep the girl.[43]

The story of Lynn Tibble, as covered by the *State Journal Register* of Springfield, Illinois, raises nearly all the issues involved in these highly contentious Indian child welfare cases. Here were several familiar tropes—that the care of Indian children by grandparents or other extended family members constituted neglect and that Indian people were hopeless alcoholics. Hirsch, the attorney for Half and Walks, asserted that neither woman drank alcohol at all. Tibble also turned to another timeworn stereotype to make her case: that these Indian mothers only wanted their children because they would benefit financially from them. She claimed she never heard from the mothers until a Shell Oil coal-rights royalty settlement was made public. "Apparently," Tibble claimed, "the mothers decided they wanted their children back because the money was to be paid per capita. So much a head." Hirsch countered Tibble's claim; he stated that when Tibble left, she claimed to be leaving for just two weeks but had lived in Illinois ever since. For seven years the mothers repeatedly wrote to and called Tibble, but she tore up their letters and hung up the phone on the mothers.[44]

Another common element of this story is that the tone of press coverage is decidedly in favor of Tibble. For the past seven years, a reporter asserted, Tibble had had custody of the children, "and yet because of a treaty signed 109 years ago by the Crow Indians and the federal government Miss Tibble says she may lose her wards to mothers who willingly signed the children away in a court of law." The supposedly objective article ends by mentioning a fund to help Miss Tibble defray her court costs![45] Up to the present day, media accounts of contentious Indian child welfare cases often side with the adoptive non-Indian families in a similar manner.

One astute Standing Rock Sioux observer, Sam Deloria, an attorney and director of the American Indian Law Center in Albuquerque in the 1970s, encountered these attitudes among VISTA volunteers so frequently that he coined the term "VISTA syndrome" for "people who were raised believing . . . poor people are saints, . . . and they really find that poor people, when they confront them, also make stupid decisions sometimes. Some poor people are unattractive, particularly to middle-class people, and it's very disturbing and disillusioning, with a great temptation to turn around and use their power against the people who have disappointed them very greatly."[46] Other VISTA volunteers, perhaps disillusioned by conditions within Indian communities, absconded with Indian children, firm in the conviction of providing a better life for them.

Many Indian families also lost their children through their initial placement in temporary foster care. Social workers often placed in foster care the children of Indian parents who were hospitalized or jailed for petty offenses. In many cases these foster families later petitioned to adopt the children and to terminate parental rights. Indian social workers and AAIA attorneys found that once in foster care, an Indian child started down a path that was difficult to reverse. AAIA western staff attorney William Lamb explained that in his experience, "While the child is with the foster parent, there is no effective effort by County Welfare workers to restore the child to his or her Indian home, and little effort is made to find Indian foster parents, or foster parents who will assist in the goal of preserving contact with the natural parents. Foster placement is too often treated as a *de facto* adoptive placement. The majority of Indian adoptions which are later accomplished are on behalf of the foster parents."[47] Thus there was a close correlation between fostering and adoption during the Indian child welfare crisis.

Indeed, in a twisted logic, the longer children lived in a foster home, social workers argued, the more traumatic it would be to remove them and return them to their natural parents. (Ironically, many of these social workers minimized the trauma involved in initially separating children from their natural parents.) Lamb detailed one case in which an attorney representing a Hoopa child who had been placed in foster care argued that removal from the foster home would cause a traumatic disruption to the child's life. The foster parents petitioned to adopt and to terminate the birth mother's parental rights. "The rights of 'psychological parents' were argued over those of natural parents," Lamb stated. A lower court had ruled against termination of parental rights, but a court of appeals reversed this ruling and denied a new trial and rehearing, "even after evidence of sexual abuse of the child by the foster father was offered." In some states, biological parents had only one opportunity each year at an annual review hearing to argue for the return of their children, which ultimately undermined the possibility of family reunification. "The longer the delay in seeking a parent-child reunion," an AAIA attorney wrote, "the more chance there is for the court to determine that to disturb existing custody arrangements would traumatize the child."[48] Hence once taken from the home and put in foster care, Indian children were more likely to be adopted eventually and to lose all contact with their families and tribes of origin.

Thousands of Indian women lost children through one of the means described, and thousands more suffered an additional indignity: involuntary sterilization, yet another practice that even more blatantly and openly undermined Indian families. This can be seen particularly in the case of Norma Jean Serena, a thirty-seven-year-old Creek-Shawnee woman whom doctors sterilized involuntarily at the age of thirty-two in a hospital outside Pittsburgh and whose three young children were removed and placed in foster homes. Serena had been born in Elreno, Oklahoma, in 1937. She contracted typhoid fever as a child and suffered from hearing loss. She spoke three Indian languages but did not learn English until the age of nine. She married in her twenties and moved with her husband to Pennsylvania in the mid-1960s. Abandoned by her husband, she turned to public assistance. Child Welfare Services in Armstrong County, Pennsylvania, intervened in her personal life in early 1970, allegedly because of reports that she was associating with black people. Caseworkers told Serena she must come with her children to Pittsburgh for a medical exam. The doctor found nothing wrong with her two children, but social workers placed them in foster care. They told Serena it was only temporary but informed the foster parents it was permanent. Serena was pregnant at the time. Without her knowledge or consent, doctors sterilized her on August 18, 1970, less than forty-eight hours after her third child had been born. She did sign an official consent form the day after the operation, but at the time she was still medicated. Medical personnel listed the reason for sterilization as "socioeconomic." Serena repeatedly attempted to get her children back but was thwarted by social workers. A jury ruled in 1973 that her children should be returned to her and awarded her seventeen thousand dollars in damages, but authorities delayed the children's return for almost a year. She filed a lawsuit in federal court against six caseworkers, two physicians, and an administrator of various child welfare services, but she lost this case in 1979.[49]

The widespread involuntarily sterilization of Indian women came to the attention of some concerned legislators in the 1970s. A doctor in the Indian Health Service (IHS) alerted Senator James Abourezk of South Dakota—the same senator who sponsored hearings for the Indian Child Welfare Act—to the practice, and he requested a General Accounting Office (GAO) investigation. Investigators gathered data in just four of twelve IHS hospitals for a limited forty-six-month period, so the study did not reveal the total number of Indian women who underwent this procedure. Nevertheless researchers discovered that 3,406 Native American women had been sterilized. The GAO report "identified several violations of the waiting period and informed consent process," but it ultimately concluded that the IHS had not acted improperly. Many Indian women like Serena, however, reported that they were pressured into sterilization or never gave their consent.[50]

Sterilization, whether overtly coerced as in Serena's case or a result of more subtle pressure, seems to have been premised, like Indian child removal, on notions of Indian families as unfit and on the desire to terminate Indianness once and for all. Such termination did not occur through the dissolution of Indian tribal assets or through relocation alone; it also occurred through this kind of intervention into Indian women's reproductive work, in both a physical and cultural sense. Some Indian women put the matter in these exact terms. A Devils Lake Sioux mother, Jeannette Goodhouse, wife of the tribal chairman at the reservation in Fort Totten, North Dakota, told a reporter that she feared the placing of Indian children in white homes was part of a plan for the "slow termination" of the tribe.[51]

Through these myriad ways, Indian families were losing their children at an unprecedented rate. Compared to other children, Indian children were up to twenty-two times more likely to be in foster care and up to nineteen times more likely to be adopted out. When boarding school placements are factored in, some states were separating Indian children from their families at seventy-four times the rate for non-Indian children. This meant that in most Indian communities, 25–35 percent of all Indian children were living apart from their families.[52] This was a crisis of epic proportions. It is impossible to know how many of these children were voluntarily relinquished by birth mothers or were removed by court order from families who truly were not caring for them properly. But whether removal was warranted or not—and this is of course a highly contested question—the fact that such a disproportionate number of Indian children were in care should have alerted officials that they had a serious problem on their hands. How could BIA and state welfare authorities have failed to notice this Indian child welfare crisis? It seems that the common view that Indian families were hopelessly dysfunctional had become so normalized by the 1960s that authorities simply took it as a matter of course. Sadly, the removal of children became the official default response to the "plight" of Indian people in the late twentieth century.

Far from being a solution to the perennial Indian problem, child removal often exacerbated Indian family problems. Westermeyer found that after authorities removed the children from the eight Indian families who had approached a social service agency for welfare assistance, the couples all separated, their drinking problems worsened, and one woman attempted suicide. The removal of the children "effectively destroyed the family as an intact unit."[53] The loss of a child was the ultimate defeat and shame for many Indian families. They believed that it was their own personal problem rather than part of a larger systemic pattern. The crisis remained hidden from their view as well as from the general public. It would take the courage of Indian women who fought against the removal of their children to break the silence. Together with tribal leaders, community organizers, and a national Indian advocacy group, they would make this crisis visible and palpable to the American public.

I found a dissertation in early 2011 about the Indian Child Welfare Act by Steven Unger. Unger had been a staff member for the Association on American Indian Affairs in the 1970s and had edited an important collection of essays called *The Destruction of American Indian Families*. Reading his dissertation is a revelation. He includes a lengthy section on Indian boarding schools as a precedent for the fostering and adoption of Indian children in the 1960s and 1970s.

I marveled that he and I had never met one another; nor had we read or cited one another's work. Yet independently—in our different worlds—we had reached very similar conclusions about Indigenous child removal. I felt compelled to contact Steve, but I couldn't find any trace of him on the Internet. Eventually I tracked down his dissertation advisor, and he sent me Steve's email address. I sent him a fan letter, and he wrote a gracious reply.

A few months later I was at the University of Massachusetts in Amherst for the Berkshire Conference on the History of Women (the "Berks"), a gathering of thousands of historians that occurs only every three years. I had organized a special workshop on Gender and Indigenous Adoption in Settler Colonial Nations. Steve lived not too far away in upstate New York, and he agreed to come to our workshop.

When he arrived, his presence exerted an added layer of meaning and gravity to our proceedings. We historians from Canada and the United States knew about the important work Steve and the AAIA had done to bring about the Indian Child Welfare Act (ICWA). We had all read his work from the 1970s, and many of us had also studied his dissertation. After we all discussed our papers, Steve stood up and made an eloquent off-the-cuff speech.

We were all moved by his presence. It is rare that historians get to meet and talk with our subjects and our sources in such a gathering. In my case, as a historian who works primarily on the turn of the twentieth century, I usually only get to know my historical subjects as two-dimensional figures in the dusty papers they leave behind.

After the workshop, the final event of the conference, Steve and I went out to lunch. He told me a little about his work with the AAIA, especially how he gained great admiration for all the American Indian women who were involved, whom he later told me were the real heroes of the movement for ICWA. After Steve and I parted, I boarded a train to Princeton, New Jersey, and for the next several days, I hunched over a table at the archives at the Seeley Mudd Library, ordering boxes of files from the AAIA papers. I found letter after letter from Steve, and from other AAIA staff members, all documenting the struggle to return the care of American Indian children to their tribes.

CHAPTER 4

# Reclaiming Care

Mrs. Fournier, a sixty-two-year-old Mandan woman, was taking care of two-year-old Ivan Brown at her home on the Fort Totten Reservation of the Devils Lake (now Spirit Lake) Sioux in North Dakota one day in 1968 when a pair of men showed up at her door. Robert Barrett, the director of the Benson County Welfare Board in North Dakota, and the Benson County sheriff had come to remove Ivan Brown and place him for adoption with a white doctor and his wife in Bismarck. Mrs. Fournier had mothered eighteen other children, some her biological children, others foster children. Ivan had been just three weeks old when social welfare authorities had removed him from his mother and placed him with Mrs. Fournier. They told her it would only be temporary, but no state welfare workers contacted her again until Barrett and the sheriff arrived unannounced at her home. In the intervening two years Ivan's birth mother had died in a fire, and Mrs. Fournier had become deeply attached to Ivan. She refused to give him up when Barrett and the sheriff barged into her home. "They tried to take him, and when they came after him I said no," Mrs. Fournier told the Senate Subcommittee on Indian Affairs in 1974. "He started crying and hanging on to me." According to an investigator in 1968, "only by the immediate on-the-spot intervention of Mrs. Joshua, another Indian woman, and the later imposition of Mr. Goodhouse, the tribal chairman, was the forcible removal of the child prevented at that time." The investigator added, "Mrs. Fournier has threatened to kill herself or person or persons attempting to take the child from her, and that threat was not taken lightly by any of the persons to whom I talked."[1]

Mrs. Fournier's story might have ended in trauma, as was all too common for Indian families who lost their children. She, however, decided to fight back. Her resistance helped to ignite a national and ultimately transnational Indigenous social movement. This drive to reclaim the care of Indian children found support among a group of Indian social workers and social service providers, most of them women, who began to notice the highly disproportionate numbers of Indian children in the child welfare systems within their own states and to recognize systemic patterns of state intervention into childbearing and childrearing in Indian communities. Some Indian men were involved and supportive, but American Indian women were particularly active in organizing on this issue. Community organizers and determined women such as Mrs. Fournier built a grassroots movement to challenge state intervention into Indian families and to create alternative Indian-run programs to provide social services to Indian families in crisis.

This movement was one crucial component of the self-determination movement of Indigenous people. To further their cause, many Indian women, families, and tribes who had lost children to their state child welfare systems asked for the help of the Association on American Indian Affairs, an advocacy organization dating back to 1922. This group became deeply committed to the cause of Indian families; they gathered data, mounted legal defenses of Indian families, raised public awareness, and promoted legislation to combat this phenomenon, eventually resulting in the passage of the Indian Child Welfare Act in 1978. American Indian women played a vital role in this struggle for Indian self-determination.[2]

Indian opposition to the unprecedented loss of their children erupted spontaneously in many different locales in the 1960s and 1970s. Women on the Fort Totten Reservation near Devils Lake, North Dakota, became some of the first to voice their resistance nationally. Tribal members had been struggling with local and state welfare authorities over the care of their children since the mid-1960s. Matters came to a head in 1967. The Fort Totten tribal council was fed up with the reckless manner in which they believed the Benson County Welfare Board was removing Indian children and placing them in white foster homes, so they "passed an ordinance forbidding the placement of an Indian child in a foster or adoptive home off the reservation." The Welfare Board "promptly certified fourteen Indian homes as suitable foster homes, whereas prior to this they

Fig. 5. Ivan Brown, seven, with his foster grandmother, Mrs. Alec Fournier, 1973. From *Indian Affairs* 84 (January 1973): 3. Courtesy and permission of the American Association on Indian Affairs.

had indicated they had found no Indian homes suitable."[3] Local authorities were responsive at first to the tribe's concerns and compliant with their contract with the Bureau of Indian Affairs to provide social services to the North Dakota tribes.

However, Robert Barrett, the director of the Benson County Welfare Board, deeply resented the tribe's move, and he decided to pursue Ivan Brown and his three siblings as a test case. In 1968 the four Brown children had all been living for some time with elderly Indian foster parents on the reservation. Ivan's older brother Tommy, five, lived with Ben DuBois, sixty-nine, and his wife, Mary, sixty-eight, who had raised him since he was two and a half weeks old. The two other Brown siblings, Bernadette, six, and Wesley, seven, lived with Frank Jetty, seventy-one, and his wife Algenia, sixty-three, who had fostered Bernadette since she was seven months old and Wesley since he was three years old. In April 1967 a North Dakota circuit court had terminated the mother's parental rights over all four Brown children, and soon thereafter Barrett contended that he had "the authority to remove any of the Brown children and place them for prompt adoption wherever he [could], in or out of the State." He hoped to "have all these points tested in court, and he indicated that he would move as soon as possible . . . to remove at least Ivan Brown from the reservation." According to one investigator, "the procedure used to put the Brown children up for adoption was to circulate their pictures with brief histories of them and, presumably, of their family background, throughout the appropriate agencies and persons in the State." While the state marketed these children, however, "the Indian families with whom the children resided were not given any opportunity to adopt the children or to prevent their foster care placement elsewhere."[4] Barrett, in short, was determined to have a showdown with the Devils Lake Sioux over the care of Indian children.

Barrett not only showed up at the Fourniers' home to remove Ivan but also appeared at the homes of the Dubois and Jetty families. These families, like Mrs. Fournier, also resisted Barrett's attempts to separate their foster children from them. One journalist reported that "attempts since April [1968] to take them have resulted in children hiding under beds and in woods, and have sent foster parents fleeing over the reservation's back roads with their youngsters in an attempt to avoid welfare workers."[5] Clearly the foster families at Fort Totten, with the support of their tribal council, were no longer willing to accept the loss of their children.

Barrett was equally determined to wrest the children away from their elderly caregivers. He refused to back down, explaining to a reporter, "Basically what we look at is: Is this the type of home that you would place your own child into? . . . And I don't mean from a physical standpoint. I mean, are these foster parents the kinds of people you would want to be caring for your child?"[6] Barrett did not elaborate on what kind of people were caring for the Brown children, but clearly he held these seasoned Indian caregivers in contempt—simply, it seems, because they were elderly Indians. Members of the Devils Lake Sioux and other tribes, however, revered elders and regarded them as *just* the kind of people you would want to care for your child.

Fort Totten families found a supportive ally in a national Indian advocacy organization. The AAIA had been working with the Devils Lake

Sioux on other issues when staff members learned of Barrett's intervention. Local families asked the AAIA for help, and they sprang into action. They arranged for a delegation to come from Devils Lake to New York City and Washington DC in July 1968 for a press conference and lobbying efforts. Lewis Goodhouse, the tribal chair, accompanied the group, but the AAIA billed it as a "mothers' delegation." It included five outspoken women: Lewis's wife Jeanette Goodhouse, a mother of ten children in her forties who was described as "a volunteer community health worker and [as] leading the mothers' effort to alleviate child welfare problems;" Mrs. Alvina Alberts, a mother of eight children in her fifties and a BIA education counselor; Mrs. Left Bear, a mother of six in her forties, all of whose children were living in non-Indian foster homes off the reservation; Mrs. Elsie Greywind, a mother of five in her fifties who cared for her grandchildren; and Mrs. Fournier.[7] The Devils Lake mothers' delegation presaged the prominent role that Indian women would play in the decade-long movement to preserve Indian families.

The AAIA sought to frame the issue in dramatic terms by highlighting the mothers' and grandmothers' laments. AAIA Executive Director William "Bill" Byler condemned the state actions as "child snatching" and charged that the "forcible removal of Indian youngsters without due process of law ... has reached epidemic proportions."[8] The AAIA marshaled solid evidence to support their claims. They distributed a fact sheet noting that out of 1,100 Devils Lake Sioux Indians under twenty-one years of age living on the Fort Totten Reservation, 275 or 25 percent had been separated from their families. The AAIA called upon Secretary Wilbur Cohen of the federal Department of Health, Education, and Welfare (HEW) to "probe charges by American Indian parents that many of them are unjustly deprived of their children."[9]

As intended, the mothers' delegation generated publicity and political action. Journalists who attended the press conference were largely sympathetic. Murray Kempton wrote a scathing opinion piece for the *New York Post*, pointing out that Mrs. Fournier had been "taking in the lost children of other Devils Lake families for more than 30 years now. There ought to be a time when Mrs. Fournier is recognized as a woman of a peculiar and special nobility instead of the object of a sheriff's pursuit."[10] The delegation also had success in convincing federal officials in Washington DC

Fig. 6. The Devils Lake Sioux Mothers' Delegation with Tribal Chairman Lewis Good-house and AAIA Executive Director William Byler at a New York City press conference on July 16, 1968. The women are (left to right) Jeannette Goodhouse, Alvina Alberts, and Mrs. Alex Fournier. Courtesy and permission of the Association on American Indian Affairs.

to take action. According to Bertram Hirsch, an AAIA staff member and attorney, the president ordered Cohen as well as Secretary of the Interior Stewart Udall to conduct an inquiry into the allegations and make recompense if they were found to be true. Cohen brought up the allegations with the child welfare consultants of the BIA, who sought to facilitate meetings between North Dakota authorities, BIA officials, and representatives from the Children's Bureau.[11] This flurry of activity initiated a decade-long campaign jointly mustered by grassroots Indian activists and tribal leaders, Indians working in the field of social work, nursing, and other service occupations, and the AAIA to reverse decades of Indian child removal and enact a law that would prevent such abuses from taking place: the Indian Child Welfare Act of 1978.

Indian activists and their AAIA advocates first had to find out whether Fort Totten represented a unique case or was part of a wider pattern of intervention into Indian families across the nation. The AAIA suspected the latter, and the response to their coverage of the Devils Lake Sioux protest delegation in their publication, *Indian Affairs*, confirmed their suspicions. Florence Kinley of Marietta, Washington, wrote to the editor that "this article is very close to me as we have experienced the same type of abuses here in the State of Washington."[12] The AAIA charged Hirsch with proving its hunch. Hirsch was pursuing a triple major in history, sociology and political science at Queens College at the City University of New York when he began working for the AAIA. He set out to collect data from BIA regional offices and hundreds of state and private agencies regarding the numbers of Indian children who were being removed from their homes to be institutionalized, fostered, or adopted.[13]

The compilation of this data proved to be an "ordeal," as Hirsch put it in 1974. "Those statistics are extremely difficult to get," he explained to a number of Indian activists. "After much badgering, they supplied me with some statistics."[14] Hirsch first requested that the BIA provide data about the numbers of fostered and adopted Indian children for the last five to ten years, preferably broken down by state and tribe. The BIA had not compiled this information and claimed that "since the BIA does not make adoption placements, we cannot provide you with a breakdown of children by age who are currently in adoptive placement."[15] Hirsch next contacted state and private agencies, which all used different approaches to tracking Indian children. Some state agencies claimed they did not keep statistics on Indian children. The Idaho Department of Public Assistance in 1969 responded, "Statistically, all children of all races and colors are lumped together." Other states went in the opposite direction. Wyoming broke their racial statistics down by "full Indian" and "half Indian."[16] Eventually Hirsch gathered some substantive preliminary data, and the AAIA continued to gather statistics on Indian child placement throughout the 1970s.[17] Their shocking data showed that in states with large Indian populations, an average of 25–35 percent of Indian children had been removed from their tribal communities and families. In every state they found that Indian children were vastly overrepresented in the child welfare system.[18]

Hirsch's gathering of statistical data was invaluable, not only in proving to state and federal authorities that there was a crisis but also in helping Indian families understand that their personal traumas were part of a larger pattern. When he began this tedious task, Hirsch recalls, "[Indian] people thought, 'this is my problem.' They didn't know that the family . . .

a mile down the road or over the next butte . . . was experiencing the same thing. Everybody feeling shame about it and not talking about it. They thought it was their own personal circumstance. . . . . . So . . . people kind of kept it to themselves and they did not seek out assistance from their own tribes."[19] Bill Byler agreed, mentioning at a 1974 strategy session, "It's an individual's tragedy, and the tribal council generally do not know about it."[20]

Not only did many Indian caregivers blame themselves for the loss of their children, but most also assumed they could do little to stop it. American Indian social worker and activist Evelyn Blanchard explains, "It's kind of hard for some people to comprehend the power that the government had over Indian people. Incorrect and harmful things were done and the people wouldn't say a word. They would just let it happen because they didn't think they could do anything. They didn't think they had the right to object. The government had so much power that [welfare] workers could do just about anything they chose."[21] Margaret Townsend of Fallon, Nevada, confirmed this sense of powerlessness in her testimony to Congress in 1974. "I think that most of the Indian women are usually overwhelmed by people who think their children should be taken away from them," Townsend observed, "and they really don't stand up to anybody and they don't have anybody to tell."[22] Once Mrs. Fournier and the mothers' delegation made their stand and the AAIA started their campaign, more Indian women and families became emboldened to challenge the removal of their children.

Many Indian women who had lost children asked for the AAIA's legal assistance in winning their children back. Hirsch, who by 1971 had finished law school at New York University and was a staff attorney with the AAIA, became one of the only litigators in the country who took on such cases. "For a good many years, I was the only lawyer doing it anywhere," Hirsch recalls. "After a bit I was able to engage primarily Legal Services lawyers that were working out on various reservations or near reservations to also participate in this. I was trying my best to find other people to jump in because it was too overwhelming really." Hirsch's work brought him to courts in thirty-five states, and he was also "providing, constantly, . . . daily for years, advice and consultation for other lawyers all across the country who were taking on these cases."[23]

The AAIA created the Great Plains Family Defense Program for the states of North Dakota, South Dakota, and Nebraska around 1972 and then applied for grants to support a more extensive American Indian Family Defense Project. They obtained funding from the Lilly Endowment by 1976 for this project, renamed it the Indian Child Welfare Reform Program, and promptly hired additional attorneys to work with Hirsch: William Lamb, LeRoy Wilder, and Lawrence Rappaport. The program identified three goals: (1) changing federal and state policy regarding Indian child welfare; (2) expanding "legal representation of Indian families and children aimed at changing judicial behavior and at having an impact beyond the individual case"; and (3) strengthening Indian self-government in child welfare matters.[24] The AAIA legal team was remarkably successful in the defense of Indian families, claiming in 1975 that in the more than six years that AAIA had been litigating in this area, they had won every case. This alone suggests that the basis on which authorities removed Indian children was often specious.[25]

Strategically, the AAIA and Indian activists also realized they needed to raise public awareness of this issue, and in 1974 staff member Steven Unger began to edit and publish *Indian Family Defense*, a newsletter that highlighted many of Hirsch's legal cases. Through this publicity and other efforts, the AAIA mobilized many non-Indians in the Northeast to take action on this issue. Perhaps because the issue involved mothering and child welfare, it particularly galvanized women. Barbara Alovia and Anita Kobre from Spring Valley, New York, wrote to Senator Edward Kennedy in 1973, "We are housewives who have taken the time out of our normal family routine because of our awareness of this pressing problem. Our deep concern in this area came about as a result of a course in Contemporary Indian Affairs, . . . travel in the North and Southwest, attending lectures and individualized reading." Alovia and Kobre enclosed a petition with 4,200 signatures and sent similar letters to Governor Nelson Rockefeller of New York, New York senators Jacob Javits and William Buckley, and Henry Jackson, chair of the Senate Committee on Interior and Insular Affairs.[26] The AAIA proved effective in raising awareness about the issue and moving many non-Indians to lobby their legislators.

Indian people were well aware of the AAIA's efforts, and many expressed their gratitude. Eloise Lahr Doan, senior vice chair of the National Association of Blackfeet Indians in Browning, Montana, wrote to Hirsch in 1976, "Your Indian Family Defense Legal Services Program is a ray of light for families and Mothers who lose all hope when their children are swept away from them. Where there is [sic] no funds to go to Court, their explanations and pleadings go unheard. . . . We have cases come up very often and we feel helpless because there is no sincere help. Legal Aid lawyers give a half hearted defense which is as good as no help at all."[27] Non-Indian advocacy groups in earlier eras had sought to help Indians based on white middle-class notions of what was best for Indians, but the AAIA by this time was more focused on empowering Indian people to determine their own futures than on directing them along preconceived lines. Most of its core staff were non-Indians, but it had several Indians on its board, and the renowned San Juan Pueblo scholar Alfonso Ortiz served as the board's president. In addition, the personal experience of non-Indian executive director William Byler, who spent part of his childhood in an orphanage during the Great Depression, made him particularly incensed about the issue.[28]

The AAIA gave their strong support to Indian efforts to resolve the Indian child welfare crisis on Indian terms. This brought them into close alliance with a group of Indians who were working on the frontlines within their communities as social workers, nurses, and other types of service providers. Some men were involved, but Indian women were most prominent among these community organizers. Nine of twelve members of the board of directors of Wisconsin's American Indian Child Placement and Development Program were women in 1973. The following year the board included eighteen women and two men; all eighteen women had personally experienced some aspect of the Indian child welfare crisis.[29]

The movement to reclaim the care of Indian children grew in concert with a new movement of American Indian women. Sixty-eight Indian women representing forty-three tribes in twenty-three states gathered at Colorado State University in 1970 and established the North American Indian Women's Association (NAIWA). They identified their goals as "betterment of home, family life and community, betterment of health and education, promotion of intertribal communications, awareness of Indian culture and fellowship among all people." They stressed that they were "not a women's lib organization." The group highly valued the integrity of tribal governments and cultures and was reluctant to criticize them. One

Fig. 7. William Byler, executive director of AAIA, 1963. Courtesy and permission of the Association on American Indian Affairs records, 1851–2010, Public Policy Papers, Department of Rare Books and Manuscripts, Princeton University Library, Princeton, New Jersey.

NAIWA spokeswoman explained that "NAIWA does favor Indian Tribal Councils and would never work against [them], because we believe if the Tribal Council is lost then tribal identity is lost."[30]

Other more militant Native women's groups sprouted up in the same period. Janet McCloud (Tulalip and Nisqually) announced the formation of a Northwest Indian Women's Council in 1979 that was concerned with such issues as "sterilization abuses of Indian women and the need for more effective social service programs that can reach and help Indian women." McCloud invited any Indian woman in western Washington to join who had a "desire to change and improve her status in the world and ensure the survival of Indian people."[31] McCloud had also helped to found Women of All Red Nations in 1974 with many other women activists from the American Indian Movement. These groups were deeply concerned with Native women's reproductive roles as childbearers and nurturers, and they may have been more inclined to challenge male leaders whom they believed to be working against the interests of women and children.

Ramona Bennett, elected chair of the Puyallup tribe in Washington State in 1972, did so when she attended the National Tribal Chairmen's Association meeting in Denver. When she arrived, they told her that her tribe had been terminated, and they could not recognize her. Instead they suggested that she should have brought the vice chair, a man, to represent her tribe, and that she should sit in the lobby with chairmen's wives. The group finally allowed her into the meeting, but she was the only woman there. Bennett recalls, "They're talking about fishing, housing, so many topics. They're listing natural resources they need to protect: timber, minerals, land, water, fish, and I step forward and say, 'I'd like to make a motion that you add our Indian children to that list of endangered resources. They're being alienated from their tribes through interracial adoptions, they have such a hard time finding their way back, they never belong anywhere.'" The other tribal chairs were skeptical at first and pelted Bennett with sexist jokes. Several tribal chairs eventually backed Bennett, including Joe DeLaCruz of the neighboring Quinault Tribe, who declared, "She always does her research, and if she says it's a problem, it is." "So," according to Bennett, "they voted children onto the list of endangered natural resources."[32] Bennett's experience shows that organizing to address the Indian child welfare crisis went hand in hand with the politicization of Indian women.

American Indian social workers, although few in number, were at the forefront of bringing the Indian child welfare crisis to national attention. This profession particularly attracted dynamic and visionary Indian women, many of whom worked for the BIA or state agencies and attempted to revamp their practices. Evelyn Blanchard, of Laguna Pueblo and Pascua

Yaqui descent, obtained her masters in social work at the University of Denver in 1969 and then worked at the BIA's Albuquerque area office as social worker in support of education for a year before becoming the assistant area social worker for the BIA's Social Services Branch. She engaged in "program oversight, consultation, and technical assistance" for twenty-three tribes in seven BIA agencies and saw firsthand the problems leading to the overrepresentation of Indian children in the child welfare system. Blanchard did what she could through her position to "encourage changes in family and children's services throughout the Area," including developing a new training agenda for BIA social workers and drafting a "policy that no children under the age of ten would be removed to boarding schools." Blanchard, too, worked with tribal leaders to reinforce their authority "so that they came to see," as Blanchard put it, that "no, ... we don't have to let our kids be carted off any time somebody outside ... who doesn't even live here, doesn't know the resources here, doesn't know the circumstances here, makes a decision to just remove our children." Blanchard moved to the Pacific Northwest in the mid-1970s to assist Washington state tribes in their efforts to enact changes in the state's administrative codes regarding Indian child welfare.[33]

There Blanchard found that Native women were actively addressing Indian child welfare. Maxine Robbins (Yakima) had worked in the Yakima County office of the state Department of Social and Health Services from 1964 to 1974. She had become deeply concerned about the numbers of Yakima children who were removed from their families each year, taken off the reservation, and placed with non-Indian foster or adoptive families. The Washington Public Health Service assigned Robbins to work with the Yakima tribe from 1974 to 1980. She applied for and received a grant of nearly $170,000 from a program of the Department of Health, Education, and Welfare for a three-year demonstration project. Robbins created the project Ku-nak-we-sha, or "the caring place," which provided preventative services to Yakima families, offered short-term emergency facilities for children who had to be removed from their homes, and recruited and compensated Yakima foster families. Prior to Robbins's program, state social service workers had apprehended an average of thirty-five Yakima children each year. Authorities removed no Yakima children from the reservation in 1975, when Robbins's program had been in operation only one year. Her project was innovative (in the 1980s, they used the slogan, "Superman Had Foster Parents" to recruit families) and served as a model for many other Indian tribes and urban Indian groups and even for Aboriginal groups in Australia. The National Association of Social Workers named Robbins Social Worker of the Year in 1980.[34]

Indian women galvanized around this issue in part because Indian societies had long prized women's caring roles. Indian societies treasured their children, and they invested Indian women with highly valued roles as primary stewards of this priceless resource. The Canadian Métis scholar Kim Anderson uses Cree/Métis writer Maria Campbell's metaphor of concentric circles to explain:

> In this worldview, children are at the centre of the community. The elders sit [in the next circle] next to the children, as it is their job to teach the spiritual, social and cultural lifeways of the nation. The women sit [in the next circle] next to the elders and the men sit on the outside [circle]. From these points they perform their respective economic and social roles, as protectors and providers of the two most important circles in our community. [In this view] everyone in the community has a connection to the children, and everyone has an obligation to work for their well-being.[35]

Anderson further elaborates on the esteemed role of women. "Motherhood accorded Native women tremendous status in the family, community and nation," she writes. Gender roles and relations varied among Indigenous cultures throughout North America, but in every Indigenous society, "producing life and raising children are understood as the creation of a people, a nation and a future." Therefore "all women have the right to make decisions on behalf of the children, the community and the nation."[36]

Official and popular discourse since the turn of the twentieth century, however, had often portrayed Indian women as unfit mothers. These rhetorical attacks had served as one of the bases for removing Indian children to boarding schools and, later, into the child welfare system.[37] Officials' bids to remove Indian children not only undermined the integrity of Indian families but also threatened Indian women's self-identities and their roles as carers, not to mention the close relationships many had with the children they tended.

Social work and other social service professions enabled Indian women to channel their traditional roles in social and cultural reproduction into viable careers that simultaneously provided them with self-supporting income, a measure of status and authority in the non-Indian world, and a set of skills that could provide meaningful help to their communities. Makah Mary Jo Butterfield reminded her audience at one conference of Indian social service providers, mostly women, that "you are the service provider and the things that you are doing are going to provide perpetuity for your tribe."[38] Indian women's social service work represented a modern manifestation of their traditional care work.

Many Indian women may have gravitated to Indian child welfare work, too, because they had known firsthand the pain of family separation. Goldie Denny (Quinault), who in the 1970s oversaw child welfare on her reservation as director of the Quinault Nation Social Services, had herself been removed from her family in the small community she lived in on the Washington peninsula. Denny's mother had died when Denny was young, and she was left as the eldest of three sisters while her single father worked as a logger. Denny's close friend Evelyn Blanchard explained that "as a small child, she and her sisters were removed from their home because the local welfare worker decided that the children were neglected, when she came upon them wading in mud puddles." Although "the communities were closely knit and there was always someone who could help," authorities briefly held Denny and her sisters in state custody before returning them to their father. Blanchard knows that "the removal was a deeply significant event in her life. In some ways, it imprinted a purpose in her life."[39] Blanchard and Denny shared this common experience.

Blanchard's family had experienced child removal for generations. The Mexican government had removed her Pascua Yaqui grandmother from her family as a very young child to live with a family in Guadalajara, where she "was essentially a servant." Later her grandmother settled in Fierro, a small town in southwestern New Mexico, as a single mother with four children, and operated a bootlegging business in the 1920s to support her family. Authorities arrested and jailed Blanchard's grandmother and then removed Blanchard's mother, twelve years old, to the Girls Welfare Home, a juvenile prison in New Mexico, and her brothers to St. Anthony's Orphanage. Her mother spent six years in the Girls Welfare Home. Authorities

Fig. 8. Evelyn Blanchard, Goldie Denny, and John J. Alonzo, Blanchard's father, Pacific Beach, Washington, ca. 1985. Courtesy and permission of Evelyn Blanchard.

released her at the age of eighteen on the streets of Albuquerque. Homeless, she eked out a living selling jewelry in a park. Eventually Evelyn's mother met her father, a young man from Laguna Pueblo who had been removed from his family to attend the most famous of the Indian boarding schools, Carlisle Institute in Pennsylvania. Blanchard herself would face removal from her parents as a teenager. After she and some friends drove on a lark to Utah for a weekend, a judge placed her on probation and gave her a choice of living at either the Girls Welfare Home where her mother had been confined or the Albuquerque Indian School. Blanchard chose the school. This intergenerational experience with child removal and institutionalization undoubtedly influenced Blanchard's sensitivity to and awareness of Indian child removal.[40]

Other Indian women activists had had firsthand experience as mothers with losing children to the child welfare system. Betty Jack, a Chippewa originally from the Lac du Flambeau reservation in Wisconsin, became involved in Indian child welfare through her personal crisis. After she had

Fig. 9. Evelyn Blanchard, 1974. Courtesy and permission of Evelyn Blanchard.

relocated to Chicago in 1962, the state of Wisconsin removed two of her children. The Evangelical and Welfare Society placed them for adoption without involving Jack in any legal proceedings. She learned only in 1973 that they had been adopted. She sent her other three children home from Chicago to live with their father on the reservation, but welfare authorities removed them as well and placed them in multiple foster homes over several years. Jack was able to regain custody of her youngest daughter, but her daughter regarded Indians as "nothing but lazy, dirty drunks, and she had her hair bleached blonde." Jack had reunited with her two other fostered children but felt as if "the minds of my kids have been damaged so terribly." Authorities had ruled Jack an unfit mother and proceeded as if she were a hopeless case, but Jack underwent treatment for alcoholism and got sober. She became a welfare specialist for the Indian Urban Affairs Council, a staff member of the Young Women's Christian Association in Milwaukee, and chair of the Board of Directors of the American Indian Child Development Program for the State of Wisconsin.[41] She thus had a personal as well as a professional stake in Indian child welfare.

Other Indian women who became activists in the Indian child welfare movement had extensive experience as foster parents. Mary Jo Butterfield cared for twenty-two foster children at her home in Neah Bay, Washington.[42] Others had been raised in the traditional Indian way by grandparents or great-grandparents, including Maxine Robbins, who was raised by her great-grandmother.[43] Indian child welfare was rarely an abstract issue for the Indian women social workers and activists who labored within their communities or through the BIA, state, or private agencies to rectify the situation. Rather it was a lived experience from which they gained determination to improve the lives of Indian children.

These Indian women social workers, as well as some male colleagues, established the Association of American Indian and Alaskan Native Social Workers in the early 1970s and set out to challenge the dominant pro-adoption discourses and practices so popular in the broader society. They particularly objected to plight narratives that reduced Indian people to a series of grim statistics. When they met in conference at Bottle Hollow, Utah, in 1977, Denny commented regarding granting agency requests for proposals that "federal RFP's and resulting proposals are humiliating—they force us to present ourselves as drunk and incompetent." Conference attendees recommended, "The media must be assisted at every opportunity to recognize the positive values of Indian culture and avoid stereotyping." They opened their final report of the conference with this caveat: "We ask our readers to keep in mind, while reading the statistics below that we are aware that the inner strength of Indian families often enables them to remain stable and together even in the face of poverty."[44]

The very nature of how Indian social service providers ran the conference at Bottle Hollow showed the ongoing vitality of Indian tribes and Indian ways. The American Academy of Child Psychiatry sponsored the conference in 1977; it brought together about 150 "actively involved Indian persons and 40 specially invited non-Indians" to the Uintah-Ouray Reservation to exchange strategies for strengthening Indian families and improving Indian child welfare. On the last morning of the conference, "the entire group sat in concentric circles (together and equal) as a spokesperson from each small group read its report and made its recommendations." Participants recounted that "it was a spirited morning with an overwhelming and enlivening sense of unity." When groups suggested "especially appealing ideas," they "were greeted with piping cries of 'Yip! Yip! Yip!'"[45] The liveliness of the participants belies the usual depiction of Indian people in the era as irrevocably beaten down and incapable of recovery. These women and men were living proof that Indian people possessed the skills and determination to address their own problems in ways that honored and sustained their own traditions and ideals.

These social workers sought to counter dominant narratives that emphasized Indian family dysfunction, but they did not deny that problems regarding Indian child welfare existed within Indian communities. At their conference in Boston in 1978, the group discussed "urban Indian and cultural family value conflicts," "parents not accepting responsibility for their children," high rates of suicide, the number of unwed mothers, and alcoholism.[46] Yet they offered a different analysis of why Indian children suffered.

These social workers identified past and ongoing federal Indian policies as major contributors to Indian family problems. The ubiquitous experience of institutionalizing children had led to disastrous consequences. "The impact of Indian boarding schools must not be minimized," they wrote. "It was often in such schools that Indian children first were introduced to physical punishment, or even abuse. Also, there was little 'mothering' or 'nurturing' going on in these rigidly authoritarian institutions. . . . Thus there is little example shown of good parenting models." As a result, they asserted, "many of today's abusive and neglectful Indian parents were victims as children in these very same institutions."[47] The postwar relocation program and its emphasis on the nuclear family had also taken its toll on Indian communities, they argued. "As more and more younger Indians begin to adopt Anglo family structures and relationships, and the extended family support network is broken down," the social workers asserted, "the same isolation occurs as with Anglo parents, and isolation and lack of a support network for occasional relief from parenting responsibilities are two of the major factors mitigating child abuse and neglect."[48]

Indian people's unique history in relation to the American state also contributed to the problem. "Dependency and immaturity that is so prevalent among young Indian parents results from a long history of wardship with the BIA and other . . . agencies dealing with Indians as incompetent children, incapable of handling their own affairs," they pointed out.[49] To compound the problem, Indian social workers asserted that "Indian peoples suffer greater economic deprivation, lower per capita income, lower educational achievement rates, poorer housing, higher unemployment, higher rates of alcoholism and suicide, and higher rates of teenage pregnancy," all factors intensifying risks of child abuse and neglect.[50] Thus Indian social workers acknowledged that Indian families confronted serious problems.

They put forth unique solutions for these problems, however. Indian social workers believed that child removal was a form of punishing parents that only worsened the problem and continued a damaging cycle. "For many years the prevalent feeling about parents who abuse or neglect their children has been shock and anger and a desire to punish them, either by jailing them or taking their children away and placing them in a 'good, stable, secure, loving home' (often a non-Indian home). Experience has taught us, however, that such punitive measures do not help stem the rising incidence of child abuse and neglect."[51] Indian social workers instead proposed a holistic solution: treating the Indian child as part of an Indian family, all of whose members deserved care. "We must look at the abusive parent as a victim as well," they wrote, "and think of ways that help and treatment can be provided, rather than punishment, in order to keep the family together. We also see the great damage that has been done to Indian people as a whole by the wholesale removal of their children."[52]

This holistic approach can best be seen in the proposal for an American Indian Youth and Family Program put forward by the American Indian Child Placement Development Program (AICPDP) in cooperation with the Young Women's Christian Association of greater Milwaukee. The AICPDP, which social service providers and activists initiated in Milwaukee in 1973, discovered that rates of juvenile delinquency among Indian youth had increased sharply. The group attempted to work with existing agencies to address the problem, but they found that most youth programs had little family involvement and that county social service departments provided few if any services to prevent the breakup of Indian families. AICPDP organizers envisioned a whole-family approach instead, explaining, "It has been traditional in the Indian country to involve all of the family in whatever undertaking, and this approach kept the family unified, leaving no room for delinquency problems." As Indian families moved to urban areas, the "predominantly white approach of fragmented family activity" became more common. The AICPDP proposed "a strong family program of recreation, counseling, and family advocacy when problems arise." The group planned family-oriented activities such as monthly family weekends in a camp setting; discussions related to family survival; family planning classes; pregnancy and prenatal care classes; childcare classes; leadership training; and a co-ed bowling league. In particular, organizers highlighted the services they planned to extend to unwed mothers, whom they noted, in contrast to non-Indian attitudes, "are not ostracized but are accepted within the families and communities without any particular stigma."[53]

Most important, Indian community organizers focused on recovering Indian ways of raising children that had been undermined by generations of child removal. It was particularly galling to Indian social service providers, who were steeped in their own tribal cultures, to be bombarded with popular notions of Indian family unfitness. The AAIA reported that "Indian communities are often shocked to learn that parents they regard as excellent care-givers have been judged unfit by non-Indian social workers."[54] Every Indian society prized and carefully prescribed the proper care of children. Victor Sarracino of Laguna Pueblo explains that "when a child is born, a kind of rededication of the entire family takes place. We become child-centered again. We say, 'Here is one who is newly born and who calls for our full attention.'"[55] Indian organizers sought to educate themselves, their communities, and the broader American society about their own viable means of raising children.

They also envisioned that tribal childrearing traditions could provide the key to developing modern Indian child welfare programs. For her keynote address at the Bottle Hollow conference, Pat Locke, director of planning resources in minority education for the Western Interstate Commission for Higher Education, declared, "I say that we must reach back as far as we can into the ceremonies that will help us understand what a child means to a particular tribal society." Speaking of her own tradition, she explained,

> The Dakota people have the concept of the 'Beloved Child.' The Beloved Child is one born after a time of travail and that is a gift from God. This child is treated in a very special way: even the soles of his [or her] moccasins are beaded and many people are invited to a feast and celebration to see him or her. The Beloved Child is a symbol: in a real sense, *all* our children are beloved because we, as Indian people have been through a terrible time of travail. It is amazing to me that we are as mentally healthy as we are, and that we have survived to such a degree with our societies intact.[56]

Participants at the Bottle Hollow conference drew up a long list of recommendations, but they emphasized one in particular, which they put in all capital letters: "WHEN IN DOUBT GO INDIAN."[57] Indian community organizers identified the recovery of American Indian systems of childrearing as key to both Indian survival and self-determination.

Even as they longed to restore these caring ideals, many social workers realized the magnitude of their undertaking. Maxine Robbins ruminated on the breakdown of traditional caring and whether it was possible to reclaim such traditions. At one strategy conference, she asserted:

> But these are the things that we have lost, the tradition of families— extended families, as it has come to be called now—being the agent

that socializes the children and raises them. This has broken down, in part by the mobility of the mother and father, the kind of family intermarriages with outside people. Certainly the most critical issue is: How can we at the reservation level begin to provide for some kind of tribal institutions that will do the work that the generations did in the past? I'm not at all certain, of course, that we can go back and recreate what was. I'm not sure that it is desirable if we could. There have been too many changes. Certainly, the concept is still there, and I think we should attempt to support it at the tribal level.[58]

Indian social workers such as Robbins combined a fervent desire to reinvigorate their cultural traditions of childrearing with a pragmatic commitment to improving the lives of Indian families.

Many Indian activists and leaders proposed a number of solutions to the Indian child welfare crisis at the grassroots level, from passing tribal resolutions, articulating vision statements, revising their legal codes, and developing their own social service programs. Like the Devils Lake Sioux at Fort Totten, some tribes passed ordinances conveying their intent to place Indian children with Indian families. The Three Affiliated Tribes of the Fort Berthold Reservation in North Dakota passed a resolution in 1971 declaring that "all agencies involved with the placement of Indian children in foster homes place such children with Indian families wherever and whenever possible."[59] Some tribes developed statements that demonstrated their unique vision of childrearing. The Tribal Council of the Mississippi Band of Choctaw Indians ratified a Choctaw Children's Bill of Rights in 1975. The statement prioritized children's needs, as for example in article 4, which asserted the child's right "to receive continuing loving care and respect as a unique human being." It also asserted that it was in an Indian child's best interest to remain within his or her biological or extended family, if possible. The Choctaw statement emphasized family reunification through the provision of "readily available services and supports to reassume [the child's] care" or, if this was not possible, Choctaw foster parents "or as a last alternative an adoptive family." Even if the Choctaw child was adopted, the Bill of Rights asserted the need for continued communication with the child's biological parents. Proponents insisted that growing up within their Indian communities was key to an

Indian child's full development. Article 5 of the Choctaw's Bill of Rights asserted the Choctaw child's right "to grow up in freedom and dignity in a neighborhood of people who accept him with understanding, respect and friendship," while article 8 granted the child the right "to receive preparation for citizenship and parenthood through interaction with Choctaw parents and other adults who are consistent role models."[60]

The Navajos from a very early date developed their own legal codes regarding fostering and adoption. The Navajo Tribal Council set up their own Tribal Welfare Committee in 1957 and passed a resolution providing "Regulations for the Care, Custody, and Control of Abandoned, Neglected and Delinquent Navajo Children." They approved a "Tribal Policy on Adoption of Navajo Orphans or Neglected and Abandoned Children" in 1960 in response to unauthorized child removal by unnamed religious organizations, most likely the Church of Latter Day Saints and its Indian Student Placement Program. This policy asserted that no Navajo child could be removed from the reservation "without prior approval of the Advisory Committee of the Navajo Tribal Council, except for the purpose of attending school under a non-sectarian program approved by the Bureau of Indian Affairs."[61] Their legal code enshrined these regulations by outlining who could be adopted and who could adopt and by including detailed adoption procedures. Unlike most state codes and mainstream adoption practices, the Navajo code allowed unmarried and divorced persons to adopt. This code designated the tribal court as the proper adjudicator of Indian child welfare cases, a stipulation that the Indian Child Welfare Act would also include.[62]

The Navajos were particularly resistant to the Indian Adoption Project as a result of their legal code. IAP director Arnold Lyslo regularly met with the Tribal Welfare Committee of the Navajos in the early 1960s "to discuss the necessity of providing some protection for Navajo children in need of adoption," as he put it. He noted, however, that many tribal officials were concerned that Navajo children were being adopted by non-Indians "through missionary channels, and that little is known about the suitability of these adoptions." In exasperation, Lyslo complained, "For whatever reason, the Tribal Welfare Committee has been unable to accept any organized program like our project for the adoption of their children. Rather, they prefer that all adoptions go through the Navajo Tribal Court, with the Bureau social worker at Window Rock acting as their agent." Lyslo believed Navajo resistance to the IAP and state intervention derived from blatant greed, not love for their children. He contended that "such [outside] adoptions represent division of the tribe and may eventually mean loss of tribal wealth. . . . With the Navajo's recent accumulation of wealth, it may be more important to them to protect their accumulated wealth than the life of a Navajo child." Perhaps aware of his contemptuous attitudes, the Navajos politely rejected Lyslo. One official told Lyslo that the Child Welfare League "'should come back to see us in ten years to see if we are then ready to consider your adoption program.'"[63]

Many tribes created their own social service agencies. They often sought to bypass the BIA as well as state agencies; like Maxine Robbins, some tribal representatives started applying directly to new federal funding sources to set up their own programs. With the help of the AAIA, the Devils Lake Sioux established a Family Development Center on the Fort Totten Reservation that was funded through HEW. The tribe noticed that on many occasions, children were removed when their parents were incarcerated for petty offenses. So they created a holistic family approach; "as an alternative to incarcerating the parents, the tribe developed a center where the parents and the children were able to live together and receive counseling in a homelike environment." The center also provided outreach services to families in trouble.[64]

A group of Sisseton-Wahpeton Sioux women on the Lake Traverse reservation in South Dakota formed a Welfare Committee that addressed all manner of issues, including people needing assistance, drug problems, and children needing care. Dorothy Gill explained its origins and work at the Bottle Hollow conference. "Throughout the history of the Sisseton-Wahpeton Sioux Tribe," she said, "womenfolk sometimes referred to as kum-shis, or grandmas, have been concerned with bettering living conditions for tribal members." During the 1950s a group of those grandmas joined forces and pledged to work together, monitoring the programs and agencies that were developing for Indian people and making sure that services intended for tribal members were provided and were consistent with their needs. They were sometimes called "the mad grandmas." These women joined forces with the Lakota TB and Health Association, initially to address high rates of tuberculosis among their communities, but later to tackle other health problems, including alcoholism. In 1973 the tribe organized a Tribal Welfare Committee, which was "concerned with emergency and permanent placement of our Indian children." At Bottle Hollow, Gill concluded, "We have a long way to go, but the 'mad grandmas' are our driving force and keep us focused on our common interest: Indian child welfare services."[65]

The minutes of the Lake Traverse Welfare Committee's meetings reveal the complicated nature of Indian child welfare issues and the sophisticated way in which this group of mad grandmas approached their work. In one case a young woman "left her baby with a couple of vista's [VISTA volunteers] and she never came back after him. They want to adopt the [baby]." The committee vowed to "Check on this. Talk to [the mother] and the couple that want this child." In another case, a sixteen-year-old living with her grandparents "went up to the school and enrolled herself so she wants to go to school. . . . She went to the State Welfare and asked them to take custody of her and place her in a foster home. She does not want to stay with her grandparents because they are mean to her. We would like to grant her wishes." The committee passed a motion to honor her request.[66] These Indian women understood the complexity of Indian child welfare, from the point of view of desperate Indian women who truly might not have wished to keep their babies to the perspective of children themselves, who were frustrated and sought to exert their own agency. When Indian parents sought to regain custody of children who had been removed, the Welfare Committee provided support. Authorities had denied one woman visits with her four children, ages fifteen, thirteen, twelve, and eight. The group declared that she must have an attorney. The Welfare Committee's influential chair Etta Finley declared, "We will help [her] get them back and [the] committee will back [her] up."[67]

The Welfare Committee sought out an alliance with the AAIA. Hirsch and two psychiatrists from the American Academy of Child Psychiatry visited the Lake Traverse reservation in November 1973 to learn from members of the Welfare Committee about their concerns and how they could support them. The doctors remarked that their visit was influenced by "a knowledgeable and dynamic person who clearly illustrated 'koonshee [kum-shi] power' or grandmother power. This was Mrs. Etta Finley, a 68-year old grandmother and chairman of the Welfare Committee."[68]

As Indian women worked within their own communities to resolve their problems, they often found themselves in conflict with state authorities. Many Indian groups, for example, sought to recruit Indian foster families, often running afoul of their states because many foster families could not meet middle-class or age criteria for fostering. One resourceful group at the Warm Springs Reservation in Oregon devised their own standards for licensing foster homes. Cheryl Ann Kennedy shared the Warm Springs Foster Home Program and Standards with attendees at the Bottle Hollow conference. Foster homes needed "to be safe in regard to fire, sanitation and accidents"; to protect the child from guns, poisons, and drugs; and to "maintain a standard of cleanliness." Children did not need to have their own bedrooms but did have to have their own bed in a room with other children of the same sex and appropriate age. Their standards also stipulated that foster parents could "not use severe or harsh punishment" and that they must provide a "nutritious and sufficient diet." They required, too, that foster parents "possess character traits and habits which are wholesome, such as responsible use of alcohol, no felony convictions or illegal drug use and have a good standing in the community."[69]

Not only did Indian social workers seek to challenge mainstream standards for foster care and devise their own, they also fought against the notion that extended family caregivers were not appropriate foster parents. In Alaska, an attorney for the Alaska Legal Services Corporation submitted a statement to the Superior Court in 1971 in support of legally recognizing Alaska Native adoption customs on grounds that it would provide "legal sanction to an already existing, stable family life."[70]

Not all adoption agencies took an adversarial stance toward Indian self-determination efforts, and Indian women sometimes found ways to work within such agencies to further their goals. Charlotte Goodluck, a Navajo social worker, advocated for more appropriate and caring child welfare services for Indians. Beginning in 1973 she directed the Indian Adoption Program for the Jewish Family and Children's Services in Phoenix, an adoption agency that quickly grasped the nature of the Indian child welfare crisis.[71] Goodluck actively recruited Indian foster and adoptive families while also providing services to birth mothers. She observed that the young birth mothers she worked with "have been generally non-delinquent with no significant history of alcohol or drug abuse." Over two-thirds of the young mothers who had come to the program up to the late 1970s had kept their children and returned to live on the reservation.[72]

Indian social service providers and activists devised creative solutions to the Indian child welfare crisis in the 1970s. They proved that Indian people had the knowledge and skill to take care of their own children. To do so, however, they needed resources and support, and they required a sea-change in the way that federal and state authorities approached Indian child welfare. The tide began to turn when Mrs. Fournier refused to give up Ivan Brown in 1968. This "mad grandma" probably had little sense that her actions would ripple far beyond her North Dakota reservation. She and the other Indian women who traveled to New York and Washington DC for a "mothers' delegation" simply wanted to stop the practices of state intervention into their families. The AAIA spread the word about their grievances and discovered a widespread pattern of unwarranted Indian child removal. Many Indian women and some male allies mobilized to address the Indian child welfare crisis and seized the initiative to reclaim the care of their children. These women found a staunch ally in the AAIA. Together in the 1970s they would work for a national solution to the Indian child welfare crisis.

Historians are like detectives. We gain one bit of information and then follow its clues to new sources. Eventually we accumulate enough evidence to build a case. From sifting through a lot of disparate material we start to see patterns. Steve Unger was the first person I interviewed for this book. He not only shared his firsthand experience of the Indian child welfare crisis with me, but he also led me to other sources. He put me in contact with his former AAIA colleagues Bertram "Bert" Hirsch and Mary Lou Byler and the Indian activist and social worker Evelyn Blanchard. Bert and Evelyn put me in touch with other lawyers and activists who had been involved in Indian child welfare. I emailed or called each potential lead to see if he or she would be willing to speak with me. Some were eager to talk; others never replied or returned my phone calls. For some, the subject seemed painful. One replied to my email to say that he had no interest in digging back in his memory. Others no doubt had grave suspicions about a non-Indigenous researcher writing about this topic.

Bert and Evelyn were passionate about the subject. After preliminary phone calls, I arranged formal oral history interviews with each of them. On two successive days in September 2011, they each recounted their stories with me for about ninety minutes. We barely scratched the surface. One week later I interviewed each of them for another ninety minutes. Bert told me that now we had gotten to about 5 percent of what he could tell me about Indian child welfare. He sent me a lengthy videotape of an ICWA workshop he conducted in Alaska in the 1980s. Evelyn sent me a copy of the dissertation she had just completed about the congressional testimony leading up to ICWA.

Evelyn has been involved with strengthening Indian families and promoting Indian child welfare since the 1960s. I had the opportunity to meet her in person in the summer of 2012. I was visiting my mother in southern Colorado. One day I drove to Taos, New Mexico, just two hours southwest of my mother's home, and Evelyn drove up from her home in Albuquerque. We met at a classic old inn. They were closed for lunch that day, but we asked the bartender to take our photo on our phones. I felt awkward and gangly next to her tiny elegance. I brought her a pair of hand-knit wrist warmers, and she gave me a beautiful pair of earrings made by her son. We found a roomy restaurant nearby and ordered northern New Mexico fare. We then talked for three and a half hours. She told me stories about the Native women in the Pacific Northwest with whom she had worked on Indian child welfare in the 1970s and 1980s. She recounted the days, too, when she regularly drove from Santa Fe to Taos, trying to avoid using her brakes the whole way. Although Evelyn is in her seventies, she has just finished working on a political campaign and is now starting a new job to help Indian children get health care benefits. She is still not using her brakes, it seems.

Both she and Bert worked extremely hard to defend Indian families and to pass ICWA in the 1960s and 1970s. The Baby Veronica case and attempts to overturn ICWA grieve them deeply. They shared so much with me, I think, because they see similar trends in Indian child welfare happening again, and they fear that the arduous labor of a generation of activists might be undone. Perhaps some historical detective work can help to solve the crimes of the past.

# CHAPTER 5

# The Campaign for the Indian Child Welfare Act

Leon "Lee" Cook had been raised traditionally by members of his extended family on the Red Lake Indian Reservation in northwest Minnesota. His mother had died shortly after giving birth to him, and his father and his mother's sisters cared for him until his father died. Then he went to live with his paternal grandfather, until he too died, when Cook was just ten years old. Then his father's older sister took over his care. To many non-Indian social workers, Cook's upbringing showed the lack of a stable and permanent home, and he might well have been swept into the child welfare system. But Cook treasured his upbringing and contrasted it to that of his "good buddy" who was also orphaned but placed in a foster home off the reservation. "Our lives have never been parallel since," he told a group of Indian child welfare advocates. "I went to prep school; he wound up in Redwing State School. I went to college, and he went to reformatory. I went to graduate school, and he wound up in Stillwater State Prison." In 1966 Cook became the first Minnesota Ojibwe to graduate from the University of Minnesota's School of Social Work. He worked in anti-poverty programs in Minnesota and later as a senior field coordinator for the Department of Commerce and director of economic development for the Bureau of Indian Affairs. He was elected president of the National Congress of American Indians (NCAI) in 1971.[1] Cook disagreed with non-Indian social workers who believed that Indian children from "broken" families would turn out better if raised in non-Indian families. He offered his own story as a counter-assertion, that Indian children could thrive and even succeed in the non-Indian world through being raised in traditional Indian ways through strong extended family networks.

Cook was one of many key Indian activists and social workers in the early 1970s who convened with allies in the Association on American Indian Affairs and the American Academy of Child Psychiatry (AACP) to strategize about how best to confront the Indian child welfare crisis. These activists decided to fight for comprehensive national legislation, leading to three remarkable sets of hearings before Congress in the mid-1970s. Activism for ICWA linked the control of Indian child welfare to the overall goals of the Red Power movement of this era: self-determination and sovereignty. Grassroots Indian activists, Indian social service providers, and advocates in the AAIA and AACP achieved the passage of the Indian Child Welfare Act in 1978, a radical piece of legislation that enabled tribes to take unprecedented sovereignty over child welfare. ICWA acknowledged that past policies and practices of child removal had deeply wronged Indian people and empowered them to reclaim the care of their own children.

To thousands of non-Indian Americans, the testimony of Indian activists and the passage of ICWA came as a shock. Many social workers, adoptive families, and nonprofit agency directors were accustomed to seeing themselves as caring rescuers. Now some perceived themselves anew through Indian eyes: as child snatchers. For some this was a sobering moment that led to self-questioning. Others resisted the implications of ICWA and opposed it wholeheartedly. For most Indians, the passage of ICWA brought a new mood of hopefulness as Indian social workers and tribal leaders organized to put the act into full effect.

As Indian social service providers, community organizers, and their allies built a national movement to confront the Indian child welfare crisis, other Indian activists were making national headlines through exerting a new militancy: Red Power. The National Indian Youth Council helped to sponsor fish-ins among Northwest Coast tribes in the early 1960s, urban Indians in the San Francisco Bay Area occupied Alcatraz Island in the late 1960s and early 1970s, and the American Indian Movement, or AIM, took over the site of the 1890 Wounded Knee massacre in the mid-1970s.[2] A quieter but no less significant battle played out, however, in the movement to reclaim control of Indian child welfare. This more behind-the-scenes activism had a profound impact on promoting Indian self-determination and changing the day-to-day lives of Indian families.

This child welfare movement occurred at a time when federal Indian policy shifted from termination to self-determination. American Indians began testing their powers to practice self-determination in the mid-1960s with the programs of Lyndon B. Johnson's Great Society. Tribes now could apply directly to federal programs administered through the Office of Economic Opportunity (OEO) and bypass the BIA. The OEO proved to be a boon to Indian efforts to control their own destiny. Now more than a thousand Indian people, according to Charles Wilkinson, "never before given the chance to assume major responsibilities, took the reins of OEO projects and then moved into leadership positions in the tribal councils, national and regional Indian organizations, and federal and state offices."[3]

President Johnson articulated "self-determination" as the new aim of Indian programs in a speech to Congress in 1968, and President Nixon reaffirmed this more forcefully in a 1970 speech. In the 1970s key members of Congress took an interest in Indian affairs and Forest Gerard (Blackfeet) and Frank Ducheneaux (Cheyenne River Sioux) gained significant staff positions on Senate and House Interior Committees. A crop of legislation grew out of this period, including the Indian Self Determination and Education Assistance Act of 1975, which allowed tribes to contract directly with the BIA and the Indian Health Service to administer many of their own programs.[4] It was within this context that the Indian child welfare crisis became visible and the movement to solve it arose and played out.

Indian activists and service providers employed a number of strategies to gain greater control over Indian child welfare. Usually they avoided the high-profile demonstrations, occupations, and public confrontations that AIM and the National Indian Youth Council carried out. Instead they did painstaking, often behind-the-scenes work to build and gain funding for alternative social service programs for their communities and to chisel out agreements with state authorities to revise existing standards, codes, policies, and practices that affected Indian child welfare.

As the AAIA and some other national organizations became active on the issue, on-the-ground activists and service providers sought to balance the desire for practical, tribally specific action, initiated by Native people themselves, and the need for a national remedy. Indian activists and social service providers wrestled with this issue at the conference at Bottle Hollow, Utah, in April 1977. Organizer Marlene EchoHawk discussed the simultaneous need for political action at the grassroots level "among tribal members to influence their councils" and for a broader national movement. She pointed out, however, that "any national political action requires this purpose and clarity at the grass roots level. A national lobbying effort in Washington would be largely ineffective without this support."[5] The campaign for ICWA proved successful, in part, because of the ongoing dialogue between national advocates and grassroots activists.

The AAIA led the national effort. It initially proposed a government investigation into alleged abuses; the development of new guidelines for state welfare agencies; training of state and local court as well as welfare workers; and more preventive services to Indian families.[6] These solutions were helpful but they focused primarily on changing the way non-Indian social workers and state agencies viewed and responded to Indian families. As attorney Bertram Hirsch defended dozens of distraught Indian families who had lost their children, he and AAIA executive director William Byler realized that a more drastic solution was necessary. The AAIA turned toward a goal of passing broad legislation that would empower Indian tribes to take over the provision of Indian child welfare services. The AAIA developed a three-pronged strategy of allying with local and regional Indian groups to revise state codes and practices; carefully selecting Indian family defense cases to litigate that would help to build a strong foundation for federal legislation; and working with key members of Congress to enact national legislation.[7] Their legal work and efforts to revise state codes kept them in constant contact with grassroots and tribally based activists.

Grassroots activists and the AAIA teamed up to negotiate new state codes and practices with state child welfare authorities. After years of confronting hostile welfare authorities in North Dakota, the AAIA and tribal leaders developed a positive relationship with state officials and helped to revise state codes there in the mid-1970s.[8] In South Dakota, AAIA attorneys Hirsch and Lawrence Rappaport consulted with tribal leaders and wrote up new regulations governing state-licensed child placement agencies that "provide[d] substantial protections for the continuity of the [Indian] child's cultural heritage in placement decisions." The state approved these "drastic" changes to their regulations in September 1976. The AAIA team also held meetings with state officials in Oklahoma, Minnesota, California, New Mexico, Wisconsin, Arizona, and Michigan.[9]

Tribal leaders, activists, and the AAIA enjoyed their greatest success in 1976 in Washington State, where after a "long struggle," they "were able to get changes in the state's administrative codes enacted even before the passage of the Indian Child Welfare Act." Social worker Evelyn Blanchard took a leave from her work with the BIA in New Mexico to work with the Washington tribes. Because "the Bureau was getting tired of my activism," Blanchard recounts, "frankly, the agency was anxious to see me find someplace else to go." Tribal representatives, Blanchard, and AAIA attorneys Hirsch, William Lamb, and LeRoy Wilder convinced Washington's Department of Social and Health Services to adopt new regulations that provided for significant involvement by Indians in all placement decisions affecting Indian children. The AAIA asserted that the new regulations were "the most far-reaching of any in the U.S. and should substantially decrease the large numbers of Indian children placed away from their families in the State of Washington." Blanchard noted that "enactment of code changes did not solve the problem overnight, but at least it gave the [Washington tribes] a greater control in their dealings with the state Department of Social and Health Services. It gave them some power."[10] This was particularly important in that Washington was a Public Law 280 (PL-280) state in which the federal government had transferred much of its jurisdiction over Indian criminal and civil matters to the state.

The AAIA and Indian tribes worked together closely through the AAIA's legal work on behalf of Indian families. The AAIA, like many other civil rights organizations, became increasingly selective about the Indian family defense cases it accepted in the 1970s, as it sought to create a new legal framework for respecting Indian family rights. They reported in 1976 to one of their funding agencies that they had "determined that selective litigation would be commenced and pursued, with a view toward establishing precedents offering greater protection for Indian children and parents, and attacking administrative bias and arbitrariness."[11] Through its legal defense of Indian families, the AAIA came to understand what crucial provisions should be in any federal legislation; Hirsch asserts that Title I of ICWA incorporated many of the lessons AAIA attorneys learned through their litigation.[12]

AAIA attorneys encountered many cases in which authorities removed Indian children from extended families or refused to grant custody to aunts, grandparents, or other relatives, so they particularly worked to establish a precedent for extended family rights. William Lamb, western staff attorney of the AAIA's Indian Child Welfare Program, reported in 1976:

> The many service requests received by the Program from members of Indian families disclose a customary pattern of extended family-child relationships among Indian people that reflect deep-seated traditions and responsibilities within the Indian community for the care and upbringing of Indian children. Many non-Indian welfare administrators, however, view such arrangements as transitory and haphazard, and as evidence that the biological parents are not properly caring for their children. As a result, children placed in informal extended family arrangements often end up in foster care. An important goal of the [AAIA] Program is to secure and protect these extended family relationships until a right is established in the law to an extended-family child relationship that is inviolable, absent extended family child abuse or neglect.[13]

This was one area, however, that proved particularly difficult to litigate, as illustrated in the Elk case in Oregon, covered in chapter 3, and a high-profile case in New Mexico, in which grandparents failed to gain custody of their grandchildren.[14]

The AAIA noted that the closed nature of most adoption proceedings worked against the maintenance of tribal ties, especially between siblings, who might be split up in child welfare cases. Lamb defended a California Mission Indian grandmother who had lost four of her six grandchildren. He contacted the adoptive family of one of the children, and they agreed to sue for the rights of siblings to maintain their relationships. Lamb noted that "raising the issues strikes directly at the confidentiality of adoptive placements and at the principle that an adoption severs all ties between a child and any former parents, relatives, and siblings."[15] The AAIA's litigation challenged the strict confidentiality of most adoption proceedings, a core principle of adoption practices in the era.

The AAIA's legal defense of Indian families revealed, too, the ubiquity of legal irregularities and abuses in Indian child welfare cases. State and county courts routinely failed to notify Indian parents and caregivers of court hearings. Typically, they did not provide legal counsel for poor Indian families who did go to court. The AAIA dealt with several instances in which jurisdiction issues clouded Indian child welfare cases—for example, when a tribal court's ruling conflicted with a state court ruling. Hirsch eventually would incorporate his experience with legal abuses and jurisdictional issues into the drafting of ICWA.

Indian and AAIA activists had some success with these measures, but there were limits to the state-by-state approach and litigation. Many activists saw the need for comprehensive federal legislation that would provide protection to Indian families from the abuses that had led to the Indian child welfare crisis. The AAIA took the lead in organizing a campaign for federal legislation. They convened a one-day Indian Child Welfare and Family Services Conference at the Biltmore Hotel in New York City in January 1974. This conference constituted a strategy session involving about twenty people, including AAIA staff members, national Indian leaders, local Indian activists, child psychiatrists, legal experts, and at least one journalist. Curiously, given the prominent role of women, it involved just one Indian woman, Maxine Robbins, and one white woman, Judge Justine Wise Polier, who substituted for a young attorney specializing in child advocacy, Hillary Rodham.[16]

The AAIA did not set a strict agenda and the resulting discussion was freewheeling. Participants discussed the nature of the Indian child welfare crisis, from the breakdown of the extended family to insensitive social workers and "bureaucratic paralysis," from jurisdictional issues and working with hostile state agencies to standards for licensing foster homes and lack of due process. Yet mostly the Biltmore conference attendees discussed solutions to the crisis, debating big philosophical issues as well as nitty-gritty strategies for effecting legislation.

Attendees agreed that an Indian child welfare crisis imperiled Indian communities. Some blamed the crisis entirely on insensitive, opportunistic, and downright vindictive BIA and welfare authorities. Byler summed up this view. "The children in . . . so many cases," he asserted, "are taken away from the parents to punish the parents, not to save the child. There's nothing wrong with the way these kids are being taken care of."[17] Other advocates for Indian child welfare, including Maxine Robbins, conceded that because the extended family tradition had broken down to some extent, many Indian families were struggling, and there were cases in which children were neglected and in need of protective services outside their families.[18] Unlike most non-Indian social welfare authorities, however, Robbins believed Indian people themselves possessed the skills and knowledge to reverse the situation.

Participants also divided over the solution to the crisis. Robbins and Lee Cook, by this time director of Minnesota Indian Resource Development, a center for urban Indians in the Minneapolis–St. Paul region, discussed the value of reclaiming extended family arrangements or creating tribal institutions to replace them. Sam Deloria of the Indian Law Center at the University of New Mexico disagreed. "When you are in a persistent economic depression that lasts for generations, that kind of system can't do you much good," he asserted. "If everybody is equally poor, then sharing child raising responsibilities doesn't really help solve your problems very much." Taking an economic determinist argument, Deloria argued that if the economy improved on reservations, the "extended family would revive."[19] Carl Mindell, a medical doctor with Eleanor Roosevelt Developmental Services in New York City and co-chair of the AACP's Committee on the American Indian Child, seconded Deloria's view that economic problems were at the root of the issue. He believed "families do better with money than they do with services" and that "providing people with a reasonable . . . standard of living" was key to resolving the crisis.

Other participants turned this logic on its head. If Indian communities waited until their economies improved, what would happen to Indian families in the meantime? Byler questioned whether there was "an economic route [sic] to all of these things" and asked about reservations that were unlikely to have any extensive economic development. "Are they to be written off as an insoluble problem?" he queried.[20] Participants did not resolve this issue, but activists incorporated both of these contrasting priorities into ICWA.

Strategists disagreed, too, on whether the Indian child welfare crisis could be resolved through broad legislation for all manner of American Indian issues or if it needed a specific effort. Sherwin Broadhead, a Cherokee attorney with the Institute for the Development of Indian Law, onetime congressional relations officer for the BIA, and special assistant for Indian Affairs on the staff of Senator James Abourezk of South Dakota, supported the inclusion of child welfare in a broader bill that was soon to pass: the Indian Self-Determination and Education Act. Many in attendance, however, believed it was too late to amend the act in that direction.[21] Broadhead also recommended the general approach of creating an American Indian Policy Review Commission (which eventually did transpire), but Byler and others worried that such a general approach would once again "drift away from the child."[22]

Conference participants also debated whether to hammer out new criteria for neglect and abuse that would prevent the widespread removal of Indian children, and whether to generate new standards for licensing foster homes that would enable more Indian families to take in foster children. Many attendees lamented that current state requirements for minimal square footage and individual rooms for children prevented many Indians from being licensed as foster parents.[23] Byler was particularly intent on developing new standards. When discussion veered away from the topic, he sought to turn it back to specific requirements that the bill might spell out. Others believed any federal legislation would be doomed if it dictated these standards to Indian tribes. Instead, the legislation should protect tribes' rights to develop their own policies and practices regarding Indian child welfare. Dr. Alan Gurwitt, a psychiatrist working at the Yale Child Study Center and co-chair of the AACP's Committee on the American Indian Child, pointed out that "instead of coming up with specific standards, which might vary very much, you are looking for the power—the financial power and decision power—to be placed in the tribe, and however they decide to do it, that's where it will rest." Given these differences, the participants did not get very far in brainstorming the actual provisions of a potential Indian child welfare bill. (As it turned out, the ICWA would lean toward Gurwitt's—and Indian activists'—vision).[24]

The group realized that any Indian Child Welfare bill would need to encompass both reservation-based and urban Indians. Cook recounted that a group of Minnesota Indian leaders had recently met in Duluth to discuss how to work with the state. "One of the things that we are looking at across the board is recognizing that, like in the City of Minneapolis or any other place in the country," he noted, "we simply have a first generation urban people, and recognizing that more than half of our people live off the reservation, it has necessitated, if we are going to survive, dealing with the city governments, county governments, state governments."[25] The concerns of urban Indians led to important provisions of ICWA that recognized ongoing tribal connection and viability, even when Indian families lived off reservations.

The attendees also recognized the difficult jurisdictional issues that confronted them, especially in PL-280 states in which the federal government had transferred some jurisdiction to state governments.[26] Robbins explained that in her work with the Yakima Tribal Council to form a tribal family and child service agency, "One of the hangups is Public Law 280. We're still fighting that in the courts." She offered "We'd be happy to become the model test case, guinea pig, or whatever you call it. We most definitely are going to challenge Public Law 280. We most definitely are going to create our own child welfare agency on a tribal basis, with a recognized tribal court."[27] Jurisdiction, a longstanding and vexing issue, became a central component of the Indian Child Welfare Act.

The conference recognized, too, the need to gain more media attention. Participants expressed frustration that the press had not covered child welfare significantly and preferred to highlight militant activism. Broadhead quipped that the coverage of Wounded Knee "always ended up showing some Indian standing up in silhouette, or some confrontation."[28] Byler lamented that even in local newspapers, most of the stories did not get covered; instead, "the children are just taken silently." The AAIA had foreseen this issue and had invited a journalist from the *Wall Street Journal,* Edwin McDowell. He piped up at the end of the meeting that he would write an article for his influential newspaper. (McDowell ran one article in July 1974.)[29]

The Biltmore conference cemented relations between the AAIA, tribal leaders, and activists who were concerned with Indian child welfare. One participant at the Biltmore conference, John Woodenlegs, tribal chair of the Northern Cheyenne, ended the day by saying, "Mr. Byler, could I just thank the Association on behalf of the Cheyenne people for their help and encouragement? We were one of the poorest tribes in Montana, or in the United States—sick and poor, trodden down to next to nothing— but we have been built up by the encouragement of the Association."[30] The fruitful alliance that tribes had established with the AAIA paid off in the congressional hearings for ICWA.

Yet the AAIA was not the only national agency that allied with Indian people on child welfare. The American Academy of Child Psychiatry also became a staunch supporter of Indian peoples' efforts to stem the tide of child removal, in part through the influence of the AAIA. The AACP established its Committee on the American Indian Child in 1973. Soon after, several members attended the AAIA's Biltmore conference, including doctors Gurwitt and Mindell. Gurwitt stated his intention to work with the Academy to inform people of Indian child welfare issues. Gurwitt was sensitive, however, to the need to help "at the behest of tribal groups," and he wanted to learn from and be educated by tribes. (In fact, he and Mindell had already made efforts in this direction, visiting through the AAIA two Sioux reservations—the Sisseton-Wahpeton reservation in Lake Traverse, South Dakota, and the Devils Lake reservation in Fort Totten, North Dakota—in November 1973.) Another AACP member, Dr. Edward Greenwood with the Menninger Foundation, proposed that the Academy's task force could recruit and provide expert witnesses in child welfare cases, help draft standards, and develop articles about boarding schools.[31]

Soon after attending the Biltmore conference, Mindell and Gurwitt drafted a position statement, "The Placement of American Indian Children—The Need for Change," that the AACP formally adopted on January 25, 1975. It was premised on a "belief in the inherent strengths of the American Indian family." Gurwitt and Mindell worked closely with non-Indian mental health professionals who treated Indian people: Robert "Bob" Bergman, the first director of the IHS's Mental Health Branch in Albuquerque, and George Goldstein, deputy director of the Mental Health Branch.[32]

The AACP did not merely pontificate on these matters while remaining distant from Indian people. The AAIA connected Gurwitt with Indian mental health and social service providers, and the AACP quickly became acquainted with and supportive of that dynamic group of Indian women community organizers, the "mad grandmas" and energetic dynamos who worked at the tribal level or in urban Indian centers to reverse the devastating practices of Indian child removal. Bergman, for example, came to know the dedicated social worker Evelyn Blanchard. He put her in touch with Hirsch, who asked her to serve as an "an advocate and expert witness in an Indian child custody proceeding," the first of many cases in which she was involved.[33] In April 1977 the AACP funded and sponsored the important conference at Bottle Hollow, Utah, on the Uintah-Ouray Reservation. Gurwitt and Mindell co-chaired the conference and Marlene EchoHawk, a clinical psychologist, PhD, and member of the Otoe-Missouri Tribe, coordinated it. The gathering enabled Indian social workers and other social service providers to meet one another, share their experiences, and strategize for the future. This proved to be a crucial act of support in the movement for the Indian Child Welfare Act that did not go unnoticed by Indian people. EchoHawk in fact praised the "remarkable advocacy of AACP for American Indian children."[34]

With the backing of Indian activists and the alliance of the AACP, the AAIA soon took action after the Biltmore conference to enact federal legislation. Byler contacted the chair of the Senate Select Committee on Indian Affairs, Senator James Abourezk of South Dakota, and presented him with a report from the Biltmore conference and statistics documenting the gross overrepresentation of Indian children in nearly every state's child welfare system. Abourezk committed to holding oversight hearings on the issue, which he convened in April 1974, to determine if the problem merited legislation.[35]

Senator Abourezk proved an invaluable ally in the campaign for the ICWA. During the subsequent 1977 hearings, he shared something of his personal background that led him to become an advocate for Indians generally. "I grew up on an Indian reservation in South Dakota," he declared. "I can remember going through stages in my life where I thought, 'Well, the Indians aren't very well off, and they probably ought to act like those of us who are not Indian. If they could act like the whites, maybe they would be very well off. But," Abourezk continued, "I have changed my views a great deal in the past number of years. . . . I do not believe we have all the answers. I think the attitude I used to take personally was a very arrogant one. I certainly do not take it today. But I think a lot of people living out around the reservations and, in fact, in cities away from the reservations probably still have the same attitude I used to have before I began to see things from a different perspective."[36] Abourezk was uncommonly sympathetic and committed to Indian self-determination.

Once Senator Abourezk had set a date for the 1974 hearings, he asked the AAIA to prepare a witness list. The AAIA sprang into action to gather

Indian witnesses who could testify personally and professionally to the Indian child welfare crisis. As Hirsch recalls, "To generate this list of witnesses, I contacted a lot of my clients who had been victims of losing their children. A lot of them agreed. A lot of those battles I had won; they had gotten their children back. They came to the Congress with their children along with a handful of experts. Indian social workers, psychiatrists who were committed to Indian child welfare."[37] Hirsch's many years of litigation paid off in mobilizing Indian people who had been personally affected by and involved in the Indian child welfare crisis.

The AAIA and the AACP also approached sympathetic non-Indian social scientists and potential Indian professionals to testify at the hearings. Blanchard's experience of becoming a witness at the 1974 hearings reveals the networks the AAIA had helped to established and now were able to activate. "In 1974 when the preparations were being made by Senator James Abourezk's . . . office for the first hearings related to the Indian Child Welfare Act," Blanchard recalls, "members of his staff contacted Dr. George Goldstein, then deputy director of the [BIA's] Mental Health Branch to ask for the Branch's assistance in the identification of witnesses. I was sitting in Goldstein's office when he got the call. He recommended that I be called as a witness and shortly thereafter I was invited to testify at the hearings." As Blanchard notes, "It was the event that cast me into the role of national advocate for Native children and their families."[38] Like Blanchard, other Indian women who had been active in addressing Indian child welfare in their communities or through the BIA, such as Goldie Denny, Victoria Gokee, Betty Jack, and Ramona Bennett, similarly became part of a national movement through their testimony in the 1974 hearings. Indian activist men such as Mike Chosa and Lee Cook also provided testimony at the hearings.

At these hearings advocates for an Indian Child Welfare Act documented the abuses and injustices Indian families had suffered as a result of the unwarranted removal of children and their placement in non-Indian families. Many Indian women testified to the intense pressure they had experienced from social workers and missionaries to give up their newborns. Other Indian witnesses claimed that social workers had unfairly removed their children, while still others reported on the veritable kidnapping of their children by missionaries or VISTA volunteers. As the

AAIA interwove testimony from Indian families with that of legal and mental health experts, they developed three main arguments in support of a national Indian Child Welfare Act: that Indian families' legal rights had been trampled; that Indian children's best interests had been compromised; and that complicated funding mechanisms through divided jurisdiction had deprived Indian communities of the necessary economic support they needed to keep Indian children within their families.

Multiple witnesses testified to the ways in which Indian people had been denied due process in regard to child welfare. The AAIA and many Indian witnesses pointed to a pattern in which Indian child removals occurred without any court order. In many cases, social workers talked Indian mothers into signing a voluntary relinquishment form for their children, so Indian parents had no opportunity to defend their rights in court. As Byler explained, "Many cases do not go through an adjudicatory process at all, since the voluntary waiver of parental rights is a device widely employed by social workers to gain custody of children."[39] In other instances, social workers and courts seem to have simply bypassed Indian families altogether. "In 1962, I had two of my children taken from me in Chicago and they were placed by the Evangelical and Welfare Society," testified Betty Jack, a Chippewa originally from the Lac du Flambeau reservation in Wisconsin. "They were taken from [me by] the State of Wisconsin and I have never seen them again." Jack asserted that "the courts said I was unfit to take care of my children, but I had never gone to court and I never knew they were legally adopted until a year ago."[40]

Even when cases did make it into court, officials often failed to inform Indian families properly of court hearings. During his testimony to Congress in 1974, Hirsch declared that the case of Cheryl Spider DeCoteau "was one of the grossest violations of due process that I have ever encountered." Court officials did not inform DeCoteau of court hearings in relation to her son John. Thus she was not present at the first hearing, at which a social worker successfully petitioned the court to place DeCoteau's son in emergency custody with a foster family. Hirsch pointed out the ways in which such legal irregularities disadvantaged the Indian mother. "They already took the child away from her prior to having any hearing on unfitness," Hirsch testified, "and the burden of proof was very clearly shifted on Mrs. DeCoteau to prove she was fit, rather than the State proving that she

Fig. 10. (Clockwise from left): Bert Hirsch, Joseph Westermeyer, Melinda Spider, and Cheryl Spider DeCoteau in the Roberts County Courthouse in Sisseton, South Dakota. From *Indian Affairs* 85 (July 1973): 1. Courtesy and permission of the American Association on Indian Affairs.

was unfit." Eventually the judge set another hearing date on the issues of dependency and neglect, more than seven months later, but once again court officials failed to inform DeCoteau directly. Instead, they simply published notification of the hearing in the local newspaper, which DeCoteau did not read. If another tribal member had not seen the notice the day before the court date and informed DeCoteau, she would not have known about the hearing or shown up for it. Thus her parental rights would have been permanently terminated without her presence in court. Hirsch learned that it was a common practice of the welfare department to place notices of hearings in the paper instead of serving Indian people directly.[41]

The AAIA also charged that Indian families rarely had adequate legal representation if they did appear in court and that social workers possessed undue influence in court hearings. Hirsch claimed that "the imperious atti-tude of many social workers and their use of professional jargon may obscure the real issues and deceptively manipulate . . . the . . . court into submitting to a seemingly valid legal position. The testimony of a social worker at a . . . court hearing, even if only in the form of a social history report, places the social worker in the role of more than a natural observer."[42] The legal sys-tem, the AAIA argued, did not play the role of a neutral arbiter of contend-ing interests in the Indian child welfare process. Instead it seemed to favor the interests of the state and adoptive families and discriminate against Indian families. Through this line of argument and testimony, the AAIA and Indian witnesses argued that a key reason for passing an Indian Child Wel-fare Act would be to restore and protect *Indian families'* legal rights.

Other witnesses at the 1974 hearings, primarily from the AACP, focused their arguments on the rights of the *Indian child*. Advocates who favored the removal of Indian children and their placement in non-Indian homes had routinely declared that they prized the "best interests of the child." They built their arguments on popular notions of rescuing "forgotten" Indian children from unfit Indian mothers and dysfunctional Indian fami-lies and communities. Proponents of ICWA argued instead that the best interests of the *Indian* child must take into account the unique historical background and identity of Indian children. Non-Indian social scientists led the charge to articulate this alternative view, including Joseph Wes-termeyer, a psychiatrist on the faculty at the University of Minnesota, AACP members Gurwitt and Mindell, and BIA mental health specialists such as Bergman.

Some witnesses argued that the placement of Indian children in non-Indian homes did not result in positive outcomes for the children. Wes-termeyer testified that of the 120 Indian patients he had treated in the previous five years, half of them had been placed out of their homes, the majority in multiple foster care placements. He noted that often the chil-dren did reasonably well in childhood, and social workers thus believed such placements were positive. "However, once they get into adolescence," Westermeyer found, "runaway problems, suicide attempts, drug usage, and truancy are extremely common among them." Almost all of his foster care patients had the experience of not being allowed to date whites and being called derogatory names; they also had more difficulty getting jobs and bank loans. While other Indians experienced this kind of prejudice, too, these children "had virtually no viable Indian identity," and no support systems from Indian peers or family members.[43] AACP psychiatrists Gurwitt and Mindell backed up Westermeyer's testimony and claimed that based on their studies, problems among Indian foster children and adoptees even showed up earlier than adolescence.[44]

Other witnesses confirmed the psychiatrists' findings. Wallace Galluzzi, the superintendent of Haskell Indian Junior College, recounted stories of failed Indian adoptions. One nineteen-year-old Navajo adoptee he encountered "had the normal teenage problems and they [her adoptive parents] completely rejected her. They said they just couldn't cope with her. She was acting out her frustrations in being abandoned or rejected. She was very much disturbed." After her adoptive parents returned her to state custody, the girl ended up at Haskell, a former boarding school, but Galluzzi noted, "we have no resources for such a severe problem here."[45]

Outcome studies of non-Indian families who adopted Indian children confirmed some of these assertions. Many adoptive parents tended to minimize the role that prejudice would play in their adopted child's life. David Fanshel found in his 1972 longitudinal study of adoptive families in the Indian Adoption Project that only one in ten adoptive mothers "anticipated prejudice against the child."[46] When it came to fostering a tribal identity within their adopted children, many adoptive families, according to Catherine Roherty's Wisconsin study, found it "threatening." One mother told Roherty of her adoptive son, "If he wants to he can do it on his own, I'm not going to make anything of it." Another father agreed, stating that "there are all sorts of books around if they are interested, we plan nothing special."[47]

Despite parental intentions and expectations, the outcome studies reveal that Indian children became aware of their Indianness quite early, just as Mindell and Gurwitt observed. Fanshel described the case of "Cal," who was four and a half years old at the time Fanshel interviewed his family. He noted that "the adoptive parents indicate that they are not planning to initiate discussion of the child's adoptive status with respect to his Indian background until he finds out," and "they imply that they feel he is so secure within the family that their telling him the facts as they know them when he asks will suffice." Fanshel interviewed Cal's family one year later, and learned from his mother that now Cal was "more aware of being Indian. . . . He does not talk about it, but I have noticed he is doing Indian drawings and seems to enjoy his Indian books."[48] Findings of this kind reinforced the views of Indian activists that the non-Indian families were neither realistic about the racism their adopted children would face nor properly equipped to help the children gain knowledge of and pride in their Indian heritage. Instead, the findings confirmed psychiatrists' and Indian activists' worst fears: that adoption profoundly alienated Indian children from their tribal heritage. This, ICWA proponents argued, was not in the best interests of the Indian child.

In their congressional testimony, these mental health professionals, too, criticized state social workers for holding biases against Indian families and thereby failing "to keep the family intact." Mindell and Gurwitt explained that the principle governing state intrusion into a family to remove a child "has generally been 'the best interests of the child.'" However, citing a 1973 *Harvard Law Review* article by Hillary Rodham, they argued that "this principle has few standards or criteria facilitating its interpretation and therefore allows for wide variations in how individual states' agents or courts put it into practice." Consequently, they asserted, "this at least allows for, and perhaps encourages the state's agent to use his own value and moral system in evaluating the childrearing of any particular family who comes before it. Thus, the judge's (social worker's, probation officer's) estimates of the child's needs and family's ability to meet those needs may be based on his own individual and class values which may differ from the child and his family."[49] Often as a result of such biases, social workers rushed to remove Indian children. Westermeyer contended that social workers "will not use the extended family resources. They won't use homemaker or mental health facilities or collaborate with Indian community resources. There seems to be an early recourse to foster placement. . . . There's the stress to sort of whip the family into shape when they experience difficulties in living, rather than to foster family strength and help the family through a crisis."[50] Mindell and Gurwitt seconded Westermeyer's views that too often "little effort [by social workers] has been made to intervene early with support for the [Indian] child and his family by the State and Federal agencies," so that the only option appears to be placement.[51]

Overall these psychological experts countered the popular view that "forgotten" Indian children from "broken" families would turn out better if raised in non-Indian families. AACP representatives advised that Indian tribal courts, not state courts, were in the best position to make decisions about the placement of Indian children.[52] They recommended that Congress empower Indian communities and give them financial support to develop their own child welfare agencies.[53]

Many witnesses at the congressional hearings also brought out the ways in which economic considerations played a role in the Indian child welfare crisis. Not only did social welfare authorities often remove Indian children simply because their families were impoverished, witnesses claimed, but complicated funding mechanisms, exacerbated by jurisdictional confusion, led to elevated levels of Indian child removal, fostering, and adoption. Some witnesses documented that the federal government, through the BIA, paid tribes less to provide child protective services than other federal agencies paid state or private agencies that performed the same functions. Richard Lone Dog, director of the Detention Center at the Rosebud Sioux reservation, testified that his center provided identical foster care services to those of Lutheran Social Services, but while his center was paid just $8.36 a day per child from the state and BIA, the Lutheran program was reimbursed $30 a day per child.[54] States often paid Indian families less to foster children than they paid non-Indian families. In one civil rights suit, *Clampett v. Madigan*, an Indian couple was taking care of related children who had been placed with them by the South Dakota Department of Public Welfare in accordance with court orders of the Rosebud Sioux Tribal Court. This couple was "receiving $38 a month under AFDC [Aid to Families with Dependent Children] rather than the $65 a month [paid to non-Indian foster parents] . . . although they qualified as foster parents." In this case the judge "agreed with the petitioners' contention that the state regulations "discouraged maintenance of family life between dependent children and related foster parents," and that the "state manual does not determine need and the amount of assistance on an objective and equitable basis as demanded by HEW [Department of Health, Education, and Welfare] regulations."[55]

Advocates had discovered, too, that while Indian families could not call upon the same level of financial support available to non-Indian families, complicated funding mechanisms had "built in incentive[s] to remove Indian children." For non-Indian children the Social Security Act required the federal government to pay 25 percent of the total cost of the foster care services, while the states had to cover the remaining 75 percent of costs. This shared funding encouraged the states to make a continuing review of the rates of placement. However, by contrast, "the BIA contracts for services covered 100 percent of the costs and [often] . . . administrative expenses as well, so that a financial incentive or at least no disincentive to remove Indian children from their homes was built in." As Broadhead pointed out at the Biltmore conference, state agencies became "very anxious to take these children into their empire, because it wasn't costing the state anything, because every year when the per capita time came around, the BIA makes one large payment to the state covering all these children, and many times the kind of care they were getting cost the state less than the amount they were getting. They were making money off of them."[56] At the same time, the BIA and the states rarely dedicated funding to providing preventative and rehabilitative services to Indian people. Blanchard testified that "state and local governments [slough] off their responsibilities to Indians, often by bureaucratic technicalities and thereby avoid providing meaningful services."[57] Thus structural inequities that undermined Indian families were embedded within the bureaucracies that Indian communities had to navigate.

Indian activists at the congressional hearings proposed a number of means to rectify these inequities. Mike Chosa of the American Indian Child Development Program for the State of Wisconsin recommended that Congress amend the Aid to Families with Dependent Children law "to permit the separate tribes to receive reimbursement for foster care services as units of government."[58] Chosa hoped to use the power of the purse to compel states to change their behavior; he also recommended that Congress pass legislation that "would prevent reimbursement to States, counties, and private agencies for foster care services unless plans are developed and implemented by them to begin rehabilitative work with children and natural parents, with the objective of eventual return to their natural homes."[59] The economic analysis provided by a number of witnesses served as an important complement to the legal and psychological justifications for ICWA. They showed that far from enacting a color-blind policy, the BIA and states were actually failing to provide Indian families and communities with the same level of funding for and range of child welfare services that were accessible to other American citizens.

Through powerful personal testimonies and the accretion of these legal, psychological, and economic arguments, the 1974 hearings produced three main outcomes. First, they brought together many people who had been working independently in their own corners to address the crisis: tribal and urban activists and social service providers, child psychiatrists affiliated with the AACP, and the AAIA staff. Now they strengthened their bonds with one another and created a national network. Second, the hearings built commitment and momentum in Congress. Hirsch later recalled to an Alaska Native group, "It was an extraordinary hearing—what we had at this hearing is something the U.S. Congress has not seen then or since." It was "extremely moving—the Senators were sitting there crying." He contends that when the testimony was over, the Senators were committed.[60] Finally, the content of the testimony provided the basis for drafting an Indian Child Welfare Act.

Senator Abourezk initiated other efforts that built on the 1974 hearings. In 1973 he had introduced Senate Resolution 133 to establish a special commission to review federal Indian policy, law, and administration. Authorized by the president in early 1975, the American Indian Policy Review Commission, chaired by Abourezk himself, carried out extensive investigations on all aspects of Indian policy. Its Task Force Four on Federal, State, and Tribal Jurisdiction concerned itself in part with Indian child welfare. Its final report, issued in 1976, included an updated AAIA statistical survey of Indian child placement in several states and formal recommendations for broad and comprehensive legislation that would address the Indian child welfare crisis. Broadhead chaired Task Force Four, and in its year of existence he held 28 days of hearings at which 250 witnesses testified, and the task force gathered 4,500 pages of testimony and 3,000 pages of additional submissions. An estimated ninety tribes participated. Task Force Four recommended the enactment of comprehensive legislation by Congress that granted tribal courts exclusive jurisdiction over Indian children domiciled on a reservation.[61]

## 1976 Foster Care and Adoption Rates of American Indian and Alaska Native Children

| STATES | NUMBER OF NATIVE AMERICAN CHILDREN | NUMBER ADOPTED | PROPORTION TO NON-NATIVE ADOPTIONS |
|---|---|---|---|
| Alaska | 28,334 | 957 | 4.6x |
| Arizona | 54,709 | 1,039 | 4.2x |
| California | 39,579 | 1,507 | 8.4x |
| Idaho | 3,808 | ** | 11.0x |
| Maine | 1,084 | ** | as often |
| Michigan | 7,404 | 912 | 3.7x |
| Minnesota | 12,672 | 1,594 | 3.9x |
| Montana | 15,124 | 541 | 4.8x |
| Nevada | 3,739 | ** | as often |
| New Mexico | 41,316 | ** | 1.5x |
| New York | 10,627 | ** | 3.3x |
| North Dakota | 8,186 | 269 | 2.8x |
| Oklahoma | 45,489 | 1,116 | 4.4x |
| Oregon | 6,839 | 402 | 1.1x |
| South Dakota | 18,322 | 1,019 | 1.6x |
| Utah | 6,690 | 328 | 3.4x |
| Washington | 15,980 | 740 | 18.8x |
| Wisconsin | 10,176 | 733 | 17.9x |
| Wyoming | 2,832 | ** | 4.0x |

\* No data available.
\*\* Data reported considered too small to allow for a realistic projection of the total number of Indian children in adoptive care.
\# Using the most conservative assumption included in the report appendix.

Based on the overwhelming testimony presented at the 1974 hearings and the recommendations of the Task Force Four report, Abourezk and the Senate Interior Committee asked the AAIA to draft legislation to address the Indian child welfare crisis. Hirsch worked on the first draft of the legislation in consultation with Arthur Lazarus, a specialist in Indian law who had worked with Felix Cohen, the highly respected author of the *Handbook of Federal Indian Law*. Bill Byler, Congressional staffers Franklin Ducheneaux and Peter Taylor, and many representatives from federal

| PERCENT IN NON-NATIVE HOMES | NUMBER FOSTERED | PROPORTION TO NON-NATIVE | PERCENT IN NON-NATIVE HOMES |
|---|---|---|---|
| 93 | 393 | 3.0x | * |
| * | 558# | 2.7x | * |
| 92.5 | 319 | 2.7x | * |
| * | 296 | 6.4x | * |
| * | 82 | 19.1x | 64 |
| * | 82 | 7.1x | * |
| 97.5 | 737 | 16.5x | * |
| 87 | 534 | 12.8x | * |
| * | 73 | 7.0x | * |
| * | 287 | 2.4x | .* |
| * | 142 | 3.0x | 96.5 |
| 75 | 296 | 20.1x | * |
| * | 337 | 3.9x | * |
| * | 247 | 8.2x | * |
| * | 832 | 22.4x | * |
| * | 249 | 15.0x | 88 |
| * | 558 | 9.6x | 80 |
| * | 545 | 13.4x | * |
| * | 98 | 10.4x | 51–57+ |

+ 51 percent of those in BIA-administered care and 57 percent of those in state-administered care were placed in non-Indian homes.

Source: Task Force Four, *Report on Federal, State, and Tribal Jurisdiction*; table created by Teresa Houser.

agencies contributed to the final version of the bill. Senator Abourezk first introduced the bill on August 27, 1976, as the Indian Child Welfare Act of 1976 (S. 3777), then again the following year on April 1 as S. 1214.[62]

The Senate Select Committee on Indian Affairs held a second set of hearings in August 1977, at which they debated S. 1214. By this time opponents to the bill had mobilized. Some came from likely sources: the Child Welfare League of America (CWLA) and religious groups such as the Church of Latter Day Saints, both of which were integrally involved in removing and placing Indian children with non-Indian families. Other government entities that might have been expected to take a more neutral stance, however, came out forcefully against S. 1214.

The BIA and the HEW provided the first witnesses to testify against it on the basis that it was unnecessary. The BIA's representative, Acting Deputy Commissioner Raymond Butler, asserted that amendments to the Social Security Act through another bill, S. 1928, would accomplish the same thing and that ICWA therefore might conflict with or duplicate the HEW's policies.[63] The BIA marshaled other arguments as well. In a cynical way, it co-opted arguments that Indian people had made in other contexts and turned them against ICWA. The bill, Butler testified, imposed "one uniform set of Federal standards over all tribes without considering the wide cultural diversity and values of Indians throughout the country." Ironically, too, Butler claimed that the BIA—notorious for its interference in the lives of Indian people—opposed Title I of S. 1214 because it increased federal intrusion into tribal domestic matters.

Butler's testimony outraged Indian activists and service providers who were in attendance. Goldie Denny, director of social services for the Quinault Nation and a representative of the National Congress of American Indians, testified that she was appalled by what she had just heard from the BIA's representative. She labeled it a "gross neglect of responsibility" that did not reflect "the thinking of people in Indian country, . . . the people who deal with Indian child welfare problems on a day-to-day basis." She relayed that at the NCAI's thirty-third annual convention in 1976, 130 tribes had unanimously passed a resolution in support of the basic concepts of S. 1214. "The BIA is supposed to represent the Indian view," Denny pointed out. "But when 130 Indian tribes say, 'This is what we want,' the BIA says, 'We don't want this for the Indians.'"[64] Indian witnesses were deeply angered that the BIA failed to support S. 1214 and their aspirations to take back control of their children.

Other federal representatives similarly opposed the bill. An HEW representative testified that her agency supported a general overhaul of the entire child welfare system rather than a separate bill regarding Indian child welfare.[65] She raised another point of opposition to ICWA: that it represented a policy of racial discrimination by requiring that Indian children be placed with Indian families.[66] Some individuals who wrote in against S. 1214 similarly portrayed it as a racist bill. One couple from Arizona contended, "This bill is an extremely misguided attempt to help Indian families. It is outrageously discriminatory! It takes away individual rights and freedoms. It appears to us that this bill is trying to confine Indians to the reservation with no concern for their well being, personal desires, or future welfare."[67]

Indian activists and advocates were at pains to educate many non-Indians that this was not an issue of race but of tribal sovereignty and survival. They were concerned that children grow up not to be "Indian," per se, but to be Standing Rock Sioux, Navajo (Diné), Zuni, or Winnebago (Ho-Chunk). These are not "races" but tribes with distinctive languages, histories, and cultures as well as some degree of sovereignty. Even Butler, the BIA representative who opposed S. 1214, explained that giving tribes greater jurisdiction over the disposition of their children was not an issue of race or ethnicity but amounted to giving "full recognition to the unique Federal relationship to Indian people."[68] Further, Senator Abourezk pointed out, "the civil rights laws would [not] apply in this instance because of the modified sovereignty concept that Indian tribes are in possession of at this time."[69]

Senator Abourezk evinced little support for the BIA or HEW position. After each agency representative testified against the bill, he mentioned that "the Indian witnesses have requested that all the [HEW and BIA] administration people remain to hear their testimony. I think it would be very valuable for you to hear them. Much better than me preaching to you about abuses of child welfare."[70] Here as elsewhere during the hearings, Abourezk proved a committed ally to Indians in their self-determination efforts.

Other testimony against ICWA at the 1977 hearings raised concerns related to the "best interests of the child." The CWLA's representative, Mary Jane Fales, director of the Adoption Resource Exchange of North America, claimed that her organization supported "the concepts behind the bill" but could not approve S. 1214 as currently written because "the Bill appears to encourage placement within the culture to the point of preference of temporary foster care or institutions rather than permanent placement outside of the Indian culture."[71] As they had in the past, the CWLA put great emphasis on permanency and emphasized the rescue of the individual Indian child over the preservation and strengthening of Indian families as a whole.

The most organized opposition to S. 1214 derived from representatives of the Mormon or LDS Church, who worried that the bill would threaten their Indian Student Placement Program if it were not amended. Harold C. Brown, commissioner of LDS social services and director of personal welfare services, came armed not only with a formal statement but with letters written by Indian parents and students who sang the praises of the ISPP. Church elder George Lee, a Navajo who had participated in the program, also testified to its benefits. The LDS argument against the bill centered on the claim that it would interfere with the free choice of Indian parents to place their children where they wished.[72]

The Navajo tribal representative disputed the LDS church position and took a critical view of the ISPP. Bobby George, acting director of the Navajo Office of Resource Security, testified that religious groups have "disrupted family relationships and separated children from their families." Because of past abuses, the Navajos now required court approval of children in non-Navajo families. "We would suggest . . . that in the vast majority of cases it is far more appropriate for . . . religious and non-sectarian institutions to expend their time, effort and money in improving the lives of Indian families within Indian nations rather than removing the children to strange lands and strange people."[73] The Navajo tribe questioned the whole premise of child removal, fostering, and adoption. If non-Indians truly cared about Indian children, they would strive to help Indian families and nations as a whole, not just remove their children.

Abourezk seemed respectful of the LDS position, questioning them only as to whether they carried out the program in accordance with the Interstate Compact on the Placement of Children (which required notification to state agencies when children crossed state lines) and asking them whether they could share information about the students in the program with tribal entities, rather than just states. When Brown declared that it was difficult to identify viable tribal governing institutions in many cases, an uproar erupted among Indian spectators, and Abourezk had to call for order in the legislative chamber. This was a maddening issue for Indian people; the NCAI had passed a resolution condemning the LDS program for failing to inform tribes properly about the children who were on placement. They wanted the LDS church to acknowledge tribal jurisdiction and authority over their children.[74]

Additional opposition to the bill derived from some adoptive families and their supporters who wrote letters to Congress. Almost all were non-Indian women from the state of Washington who used similar wording in their letters, suggesting that some individual or group had orchestrated a letter campaign. Their arguments against the act centered on one section of the bill, Section 204 in Title II, which gave the secretary of the interior authority to review all placements of Indian children in the prior sixteen years to determine if a child had been removed illegally and without cause. In such cases the government could move to have children returned to their natural parents or extended family. Although many writers mentioned that this would be damaging to children, most focused on how it would "be a great injustice to all adoptive families." One even asserted that it would be akin to "allowing a type of Hitler's Germany in America."[75]

Several writers expressed how frightening it would be to lose children through such heavy-handedness. Washington State social worker Mildred Wright asked, "Can you imagine what havoc that will play in the lives of the adopted children and their adoptive parents? Can you imagine the fear that will be struck into the hearts of all such families when they learn they may or will have to fight in court (at great expense while the other side has government paid lawyers) to keep adopted children whom they have loved, supported, and nurtured all these years?"[76] Interestingly, letter writers seemed to reserve all their empathy for adoptive families who might lose their children, without acknowledging the heartache, fear, and trauma that many Indian families had already experienced—in just this fashion—at the hands of government authorities. Additionally these letter writers opposed the bill because they contended it was "merely a way to add possible numbers to the Indian count" and that "the bill turns Indian children into "mere pawns in the hands of people interested in the *cause* rather than the *children*."[77]

This concern was not borne out by the testimony of many Indian tribes on S. 1214 at the 1977 congressional hearings. The Cheyenne River Sioux tribe of South Dakota submitted a statement that took issue with several clauses of the bill as written. "We disagree with the section [that] alcohol abuse or misconduct caused by alcohol abuse should not be utilized in child protection cases," they wrote. They and many other tribes also objected to clauses in the bill that allowed the return of children in long-term foster care to their natural families because of "possible trauma that would be experienced by the foster child."[78] Ramona Bennett, chair of the Puyallup Tribe, similarly worried that the bill's standards for removal might leave children for years in "semi dangerous, semi functioning family structures." She wanted more discretion left to tribal agencies.[79] Many tribes or Indian organizations opposed Section 204, including the National Tribal Chairmen's Association. Indian people were at pains to look out for the best interests of their children, balancing the desire for maintaining kinship and tribal ties with the interests of individual children.

As this testimony from Indian people makes clear, they did not blindly support ICWA, and they read its provisions carefully. Neither did all non-Indian people blindly oppose it; some adoptive families in fact took a strong stand in its favor. Don and Barbara Reeves, a white Quaker family from Nebraska who had adopted three Indian children, testified in favor of S. 1214 and told the Senate subcommittee that "state courts had judged that their [adopted children's] natural families could not care for them." The Reeveses laid the blame for this at the feet of federal authorities, stating, "It would seem likely . . . that the difficult straits of these three youngsters derived indirectly from national policies toward Indians." The Reeveses added: "Much of what have been termed 'causes' of Indian family instability are more correctly judged symptoms of the destruction of the Indians' value systems and tribal structures and of the often direct attacks on Indian family life as part of this process."[80]

The Reeveses' statement reflects a perspective that some liberal Americans adopted when they were confronted by the anger of Indian activists. Rather than holding tenaciously to their views, they challenged their own assumptions. Reeves explained, "Looking back, I think it is clear to many of us within the Religious Society of Friends that we assume some things particularly in the realm of values, in a kind of arrogant way; that we have insights and values which Indians ought to adopt. Our programs were based on these insights and values with not enough regard for traditional Indian values. Today, the character of some of our programs has changed. With it comes a certain degree of humility about the kinds of judgments that we have made in past times."[81] Thus many white Americans, including a majority of senators, became convinced by the arguments of the bill's supporters.

Activists had carefully cultivated support for the bill through the poignant testimony of Indian witnesses at the 1974 hearings coupled with the hard statistical evidence compiled by the AAIA at the request of the American Indian Policy Review Commission. The AAIA's state-by-state statistics made up the final sixty-six pages of the 1977 hearings report and provided irrefutable evidence of a dramatic disparity in placement rates for Indian and non-Indian children in nineteen states with large Indian populations.[82] Without the controversial Section 204 of Title II, the Senate passed S. 1214 on November 4, 1977. This version included Title IV, which addressed concerns with the ongoing use of boarding schools in certain Native communities. It provided for a placement prevention study to develop a plan for providing schools for Indian children within their communities.[83]

However, the bill still needed to be considered by the House of Representatives. On two separate occasions, on February 9 and March 9, 1978, the House held hearings before its Committee on Interior and Insular Affairs, chaired by Morris Udall, a representative from Arizona who was sympathetic to Indian self-determination. At this final set of hearings, urban Indian groups made known their concerns with a restrictive definition of Indian and Indian child that would mean ICWA would not apply to the thousands of Indian children who lived in urban areas. Suzanne Letendre, director of the Northeast Indian Family Structure Project of the Boston Indian Council pointed out:

> Those native Americans who are faced with adjusting to off-reservation living, who lack the support and assistance of their tribal courts and councils, who are alienated in urban settings and lost in a world unaccustomed to the Indian way of life and the Indian family structure, and who, in fact, make up a significant portion of the alarming national statistics on Indian family disruption, are ignored by this bill, left stranded, unassisted while they watch in bewilderment the termination of their parental rights and the placement of their children with people who are total strangers to them.[84]

She and many other urban Indian service providers called for using a less restrictive definition of Indian that would include urban Indians. Similarly Alaska Natives lobbied for a definition that would include their children.

Opponents of the bill, including the BIA, the Department of Justice, HEW, and the CWLA, took a new tack. They argued that the bill would violate the privacy rights of Indian parents living off the reservation, especially unwed Indian mothers. Mary Jane Fales, director of ARENA, asked rhetorically, "If [Indian people] chose not to remain on the reservation, shouldn't they have some right to privacy of what happens to their lives off the reservation?" "By putting control of Indian child welfare matters into tribal hands," Fales and her colleague Dorothy Buzawa argued, "it does not respect the confidentiality and autonomy of the birth parents to determine the future of their child. Non-Indian birth parents thus have more rights and privacy than Indian parents."[85] They suggested that Indian families could not wait to leave the reservations and would not want their children placed with families who still lived there.

There were undoubtedly some urban Indians who felt this way, but many others maintained vital relations with their reservation communities or homelands, as illustrated by the testimony of Indian social service providers in urban areas who worked with Indian families on a daily basis. Jacquelyne Arrowsmith from the Urban Indian Child Resource Center in Oakland, California, testified: "Eighty percent of the Indians are mobile and often return to their homeland. With this fact in mind, the center provides a linkage between urban and reservation living." Arrowsmith's contention has been confirmed by recent scholarly work, such as Renya Ramirez's *Native Hubs*.[86] Further, many Indian social service providers sought to respect the rights of unwed Indian mothers. Faye La Pointe, for example, coordinator of social service for child welfare for the Puyallup Tribe, declared that in most cases a young Indian mother would want her child to be placed with Indian parents if they "were known to be reliable, stable, sober adults."[87]

Other Indian activists challenged ICWA opponents on the issue of personal choice. Representatives from the LDS Church argued that ICWA might interfere with the choice of Indian parents to send their children to Mormon homes for nine months of the year.[88] Many Indian witnesses, however, questioned how much choice Indian people actually had regarding participation in the Mormon program when there were no day schools in their own communities. La Pointe countered, "Every Indian person should, indeed, have the right to choose what is best for their child. A choice that is uninhibited by such conditions as poverty, illiteracy, physical, emotional, or mental handicaps. When these conditions become rare rather than commonplace in Indian country, we will believe that Indian people truly have the right of free choice."[89]

As these interchanges show, a fundamental disagreement surfaced that pitted individual rights versus group rights. Sister Mary Clare of the National Conference of Catholic Charities represented the side of individual rights. She asserted that Indian opposition to the relinquishment of Indian newborns was unfounded because "in the case of infants, . . . no cultural purpose is served [in keeping the child with the tribe] since the child is not removed from a culture he has grown up with."[90] Sister Mary Clare and other opponents of ICWA just could not see what all the fuss was about. Non-Indians were embedded within a liberal culture that prized individual rights and had long been exposed to "plight" narratives that found little of worth to preserve in Indian cultures. They believed that individual Indians longed to flee reservations and live like middle-class Americans.

Indian witnesses tried to educate them about the importance of tribal heritage, sovereignty, and a different conception of group rights. Calvin Isaac, chair of the Mississippi Band of Choctaws and representative of the National Tribal Chairmen's Association, explained: "Culturally, the chances of Indian survival are significantly reduced if our children, the only real means for the transmission of the tribal heritage, are to be raised in non-Indian homes and denied exposure to the ways of their People. Furthermore, these practices seriously undercut the tribes' ability to continue as self-governing communities. Probably in no area is it more important that tribal sovereignty be respected than in an area as socially and culturally determinative as family relationships."[91] Advocates for ICWA argued that ongoing removal of Indian children undermined the group rights and sovereignty of Indian people.

After the 1978 hearings Udall made a final set of revisions to the legislation and introduced his subcommittee's version as HR 12533 on May 3, 1978. The bill then had to make its way through a circuitous legislative path. It finally passed the House on October 14, 1978, and the Senate agreed to their version of the bill on that same night in the very last minutes of the 95th Congress. Although HEW and the Departments of Justice and the Interior all opposed the bill, President Jimmy Carter signed it into law on November 8, 1978. AAIA staffer Steven Unger surmises that Carter signed it because Udall strategically linked the bill with a civil service reform bill and other legislation that Carter favored.[92] A long battle spanning at least ten years came to fruition through a well-designed campaign that linked grassroots tribal groups, Indian community organizers and social service providers, and national advocacy organizations, most prominently the AAIA.

ICWA embodied Indian self-determination through recognizing the jurisdiction and sovereignty of Indian tribes. Its primary provision affirmed tribes' rights to take unprecedented sovereignty over most child welfare matters involving Indian children, which the act defined capaciously as either a tribal member or a minor eligible for membership in a tribe. This rendering of the law meant that tribal courts held jurisdiction over not only children on tribal lands but also children who lived off the reservation. ICWA granted the right of the Indian custodian or tribe to intervene in the state court proceedings and to request transfer of child welfare proceedings to the child's tribal court under certain conditions.

ICWA sought to provide strong legal protections to Indian families to prevent the abuses that had led to the Indian child welfare crisis. It attempted to remedy violations of due process by stipulating that Indian custodians of children who were threatened with removal must be given written notice through registered mail at least ten days prior to a court hearing. It also guaranteed Indian caretakers the right to court-appointed counsel. In an effort to stop the unwarranted removal of Indian children on vague grounds, the act required the highest level of proof of neglect or abuse. Parental rights could not be terminated without a "determination, supported by evidence *beyond a reasonable doubt*, including testimony by expert witnesses, that the continued custody of the child by the parent or Indian custodian is likely to result in serious emotional or physical damage to the child." To honor Indian extended family arrangements and the importance of sustaining tribes, the act created a hierarchy of placement preference for Indian children who were removed from a parent or custodian. Ideally, a child would be placed first with a member of the extended family, second with other members of the child's tribe, or third with another Indian family. Only if all three of these options were unavailable were courts to place a child with a non-Indian family.[93]

ICWA sought, too, to strengthen rather than tear asunder Indian families. It contained a number of provisions that were aimed at providing services to Indian families—through Indian tribes and organizations—that would prevent Indian children from being removed. One provision required that before a child could be removed, preventative services had to have been extended to Indian families. Title II of the act provided for grants for Indian programs to engage in such matters as licensing of Indian foster and adoptive homes, counseling and treatment facilities for Indian families, in-home family assistance, and employment and training of professionals in child welfare, Indian tribal court judges, and staff. ICWA recognized, too, that the lack of local day schools for Indian children in some remote locations had led to children's removal and institutionalization at distant boarding schools, and it authorized the secretary of the interior to work with the Department of Health and Human Services to "report on the feasibility of providing Indian children with schools located near their homes." Soon after the act passed, Congress appropriated $5.5 million to which tribes could apply to "operate their own family development centers" in order to "strengthen Indian family life and prevent the unwarranted removal of Indian children from their families." This raised hopes, as Steven Unger put it, of "a blossoming of tribally operated and controlled programs in the area of child and family services."[94]

An optimistic mood swept through Indian country among many grassroots Indian activists after ICWA passed. The social service providers who had been so instrumental in its passage eagerly worked to make its potential a reality. The Association of American Indian and Alaska Native Social Workers held their second annual conference in September 1979 in Albuquerque in conjunction with the national conference of the NCAI and made its focus the newly minted ICWA.[95] Two months later, on the Warm Springs Reservation in Oregon, the AACP sponsored a three-day training seminar in conjunction with the National American Indian Court Judges Association. One hundred and fifty tribal social service and court workers attended the event, and the seminar produced a training manual in 1980.

Rather than focusing on the problems in Indian communities, the seminar wanted to "highlight the inherent survival strengths of American Indian and Alaska Native families in the belief that in their traditions, knowledge and cultures lie the true keys to survival." The group regarded ICWA and other laws as "tools for tribes to use to reinforce and renew the powers of their member families upon whom tribal community depends."[96] In his keynote address at the Warm Springs conference, Sam Deloria, who had been involved with the AAIA's earliest strategizing efforts, affirmed the important caring and reproductive work carried out by these Indian community organizers. "Indian tribes are engaged in some of the most delicate and complicated creative work that is being done in this world right now," he told the crowd.[97]

Warm Springs seminar participants contended that traditional Indian practices were in synchrony with and perhaps even ahead of the most cutting-edge theories in the child and family welfare field. Attendees asserted that, contrary to practices that had separated the interests of Indian children from their families, "helping the parents and strengthening the family is now generally recognized as being the key to helping children grow and develop in the best possible way." Taking such a holistic approach, the seminar asserted, "traditional Indian healing practices, as well as current child psychiatric principles, require that we pay attention to and deal with all aspects of the child, his or her family and all aspects of the setting within which the family lives." They asserted that it was important that removed children maintain a relationship with their non-custodial parents and that the new trend of "'open adoption' . . . is an ancient Indian practice."[98] The Warm Springs training manual thus implied that Indian people had been right all along and western social work practice was just catching up with them.

The Warm Springs conference exuded hope that the Indian child welfare crisis could be resolved through Indian self-determination. The group recognized that Indian communities had been plagued by a "cycle of family disorganization." "But the cycle can be broken," they insisted. "Strengthening the family through positive intervention *at any point in the cycle* can have far-reaching effects in preventing other problems from developing later." The Warm Springs training manual listed the resources available to Indian social service providers in their work of strengthening Indian families. Tellingly, it emphasized Indian solutions, not federal laws and programs. Its resource list included a long section on the extended family as the "bottom-line resource of any tribal community, urban or reservation" and mentioned "rituals and ceremonies" as a tribal resource, an "answer to the troubles of . . . young people." Urban Indian centers also served as a resource. Only after all these did the manual mention ICWA, the Indian Self-Determination and Education Act, and the Adoption Assistance and Child Welfare Act of 1980.[99] Clearly these Indian activists prioritized a reclamation of Indian ways as the primary means of breaking the cycle of family disorganization and saw federal legislation as a backup support. This approach enabled *every* Indian person to participate in the solution, not just those who had training in social work or the law. It emphasized the need for Indian people to seize control of their own destinies, not to depend on federal legislation, important as it was, to protect their rights.

While the Warm Springs meeting was full of hope, there were also signs that the problems surrounding Indian child welfare had not vanished overnight. Some social service providers noted that "tribes are encountering state agencies which tell them, 'Oh well, now that the Indian Child Welfare Act gives you jurisdiction over your kids, they are ineligible for state services and funds.'" The manual insisted, "*This is not true.* The 1974 Department of Health, Education and Welfare Program Instruction to all state agencies is still valid; it says, in short, that if these agencies do not provide the same services on-reservation as off, their funds will be cut back proportionately."[100]

Warm Springs meeting participants were also well aware that the enactment of ICWA and the recovery of the care of Indian children by Indian people would be a long struggle. A century of assimilation policies that had undermined and damaged Indian families and left lasting legacies could not be reversed immediately through the passage of a bill in Congress. Indian people themselves had to create their own resources and tools to make ICWA's promise real. As Indian women such as Maxine Robbins and Evelyn Blanchard sought to do just this, other Indigenous people north of the American border and across the Pacific carried out their own struggles to understand and reverse Indigenous child removal. ICWA became a tool for them as well.

# PART THREE

# The Indian Child Welfare Crisis in a Global Context

I traveled to Saskatoon and Winnipeg to spend several weeks in the Saskatchewan Archives Board and the Archives of Manitoba in the fall of 2012. On my last day in Saskatoon I found an intriguing newspaper article that referred to a case in which authorities removed three Métis children from the Doucette family in Prince Albert. I longed to know more, so in my last few hours in the archives, I combed through the archival finding guide for provincial social service agencies and ministers of the mid-1970s. There I identified numerous files related to the Doucette case.

But these files were restricted. I had to obtain permission from the originator of the files, a retired social services minister named Herman Rolfes, who still lives in Saskatoon. I wrote to him shortly after I returned home, but I didn't expect to hear back from him. I thought I would try anyway. A good detective follows every lead. Soon Mr. Rolfes emailed me, however, and told me that I could view the records. But privacy laws in Canada require that an archivist carefully go through each file to make sure no confidential information is included, so I still could not access them. I applied for permission to the archives, imagining that I probably would not be able to view the records after all. I was pleasantly surprised when an email showed up in my inbox in early 2013 to tell me that the Saskatchewan Archives Board had approved a batch of records for me to view. I eagerly paid for the copies, and a few weeks later a thick package arrived. I only had time to skim the documents before leaving the next day for a research trip to New Zealand and Australia for a month. But I was excited, and appalled, by what I saw.

When I returned from the southern hemisphere and read the documents more thoroughly, I was overwhelmed by the Doucettes' story. The files ended abruptly in 1977, and I wondered what happened to the Doucette family after the bureaucracy filed their case away. I contacted Indigenous friends in Saskatchewan, asking them if they knew any members of the Doucette family. Allyson Stevenson, at the time a PhD student at the University of Saskatchewan, told me she had interviewed Robert Doucette, one of the family's older foster children, and now the president of the Métis Nation of Saskatchewan. She gave me his contact information. I called him at his office, but he was sick that day. He didn't return my phone call. I emailed him with a request to interview him, but he didn't reply. I didn't know if I should persist. Perhaps he was just busy and I should keep trying. On the other hand, many Indigenous people don't want a non-Indigenous scholar snooping around into their past or writing about them. Why should they trust me with their stories? So many anthropologists and historians have misrepresented them. Too often scholars have compounded rather than exposed the injustices suffered by Indigenous people. Still, I longed to know what happened to the Doucettes.

I returned to Saskatoon in June 2013 for the Native American and Indigenous Studies Association Conference. I decided I would make one last effort to meet Robert Doucette. His secretary set up an interview for me. On the second morning of the conference I was to meet him at 9:00 at the restaurant in the Parkside Hotel, not far from where I was staying. It was a rainy morning, but between downpours I walked to the hotel and sat in the lobby. It reached 9:15 and he still hadn't shown up. Having gotten this close, I decided to email his secretary. She eventually tracked him down, and he showed up at about 10:00. He apologized for keeping me waiting, but I truly didn't mind. I was grateful to have the opportunity to meet him finally.

Given what I knew about his family and the situation of Indigenous people in Canada, I thought Robert Doucette would be bitter and angry. Instead he was warm and affable. He greeted me and the waitresses in the restaurant as "sister." Over many cups of coffee and tea, I learned about his promising hockey career. We discovered, too, that as children, we had both spent inordinate amounts of time in public libraries. When the conversation turned to his family's harrowing experience, he told me how much his mother hated Herman Rolfes, the Social Services minister to whom I had had to write for permission to access his records. Robert also recounted how he came to be in foster care and about reconnecting with his birth mother and the pain of never getting to know his grandfather. We agreed that he should write a book about his fascinating life.

Near the end of our interview, I asked Robert if he thought it was appropriate for me to write about his family's experience in this book. He said emphatically that he wanted me to write about it. I worried out loud, though, about whether his parents would approve. He pulled out his phone and I assumed he had to take a call. I was startled when he said, "Hi, Mom." He explained our conversation and then handed the phone to me. I knew the traumas Robert's mother, Rita Doucette, had endured, and I was nervous about talking to her. I worried that my inquiries would reignite painful memories. It seems, though, that events from almost forty years ago had never faded from her memory. She recalled all that I had read about in the files from the late 1970s as if it had happened a week ago. And she, too, told me that she wanted me to write about her family's case.

A few days later I was driving with my husband and youngest son back to Nebraska from Saskatoon. We drove for most of the day through the prairies of Saskatchewan before we reached the town of North Portal, just over the border from North Dakota, where authorities placed three of the Doucette children in another family for half of their childhood. Their story and this place means nothing to most of the travelers who slip across this remote international border, but I felt weighted down by the knowledge of their family's broken history.

# CHAPTER 6

# The Indigenous Child Welfare Crisis in Canada

Authorities with the Saskatchewan Department of Social Services decided in 1975 that it was time for three Métis foster children from Prince Albert to be permanently adopted. They advertised the nine-, ten-, and eleven-year-old children and found an interested white family, the Todds from Ann Arbor, Michigan. Officials arranged for the Todds to come to Saskatchewan in June 1975 to meet and become acquainted with the children. Yet the three Métis siblings already had a home. They had lived for eight to nine years with their foster parents, Marcien and Rita Doucette, the Doucettes' three biological children, and three older foster children. According to the Doucettes, when the Todds arrived in Prince Albert, the children were "rushed away by strangers without much p[r]eparations." At first a social worker told the children "they didn't have to go" with the Todds if they didn't want to, yet after Mrs. Doucette allegedly "refused to cooperate and was abusive toward the [social] worker," authorities decided that under no circumstances would the children be returned to the only family they had ever known. When the social worker informed the children they now must go with the Todds, "each put their jacket over their face and had a little cry."[1]

Authorities proceeded with the adoption and sent the children to live with the Todds in Michigan. According to the Doucettes, the two older children wrote to their former foster parents frequently to convey how much they wished to return to their home.[2] The loss of their children devastated the Doucettes, and they sought every means possible to regain custody of the children while "keep[ing] the children's rooms as they were before they left." The Métis community in Prince Albert responded forcefully. They organized a caravan to travel to Michigan and confront the adoptive family and authorities. Former Prime Minister John Diefenbacker, a Saskatchewan resident, condemned the removal of the children as a "wrong, unjust, cruel, and even dastardly act." He added, "'This is scandalous from beginning to end," and "whoever took these children away after eight years with their foster parents has committed a grave injustice."[3]

The Todds and the children had been in Ann Arbor just four days when the telephone began to ring and news reporters showed up at their doorstep. The family "packed up and ran," spending several nights in motels until they reached a remote cabin. Here, allegedly, "telling Mr. and Mrs. Todd they had a surprise for them, the youngsters prepared the table and set special places for their new parents." Then, according to Mrs. Todd, "'the kids decided to tell us they'd decided to be part of our family.'" Once they returned home to Ann Arbor, however, the Todds "decided the adoption would not work, not then anyway." After having the children just ten weeks, the Todds "requested the children be removed from the[ir] home," allegedly "due to adjustment problems." According to the Todds, the adoption would have been successful if they had been left alone instead of harassed by news media.[4]

Authorities brought the children back to Saskatchewan in September 1975, but they still refused to return the children to the Doucettes, placing them instead with a foster family in the community of North Portal near the North Dakota border. Officials continued to search for an adoptive placement for them far away in eastern Canada.[5] They stipulated that the Doucettes should have no contact with the three children. The Doucettes attempted, however, to see their children and to get them back. "We will never give up if we have to follow them to the end of the world," they wrote to the minister of social services. "They will always be in our hearts and on our minds and know they will never forget us and will be back as soon as they get a chance no matter where they are put."[6]

This dramatic case brought great pain to the foster parents, the foster children, and the would-be adoptive family. It reveals that the Indian child welfare crisis of the United States was not just a national occurrence but part of an international and transnational phenomenon. Indigenous children in Canada, like their counterparts in the United States, were vulnerable to removal and placement in non-Indigenous families, and a parallel Indigenous child welfare crisis arose in Canada. As Indigenous women and some men in Canada organized to challenge the loss of their children, they discovered that their struggle was intertwined with that of American Indian people in the United States. Authorities in Canada and the United States had colluded in promoting transnational adoptions of Indigenous children. As the campaign for the Indian Child Welfare Act intensified in the United States, the Adoption Resource Exchange of North America responded by increasing its placement of Canadian Indigenous children in the United States. This tactic backfired, however, as the export of Indigenous children only outraged Canadian Indigenous people and fueled their activism. When American Indians and their allies in the U.S. achieved the passage of ICWA, it inspired Canadian activists. They invited American organizers to attend their conferences and redoubled their efforts to achieve greater control over Indigenous child welfare.

The Canadian government, like that of the United States, wrestled with how to deal with its Indigenous population. Canada's administration of Indian affairs resembled that of the United States in that the federal government, not its provincial administrations, held responsibility for and jurisdiction over the Indigenous people within its borders. Yet Canada's Indian Act, first passed in 1876 and amended many times, conceptualized its Indigenous people in quite different ways than the United States. It created four categories: status or treaty Indians, non-status or non-treaty Indians, Métis, and Eskimo (or Inuit) people. In a circular way, the act defined status Indians as "those persons registered or entitled to be registered as an Indian under the terms of the Indian Act." According to the act, non-status Indians possessed Indian ancestry but had "lost or exchanged their right to be registered under the Indian Act." By voluntarily giving up their status, non-status Indians gained benefits such as the right to vote and consume alcohol. Some registered Indians involuntarily lost their status; Indian women who married non-Indian men automatically did so, as did their children. This facet of the Indian Act particularly disadvantaged women of Indian ancestry and may have exacerbated the Indigenous child welfare crisis in Canada. The Indian Act defined Métis as persons of mixed Indian and European ancestry. Most were the descendants of Indian women and early French and Scottish fur trappers. The fourth category, the Inuit, who lived in the extreme northern sections of Canada, fell under the responsibility of the federal government but were not covered by the Indian Act.[7] I refer to all these categories as Indigenous people.

Canada prided itself on dealing with its Indigenous people fairly, in contrast to its neighbor to the south, but its policies often paralleled American policy initiatives. Canada modeled its residential schools for Indigenous children on federal Indian boarding schools in the United States. Powerful religious groups, including the Catholic and Anglican churches, ran most of these schools by the late nineteenth century. As in the United States, authorities forcibly removed Indigenous children, and they also justified their policies in similar ways: as for the good of the children and as the principal means to assimilate Indigenous people.[8]

Canada sought to frame a new policy toward its Indigenous peoples after World War II. It convened from 1946 to 1948 a special joint committee of the Senate and House of Commons to examine and amend the Indian Act. The joint committee took testimony from a wide variety of organizations and agencies concerned with the administration of Indian affairs, including some newly organized Native groups. The federal government updated the Indian Act as a result in 1951. Even as it removed some of the act's coercive methods, however, it maintained its assimilative goals. Administrators increasingly defined their new policy as integration rather than assimilation. Such a change of terms held little meaning to Indian groups, who still felt the strong arm of paternalism and forced cultural change.[9]

Some Canadian policies mirrored those of the United States in this era. Clearly policymakers consulted one another across the border. The Canadian superintendent of welfare for the Indian Affairs Branch wrote to the BIA chief of welfare in the United States after reading the bureau's 1953 annual report. He admired the BIA's placement and relocation service and the "growing number of states" taking on full responsibility for Indian welfare. He asked the BIA's chief of welfare about "methods of arriving at financial terms with the States" and the length of time the BIA "retains financial responsibility" for relocated Indians. Such information would be helpful to Canadian administrators as they discussed the establishment of relocation committees in Canada.[10] These two governments communicated frequently with one another about how best to manage their Indigenous populations in the decades following World War II.

Canada's revamped policy owed much to the color-blind liberal ideology that officials and social critics increasingly espoused, as in the United States, in the post–World War II era. The newly formed Ontario Select Committee on Civil Liberties in 1953 and 1954 likened the separate status of Indians to apartheid and advocated the legalization of alcohol sales, full voting rights, and education for Indigenous Canadians. This extension of equal rights to Indians might seem laudable, but many Indian bands and organizations resented the fact that the committee made no effort to consult Indigenous people. And the committee's support for integration saw no future for distinctive Indian cultures and communities. "Indians are realizing that their language must soon be relegated to the status of a hobby if their people are to meld with the rest of the population," the report intoned. "Several generations will be born before the Indian takes his place alongside his Ontario neighbour with full equality—neither maintaining his present exceptional benefits, nor his ... disadvantages."[11] Officials regarded any attempts by Indians to sustain their cultures and their rights to the land as quaint but impossible notions.

This liberal viewpoint did not just underwrite Canadian policy toward Indigenous people; it also galvanized Canadians at the grassroots level in the 1950s and 1960s. Increased postwar urban migration brought Indigenous people to the attention of non-Indigenous city dwellers. Indigenous women made up a disproportionate number of urban migrants due to the Indian Act's disenfranchisement of status Indian women and their children if the women married non-status or non-Indian people.[12] White citizens' groups grew particularly concerned with young women migrants to the city. In Winnipeg, Manitoba, the white women of the Community Welfare Council formed a Housing for Girls of Indian Descent Committee in 1953 to determine the need for housing for Indian girls. The following year they sought to establish a hostel and training program for Indian girls to provide help with "making a living in the city and also assistance in adjusting to urban life."[13]

The work of this group led to increased overall involvement of Winnipeg's Community Welfare Council in Indian and Métis affairs. The women's committee recommended that a two-to-three-day conference be held in 1954 to discuss all aspects of the Indian and Métis "problem." The council established a standing committee on Indian and Métis people, which met for decades and started holding annual conferences in 1955.[14] From its inception until sometime in the early to mid-1960s, non-Indigenous people led this committee. It included little Indigenous participation except during the annual conference. At the suggestion of an unnamed Indian person at the annual conference in 1958, the committee established a board for a proposed Indian-Métis Friendship Centre, a referral service for Indigenous newcomers to Winnipeg, which became a prototype for other such efforts in cities across Canada. When the center opened in 1960, its board had just one Indigenous representative.[15] Liberalism in the late twentieth century continued the "friends of the Indian" tradition from the nineteenth century, in which benevolent non-Indigenous citizens provided guidance to benighted Indigenous peoples.[16]

Canadians who cared about Indigenous people avidly followed American developments. The Winnipeg Friendship Centre board concluded that "some study of the U.S. Bureau of Indian Affairs Relocation Programs might suggest possible lines of action."[17] They sent one of their members to the United States for eight weeks to visit "three of the most successful community development programs": in Chicago; Omaha, Nebraska; and Gallup, New Mexico.[18] Liberal grassroots activity on behalf of Indigenous peoples was thus a transnational endeavor.

Some Canadians established national groups to press for the liberal vision of integration for Canada's Indigenous people. The Indian and Eskimo Association (IEA) incorporated in 1960 and within a decade had a membership of more than eighty organizations and one thousand individual members, one third of them Indians or Inuit. The association marshaled the common litany of statistics showing the poor quality of life for Indigenous people and expressed concern that "the desperate plight of our native citizens is a national disgrace that is damaging Canada's image the world over." They defined their goals as "breaking the cycle of poverty among native peoples," "shifting the emphasis from relief to employment, restoring dignity and self-respect," and "helping native people who leave the reserve to adjust to modern urban life." The IEA's honorary president declared in the mid-1960s: "Our faith is rooted in the belief that Canada will be stronger, her reputation brighter, the prosperity of her industry and commerce greater, if the nearly half a million citizens of Indian and Eskimo background are helped to find their way into the national community, to stand on their own legs economically and politically, and to adjust to the white man's civilization on terms they can understand and accept."[19] The IEA was ostensibly an advocacy organization for Canada's Indigenous peoples, but its rhetoric betrays a more pressing concern with Canada's national development and its international image.

This new climate of liberalism compelled Canadian administrations in the mid-1960s to study the "plight" of Canada's Native peoples and to propose new solutions, supposedly to treat them more justly. Social scientists played a particularly prominent role in this endeavor, as they did in the United States. Scholar Hugh Shewell explains, "In many respects the social scientists were the explorers and missionaries of the mid-twentieth century, the new interpreters of the 'other' to the European mind." Through the influence of social sciences, Shewell contends, government "reinvent[ed] paternalism based on the 'benevolence' of secular understanding, knowledge, and the tools of social engineering." A 1966 report titled *Survey of the Contemporary Indians of Canada: A Report on Economic, Political, Educational Needs and Policies*, by anthropologist Harry Hawthorn and other social scientists, called for "bringing Aboriginal peoples into full rather than incomplete fellowship with other Canadians" and ending discriminatory treatment toward Indians. Hawthorn and his associates regarded the extension of provincial child welfare services to reserves as a key step in promoting equal rights for Indians.[20]

Federal authorities in Canada announced a new policy after the election in 1968 of the new liberal government of Pierre Trudeau: the "Statement of the Government of Canada on Indian Policy, 1969," which came to be known as the White Paper. The historian J. R. Miller writes that the White Paper "argued that Canada's Indians were disadvantaged because they enjoyed a unique legal status," not because "Indians lacked control of their own affairs or because they had been systematically dispossessed of their lands." The government now sought to terminate the unique status of Indian people, to repeal the Indian Act, and to dissolve the Indian affairs bureaucracy. It would transfer responsibility for delivering services to the provinces. This government effort closely paralleled the American policy of termination, which Congress had championed almost fifteen years before and which had led to disastrous consequences and Indigenous resistance.[21]

Indigenous people in Canada fiercely opposed the White Paper, but its underlying sentiment received broad support among Canadian settler citizens. Winnipeg newspaper columnist Shaun Herron declared, "We must make enormous efforts *to place the Indians in society as people, not as Indians.* They must have the same rights, the same opportunities, the same responsibilities and the same rewards as others. The fact that they were here when we came no longer has relevance."[22] Just as in the United States, Canadian Native people had become the "subject of 'equality talk,'" as Veronica Strong-Boag puts it, and a color-blind racial ideology animated many liberal programs directed at Indigenous people.[23]

Officials insisted that Indigenous people in Canada should have access to the same government programs as other Canadians, and they pronounced that provincial governments rather than the Department of Indian Affairs (DIA) should take responsibility for Indigenous children. This mandate led to a dramatic increase in the numbers of Indigenous children within the provincial child welfare systems. In Saskatchewan, admissions of Indian and Métis children rose from 366 in 1966–67 to 534 in 1967–68, an increase of 46 percent. Although the Indian and Métis people of Saskatchewan constituted only 7.5 percent of the population, by 1968–69 Indigenous children accounted for 42 percent of children in care, or 1,443 of the total of 3,444.[24] Philip Hepworth estimated the number of native children in care "as a proportion of all children in care" by 1976–77 at 9 percent in Ontario, 39 percent in British Columbia, 40 percent in Alberta, 50 percent in Saskatchewan, and 60 percent in Manitoba.[25] By emulating the American termination policy and its transfer of Indigenous child welfare to the provinces, Canada soon had Indigenous children grossly overrepresented within the provincial child welfare systems. Canada had developed a bona fide Indigenous child welfare crisis of its own.

To respond to the growing numbers of Indigenous children in care, Saskatchewan's Department of Social Services created the Adopt Indian Métis (AIM) program in 1967, an approach akin to the Indian Adoption Project in the United States. Authorities invoked the same color-blind liberalism promoted by the IAP. As one adoption proponent put it, "The 32.3 per cent of children in care who are of Métis or Indian extraction have proven they are no different from the other 67.7 per cent, except for the colour of their skin. All children have one common denominator, they need secure homes. These children are being denied that basic human right."[26] Funded jointly by the federal and provincial government, AIM sought to increase interest among white middle-class families in the adoption of the increased numbers of Indian or Métis children in provincial care.

Some Department of Social Services personnel contemplated an alternative and more preventative and holistic approach to Indigenous child welfare. One official wrote, "There is always the need to get to the root of the problems that exist in Indian, Métis and other families to avoid the need to take children into care on a permanent basis. In our discussion [of AIM] we considered briefly whether at some point there might be some merit in setting up a demonstration project of a preventive character focussed on strengthening the home life for Indian and Métis children before they are separated from their parents."[27] This was the only mention in the files of an alternative to fostering and adoption; authorities never followed up on this proposed demonstration project. Instead they turned to a timeworn child removal approach.

AIM, similar to the IAP, presented itself as offering unmarried Indian mothers a service. A reporter noted that now "unwed mothers will no longer have to go through upsetting court proceedings to relinquish rights to their children." Like the voluntary waiver form in the United States, this measure undermined Indigenous legal rights and exposed Native people to differential legal treatment.[28]

AIM pursued an aggressive advertising campaign to recruit white adoptive families, even hiring an advertising firm to develop TV and radio spots as well as newspaper ads.[29] "Successful advertising was vital to the AIM project," the Department of Social Services reported in 1970, adding:

The publicity given the project was at all times of high quality and it received a gratifying response from the better-income, better-educated sectors of the urban population. It was dignified and in good taste—as befits a governmental institution which is sponsoring a project of some delicacy. Advertisements were never stodgy but attained interest through clear, original language useage and through association with contemporary symbols that reflected favourably on the project. A low pressure approach was taken at all times, and sentimentality was avoided because the object was to stir the genuine interest of nor-

Fig. 11. Adopt Indian Métis display, Saskatchewan, ca. 1968. From Saskatchewan Archives Board, Regina, Department of Social Services, R-1721, folder #5.9 Publicity, Display, 1968–1977, used by permission.

mal, well-motivated people and to avoid any suggestions conducive to hysteria or pathos.

AIM also developed a slide show featuring three families who had adopted Indian and Métis children to show to community groups. AIM presented the show to approximately three thousand people in its first year. Television stations also ran the slide series, and one particularly enthusiastic station featured an individual child each week during its nightly newscast.[30]

Canadian promoters of the adoption of Indian children portrayed the practice as a means of racial reconciliation. One editorial said: "It is really hard to assess just who stands to gain the most from adoptions under the AIM system. The child gains the love and security of a family of his own. The family in turn gains the opportunity of immeasurably enriching the lives of its members and widening their understanding and scope. The future for children from such families is bright in its potential for mutual understanding and improved human relationships."[31] The adoption of Indigenous children would thus alchemize a post-racial world where conflict between Indigenous people and settler citizens would dissolve. Coincidentally, too, Indigenous people would cease to exist as distinct entities, thus fulfilling the settler logic of elimination.

AIM characterized adoptive families as builders of a new racially reconciled nation, but they portrayed Indigenous children and families in a manner quite similar to the IAP. AIM ads often conjured up the figure of the ubiquitous "forgotten child." Welfare minister Cy MacDonald proclaimed in 1967 that "wards of Indian heritage seem destined to get into the limbo of forgotten children without parents and without a home and family to which they belong."[32] Under a photograph of an Indian or Métis infant in a 1967 ad, the text reads as if written by the child: "I want to find a *real* home. On the outside I'm different because I'm part Indian but inside I'm just like you. I'd like to belong to someone and to be loved and wanted. It would be wonderful to have a Mummy and a Daddy."[33] This ad activates a number of common tropes. The viewer learns that beneath appearances, racial differences do not really matter—a truism of color-blind liberalism—and that some Indian children do not live in "real" homes or have a mummy and a daddy and are not truly loved and wanted.

AIM administrators publicized the program as a benevolent effort to provide care for the province's neediest children, but behind the scenes they indulged in the same kind of cost-benefit analysis that supporters of IAP did in the United States. One AIM report contended: "The short and long-term economic benefits of permanent adoption to a society are obvious. As a result of sound adoption placements [from 1967 to 1969] . . . 110 children are in a better position to become productive, contributing members of society. Moreover, foster care presently costs about $1000 per child year, and care for 110 children during the 20 years of dependency at current rates would cost some $2,200,000." Additionally, the report noted, because foster children usually had lots of problems, "giving a child a better chance to find a good home usually amounts to a sound investment that pays real dividends in the future."[34] Benevolent rhetoric regarding the adoption of Indigenous children provided a dominant melody while bureaucratic calculations provided an underlying bass line in AIM pronouncements.

THE NORTH BATTLEFORD REGIONAL OFFICE
OF THE
DEPARTMENT OF WELFARE

~PRESENTS~

A. I. M.

AND A

# PANEL DISCUSSION:

"ADOPTING CHILDREN
of
MIXED RACIAL ORIGIN"

A SLIDE PRESENTATION WILL BE INCLUDED

DATE: NOVEMBER 13
TIME: 8³⁰ p.m.
PLACE: LEGION HALL, N. BATTLEFORD
—THE GENERAL PUBLIC IS INVITED TO ATTEND—

Fig. 12. Flyer for Adopt Indian Métis panel discussion, Saskatchewan, ca. 1970. From Saskatchewan Archives Board, Regina, Department of Social Services, R-1721, File Folder #5.72, used by permission.

AIM proved a success by department standards in its first five years. Before its advent, only one in ten adopted state wards was of Indigenous ancestry (about 35 children per year); by its third year of operation, Indigenous adopted children numbered one in four (or 120). Between 1967 and 1972, AIM offices in Regina and Saskatoon placed more than 300 Indigenous children for adoption. Also like the IAP, "AIM appeared to have a stimulating effect on the number of adoption placements for Indian and Métis children outside the AIM area." In this five-year period other regional offices placed more than 300 other Indigenous children for adoption.[35]

Saskatchewan's AIM was the most developed of provincial efforts to promote the adoption of Indigenous children, but other provinces engaged in similar techniques and had comparable success. Ontario had run a newspaper column since 1964 called "Today's Child." Helen Allen penned the column, which appeared in 23 newspapers daily and in 155 weeklies. Allen estimated that the column had resulted in the adoption of eight thousand children. She used pseudonyms for younger children and never mentioned a child's ancestry, although many columns featured Indigenous children. By the 1970s Ontario was also running Family Finder television spots.[36]

Provincial authorities regularly worked in cooperation with American authorities in order to find non-Indigenous adoptive homes for Indigenous children. Manitoba partnered with Lutheran Social Services and Midwest Adoption Facilitating Exchange in the United States. The province placed 3,469 children in other provinces and 1,149 in the United States between 1960 and 1980; more than 90 percent of these children were Indigenous.[37] British Columbia regularly agreed to the placement of Indigenous children in Washington State, and Catholic Charities in Ohio routinely placed Indian children from Montreal and Toronto Catholic agencies in American homes.[38]

The Child Welfare League of America, cosponsor of the IAP, crossed the northern U.S. border frequently, holding workshops and promoting exchange with Canadian social welfare agencies.[39] Saskatchewan's AIM established close ties with the CWLA's ARENA program (the successor of the IAP) and through them started placing Indigenous Saskatchewan children in the United States in 1968. AIM administrators noted that ARENA could possibly place all the children in U.S. families in 1970, with 160 new "referrals," as they euphemistically referred to removed children. AIM also developed more informal ties in the United States. While on vacation in 1967, one Saskatchewan official discussed adoption with a county director of welfare in Kansas. The director told him they had several couples wanting Indian children, but they had no Indian children to place.[40]

Evidence suggests that as agitation for the Indian Child Welfare Act rose in the United States, the adoption of Canadian Indian children by American families increased. Historian Karen Balcom has found that after 1970 an increasing percentage of ARENA's available Indigenous children were from Canada: twenty-five of the forty-three Indigenous children that ARENA placed for adoption in August 1971 were from Ontario.[41] This practice did not extend significantly to non-Indigenous Canadian children. A 1975–76 report on Winnipeg children in care, the "Location of Foster Placements," shows that authorities placed fewer than 2 percent of non-Indigenous children outside Canada or the province, whereas they exported more than 20 percent of Indian children to the United States and about 3 percent to other provinces.[42]

The increased adoption of Canadian Indigenous children occurred against the backdrop of a new movement for Indigenous self-determination in Canada. Indigenous leaders resisted the White Paper's recommendations and condemned the government's failure to consult with them before announcing the new policy. Due to widespread Indigenous protest, the government shelved the White Paper.[43] At the local level, Indigenous people had grown weary of playing a backseat role in organizations such as Winnipeg's Community Welfare Council and its annual Indian and Métis conference. A few Indian people met to follow up on a resolution that the conference had passed in 1967 expressing that a "strong Indian organization in the city was needed." By August of that year they had signed up forty members. The Métis similarly sought greater self-determination and to be identified as a distinct group. The newly formed Manitoba Métis Federation asserted in 1968, "The Métis people in Manitoba today have all the disadvantages of the Treaty Indian with none of the advantages. The Métis have not been united in representation to government. They have been represented by white organizations and have been the pitied object of newspaper articles and radio and television programs. It is time that the Métis once again became their own spokesmen as they did when they created the Province of Manitoba."[44] Indigenous people throughout

Canada mobilized in the late 1960s and the 1970s to take greater control of their own affairs.

Indians and Métis also took over or formed new Native service agencies. By 1968 fourteen of the eighteen board members of Winnipeg's Indian and Métis Friendship Centre were Indigenous people. They transformed the center from its original conception as a "stepping stone [for urban Indian migrants] into greater society" to a new hub for social action, cultural stability, and leadership development.[45] The Native Clan organization formed in Winnipeg in the early 1970s at the request of Indigenous inmates in penal institutions. At the same time activists created a Native Club to provide for the recreational and social needs of the Indigenous population of Winnipeg. The Neeganin Task Force promoted an ambitious plan to create a Neeganin Native village with a cultural services center, a housing development designed and built by Native craftsmen, and Native business enterprises, all to serve urban Indigenous people in Winnipeg. Neeganin's organizers promoted the project as "proper housing, good schools, and business enterprises—owned, operated, and controlled by you!" and "Native people, themselves and in their own way, solving the real problems of everyday city life!"[46]

Buoyed by this new sense of self-determination, Indigenous activists challenged the paternalism they faced. Mary Richard, executive director of the Indian and Métis Friendship Centre in Winnipeg, complained in 1975 to a local health care agency, the Mount Carmel Clinic, about their proposal to open a day care facility primarily for Indian and Métis children. Richard complained that there was no meaningful involvement of Indigenous peoples in the proposal, and she contended that this "tends to perpetuate a view all too prevalent in the greater society—that sees Indian people as incapable of solving their own problems." Furthermore, Richard objected to the clinic's proposal because they indicated the need for the children "to be socialized." "To us your proposal clearly indicates a questionable attitude and lack of understanding, similar to that which historically resulted in the setting up of the Boarding School system," Richard explained, which "is credited today, by Indian leaders, Psychologists, and Sociologists as being one of the most destructive factors, in the robbing of self-esteem, spiritual base, and sense of identity" of Indigenous children. Richard noted how white social service providers in the community portrayed Indigenous people in a negative light and asked, "How can you on the one hand have such a negative image of a group of people and turn around and say you are going to solve the problems of these people?"[47] Richard's assertive stance built upon the activism of Indigenous women and their particular concerns with child welfare.

Many Canadian Indigenous women participated in the Indigenous self-determination movement while seizing the opportunity to reclaim their roles as carers within their Indigenous cultures. Treaty Indian women held the first Saskatchewan Conference of Indian Women in Fort Qu'Appelle in 1967. More than sixty delegates from thirty-four Saskatchewan reserves attended. Cree activist Mary Ann Lavallee of Broadview gave the keynote address, telling the delegates: "It is time for us Indian women to quit behaving like the ostrich . . . it is time for us Indian women to loosen our tongues, to speak out, and it is time for us to give our children a new deal, a better break and a happier home life." According to a reporter, Lavallee "spoke frankly about the worst of the Indian problems—about drunkenness and broken homes, about illegitimate and neglected children, about unemployment and wife-desertion," and "she put the responsibility of keeping children in school and in good health for learning, on the shoulders of mothers." Further, "she said it was time for Indian women to get busy and have a voice in band administration."[48] Lavallee's keynote sought to mobilize Indigenous women to reassert their traditional caring roles within their societies.

The conference designated Rose Ewack of the White Bear Reserve and Lavallee to represent them at the annual meeting of the Federation of Saskatchewan Indians (FSI). Ewack and Lavallee submitted a resolution that doubled as a submission to the provincial minister of welfare. Their statement conveyed humor at first; the women had met together in Fort Qu'Appelle to "discover and share mutual interests, mutual problems, to visit and laugh together, to boast about our husbands and families, to compare our aches and pains." Their submission took a serious turn as they moved to "our long neglected homework." Like Indigenous women in the United States, they coveted their roles as cultural reproducers and were concerned with growing family problems. "We Indian women tried to find ways and means by which we as grandmothers[,] mother[s], wives and sisters could contribute a genuine effort towards improving our homes and reserves and also look toward insuring a better tomorrow for our children and our grandchildren," they explained. Concluding that "our children in far too many cases are getting a very raw deal," they complained of parents who neglected their children. They were fully prepared to tackle this situation within their own communities. "This type of mental cruelty must not be allowed to keep on and we Indian women of Saskatchewan intend to see that constructive steps are taken to better these conditions which are a very dark blot for Indian people."[49]

Saskatchewan Indian and Métis women sought to establish the Saskatchewan Native Women's Movement (SNWM) in the early 1970s. Interestingly, unlike the separate men's organizations, they included treaty and non-treaty Indians and Métis people. Child welfare and family concerns topped their agenda. The women explained that "because of lack of knowledge," the men's organizations had not addressed areas of concern to them, including the "establishment of day-care centres" on reserves, in Métis communities, and in city neighborhoods. The group also wanted "to provide service to mothers who are working, taking training, or who are ill." They envisioned combining these with services for the elderly to create a more family-like atmosphere. They also wanted a "halfway house in conjunction with" the women's jail and counselors at the prison who "could provide for the care of children, when necessary and likewise arrange to bring the family back together on the release of the mother." Their holistic agenda included a handicrafts program, arts and recreational program, clothing depots, and "counseling services for young women moving to cities" to prevent them from "fall[ing] into a way of life on 'skidroad' and prostitution." They saw a need for "family planning information centres" and homemaking classes. Incidentally, the provision of these services would also provide employment to Indian and Métis women.[50]

The SNWM constantly connected their work with the traditional caring roles of women in Indigenous societies and the need to revive these roles to meet the unique needs of modern Indigenous women. They proposed a women's halfway house, appropriately titled the "We Care Home," in Saskatoon, and noted, "In the disintegration that took place in Native society in the past one hundred years, the role of Native women became very confused and this resulted in an increasing incidence of alcoholism, promiscuity and personal health problems among Native women."[51]

Indigenous women in other provinces began organizing their own groups at the same time, and like the SNWM, they were concerned with child welfare from their inception. In 1969 the First Indian Women's Conference in Manitoba devoted an entire morning to the subject of child welfare. The session included Lavallee on the subject of "Women's Role in Child Welfare." (Since speaking at the first Saskatchewan Indian women's conference in 1967, Lavallee had traveled to Australia, one of only two Canadians invited to attend a national conference on the advancement of Aboriginal people.) During her 1969 speech Lavallee strongly promoted the idea that "improvement rests with Indian women."[52]

In Ontario and British Columbia, Indigenous women organized through Indian Homemakers Clubs, which the DIA had originally set up in the 1950s to promote home economics among Indian women. The clubs became fertile ground for Indian women's efforts to cultivate their roles in social and cultural reproduction.[53] In 1961, according to a DIA social worker, twenty-three homemakers clubs on northern Ontario reserves held "regular meetings of their own, [to] discuss community problems such as education, sanitation, water supplies and health." They raised money for community improvements, too.[54] Indigenous women from the fifty-two Indian Homemakers Clubs in British Columbia in 1968 decided "they want to be bargaining agents between the Indian Affairs and the reserves." The clubs claimed "inequality in treatment from welfare agencies" and that "Indians are allowed to die in situations where help would be brought for non-Indians." They had begun to function as "counseling groups on the reserves and in many areas are recognized as spokesmen for their bands," and now they wanted to be officially recognized as a "pressure group."[55]

Canadian Indigenous women's efforts reveal that tension and conflict existed between Indigenous men and women as a result of the Indian Act.[56] More than American Indian women in the United States, Canadian Indigenous women fought not only against state policies and practices regarding Native child welfare but also against male chauvinism within their bands and organizations. Mrs. Albert Douglas of the British Columbia Indian Homemakers Clubs claimed in 1968 that "men don't really understand what we're trying to do," and conveyed to a Vancouver reporter that "the Indian women have much to say, but they feel no one is listening and no one is interested."[57] Indigenous women in Thunder Bay, Ontario, also believed that the local Friendship Centre ignored women's concerns; they started their own organization in the 1970s to address family violence within the Indian community. Organizing proved divisive, and activist Indian women often felt silenced or marginalized within their communities.[58]

This can be seen in the efforts of the SNWM to gain funding for their organization. The group wrote that Indian and Métis women suffered from "double domination" and mentioned that many women's groups had started in the past decade but "have failed because of domination by male parent organizations, which have male executive[s]."[59] It was a struggle, however, to make government funding agencies understand this. When the SNWM applied for provincial funds to support their group and hold their first annual conference, government officials balked, replying that they already funded the FSI and the Métis Society of Saskatchewan. "As parent organizations of your group, they should be budgeting for organizations such as yours," one official told the native women's group.[60] The Saskatchewan women's group invited Bob Mitchell, the provincial secretary of state, to a board meeting in 1973 to discuss their lack of funding. They told him they were "not getting equal treatment in Native Organizations." Activist Nora Thibodeau said, "The men have become brainwashed." The women also told him that the Métis Society gave them moral support but the FSI refused to recognize them. The women expressed their objection to the provincial government policy that their organization be dependent on male parent organizations.[61]

Despite their lack of funds the SNWM proved remarkably resourceful. They held an annual conference and published a newsletter. Local branches of the group established several "Native Women's Centres, Transition Homes, and other community-oriented services." A flood in June 1975 destroyed the women's center and day care center that the Regina branch had established. The women's center, which offered crisis intervention, general counseling, welfare rights advocacy, and coordination of a housing program, found a new location, but the group was forced to close its day care center. (Unfortunately, some non-Indian neighbors complained when the women's center moved into their neighborhood that their property had been devalued.)[62] The Native Women's Center in Prince Albert operated drug prevention and rehabilitation programs. The

Meadow Lake group ran a family planning center. The SNWM's dynamism caught the attention of Heléne Josefowicz, an employee in the province's Department of the Secretary of State; she characterized the group as a "success story, born out of struggle, determination and hard work." However, she noted that the group was "stunted by lack of funds" and pointed out that "so much energy has gone into the constant search for sustaining funds" that the group was frustrated and angry. Josefowicz disagreed with other administrators who told the SNWM that they were "duplicating existing services."[63]

Marginalization and funding problems did not stop Canadian Indigenous women from addressing the Indigenous child welfare crisis. Native women teamed up with some male allies to critique Saskatchewan's AIM program. Métis activist Howard Adams and a group of Métis women, including Phyllis Trotchie, Nora Thibodeau, and Vicki Racette, who later formed the SNWM, first protested AIM in December 1971.[64] The small group issued a statement that emphatically declared, "As Métis parents of Saskatoon, we are decidedly opposed to having our children separated from Métis homes and culture and being forced to live in white homes." The group contended, "We want our children to be brought up as Métis and not as middle class pseudo-whites. . . . Those children belong in our Métis culture and nation."[65]

The group also issued a separate statement objecting to AIM's advertising approach. The AIM ads were "racist propoganda [sic] against the Métis and Indian people," the group proclaimed, because "such ads project Métis parents as being incapable of looking after their children." Moreover the ad campaign "inferiorizes and degrades our Métis children, in that they are displayed as surplus and unwanted children." The group asserted that the AIM program "is using our children to debase and humiliate our people by playing on children's pathetic appearance to have white people care [for] and support our children." They demanded that "this kind of advertisement be stopped immediately" and objected to Métis children "being shipped out of the province of Saskatchewan for adoption to white homes in other provinces."[66]

The protest paid off for at least a few months. One Social Services official complained in 1972 that "our Adopt Indian and Métis Centres in Regina and Saskatoon have almost been immobilized because we have not been able to recruit prospective adopting parents through the media because of objections raised by the Métis Association."[67] The Department of Social Services changed the name of AIM to the Aim Centre and downplayed the Indigenous ancestry of most of its children, accentuating instead that they were hard to place because they were older and part of sibling groups.[68] Administrators, however, secretly saw this as a means to continue their program while placating Indigenous protesters. One recommended, "We should now de-emphasize the homes for children of native ancestry approach," but "we should bear in mind that the majority of children available will still be children of native ancestry." This administrator advised that the Aim Centre should add handicapped children to its agenda and have the minister of welfare issue a public statement. "This would at the same time have the effect [of] allaying the fears of the native community . . . without destroying the essential qualities of the program."[69] Indigenous women activists soon saw through this disingenuous effort.

The newly established SNWM targeted AIM for abolition during the first half of 1973. Lavallee asserted at one of their first board meetings: "We have to get to the root of the social problems that caused AIM to be established."[70] The group sent a letter to all Métis Society Locals and SNWM branches throughout the province, declaring, "We do not like the unjust way our children are being advertised on T.V. and newspapers and how we don't have any choice or voice in the way our Native children are being fostered out."[71] Then they met with Social Services minister Alex Taylor. SNWM president Nora Thibodeau told him that "it was the mother's duty to care for her children but under present conditions, this was often difficult. Then the child was taken from its parents because of these poor home conditions, but many have no chance to provide better homes." SNWM activists also asked Taylor why children were taken away without informing the parents.[72] As they protested AIM, the SNWM also developed alternatives to placing native children in non-native foster and adoptive homes. The Saskatoon branch presented to the provincial government in 1973 a proposal to establish a "Native Home for Native Children in Saskatoon."[73] The branch in Regina created a registry in 1974 of Native people in Regina interested in providing foster homes for Native children in the city and sought to work with a skeptical and hostile provincial agency.[74]

Eventually their efforts resulted in a decision by the Department of Social Services to change the name of the Aim Centre to REACH, which stood for Resources for Adoption of Children. REACH continued to deflect attention from the Indigenous ancestry of most of its children. The department also stated that they would work out an agreement with Indigenous groups in the province for those groups to provide services for Indigenous children. It made some tentative efforts to recruit native foster homes, too, querying its workers as to whether the department's policy requiring married couples as foster parents was unfairly disqualifying Indigenous applicants in common-law unions.[75]

Despite these conciliatory gestures, little actually changed. REACH still dealt mainly with and continued to advertise Indigenous children, primarily through a newspaper column called "A Child Is Waiting," begun in 1975.[76] Although one REACH ad concentrated on older children and family groups, it also mentioned that REACH had "well over 100 children waiting for parents. Many of these children are of native ancestry." The accompanying graphic featured noticeably Indigenous children.[77] The Department of Social Services failed to follow through on its agreement to work with Indigenous groups to provide child welfare services, and it never resolved the question of whether it would allow couples in common-law unions to foster or adopt children.[78] Perhaps most galling to Indigenous people, REACH continued to place many Saskatchewan Native children out of the province and even out of Canada.

As activists in Saskatchewan protested AIM and REACH, pro-ICWA campaigners in the United States became aware that the American Indian child welfare crisis had crossed international borders. AAIA attorney Bertram Hirsch had been collecting statistics from state and private adoption and social service agencies in the early 1970s when he received a letter from Mary Graves, the director of Welcome House in Doylestown, Pennsylvania. She asked him if he really wanted their statistics since most of the Indian children they placed for adoption were from northwestern Canada. "The children have entered the United States without visas because they are all over half Indian heritage and thus entering under the treaty which affords them free passage because of their Indian heritage," Graves explained to Hirsch. A public welfare agency finalized most of the adoptions of Canadian Indian children in Canada, and in most cases, she elaborated, "we do not have a clear designation of tribe and on many no native village information has been given to us because the agency in Canada wishes to protect the child's identity." Hirsch expressed his interest in the statistics, and Graves sent a chart showing that her agency had placed the following numbers of Indigenous children from Canada with adoptive families in the United States:

1970—18
1971—60
1972—24
1973—11[79]

The AAIA staff was astonished by this information, and they quickly channeled it to activists in Canada. AAIA executive director Bill Byler wrote to Alfred Ketzler, his contact in the Alaska Federation of Natives, with whom the AAIA had worked closely on the Alaska Native Claims Act of 1971, and asked him to "forward it to some of your contacts in Canada so they can raise some hell." Ketzler sent the information to George Manuel, president of the National Indian Brotherhood, and to James Wah-Shee, president of the Indian Brotherhood of the Northwest Territories. A representative of the National Indian Brotherhood called Byler, and the two organizations vowed to work together "to try to halt the flow of Canadian Indian children into the United States."[80] Wah-Shee also informed Byler, "We are currently exploring in a very discreet manner and as yet have not come up with anything substantial enough to take the kind of action this disgusting situation warrants. The Government here has been reluctant to give us any information and we are not yet ready to pressure them without more facts, but we do have the admission from an official that children are sent 'south.'"[81]

Soon Canadian Indigenous women activists contacted the AAIA. Margaret Horn-Pichovich of Quebec Native Women wrote to Byler in 1974 to inform him that they would be holding their founding conference in July in Montreal. "One of our concerns centers on the adoption of Indian children by non-Indian parents," she told him as she asked for any relevant material the AAIA had collected and published on the topic. AAIA staffer Steven Unger sent off a packet of congressional testimony, statistics, and copies of the *Indian Family Defense* publication.[82] Two other Indigenous women, identified in the written records only as Jacquie and Marie, found out from an official in the Canadian DIA that authorities in Manitoba had placed children for adoption in the United States when there were not enough adoptive homes in the province.[83]

The AAIA also sought to alert lawmakers in Canada to the issue. When a group of Canadian parliamentarians came to Washington DC, attorney Arthur Lazarus, who was working with the AAIA to draft the Indian Child Welfare Act, "raised with [them] the matter of exporting Indian children to the United States. The answer was, of course, that there are not enough Canadians, Indian or non-Indian, to adopt the children. The thought never seems to have occurred to them to subsidize Indian foster homes."[84] Soon the Indigenous child welfare crisis in Canada would become more visible to the Canadian public through the high-profile Doucette case of 1975 and 1976.

Marcien and Rita Doucette presided over a large working-class family in Prince Albert, Saskatchewan, a community with large numbers of Indian and Métis people. Marcien had worked for the Canadian National Railway for over twenty-five years, while Rita maintained the home and cared for the children. They had raised three biological children, who were adults in the mid-1970s and living on their own. They had also taken in six Métis foster children by that time. The three oldest were teenagers when authorities decided to remove the three youngest foster children: Harold, Eileen, and Geraldine Laliberté.

The ethnic background of the Doucette parents is ambiguous. Robert Doucette, one of the older foster children, believes that his foster father is Métis based on genealogical research.[85] Yet Marcien and Rita Doucette did not claim to be Métis at the time, perhaps because they calculated that authorities would consider this as one more strike against them. Robert explains that Indigenous people experienced great prejudice in the 1960s and 1970s. Many people of Métis heritage in Saskatchewan did not openly declare their background.[86] Even the Métis activist Howard Adams describes in his memoir how he came to regard his "halfbreed heritage" as an "albatross" after he was "making it in the white world" in the 1960s. After his mother's death, he "began to regret every day of the years [he] had stayed away from [his] family simply because they were halfbreed." As he puts it, "the system had succeeded in turning my love into shame. It had replaced the beauty and love of my Indianness with disgust and contempt."[87] Just as Adams embraced his Métis heritage in the 1970s, so did increasing numbers of Prince Albert residents. The Doucette case, in fact, played a critical role in mobilizing the Métis in Prince Albert to identify more fully with their heritage.[88]

The Indigenous community in Prince Albert treated the Doucettes as one of their own. According to Robert, his foster family had close relations with local Indigenous families, who gave the Doucettes their absolute support in the battle to regain the foster children. Shortly after the children were removed in July 1975, at least 250 people crowded into the local Prince Albert library auditorium to protest. The group resolved to send the Doucettes to Michigan to see their children and to accompany them with a caravan of activists. They petitioned the provincial government to return the children to the Doucette home and give the Doucettes first priority in adopting them, and they "set up a citizens' committee to conduct meetings around the province on native adoption policy, and present its findings to the government." Attendees unanimously agreed that "native foster children should be adopted by native parents" and that all Saskatchewan children should stay in the province if adopted.[89]

This meeting created a space in which families who had lost children could share their painful experiences, much like the congressional hearings did in the United States. "With emotion-laden voices," a local journalist reported, "sometimes tearful foster parents told the meeting of similar incidents which have occurred in the past. One person said that at 36 she had been told by social services that she was too old to take care of a foster child. Another woman said she was fighting a 'constant battle' to keep the department from taking five grandchildren who have been left to her care. Others complained that the department considers many 'loving families' to be too poor to adequately handle foster children or adopt them."[90] The forum enabled community members to discover the systemic nature of what many participants believed were their own personal problems and to learn that authorities often removed Indigenous children from their natal or foster homes for specious reasons—because their family suffered from poor economic conditions or because extended family members were their primary caregivers.

The Doucette case galvanized Indigenous activists and their allies in Saskatchewan. Five main groups united in their opposition to the removal of the Doucette children: the Métis Society of Saskatchewan, SNWM, Saskatchewan Human Rights Commission, Prince Albert Family Planning Centre, and Indian-Métis Friendship Centre of Prince Albert.[91] Sustained protests in Prince Albert and elsewhere in the province led to an official investigation of the Doucette case by the provincial ombudsman, Ernest Boychuk.

Boychuk's report of August 1975 affords a rare opportunity to follow a child removal case over a number of years and to gain insight into how authorities justified child removal as well as how families coped with it. Boychuk found many irregularities with the case and particularly criticized the social worker's act of telling the children that *they* could decide if they wanted to live with the Michigan adoptive family. Yet he ultimately agreed with the Department of Social Services' decision to remove the children and not to return them, on two main grounds. First, he cited "the inability of the Doucettes to handle adolescent children."[92] Boychuk highlighted officials' claims that "the Doucettes had experienced difficulties with their own children in adolescence and the prospects for the foster children 'may not be too good.'" Boychuk asserted that "little purpose could be served here by going into the private lives of the members of this family," and he referred only in vague terms to incidents in the late 1960s when the Doucettes had quarreled with their neighbors and the police had been called. He also expressed concern that one of their older foster children had run away from home. Boychuk claimed to be sparing the Doucette family from unwanted scrutiny about their other children's lives, but his subtle condemnation of the Doucettes and their parenting abilities left little room for them to refute his charges directly.[93]

The Doucettes did not have a chance to defend themselves against these insinuations, either in court or in a meeting with the ombudsman, who never interviewed them or their foster children. "It seems that they just took the social worker's word for everything without consulting anyone else," Mrs. Doucette complained.[94] Mrs. Doucette freely shared information with the press to counter official accusations, claiming that her biological son had stolen a car as a juvenile, but had since settled down. In the case of her older foster daughter, Mrs. Doucette asserted that when the girl started running around with boys, the Doucettes had called social welfare authorities, who placed the girl in a Saskatoon girls' home. Subsequently she fled from the institution, not from the Doucettes' home. Sympathetic authorities pointed out that many Canadians from all walks of life had difficulty raising adolescents. Liberal Party leader Dave Steuart, member of the Legislative Assembly for the Prince Albert area, remarked, "I wouldn't have too much difficulty finding thousands of families in Saskatchewan which have had a runaway daughter or son." Moreover, Steuart pointed out that if the Doucettes "were a good enough family for the children for nine years, then surely they were good enough to adopt them." In regard to the neighborhood quarrel, Mrs. Doucette claimed that it was the Doucettes themselves who had phoned the police for help with a "menacing neighbor" who was bothering other residents as well. Welfare authorities threatened to take the foster children away if the problem did not resolve, so the Doucette family moved to a new neighborhood, at considerable trouble and expense, where they had no trouble with their new neighbors.[95] From the Doucettes' point of view, they were bending over backwards to comply with the demands of the Department of Social Services.

The second reason Boychuk cited in support of removing the children made it unlikely that the Doucettes could ever have satisfied the department. Boychuk admitted that "the children were well established as part of the family and there was genuine mutual affection," and that "the foster children seemed to feel quite secure." But the Doucette home "seemed to be lacking in stimulation," he contended.[96] What exactly did this phrase mean? And why would it be grounds for removing children from a loving and secure home? One news story on the Todds, the adoptive couple in Michigan, provides a clue. "The Todds enjoy music," the reporter wrote admiringly. "Mr. Todd sings and his wife plays the piano. They quickly discovered the three children shared their interest." According to Mr. Todd, the children "'really have a lot of potential.... They have a really good grasp for esthetics. They enjoy music. They have a lot of talent, they really do.'"[97] This story suggests that the ombudsman, minister of Social Services, and many non-Indigenous social workers shared an unstated set of assumptions about what a child needs beyond basic comforts, love, and caring. It conveys that "stimulation" required an additional layer of middle-class trappings—proper education in western literature, art, music, and "esthetics"—that would not necessarily be available in a working-class home with nine children.

The concern with "stimulation" suggests that social workers retained unexamined middle-class standards and cultural norms that led them to regard Indigenous families as lacking and even unfit. The phrase turns up frequently in Indigenous child welfare contexts. When advertising Indigenous children for adoption, officials commonly asserted that the children had lacked early stimulation and called for adoptive families who would "provide them with love, stimulation, and guidance."[98] Scholar Amy Ogata has found that Cold War North Americans highly valued creativity in their children, and middle-class families expended much time, effort, and money in stimulating their children through the purchase of special toys, books, furniture, and educational experiences. She explains that "in the prosperous years after the end of the war, middle-class, predominantly white families interpreted children's 'needs' to include . . . early education, such as nursery school, more personal space, increased opportunities for play, and an unprecedented number of personal belongings such as books and toys."[99] The nebulous but encompassing nature of the term *stimulation* allowed authorities a great deal of discretion to remove children, as no objective or quantifiable criteria existed to measure its extent in a home or family.

When it came to the Doucette case, and presumably others, this concern with stimulation seemed to take precedence over the children's sense of security. Authorities referred the three younger Doucette foster children for a psychiatric assessment in 1974. The report, quoted by the ombudsman, is telling:

> There is no problem with any of these three children and so any decision about future placements will have to be determined on the basis of resources that are and can be provided in the present foster home. These children are all sufficiently intelligent that they could easily develop manipulative skills in setting up foster parents . . . as well, there is a distinct possibility that the children will regress in terms of

overall functioning if they do not receive stimulation from the home environment. But on the other hand, the children are well adjusted in their present foster home placement and are adamant that they do not want to be placed anywhere else and certainly do not want to be separated.... Thus, the entire problem seems to be that if the present foster home is adequate, then these three children should remain together in that home-like environment in which they are satisfied, adjusted and happy.... Leaving the children in the present home or ... placing them elsewhere would be much easier if these children were of lower mental ability because then they would not require as much stimulation and would not be as difficult to cope with.[100]

The assessor seems to think out loud, first praising the children's intelligence and noting their happiness and positive adjustment but then expressing concern about their potential for manipulating foster parents, becoming difficult to cope with, and regressing if they are not given greater mental stimulation. No assessment of the children at any point in the records indicates that any of these problems were actually present in the children. This assessor and other officials instead seemed to imagine a future moment when the children might succumb to these behaviors if they were not sufficiently "stimulated." On the eve of the children's removal, a social worker reported in 1975 that the children "continue to be so spontaneous and natural it is refreshing. It is easy to see they are a real delight, though perhaps immature for their ages ... given a more stimulating environment they should bloom."[101] For officials the amorphous concept of stimulation trumped the children's sense of adjustment, security, and happiness in their foster home.

When I shared this official justification for the removal of the three Laliberté children with their older foster brother, Robert Doucette, he appeared baffled. What did that mean, he wondered? His foster parents were always trying to find out what interested their children and to support them. He loved going to the library and playing hockey. He recounted much time spent outdoors with his foster father, who taught him the value of hard work. He remembered the time when he tried out for a hockey team and was told that he would never make it because he was Indian. His protective father, he told me, "smoked" the guy. In one letter to the minister for

Social Services, the Doucettes conveyed something of the positive home environment that Robert remembered. "Please Sir, let them come back to their loved ones here," they pleaded, "also their ponies, puppies, bikes and other toys and also little friends they had to leave behind."[102] Perhaps the Doucettes did not possess the key indicators of a middle-class lifestyle, the proper kind and quantity of material objects (a piano?), but they seem to have provided their children with plenty of other kinds of stimulation.

In a related way, authorities also contended that the Doucettes had too many children. A three-member advisory committee conducted a second investigation of the episode, concluding that although "the Doucette home offered a happy and loving environment, . . . 'The fact is however that the home environment was not equipped to take care of eight or nine children, particularly those reaching and going through adolescence and the early and mid-teen years.'"[103] Officials invoked further unstated assumptions based on the ideal of Cold War era families where mothers gave intensive attention to their properly spaced children. Conformity to such an ideal, in authorities' minds, would be nearly impossible in a family with so many children so close together in age. Mrs. Doucette conveyed an alternative ideal. A social worker expressed regret to Mrs. Doucette for having overloaded her family with so many children and told her that removing the three younger children would ease the pressure. But "Mrs. Doucette responded by pointing out that the Doucettes had never concerned themselves with having many children to look after, and indeed considered large families created a healthy atmosphere for raising children."[104] Authorities themselves had placed six children with the Doucettes, thus contributing to their large family, but now penalized them for failing to conform to predominant middle-class family norms.

The Boychuk report not only illuminates authorities' reasoning for removing Indigenous children from their long-term carers. It also shows that they were often deaf to one of the main concerns of protesters: that Indigenous children should not be placed with non-Indigenous families, especially when these were located so far from their home communities. Officials and some journalists minimized the children's heritage and the importance of growing up either within an Indigenous family or close to an Indigenous community. The three-member advisory committee concluded that "complaints about a loss of native cultural heritage by moving the children out of their Prince Albert foster home were largely unfounded, ... and any such loss would be minute and not a major factor in deciding the children's future."[105] A reporter quoted Mr. Todd as claiming that the children seemed "completely unaware of their Indian heritage." Mr. Todd said he would have helped the children learn about that heritage because he was trained in cross-cultural communication.[106] Both Todd and officials regarded Indigenous culture as a kind of kit that could be learned by anyone through books and classes and then transferred to children. By contrast, Indigenous communities regarded their cultures as embodied traditions that had to be lived and experienced through family and tribal relationships.

The Boychuk report and related documents enable us to see what effect child removal had on families and how they responded to it. The social services minister insisted that all "communication between the Doucettes and the[ir former foster] children be discontinued," but the Doucettes were so attached to the children that they wrote them many letters, all of which were returned unopened by school authorities or the children's new foster parents. Despondent, they contacted the children in person without the consent of the department, first in October 1975, then again in December of 1975, and once more in May 1976.

The Doucettes also applied repeatedly to the Department of Social Services to adopt the children. They had already tried to adopt one of the children before the entire debacle, only to be told that they would have to adopt all the children or none. This proved financially unviable for the Doucettes. As foster parents, they received a small stipend for each child, which enabled them to afford to care for the children. Adopting all the children would have meant that they would lose these subsidies and would be financially strapped. Authorities held this against the Doucettes, contending that they made no significant attempt to adopt the children. After the department removed the children, the Doucettes continued to appeal to authorities to be allowed to adopt all the children, no matter the financial consequences.[107] They made their final plea to adopt their three former foster children, as well as two older foster children still in their care, in two poignant letters in March 1976.

These letters reveal the ways in which families sought to counter the damaging stereotypes leveled at them and to appeal to liberal values of the era. To establish their respectability, the Doucettes provided the names of fourteen references from the Prince Albert community and emphasized that Mr. Doucette had worked for the Canadian National Railway for twenty-six years while Mrs. Doucette had been a housewife.[108] The Doucettes' letters also appealed to a sense of Canadian national identity in the Cold War Era. "What are they trying to put these children through?" they inquired of Herman Rolfes, the minister of social services. "We are not in Russia or a communist country, but suppose[d] to be in a free country. These children are Canadian and were in Brownies and Scouts, and are proud of their country, why send them out??"[109] The Doucettes attempted to awaken Rolfes's liberal consciousness more specifically. "We heard you speak many times over radio and TV about what you were doing for your people," they wrote. "Be the[y] in the prisons, . . . or the poor or whoever needs help and you were with them and very understanding of their needs. We do hope you can help us also and understand what these three children will be going through if they try to put them in another adopting home and if they won't stay, then put them in another foster home. If you have such a big heart for other people, we're sure you will for these children also."[110] The Doucettes' letters reveal that they were well aware of the predominant ideologies underpinning Indigenous adoption. Turning these notions on their heads, they argued that a truly Canadian and liberal response to the Doucette foster children would be to return them.

These letters, too, provide a glimpse of Indigenous critiques of provincial fostering and adoption policies. The Doucettes questioned why all contact should be severed between them and the children. "Why . . . are they kept just like prisoners there with strangers all around," the Doucettes asked, "and we cannot send them a Birthday or Valentine card even. Prisoners are allowed to write home and receive letters and have visitors once in a while, but these little darlings cannot. What have they done to *deserve* this *punishment* or us??"[111] This practice of cutting off all contact between families and removed children was very much at odds with Indigenous conceptions of care, and many Indian and Métis families and organizations challenged it.

The Doucettes' letters convey the utter desperation and powerlessness of Indigenous parents in relation to state agencies as well. "We will never give up if we have to follow them to the end of the world," they wrote to Rolfes. "They will always be in our hearts and on our minds and know they will never forget us and will be back as soon as they get a chance no matter where they are put." The Doucettes were at the mercy of state bureaucracies, and they resorted to abject supplication, frequently begging Rolfes with a Dickensian "Please sir."[112] Displaying his authority, the minister did not reply to the letters until more than two months later, and he merely reiterated that he was following the recommendation of the advisory committee and refusing to return the three younger children to the Doucettes' care.[113]

The case illustrates broader experiences of Indigenous families, who confronted stony-faced officials apparently indifferent to their pleas. The minister of social services had met with the Doucettes only once, in July 1975. He claimed to be open to their concerns, but he had prepared a press release *before* the meeting stating that he still supported the removal of their children. Mrs. Doucette emerged tearfully from the meeting, declaring that "he doesn't care a bit about those children. . . . he could have been talking about horses for all he cared."[114]

The actions of the department seemed insensitive at the least, if not downright vindictive and punitive. The department had run ads for the three children in the Prince Albert *Daily Herald* and other Saskatchewan newspapers in January 1976. Rita Doucette and two other women wrote angry letters to the editor. "It was inconceivable to me that the REACH people could be so inhuman as to subject these children to this kind of publicity," Doucette wrote. "What right do these people have to make a spectacle of these children," Mrs. B. Delorme asked, "to place their pictures in a newspaper and to give a resume concerning abilities, disabilities, etc. . . . These children are not animals in a pet shop to be placed on exhibition." Authorities angrily dismissed the uproar.[115] After the Doucettes conducted another "unauthorized visit" with the children in May 1976, the Department of Social Services stepped up its efforts to have the children adopted. They published their pictures and stories in the National Adoption Desk Bulletin, REACH distributed a special bulletin to all provinces advertising the children, and Ontario's "Today's Child" column featured the children.[116]

Still no adoptive families stepped forward, and the department even considered returning the Laliberté children to the Todds.[117] Placing the children once more in the family who had returned them after just ten weeks would have been confusing to the children. And how could authorities be sure that the Todds would not change their minds again? That authorities would even consider placing the three children with the Todds again shows that they were so fixated on the permanency of adoption that they were willing to subject children to gross emotional trauma. As Boychuk put it, approvingly, "the department is of the opinion that the difference in legal status between a permanent ward and an adopted child in a home is of sufficient significance socially and psychologically to a child to compensate for the trauma of separation involved even in the placement of older children."[118] From the evidence he had actually gathered, it appears that legal status and formal adoption mattered little to the Doucette foster children. They were safe, secure, and happy in their foster home. Legal status would have been relevant to them only in hindsight, for if they had been legally adopted by the Doucettes, they would have been spared the ordeal of being separated from the only caregivers they had ever known. In their zeal to place the children in a supposedly appropriate middle-class and "stimulating" home, authorities did not see the contradictions in their own actions. They undermined the secure and permanent home the children already enjoyed, simply because the Doucettes did not conform to official ideals.

Virtually the only action that Indigenous families could take that elicited any response from authorities was to turn to legal proceedings, a route that was often far beyond their financial means. In June 1976 the Doucettes contacted a lawyer, who conveyed to the minister of social services their wish that they be allowed to correspond with and visit their former foster children.[119] The minister threatened legal action against them, arguing that continued contact would "undermine our efforts to locate the children in a suitable home."[120] The department eventually softened its stance, however, and the Doucettes were allowed to visit the three children in October 1977. The children allegedly said that as soon as they turned sixteen, they would return to live in Prince Albert, where they could not only reunite with the Doucettes but also be close to their other siblings. The department insisted that the Doucettes would be allowed only three visits per year.[121] Robert Doucette remembers that his parents maintained contact with the three children, making the long drive to North Portal several times a year, and that all three did return to Prince Albert once they came of age. Yet, he also recalls, his parents were never the same after losing their three youngest children.[122]

The Doucettes failed in their bid to regain their foster children, but their case did lead to an overhaul of Saskatchewan's practices, a side effect that Mrs. Doucette, even in her grief, acknowledged. She hoped that no matter what happened with their case, the publicity over it "'will help other children in the future.'"[123] As a result of the Doucette case, the Saskatchewan Department of Social Services froze all placements of Indigenous children outside the country.[124] They also formed a three-member review committee to hear grievances from Indigenous community members regarding adoption and foster care and considered a program of subsidized adoptions, which would enable low-income foster parents to adopt children for whom they had been caring for many years.[125]

The Doucette case strengthened ongoing protests by Indigenous Saskatchewan groups and gave their efforts new urgency. A delegation of activists occupied the office of the deputy minister of social services in Regina in March 1976. Rod Durocher of the Métis Society led the two-hour occupation by forty Indigenous people, who represented six organizations. Indigenous women at the protest asserted that foster children in non-Indigenous homes were not being treated properly. Agnes Sinclair, president of the Regina Native Women's Movement, declared that "the foster home and adoption programs are not working because there is a lot of neglect." Her group wanted to set up a "special board . . . to deal with appeals regarding foster home placement, adoption home placement and cases where children have been removed from their homes." Alexine Nuwman, a Regina foster mother "who occupied the deputy minister's chair during the demonstration, claimed that native children are being mistreated in foster homes. With emotion in her voice, she said she has seen native children 'locked up because they're considered too filthy.'" She noted that in another foster home, "the native children were required to stand in a corner while the rest of the family ate and only afterwards were the children allowed scraps from the table."[126]

Officials initially reacted defensively to this criticism. A draft of a speech written for the minister of social services to deliver to the Saskatchewan Association of Social Workers admitted that 53 percent of all children committed to care in 1975–76 were Indigenous but declared, "There have been statements made from time to time that the department is guilty of practicing racial and cultural genocide because we place native children for adoption in non-native homes. We reject that charge." Authorities also turned to timeworn stereotypes of Indigenous families in an effort to dampen their criticism. "Let us not mistake irresponsibility, personal immaturity or open neglect of children for native culture," the minister wrote in the draft of his speech. "I am satisfied that our employees are removing native children from their parents only when it is necessary for the child's health or safety and that these considerations supercede considerations of race or culture."[127] Ultimately authorities had to respond to the increasing protests of Indigenous people despite this initial defensiveness.

Officials now sought to consult with Indigenous groups before proceeding with further promotion of Indigenous fostering and adoption rather than getting caught in another political firestorm. REACH officials met with the SNWM in October 1976, "in an effort to determine the acceptability of material prepared for us in a REACH advertising campaign." To the relief of REACH officials, "representatives at the meetings were not militant," but the women did object to the using the phrase "special needs" to describe Indigenous children, because it "made it sound like native children were equated with [the] handicapped on the television spot." The women did, however, praise REACH for the "use of parents of native ancestry [on the] TV spot."[128]

Indigenous activists continued their activism despite evidence of some détente with Saskatchewan officials, and they provided ongoing support to the Doucettes. They gathered six hundred signatures on a petition in 1977 calling for the return of the three children to the Prince Albert vicinity, if not the Doucette home. The petition declared, "We do not think this kind of treatment they are receiving is helping those children at all."[129] Activists in Saskatchewan achieved another milestone in 1977 when officials with the DIA admitted that department social workers had illegally removed Indian children from their parents on reserves in the North Battleford area without their parents' consent and without a court hearing.[130]

The passage of ICWA just a year later in the United States provided a stimulus to an already burgeoning movement to reclaim Indigenous child welfare in Canada. After ICWA's passage, cooperation and exchange between the AAIA and Canadian Indigenous groups resumed. This revival occurred in part as a result of Steven Unger's testimony to the U.S. Select Commission on Immigration and Refugee Policy in 1980. The Select Commission had asked Unger to testify about problems Native Americans faced crossing the U.S.-Canadian border, including the impact of ICWA on Canadian Indian children being adopted in the United States.[131] Unger urged the commission to investigate whether Canadian Indian children were being brought into the United States illegally to be adopted. He asserted, "It would be tragic . . . if the reforms adopted here [through ICWA], by limiting the number of Indian children available for adoptions, unintentionally exacerbate pressure to transport Canadian Indian children into the U.S. for adoption." Unger cited statistics from Minnesota and Welcome House, as well as from Maine, showing that in 1974, 114 out of 120 Indian children adopted in that year through their program were Canadian. Unger claimed that "the crisis is largely invisible" and recommended that the commission establish a joint U.S.-Canadian task force to investigate the problem. Unger forwarded his testimony to the National Indian Brotherhood in Canada.[132]

Unger's statement and his experience with ICWA proved of great interest to Canadian activists. Clem Chartier, head of the FSI, invited Unger to speak at the National Indian Child Welfare Rights Workshop in March 1981 in Regina. Unger readily accepted but suggested broadening his topic from the trafficking of Canadian Indian children to how American Indian tribes organized to protect their rights regarding children, a proposition that Chartier approved.[133] Unger and Nancy Tuthill of the American Indian Law Center gave the opening presentation of the workshop on "The American Situation Regarding Indian Child Welfare."[134] Inspiration flowed both ways across the border. Unger and the AAIA's contact with Canadian activists led them to recommend that ICWA be amended to cover Canadian Indigenous children.[135]

Other American activists also helped nurture transnational Indigenous child welfare efforts, including seasoned social worker and activist Evelyn Blanchard. She attended the first national meeting of health and social service representatives of Canadian provincial and territorial tribal organizations, held on April 13–14, 1982, in Ottawa. The meeting provided a national forum to examine varying arrangements between provinces regarding Indigenous child welfare, to analyze positive and negative U.S. Indian child welfare experiences, and to develop a draft national plan of action. Blanchard's experience in Canada led to her awareness that "the child welfare problems faced by Canadian Indians are identical to those we face as related to out-of-home placements." Blanchard learned, too, of the cross-border adoption of Canadian Indian children who were "aggressively sought for adoption by non-Indian individuals and organizations in the United States." She met Indians in Manitoba who were upset about children being taken to Louisiana and heard complaints about Indians who went over the border to Washington State to harvest crops and lost their children.[136]

Cross-border adoptions continued to trouble Indigenous communities deeply. Activists in Manitoba strenuously objected in 1982 to the placement of so many Indigenous children for adoption in non-Native homes in the United States and in other Canadian provinces. In response, the provincial government established a moratorium on all out-of-province placements of Indigenous children and appointed Judge Edwin Kimelman to conduct an inquiry. Kimelman held public hearings in major population centers from May to September 1982, and special hearings on Manitoba Indian reserves from October 1982 to November 1983. The judge also received seventeen written submissions; interviewed child care agencies, Native organizations, foster parent groups, and religious leaders; studied group homes; read one hundred books and articles, including in the AAIA periodical *Indian Family Defense*; and examined the adoption files of ninety-three Indigenous children who had been placed in the United States or outside the province in 1981. Kimelman studied the problem for two years and released six preliminary reports. He submitted his final report in 1985, which made 109 recommendations, many of which incorporated some of the provisions of ICWA.[137]

The Kimelman inquiry enabled Native peoples in Manitoba finally to have a public forum in which to air their grievances and have them taken seriously. Kimelman did not react defensively to the complaints of Indigenous people; instead he came to agree with many of their assertions. He critiqued social work practices specifically. Kimelman assumed that he would find documentation in the files showing that social workers had made efforts to locate families for children in Manitoba. He expected that social workers would explain why they had resorted to placing Indigenous children out of the province. Instead, much to his shock (which he emphasized with italicized text), Kimelman discovered a *"casual attitude to dealing with children"* that *"reflects an inappropriate position and procedure."* He found that "there was no evidence that cultural factors were even discussed with adopting families" and that child care agency staff "seemed abysmally uninformed about Native value systems." He observed that caseworkers seemed to have been "programmed to view people as carriers of the symptoms of social pathology rather than as fully rounded human beings with weaknesses and strengths." Kimelman learned, too, that when Indian people asked for help, officials often took their children into custody, as had happened in the United States. In one file he reviewed, "an Indian mother came to the agency to ask that the child be placed in a foster home for a few days to permit the mother time to recover her health, find a place to live, and get her life in order." The social worker replied that they didn't do that and "offered only one option—relinquish custody of the child."[138]

Kimelman noted that provincial social work practices did not follow proper legal procedures. He reported that "the story was told, too often to be ignored, of children taken into temporary custody and parents never again informed of their whereabouts." As in the United States, he found evidence that child welfare agencies were able to implement plans that were not approved by courts. He regarded this as "an affront to the legal process and an injustice to the children." He declared emphatically that *"Children need protection to ensure that they are not removed from their families without substantial cause."*[139]

Kimelman was frank in his condemnation: "The appalling reality is that everyone involved [in the child welfare system] believed they were doing their best and stood firm in their belief that the system was working well. Some administrators took an ostrich approach to child welfare problems— they just did not exist. The miracle is that there were not more children lost in this system run by so many well-intentioned people. The road to hell was paved with good intentions, and the child welfare system was the paving contractor." Kimelman agreed with Indigenous groups that "native people of Manitoba had been victims of cultural genocide" in his Interim Report of May 1983. Despite criticism of his viewpoint, he reiterated this point more forcefully in his 1985 report. "Having now completed the review of the files of the native children placed out of province in 1981, *the Chairman now states unequivocally that cultural genocide has been taking place in a systematic, routine manner.* This practice "took advantage of a readily available pool of adoptive parents" and *"served to delay the development of Indian resources, prevented the development of specialized services."* At least under the residential school system, Kimelman wrote, *"children knew who their parents were and they returned home for the summer months."*[140]

Kimelman was deeply sympathetic to Indigenous families, but he stopped short of fully supporting Indigenous self-determination over child welfare. He promoted the wishes of Indigenous people to have authorities recognize "custom adoption," and he opposed closed adoption files and strict standards of confidentiality. He called, too, for provincial social service agencies to become more sensitive and responsive to Indigenous needs. Yet although he studied ICWA, he did not recommend similar Canada-wide legislation. Nor did he support First Nations and Métis people in their aspirations to establish Indigenous child welfare agencies.[141]

Indigenous activists had other ideas. Under the leadership of David Ahenakew, the Assembly of First Nations "initiated negotiations with the federal government for federal child welfare legislation for Treaty Indians and for the establishment of a tribal court system." The DIA and the federal government ignored these calls, and federal legislation did not prevail. Activists noted in 1984 that "in the absence of a National Indian Child Welfare Act, the Indian child welfare agencies have been forced to work with Provincial laws."[142] Rather than achieving comprehensive federal legislation that would have covered all bands and non-status Indians, individual Indian bands and regional native child welfare groups negotiated agreements with the federal and provincial governments.

Some activists engaged in dramatic protest to achieve this. Wayne Christian, chief of the Spallumcheen Band in British Columbia, organized an Indian Child Caravan of an estimated one thousand protesters who converged in front of the home of British Columbia's minister of human resources, Grace McCarthy, on Canada's Thanksgiving Day in October 1980. Authorities had removed Christian from his parents and had placed him in a non-Indigenous foster home. He had lived there until he was seventeen, then returned to his reserve. Officials had also removed Christian's younger brother and placed him with a different family. He, too, returned to the reserve, but he eventually committed suicide. According to Christian and the protesters, state welfare workers had similarly removed 150 children since the 1960s. With just three hundred members, the Spallumcheen Band had "lost virtually an entire generation of its children to child welfare authorities." The band had passed a bylaw asserting the right to self-determination and exclusive jurisdiction over Indian children in their band, whether living off or on their reserve. As a result of the protest, McCarthy signed an agreement with the Spallumcheen Band that gave them "exclusive jurisdiction over any child custody proceeding involving an Indian child" from their band and called for returning removed children to the band where possible.[143] By 1988, 184 out of 592 bands in British Columbia had negotiated similar agreements with provincial authorities.[144]

Indigenous groups in other provinces similarly pressed for and achieved agreements with provincial authorities. The Four Nations Confederacy of Manitoba, composed of the Cree, Dakota, Dene, and Ojibway nations of the province, negotiated a tripartite agreement with the federal and provincial governments in 1982 to develop their own child welfare services.[145] They looked to ICWA as a model in their negotiations with provincial authorities. Under "Placement Priorities for Native Children," the Manitoba native caucus "recommend[ed] that placement priorities for Native children be modeled after the U.S. legislation."[146] The Federation of Saskatchewan Indian Nations (FSIN) signed an agreement with the minister of social services in 1984 that enabled the FSIN to provide services to assist Indian families in fostering and adopting Indian children who were registered for adoption with the province.[147]

Canadian provinces took a more piecemeal approach to Indigenous child welfare than in the United States. They negotiated agreements with First Nations and Métis organizations and communities rather than establishing a federal law that would apply universally across the nation.[148] To some extent these localized agreements gave Indigenous activists greater latitude. In Manitoba the Native Caucus recommended that the new proposed provincial Child Welfare Act should recognize "custom" adoptions among native communities, "which do not always involve extended family members." They commended the act's recognition of common law unions and single persons as appropriate adopters of children and asserted that the "section on subsidized adoptions should be proclaimed (long overdue) and funds be made available to provide needed care for Native children in Native homes."[149] The Canadian approach did not provide the leverage of a federal law, but it did afford Indigenous communities flexibility and localized control.

In their effort to regain control over the care of their children, Canadian Indigenous community organizers discovered not only that provincial authorities were removing Indigenous children from their families at unprecedented rates but also that such a crisis was likewise occurring south of the border. Government authorities in Ottawa and Washington DC had colluded in these parallel Indigenous child welfare crises. They had exchanged tips about how best to transfer responsibility for Indigenous children to state or provincial authorities and how to advance urban relocation. The Doucette case taught activists, too, that the fate of Indigenous children in Canada was inextricably linked to events in the United States. The Doucettes' youngest foster children were just three of hundreds or thousands of Canadian Indigenous children whom private and government agencies had exported to the United States for adoption. Indigenous child removal was thus a transnational phenomenon.

Indigenous activism to reclaim the care of children also crossed the border. American and Canadian activists made key connections in order to challenge transnational Indigenous adoptions, and the passage of ICWA offered inspiration for provincial agreements that transferred greater control for child welfare to Indigenous community organizations in Canada. As North American activists organized across the U.S.-Canadian border in the 1970s, they also learned that Indigenous child removal was not isolated to their continent. It was a global phenomenon that affected Indigenous families more than seven thousand miles away across the Pacific Ocean.

I learned of the remarkable family of Margaret Tucker on my first research trip to Australia in 1998. I sat rapt in the National Library in Canberra as I read Tucker's memoir, *If Everyone Cared*, in which she recounted her traumatic story of child removal. Tucker became a major advocate for Aboriginal people and one of the first activists to expose the traumatic experiences of the "Stolen Generations." Her daughter, Mollie Dyer, carried on Tucker's activism for Aboriginal child welfare in the 1970s and 1980s. I was stunned when Steven Unger told me he had met an Australian Indigenous activist named Mollie Dyer when she came to the United States in the 1970s. A day after meeting Steve, I found several files labeled "Child Welfare—Australia" in the Association on American Indian Affairs papers at Princeton. Steve and Mollie had exchanged dozens of letters in the 1970s. Mollie's sense of compassion and her warm humor wafted up through her letters. Steve's written words conveyed empathy and dedication. I longed to share all these serendipitous connections with the researcher at the next table, or any random stranger, but I knew from experience that not everyone shares the intellectual excitement of a historian at work.

I decided to go to Melbourne in early 2013 to learn more about Mollie Dyer's work there. I wrote to my friends and colleagues for their advice. Lynette Russell, director of the Indigenous Centre at Monash University, responded that she knew some of Mollie's relatives. "Maybe I can hook you up," she wrote. Soon I received an email from Lynette addressed to both me and "Aunty Di." I was astonished to learn that Aunty Di is Diane Singh, the Elder in Residence at Lynette's Indigenous Centre and Mollie Dyer's first foster daughter. Aunty Di generously corresponded with me in the next few weeks, and she connected me with Mollie's eldest biological son, Allan Burns, and with a Melbourne Stolen Generations organization.

I flew to Melbourne on March 17. The next morning I took a taxi out to the Indigenous Centre at Monash University. Lynette welcomed me with a warm hug and we gave each other an abbreviated update on our lives. Then she took me to meet Aunty Di in her office. As we walked down the corridor, I felt the same sense of nervous anticipation that I had experienced when meeting Steve Unger and Evelyn Blanchard. I imagine that others might feel this when meeting a favorite celebrity, athlete, or politician. Awkward and tongue-tied. Aunty Di told me about students who came to her searching for their Indigenous roots. She showed me the careful work she was doing to trace Aboriginal family genealogies in Victoria. I told her about my long-time interest in her foster mother. She gave me a thick file of material about Mollie, and I shared with her copies of correspondence between Mollie and Steve. Later we went out to lunch with Lynette. I was reluctant to leave campus that day; I wanted to keep that connection with someone who had been so close to Mollie.

A few days later I was poring over the papers of the Council for Aboriginal Rights in the State Library of Victoria. They had scrapbooks and folders full of newspaper articles from the 1950s and 1960s simply labeled "Aboriginal children." I suspected there might be some material in them on fostering and adoption; there was even more than I expected. And among the yellowed and brittle newspaper clippings was something even more surprising: two articles about fifteen-year-old "Dianne Day," who had been living with Mr. and Mrs. Burns (Mollie Dyer) for three years. Prior to that, the articles reported, Dianne had attended over twenty schools in country towns in New South Wales and Victoria as her parents migrated from job to job. The 1962 articles explained that the Burns family had six biological children and one other foster child. "Every week the Burns family opens its home for from 20 to 25 aboriginal visitors from as far as Shepparton, Nathalia, and Echuca," one reporter added. Dianne, now Diane Singh, smiled broadly in the accompanying photo.[1] As I gazed at Diane's unmistakable smile, the intervening fifty years seemed to compress into a matter of days or even hours. The thousands of miles between Australia and North America seemed to shrink. The past caught up to the present and the continents drifted back together again, if only for an afternoon.

# CHAPTER 7

# The Indigenous Child Welfare Crisis in Australia and Transnational Activism

Australian Aboriginal community activist Mollie Dyer had been working as a field officer with the Aboriginal Legal Service for a number of years in the 1970s in Fitzroy, an inner-city neighborhood of Melbourne where many Aboriginal people lived. She provided representation for Aboriginal defendants in court, offered general welfare advice and assistance, and assisted with the running of a hostel for Aboriginal people recently released from jail and for the temporarily homeless.[1] Through her work Dyer became acquainted with hundreds of Indigenous children who had been removed from their families. She responded at first in a personal way: by fostering dozens of children herself. As she wrote in 1975, "I have reared six children of my own, cared for 25 part-Aboriginal children on a fairly long term basis and many more on a short term basis. Aboriginal children are often placed with me by the Social Welfare Dep[artmen]t after they have been returned from non-Aboriginal foster-care to the care of the Department."[2]

Dyer got hold of an issue of *Indian Family Defense,* the periodical of the Association on American Indian Affairs, and in early 1976 she wrote to its editor, Steven Unger. He published a long letter from Dyer in the July 1976 issue in which Dyer described an Indigenous child welfare crisis in Australia mirroring that experienced by American Indians. "It has generally been assumed that the Aboriginal parents are not capable of caring adequately for their little ones," Dyer explained, "so the children have been fostered out to white families, and in some cases even adopted without the consent of their mothers." Dyer cited a 90 percent breakdown in these placements and noted that white families often returned the children to the care of the Social Welfare Department, which placed them in institutions. Dyer lamented that these children "have become 'lost' to us" in many cases. Her organization tried to help the children reunite with their families, but often the children could not relate to their Aboriginality after years of hearing disparagement of Aboriginal people in popular culture, schools, and from their foster or adoptive families. One girl told Dyer that "her foster mother kept a scrap book about all the terrible things that Aboriginal people do and would cut out extracts from the press and paste them in the book. She would have to read this book of cuttings at least once a month to make sure she realized 'how lucky she was to have been given a chance to live in a white family and be saved.'"[3] Dyer's letter signaled that the American Indian child welfare crisis was not restricted to North America but was a phenomenon of global proportions.

Dyer, aged forty-eight in 1975, had applied for an Aboriginal Overseas Study Award prior to the publication of her letter in *Indian Family Defense*. She wanted "to try and discover how to overcome the problem" of the overrepresentation of Aboriginal children in the child welfare system, and she wrote to Unger at the AAIA "for guidance . . . in relation to courses and work situations I could be involved in during my stay in America if my application is successful."[4] Having won the award, Dyer traveled extensively in Canada and the United States in 1976. She attended a three-week course at the newly minted Saskatchewan Indian Federated College in Prince Albert, the community that was reeling from the Doucette case. Later she spent a whirlwind day with Unger and Bert Hirsch in New York City and toured reservations and Indian communities in the United States that had developed their own Indian child welfare programs. Her most successful connection occurred on the last leg of her trip, when she stayed with Maxine Robbins, founder of the innovative Ku-Nak-We-Sha program on the Yakima Reservation. "After my long journey, it was here, at the end of it, that I would find the program that I had been searching for," wrote Dyer.[5]

Dyer's trans-Pacific correspondence and tour of Canada and the United States heralded the beginning of a significant transnational movement regarding Indigenous child welfare. Dyer invited Robbins to attend a conference in Melbourne in October 1978 to help push for greater Aboriginal control over Aboriginal child welfare. She brought both Robbins and Unger to speak at a special Aboriginal child welfare seminar in April 1979, just six months after the passage of the Indian Child Welfare Act in the United States. At the close of the seminar the Aboriginal delegates passed a resolution calling for "all states to enact Aboriginal child welfare legislation (similar to the Indian Child Welfare Act USA)."[6]

Dyer's story illuminates another facet of the Indigenous child welfare crises in the United States and Canada: thousands of miles from North America, across a vast ocean, Australia, too had developed its own Indigenous child welfare crisis at the very same time.[7] Aboriginal activists, particularly women such as Dyer, awoke to this crisis in the late 1960s and challenged it head-on in the 1970s. Their activism became a key means of shaping the broader Indigenous rights movement in Australia, articulating the true meaning of self-determination and countering liberal narratives that cast Indigenous children as victims in need of rescue. Indigenous activists discovered that the loss of their children was a common experience across national borders and immense distances, and they also found inspiration and support in significant transnational connections and exchanges.

The administration of Aboriginal affairs was left to the states in Australia, not the federal government as in Canada and the United States. Australian states also took responsibility for child welfare, similar to Canada and the United States. This might have led to identical treatment of Indigenous and settler children under the law, but in the late nineteenth and early twentieth centuries, every Australian state (except Tasmania) created a separate child welfare system for Aborigines that gave the state and its ministers unprecedented powers over Aboriginal families. State authorities became legal guardians over *all* Aboriginal children.[8]

Policies toward Aboriginal people before World War II varied from state to state. Queensland, for example, advocated "protection" for all people of Aboriginal descent, segregating Aboriginal families from the general population on reserves and missions. New South Wales (NSW), by contrast, implemented a two-pronged policy of isolating "full-blood" Aboriginal people, while dispersing and "absorbing" part-Aboriginal people into the general population. In all cases, authorities supported the removal of most Indigenous children, particularly part-Aboriginal children, from their families and communities to institutions. These special homes and missions trained Aboriginal children to be "useful," a phrase that connoted the instruction of young Aboriginals in unskilled labor such as domestic service and cattle wrangling.[9] Authorities had been separating Indigenous children from their families for generations by the second half of the twentieth century, as in the United States and Canada.

After World War II, authorities in Australia made a new plea for equal treatment of Indigenous peoples on the basis of liberalism, similar to developments in North America. Paul Hasluck, who became Australian minister for territories (responsible for Aboriginal affairs in the Northern Territory and Papua New Guinea) from 1951 to 1963, epitomized this new ethos. "We rejected the idea that race . . . made any difference between human beings," he asserted. "We tried to think of the Aborigines as we thought of ourselves, not as another race but as fellow Australians." Hasluck and other state ministers advocated the creation of one system of child welfare that would cover all children.[10]

Other parallels with the United States and Canada abounded. Officials now believed that it was better to place removed Indigenous children in foster and adoptive families rather than institutions. In New South Wales the Aborigines Protection Board had been removing and placing Aboriginal children in institutions since the turn of the twentieth century.[11] Its successor, the Aborigines Welfare Board, took over in 1940 and "launched a drive" in 1955 to find homes for 150 aboriginal children in its care, ranging from "babes in arms to boy and girls in their teens." According to the NSW director of Aboriginal welfare, H. Saxby, "We have several fine institutions where we care for aborigines who are orphans or whose parents cannot look after them adequately. But no institution can give a child the security, love and happiness of a good home. We have power under the Aborigines Protection Act to board out these children in selected foster homes. We are planning now to take full advantage of it. Our policy for the aboriginal has always been one of assimilation. What better way could there be of achieving this than to have young aborigines brought up in white homes?"[12]

Similar trends occurred in other states and territories as well. The Northern Territory saw a dramatic increase in the numbers of Aboriginal children placed in foster care from 1952 to 1971. Its foster care program reported that the percentages of various groups in foster care in 1971 were 24 percent full-Aboriginal descent, 73 percent part-Aboriginal, and 3 percent

European. Northern Territory child welfare authorities placed most part-Aboriginal children with white foster families while they sought Aboriginal families for children of full descent. The 1971 report shows the persistence of concern with "blood" despite new color-blind rhetoric.[13] The Western Australia Department of Native Affairs set up its own adoption and fostering programs in 1951. According to the historian Anna Haebich, they "printed appealing photographs of beautiful Aboriginal babies safe with their new white mothers, often juxtaposed with stories of Aboriginal parental neglect," not unlike the Indian Adoption Project in the United States and the Adopt Indian Métis program in Saskatchewan. Authorities in Queensland asserted in 1959 that "'near white children' should have 'the opportunity of entering into the white community as white girls and boys,'" and they "sought out prospective carers through advertising and media 'feel good' stories."[14]

Authorities still relied on a parallel system of institutionalization for Aboriginal children, however, as in the United States and Canada. Not until 1969 did officials in NSW close the Cootamundra home for Aboriginal girls (to which Mollie Dyer's mother Margaret Tucker had been removed) and the Kinchela Home for Aboriginal boys.[15] Queensland continued until 1965 to institutionalize Aboriginal children under the Aboriginal Preservation and Protection Act of 1939, which gave the director of the Department of Aboriginal Affairs (DAA) legal guardianship over Aboriginal children under the age of twenty-one.[16]

Each separate state Aboriginal agency in Australia took steps to divest itself of responsibility for Aboriginal child welfare and transfer this to mainstream state social service agencies after World War II, just as the Bureau of Indian Affairs in the United States and the Department of Indian Affairs in Canada sought to turn over responsibility for Indigenous child welfare to the states and provinces. New South Wales replaced its parallel white and Aboriginal child welfare systems with a single child welfare system in 1969.[17] The Queensland Department of Family and Child Services ostensibly took over responsibility for Aboriginal child welfare in 1970, but they still held overlapping authority with the state department of Aboriginal Affairs until 1984.[18]

As in the United States and Canada, this transition to new authority for Indigenous children created a bureaucratic muddle that often had dire consequences for Indigenous people. Haebich notes that in Western Australia, "The Department of Child Welfare . . . had to negotiate [with the Department of Aboriginal Affairs] over a twenty-year period from 1951 before it took full control of Aboriginal child welfare. This resulted in a period of parallel and sometimes competing services. With great surveillance of Aboriginal families and the facilities of *two* departments now available for child placements, removals began to escalate."[19]

New schemes for fostering and adoption gained popularity in part because of trends in Australia that mirrored those in Canada and the United States. Shifting gender roles and sexual norms in the 1960s and 1970s constricted the supply of so-called blue-ribbon babies available for adoption at the same time as state policies brought increasing numbers of Indigenous children into state child welfare systems. Officials told the Miller family of Bondi in NSW that they would have to wait years to adopt a baby in Australia. However, when they were in Queensland, they "'approached the Native Affairs Department and within two months the department had found [a twenty-one-month-old Aboriginal girl] and turned the adoption papers over to the State Children's Department."[20] Other would-be adopters also were able to obtain Aboriginal children easily with virtually no red tape. A British migrant couple who had taken in two other Aboriginal children simply "visited an aborigines' home and returned with 14-day-old Jonathan, son of a 13-year-old Aboriginal girl." "For people who have mildly raised their eyebrows," the couple responded, "'there is always a waiting list for white babies.'"[21]

Both religious and liberal motivations inspired white families to adopt Aboriginal children. The Matthews family were Baptist missionaries with six biological children. They spent seven years in Queensland and the Northern Territory. When they left the mission field and settled in Morwell, Victoria, they brought an eleven-year-old Aboriginal girl with them and later took in a three-year-old Aboriginal foster child. Mrs. Matthews said she "was prompted to foster aborigine children because she was a Christian and she felt white children could readily be adopted but few people were willing to take a dark child as their own."[22] A Melbourne policeman and his wife who adopted an Aboriginal girl in 1965 asserted, "We had always wanted to help the Aboriginal people, to give them the chance of leading a better life."[23] South Australian Aboriginal activist Brian

Butler observed that in his experience, "many who adopt have their own biological children but feel called to do more," which might "well have a basis in religious beliefs or in the desire to help solve what the media glibly calls 'the Aboriginal problem.'"[24] Many other Australian families who adopted Aboriginal children were recent migrants to the country; they hailed from the Netherlands, England, Yugoslavia, and other European countries.[25] Perhaps such couples sought to adopt an Aboriginal child as a means of becoming more fully Australian, of gaining a sense of belonging to their new country.[26]

We can track the new concern with Indigenous children through a distinctive Australian institution, the Harold Blair Aboriginal Children's Project and its Holiday Scheme. Authorities had removed Harold Blair as a child from his Aboriginal family and placed him in a mission in Queensland. Blair eventually obtained formal music training in Melbourne and became a well-known singer. He co-founded the Blair Project with Mrs. Pettit, whom he had met when performing in *Uncle Tom's Cabin* in Melbourne. Each year Blair's project brought seventy to eighty children from the north, primarily Queensland, to spend their holidays with white families in Victoria. Eventually the project expanded to all other states, and it placed more than two thousand children with white urban families from 1962 to 1974.[27]

Authorities, host families, and journalists all presented the Blair Project as one key means of giving Aboriginal children a chance in life. "It is not the holiday ... which is so important, it is the effect on their personalities," a reporter noted. "The children go to some wonderful families who give them a new outlook on what must seem like a pretty crummy future. These are mission children and for most there is little hope after leaving the mission. The holidays can give them an incentive to escape the dead-end of adulthood in Alice Springs."[28] Their rhetoric is nearly identical to that of the IAP's director Arnold Lyslo in the United States, who captioned a photo of an Indian toddler: "Dead end—or a chance?" They configured Aboriginal communities as hopeless dead-ends and children's holiday placements as benevolent rescue that exposed Indigenous children to new possibilities.

The Blair Project also led directly to the adoption of Aboriginal children. The Frith family of Victoria hosted Charity Carbine, an Aboriginal girl, for a holiday in 1964. "We very quickly grew to love her and before the holiday was over we wanted to adopt her," Mrs. Frith told a reporter. The Friths claimed that Carbine was an orphan, a common justification for removal and placement that ignored the importance of extended family relationships. Authorities flew her from Woorabinda in central Queensland, where she had lived the first nine years of her life, to live with the Friths. "No one in the world needs more help now than these little aboriginal children," Mrs. Frith said.[29] By increasing the demand for Aboriginal children, the holiday scheme contributed to the increase in fostering and adoption of Aboriginal children.

Non-Aboriginal adoption of Aboriginal children had become fashionable, it seems, by the late 1960s. The Aboriginal poet Kath Walker created a stir in 1967 when she asserted, "I come up against women all the time who ask me how they go about adopting 'a black baby.' It seems to be the done thing today to want to adopt an aboriginal baby. It's a status symbol." Mrs. Pettit, co-founder of the Harold Blair project, agreed that "the publicity given to the problems of aboriginals today and the people—the academics and intellectuals—who are fighting for them, have made adoptions of aboriginal children—not only babies—the 'in' thing."[30]

This desire to adopt Aboriginal children had much to do with configurations of Indigenous communities and families as hopelessly dysfunctional and Aboriginal children as unwanted, abandoned, and neglected. In regard to the placement of some forty Aboriginal children from NSW, a reporter asserted that "the children have an unhappy history of broken homes and forgotten parents."[31] A letter to the editor claimed that they were "in the main unwanted children."[32] Saxby called them "little outcast children."[33] A couple in South Australia "decided to adopt an aboriginal baby because aboriginal orphans were the most unwanted ones in the community."[34] Reports of adoption, with titles such as "From Lean-to to Luxury" and "The Aboriginal Cinderella," focused on the material aspects of what adoptive families could offer these allegedly unwanted children. A Queensland couple became foster parents to a five-year-old Aboriginal girl in order to "give her a loving home background, a wardrobe of pretty clothes—and an education to fit her to compete for a worthwhile job in later life."[35] Such sentiments echoed those of authorities and white adopters in the United States and Canada who regularly alluded to "forgotten" Indigenous children.

There was a self-congratulatory aspect to white adoption of Indigenous children, a sense of national color-blind triumph. Dozens of white families responded positively to an advertisement for 150 Aboriginal children in the 1950s in NSW. A reporter concluded: "The warm-hearted response to the plight of these children seems to illustrate the point that the color bar does not exist in Australia. It seems that in helping our aboriginals we have helped ourselves."[36] Only decades later during the Stolen Generations inquiry in the 1990s would white Australians realize just how devastatingly discriminatory such practices really were.

These families confidently breached the color line, but they had to grapple with the broader society's attitudes toward Aboriginal people. Some adopters simply denied that their children experienced any prejudice whatsoever. Mrs. Schulz of Adelaide declared proudly in a letter to the editor, "Our aboriginal son has been at school for 18 months, and it is no problem to him that he is 'different.' . . . Neighbors and teachers have gone out of their way to be helpful."[37] Others, however, acknowledged that many of their neighbors displayed blatant racism upon encountering adopted children. The Manclarks in Western Australia, an English couple with three older biological children, had adopted two Aboriginal babies. Peers of their older children taunted them, "You mean that nigger's your brother?" And a delivery boy asked, "You're not bringing another dirty Aborigine into this house?" A friend of the husband's quipped, "It's all very well, he's cute now. But wait until he grows up. I wouldn't have an Aboriginal in my house." The Manclarks and other families dismissed such prejudice as a trivial matter that would have little impact on their family. One Manclark son, aged fourteen, declared, "Whatever skin colour people have it does not matter. I would like to see the colour bar dropped."[38] Such colorblindness would prove to be easier for white families to profess than for Aboriginal adoptees to realize on a daily basis.

Some authorities now deemphasized the racial basis for removing Aboriginal children and supported in theory the notion that Aboriginal children should stay with their families, if at all possible. Stanley Middleton, who took up the position of commissioner for native affairs in Western Australia in 1948, asserted that the "need to split families no longer exists when better living accommodation and conditions have been provided or obtained. The retention of the family unit . . . [is] considered to be preferable [to] the best institutions available."[39] Ironically, however, Aboriginal child removals actually increased under Middleton's watch. Haebich found that "removals more than doubled from 151 in 1957 to 379 in 1960." The number of "coloured" children "committed to the care of the Child Welfare Department increased from nine in 1955 to 161 in 1963, making up 6 per cent of state children in care."[40] Now authorities justified removal on other standards than race. They lionized the nuclear family, as in the United States and Canada, and demonized extended family care arrangements that were common among Indigenous people. And the economic distress of most Aboriginal families and communities, due to longstanding government policies and settler discrimination, made it difficult for Aboriginal families to live up to the material standards that social welfare authorities thought were necessary to children's well-being. Middleton, in fact, supported the removal of Aboriginal children who were "living under unsatisfactory circumstances."[41]

Concerns with race and the desire to assimilate Indigenous peoples remained an underlying issue that lurked not far below the color-blind concern with the "best interests of the child." Australians continued to be haunted by earlier racial categories that divided Indigenous people into "full-bloods" versus "half-castes," now more sensitively called part-Aboriginal children. The NSW 1955 campaign to promote the fostering and adoption of Aboriginal children, according to a reporter, "emphasized the point that the Australian aboriginal is one of the few native races which does not have any 'throw-backs' after inter-marriage. The white blood always predominates, and after marriage into white families the next generation is always a lighter color, so that the assimilation of the aboriginal is purely a matter of time."[42] These notions persisted into the 1960s and 1970s. Mrs. R. P. Hoffmann, an adoptive mother in Adelaide who had taken in two Aboriginal children, told a reporter in 1966 that the reason more people had been accepting "half-caste" children as little different from their own was "'because by the third generation all traces of aboriginal features are gone. . . . It is really our responsibility to see that we accept half-castes, and treat them equally. . . . My husband and I firmly believe that this is the only way to successfully assimilate aborigines.'"[43] As one researcher found in the 1970s, "In Victoria, where few Aboriginals today are genetically 'fullblood' Aboriginals, there is controversy over whether part-Aboriginal children should be brought up 'as white,' or as Aboriginals, or in contact with both Aboriginal and non-Aboriginal cultures."[44] Color-blind rhetoric thinly masked a persistent concern with race and color in Australia.

While authorities promoted a liberal assimilationist agenda, Aboriginal activists and their non-Aboriginal allies developed a self-determination movement akin to that of Indigenous people in the United States and Canada. This movement had its roots in the pre–World War II era, when in 1939, people from the Aboriginal community of Cumeroogunga on the NSW side of the Murray River walked off the reserve and crossed the river to Victoria. Cumeroogunga's residents had created a thriving, largely self-sufficient community by 1908 through raising wheat and other crops on small family blocks, while pursuing seasonal labor nearby. Cumeroogunga's Aboriginal residents seemed to be models of assimilation, but the Aborigines Protection Board instituted policies that undermined the community's self-sufficiency. They took back the men's rights to use the land and leased it to local white farmers instead. They promoted a policy of "dispersal," whereby authorities forced so-called half-castes to leave reserves and missions to earn their living among the settler population. Dispersal required, too, the removal of children to institutions, where they were to be trained to be useful. The Aborigines Protection Board's forcible seizures of Aboriginal family farm blocks from 1915 to 1919 naturally led to resentment on the part of Aboriginal families, some of whom openly resisted the policy. Many families fled across the river, or were "dispersed," and by 1925, the once-thriving population of Cumeroogunga had decreased from 400 to 147. Across the river in Victoria, a Cumeroogunga exile, William Cooper, organized the Australian Aborigines' League (AAL) in the 1930s. Other former residents served as vice presidents of the league: Doug Nicholls and Margaret Tucker, Mollie Dyer's mother. Together they pressed for a return of land that would help restore their independence, culminating in a high-profile Day of Mourning on Australia Day, 1938, a day other Australians celebrated as the sesquicentenary of Australia's founding.[45]

The Great Depression of the 1930s conspired against the AAL's vision, however, as widespread unemployment and racial discrimination dampened any possibility that Aboriginal people might regain their land allotments. Under pressure from settlers who no longer needed Aboriginal labor, the board reversed its dispersal policy and now forced Aboriginal people, including so-called half-castes, back to supervised reserves. Aboriginal people had to comply if they hoped to obtain rations or any other economic relief. Reserves such as Cumeroogunga suffered from overcrowding, poor sanitation, and extreme poverty as well as the newly enhanced dictatorial powers of the board against Aboriginal people. The threat of renewed forcible removal of children caused particular alarm and consternation. Local residents petitioned officials and sought the help of the AAL. The AAL joined with the Aborigines Progressive Association, established in 1937 by three NSW Aboriginal activists, to protest these conditions vigorously. They rallied community residents to walk off (or actually row off) the reserve by crossing the river. An estimated one hundred residents left the reserve during one week in February 1939. The AAL and the Aborigines Progressive Association gained the support of some left-wing individuals and organizations in Melbourne, and in unison they called for an inquiry by the NSW government. Nine months later, as a core group of Aboriginal activists remained camped across the river, the NSW administration still refused to hold an inquiry, while the Victorian government cut off support to the protesters. Protesters failed to obtain concessions, but some, such as Margaret Tucker's mother Theresa Clements, remembered the walk-off as a means of restoring their dignity.[46]

The Aboriginal rights movement in Victoria and elsewhere around the continent revived after World War II. Doug Nicholls of the AAL, trade unionists, and the Communist Party of Australia held a public protest meeting in Melbourne in 1951, which led to the formation of a new multiracial and nationally focused organization called the Council for Aboriginal Rights (CAR). The group sought to bring Aboriginal affairs under the federal government rather than the states and to enact a uniform federal policy for Aborigines. Nicholls and Tucker served on the executive board of CAR throughout the 1950s; by the late 1950s, they had founded the Victorian Aborigines Advancement League. These and several other organizations convened a conference in 1958, which led to yet another organization—the Federal Council for Aboriginal Advancement.[47] This group headed the campaign for a 1967 referendum that asked Australian voters "whether Aborigines should be granted the same rights as other

Australians, [ir]respective of race." The passage of this referendum eliminated a racially discriminatory clause from the constitution and provided for the counting of Aboriginal people for the first time in the nation's census. Many observers heralded the referendum as a grand change, but it mostly concerned what historian Bain Attwood calls "mundane" changes in Australia's constitution, while failing to embrace new policies that would grant Aboriginal people full citizenship, equal rights, or sovereignty.[48]

The campaign for the referendum energized a new generation of Aboriginal activists, who in the 1960s and 1970s increasingly sought to form and take control of their own organizations, to assert Aboriginality and "black power," and to challenge assimilation.[49] Such activism eventually had an impact. The federal government funded a number of new Aboriginal agencies, including the Aboriginal Legal Service and the Aboriginal Health Service. A new Labour government, led by Gough Whitlam, took power briefly in 1972 and ended the policy of assimilation. Whitlam emphasized "community self-government" and development through the establishment of Aboriginal land councils in the Northern Territory, a "type of parallel government for Aboriginal peoples residing on reserves."[50] A Liberal Party administration (which in Australian terms was conservative) took over in 1975, and promptly defunded the Aboriginal Health Service, but the Aboriginal self-determination movement could not be re-contained.[51]

As the daughter of Margaret Tucker, Mollie Dyer grew up with the Aboriginal rights movement and would become an activist in her own right. She proved central to integrating Indigenous child welfare into the Aboriginal self-determination movement. The specter of involuntary Indigenous child removal had haunted Dyer from a young age. She told a reporter in 1979 that "all her life she remembers seeing Aboriginal mothers fretting for children who had been removed from their care."[52] It was also a deeply personal issue that had affected her own family. Authorities had brutally removed her mother, Margaret Tucker, and aunt from their family and placed them in the Cootamundra girls home in the early twentieth century. When Dyer first contacted Steven Unger at the AAIA in the United States, Tucker was working on her memoir, *If Everyone Cared*. The book reached a wide non-Indigenous audience when it was published in 1977. Many Australians became aware for the first time of the widespread practice of Aboriginal child removal that had gone on since the late nineteenth century.

Dyer was not removed involuntarily from her mother, but her own family background also reflected some of the experiences of removed children. When her mother separated from her white father, Dyer lived with her paternal white grandparents. Unlike children who had been removed, however, Dyer frequently saw her mother and members of the Aboriginal community. Her grandparents, in fact, insisted that "she spent equally as much time with her mother's aboriginal family as she spent with them." Dyer's family sent her to boarding school at age nine, where she would experience some of the same loneliness of the Stolen Generations of Aboriginal children who had been involuntarily institutionalized. Dyer's situation was qualitatively different, however, as her family freely chose this experience.[53]

Dyer inherited her mother's activist fervor and determination. She began her community work with Nicholls in the AAL in Victoria and later spent five years as a field officer with the Aboriginal Legal Service. She also carried on Aboriginal ways of caring. Dyer began fostering Aboriginal children alongside her own six children beginning in 1959. Social welfare authorities had separated many of these children from their families and put them in white homes, but their placements had broken down.[54] Jenny Munro, an Aboriginal activist in Victoria, considered Dyer's eventual fostering of twenty-five Aboriginal children as the "grandmother law coming out in Mollie without her even realising." Munro explains,

> Every child that presented, they were hers. It didn't matter whose child they were. She looked after them. My grandmother was the same and she looked after my auntie's kids, looked after my uncle's kids.... Those old girls in the 70s and 80s. Didn't even know it then, but we were articulating it—the old law, the old way, the old system. The extended family. The way we looked after our own family was the way that we would survive, not the way these white people wanted us to be confined into their squares or circles.[55]

While working with the Aboriginal Legal Service, Dyer became aware that her personal care work reflected a much greater crisis in Indigenous

Fig. 13. Mollie Dyer with May Walker and Robbie Dyer, two of her foster children, ca. 1979. Courtesy and permission of Diane Singh.

child care. She witnessed "young Aboriginal mothers living in hopelessness and poverty [who] often give their children to white families in the belief that when they themselves are in a better position, the children will be given back. Experience indicates that the children are seldom reunited at an early age with their natural mother; they grow into teenagers who often cannot relate to either the Aboriginal community or the non-Aboriginal community."[56]

Dyer parlayed her personal and professional experience into a distinctive activist role and put Aboriginal child welfare on the agenda of the self-determination movement. She observed that "there are not many Aboriginal people in Australia who concentrate solely on the problems of children and families." Most worked on issues affecting adults such as "health services, legal services, education programs, land rights, alcohol rehab centres, etc." "I seem to have been the only person to concentrate solely on issues concerning children and the family, so whilst it is far from the truth, I seem to be considered an 'expert' in the field," Dyer recounted.[57] As she carried out this work, Dyer articulated an Indigenous feminist ideal centered around Indigenous women's esteemed caring roles.

Whether intentional or not, the title of Dyer's autobiography, *Room for One More*, seems to challenge the Virginia Woolf book that became so central to white feminists' visions in the 1970s and 1980s: *A Room of One's Own*.

As Dyer had, Aboriginal women in other locales organized around their own vision of feminism. In Redfern, a suburb in Sydney that was home to many urban Aboriginal people, a dynamic group of women founded Murawina (meaning "black woman") in 1972 to provide services for Aboriginal women and children in the city; the founders included Norma Williams, Naomi Mayers, Pam Hunter, Lyn Thompson, Bobbi Sykes, and Sandra McGuinness. As one reporter put it, "The women of Redfern are battlers—they have had to be. First they decided that their children and those of other poor families should have breakfast in their stomachs to give them a fair chance of getting through the day when they went to school. Then they saw the pressing need to keep the little children off the streets, help the working mothers, give them a place to meet and learn about their Aboriginal culture and heritage." They established a preschool for Aboriginal children and by 1979 had obtained funds to buy a building for their preschool and a hostel for Aboriginal women.[58]

Some Aboriginal activists and their allies spoke out against the fostering and adoption of Indigenous children in the 1960s. Doris Blackburn, a white ally who had been president of the AAL and was an independent Labour Party parliamentarian, forcefully declared her opposition to the practice. When she addressed the Traralgon Presbyterian Women's Mission Union in 1966, "a member asked her opinion on whether the children should be taken away from their parents and 'given a chance.'" Blackburn responded that "taking aboriginal children away from their parents was *not* the answer to smoother assimilation," and that "problems could not be solved by taking the children away."[59] Blackburn's colleague Stan Davey, another non-Indigenous activist, who was president of the AAL in Victoria after Blackburn, wrote a letter to the editor of a Melbourne newspaper the following year regarding the many Aboriginal children who had been brought from Queensland and the Northern Territory "to be fostered by well-meaning, sincere European-Australian families." "Spurred on by being able to do something positive for an aboriginal child as a contribution to solving 'the aboriginal problem,'" he wrote, "few appear to have considered the consequences of the child's loss of identity with his own people."

Davey pointed out the need for proper research on the long-term consequences of this scheme before bringing more children. In the meantime, he argued, "Victorians who are really concerned for these children should rather channel their energies into having the Queensland and Northern Territory authorities change their racially-destructive policies to enable aboriginal communities to repossess and care for their own children."[60]

A campaign against the placement of Indigenous children in non-Indigenous homes did not develop fully until the 1970s, in concert with the Indigenous self-determination movement. Activists discovered the Aboriginal child welfare crisis while working on other pressing concerns. Dyer, while employed with the newly established Aboriginal Legal Service in Melbourne, became concerned with the number of juvenile offenders who had been in the child welfare system. She called for a formal investigation of the rates of removal in her home state of Victoria in the mid-1970s. Her efforts led to a report by Christine Watson showing that in Victoria in August 1974, 323 or 9.6 percent of all Aboriginal children were wards of the state; this was sixteen to twenty times higher than for non-Aboriginal children, who were only 0.5 percent of those in care. Two thirds of these Aboriginal wards were in children's homes; many had been there at least five years.[61] A few years later Gabrielle Schneeman, a Melbourne student who worked with Dyer, found that Aboriginal children made up less than 1 percent of Victoria's population but were placed in foster care or adoptive homes at twenty-six times the rate of non-Aboriginal children.[62]

Activists and scholars in other Australian states found similar high levels of removal. Authorities had removed an estimated 30–40 percent of Aboriginal children in Queensland from 1939 to 1965, most of them to be institutionalized.[63] One out of every three Aboriginal families in Western Australia in the mid-1970s had a child under notice of the Department of Child Welfare, compared with one of every thirty-four white families. In NSW at least 20 percent of Aboriginal children were under state welfare control in the late 1970s. More than 25 percent of Aboriginal children in the Northern Territory had been separated from their families.[64] In South Australia one in six Aboriginal children were wards of the state in the 1970s.[65] These were deeply disturbing statistics proving that Aboriginal children were suffering from a crisis just as devastating as that experienced by Indigenous children in the United States and Canada.

Gathering statistics was only the first step in addressing the crisis. Once aware of the scope of the problem, activists then sought to understand and critique the practice of Aboriginal child removal. They discovered that Australian social workers and police officers seldom removed Aboriginal children on the grounds of physical abuse but instead used the basis of neglect. Researcher Christine Watson found that in Victoria virtually all Aboriginal children came into state care involuntarily through apprehension by a police officer followed by a court hearing. Bases for apprehending children included some well-defined conditions of neglect: the child was found begging, wandering, abandoned, or sleeping in a public place; "no visible means of support and no settled home"; living with or in company with vagrants or criminals; "is ill treated or exposed"; and "employed in street trading." Other bases for removal seem more value-laden, however: "not sufficiently provided for"; "is involved in physically dangerous entertainment"; "is under unfit guardianship"; "is likely to lapse into violence or crime"; and "is exposed to moral danger." These vague criteria gave social workers and police wide latitude to apprehend Aboriginal children.[66]

Dyer and others argued that these ill-defined standards of neglect often betrayed a cultural bias against Aboriginal families. Authorities might remove children without good cause if they were in the care of an extended family member, Dyer charged, or if parents were deemed too permissive, although this might "simply be a different but effective way of disciplining children." Dyer also noted that authorities often removed a child if they regarded a family as too impoverished.[67]

Many Aboriginal people lost their children as a result of their own poor health. In one high-profile case, an Aboriginal couple had met and married while undergoing treatment at the leprosarium in Darwin and had had four children while institutionalized. Authorities baptized and removed each child at birth to the Bathurst Island Catholic Mission. When the couple were still suffering from leprosy, they conceded the wisdom of their children's removal, but in 1958, "when their disease ceased to be contagious and they returned to [the father's] tribal country at the Oenpelli Mission in western Arnhem Land," they immediately sought to regain custody of their children, now aged four, six, eight, and eleven. Authorities refused to return them, but the couple persisted, contacting authorities every six months for seven years. A Northern Territory judge in 1965 finally returned the children to the couple. When the couple sought to regain legal custody, however, the Northern Territory Supreme Court denied their request and returned the children to their foster parents, a Torres Strait Islander couple.[68] Higher rates of disease and lower life expectancies among Indigenous people in Australia, just as in the United States and Canada, could lead to a further indignity—the removal of their children.

Many activists found that social workers removed Aboriginal newborns or infants under suspicious circumstances, as in North America. Single Aboriginal women often faced intense scrutiny and pressure to give up their children when they went into a hospital to deliver a baby or for other health reasons. A nineteen-year-old Aboriginal mother, Jennifer Thomas, alleged that while she was ill and recuperating in the hospital in 1978, she had handed over her one-year-old son Richard to two women for temporary care. The women took Richard without Thomas's permission. A year later Thomas still had not heard from the women or Richard, now two years old. Dyer got involved in the case and made allegations of baby stealing, which led to a police investigation. Police traced Richard to Brisbane, in Queensland, and eventually returned him to his mother.[69]

Richard Thomas's case inspired other Aboriginal mothers in Victoria to come forward with charges of involuntary child removal. This led to a police investigation that involved the removal from a foster home of seven Aboriginal children who had allegedly been taken from their mothers without proper court procedures. An Aboriginal activist from the Bairnsdale Aboriginal community, Nessie Scooter, also prepared a report citing "examples of Aboriginal babies allegedly taken from their mothers for extended periods without proper permission." Scooter charged that the people who took the children had scouts out in the Gippsland area to check on which Aboriginal girls became pregnant. "They try to get the children as young as possible. Something will have to be done to blow the top off this situation," she told a reporter.[70]

Dyer and other activists found that lack of due legal process led to increased rates of removal of Aboriginal children. They documented the informal removal of Aboriginal children by "well meaning people" and their informal placement with foster families. Some non-Aboriginal people simply took children "for a holiday" and never returned them. "When parents request the return of their children, some cannot be traced," Dyer's agency noted. It added that "some of these children have even been taken Interstate and may never again be seen by their families."[71]

One particular case is so egregious that it seems like the plot of a B-movie. Kathleen Trimmer, a twenty-five-year-old Aboriginal mother studying to be a nurse's aide in Perth, allowed her two-year-old son, Barry, to go on a holiday to Victoria in 1963 with one of her friends, a white woman who worked at a nearby school and offered to "'to give his mother a rest.'" The white woman disappeared with Barry, and police had no success in tracking them. With the help of news reporters, however, the determined Trimmer found her son living in a Sydney suburb with the white woman. According to a reporter, the white kidnapper "declared that she would never send Barry back. . . . 'I want him to grow up as a human being, not as a shabbily-treated native,' she said." Although Trimmer reported the whereabouts of her son to police, the kidnapper took Barry out of Australia on a family passport under a false name. Trimmer was bitter. "I can't get it out of my head that if a white woman had disclosed publicly what I did nearly 14 months ago . . . it would have become a serious police matter straight away," she asserted. "When the authorities had so much warning, it's hard to understand how Barry could have been sneaked out of Australia so easily."[72] Eventually, as a result of press reports (but not a police investigation), a relative of the kidnapper came forward to reveal that she had received a letter from the white woman, now in East Germany. Another white woman had taken Barry to Cuba when it became clear that East Germany did not welcome the little boy. The kidnapper's relative agreed with Trimmer's assessment of the police. "They don't seem to regard Barry—or his mother—as humans of any importance. . . . If she and Barry had been white, this thing *couldn't* have happened."[73] Activists expressed outrage at such blatant indifference to Aboriginal families.

They also sought to expose the devastating consequences of such removal for adoptees as well as their families and communities of origin. Activists became particularly concerned with the high rates of adoption placement breakdowns, a situation in which adoptive families decided to "return" children before formally adopting them. Christine Watson noted the case of "Cheryl," adopted at age of two by a white couple who, in their words, wanted "'a handicapped or Aboriginal child or something.'" The parents encouraged Cheryl to be a "beautiful doll-like creature," and she acted the part until adolescence, when she got interested in boys. As she became "more difficult to handle," in the parents' view, they tried placing her in boarding school and factory work. According to Watson, the parents "began to resent the money they had spent on Cheryl who did not now 'have their standards.' Cheryl became more Aboriginal in their eyes." The family contacted some Aboriginal organizations to see if they could help, but infrequent contact with Aboriginal people did not resolve the problem. The parents "decided Cheryl was uncontrollable, and allowed Police to bring a Protection Application against her." The Aboriginal Legal Service defended Cheryl, and she was put on twelve months' probation and returned to her adoptive parents, since "they were the only ones with any close contact with her," and they were willing to take her back.[74] Interestingly, white adoptive families seem to have had a great deal of choice in their dealings with child welfare authorities. Cheryl's adoptive parents could *allow* a protection order to be made and choose whether to maintain custody, whereas Aboriginal parents often had little say in the matter.

Cheryl's case, unfortunately, was not unique. Many Aboriginal adoptees became "difficult to handle," according to their adoptive parents, when they reached adolescence. Dyer developed an extended analysis of the phenomenon: "An Aboriginal child raised without an understanding of his roots and without association with Aboriginal people, is most likely to suffer an identity crisis in adolescence," she told a reporter. "That is when society throws his aboriginality up in his face," she relayed. "It is misguided and unrealistic to think that because [children] have been raised in the white way they can survive in the white world,'" she added. Dyer continued, "'Most of the kids who break down in placements come from families where there was a very negative attitude about Aborigines— they were all supposed to be dirty, thieving drunks. The family considered they were saving their child from being one of the stereotypes." Dyer believed that "the family contributed to the child's confusion and sense of worthlessness. He had no defence when society reminded him that he belonged to the people his white family had so crushingly disparaged."[75] Aboriginal activists highlighted the high rates of adoption breakdown to show that removing Aboriginal children from their families and communities and placing them within white families was not truly in the children's best interests.

Such adoption breakdowns resulted in long-term problems not only for the adoptees but also for Australian society at large. Dyer observed many Aboriginal children who were "the product of the Social Welfare 'shuffle'" and who ended up in Children's Court for criminal offenses and accounted for high rates of adult Aboriginal incarceration.[76] Dyer and Watson both estimated that nine out of ten Aboriginal people seeking advice from the Aboriginal Legal Service agencies in Victoria and NSW had been in white foster homes or institutions as children.[77] Activists made the case that the placement of Aboriginal children in non-Aboriginal homes led to increased crime and other social ills.

Activists also sought to demonstrate how this practice of destroying Aboriginal families devastated Indigenous communities. "If one makes a cross study of a section of Aboriginal families," Dyer asserted, "it would soon become apparent that 'decimation' is the only appropriately descriptive word which sums up the results of one hundred years of European policy on Aboriginal families." Further, she added, "The lack of a sensitized policy on the part of housing, health, education and welfare authorities has resulted in nothing short of a total break-up, social dislocation and alienation of Aboriginal people."[78]

The Aboriginal self-determination movement and its critique of the removal of Aboriginal children rippled out to other non-Indigenous Australians, some of whom embraced and acted upon the message. A Northern Territory social worker named John Tomlinson, working in concert with the North Australian Aboriginal Legal Aid Service, "abducted" an Aboriginal girl, Nola Bambiaga, in 1973 from her white foster parents and returned her to her Aboriginal parents in an Arnhem Land tribal community. Tomlinson acted "against the opinions of those who argued that after six years in a white foster home, Nola was for all intents and purposes a white child." He "insisted that Nola's parents had complete legal rights to the child and saw it as his duty to 'abduct' Nola and return her to her natural parents." Authorities tried Tomlinson on five charges and the Northern Territory government demoted him. Other social workers went on strike in support of him, however, and he regained his position. According to writer Ken White, "the return of Nola outraged public opinion in the Territory," but it led the Community Welfare Division to phase out its exportation of Aboriginal children to the south to be fostered and adopted. Instead the

Northern Territory articulated a new, but often unimplemented, policy to place Aboriginal children only with Aboriginal families.[79]

Aboriginal activists no doubt appreciated an ally among white social workers, but like Indigenous activists in the United States and Canada, they hoped to develop Aboriginal-centric institutions that fully reclaimed care for Aboriginal children within Indigenous communities. Aboriginal community leaders such as Dyer and other representatives from Victoria, NSW, and the Northern Territory formed an Aboriginal Task Force at the first Australian Conference on Adoption, held in Sydney in February 1976. They made a forceful statement against the adoption of Aboriginal children by non-Aboriginal families, arguing that "any aboriginal child growing up in Australian society today will be confronted by racism. His best weapons against entrenched prejudice are a pride in his aboriginal identity and cultural heritage, and strong support from other members of the aboriginal community." Aboriginal representatives believed it was nearly impossible for Aboriginal children to develop their identity and pride in a non-Aboriginal family. They also argued that the placement of Aboriginal children should be the "sole prerogative of the aboriginal people." The entire conference endorsed the Aboriginal Task Force's resolution with only one dissension. One white observer at the conference noted, "Today, aborigines regard any attempt to assimilate them into white society as genocide." She added "The fear of cultural genocide stems from the increased racial pride among aborigines, and the belief that any dilution of identification will threaten their unity in the struggle against an oppressive society."[80]

Authorities took heed of activists' demands. The DAA adopted new policy guidelines on Aboriginal adoption and fostering not long after the conference, conceding that the removal of an Aboriginal child should be the "last resort," recommending more preventative services that would "encourage family and community self-management and self-sufficiency," and encouraging the fostering or adoption of Aboriginal children with Aboriginal parents.[81] Yet it would take many more years for state social workers to enact such initiatives fully. It was only through the ongoing pressure of Aboriginal activists that these new standards took hold.

Aboriginal activists in Sydney established the Aboriginal Children's Service after the 1976 Conference on Adoption, while those in Melbourne set up the Aboriginal Child Placement Agency (ACPA) to meet the needs of Aboriginal children. The impetus came from "the experience of the Aboriginal Legal Service and after unceasing requests from Social Workers from all over the State to help in finding alternatives and supports from within our community for Aboriginal children who were the victims of breakdown in non-Aboriginal adoption and foster care."[82] The establishment of these new Indigenous child welfare agencies represented an act of both self-determination and self-help.

The ACPA sought to gain control over Aboriginal child welfare and to strengthen Aboriginal families, primarily through making use of extended family networks. Aboriginal activists, like their counterparts in North America, emphasized the persistence of the extended family despite the assaults it had endured from settler colonial policies. The group noted that "in the traditional Aboriginal community our children were cared for by the combined efforts of a number of relatives. Traditional cultural values included an emphasis on the extended family as the basic unit, with responsibility for the welfare of each member of that extended family or tribe being shared by all." Colonization had decimated this family structure. The ACPA contended: "Removal polices, the establishment of Missions, a break-up of traditional family units into single housing and intervention by the State by means of Child Welfare legislation have the effect of superimposing a completely different sub-culture, a system of child care which was totally alien to our own traditional child welfare system." Still, Aboriginal childrearing ways had persisted. "The prevalent Aboriginal viewpoint is still that if a child is both well loved and well cared for the parents cannot justly be criticized for their poverty or non-material outlook," the ACPA insisted. Under these criteria incidences of neglect were minimal, yet "in Victoria a high proportion of our children have been removed from their families and placed elsewhere without the consent or the approval of our extended family unit."[83]

Dyer and other activists championed the Aboriginal extended family as a foundational strength of Aboriginal community life rather than an aberrant and substandard family arrangement, as non-Aboriginal social workers so often characterized it. The ACPA newsletter editor wrote in 1978, "We are attempting to normalize our living experiences within our own traditions and establishing ways of life to negate the pressures to adopt the private and competitive lifestyle of the non-Aboriginal." ACPA's basic principles and philosophy included "the re-affirmation of the Aboriginal extended family in the nurturing and caring of youth." The ACPA often had to fight against Social Welfare Department double standards, which deemed an Aboriginal family unfit to be a foster family because they had five children but allowed a non-Aboriginal family to foster eleven Aboriginal children.[84]

Dyer's agency also wanted to improve the existing situation of Aboriginal children in out-of-home care. A number of non-Aboriginal parents who had adopted Aboriginal children were alarmed by statements made by the Aboriginal Task Force at the first Conference on Adoption, and they asked to talk with Dyer. She was nervous about meeting them, but it led to the formation of an adoptive parents group that met regularly with ACPA to learn about the importance of Aboriginal heritage to their children. "This group has strengthened my belief that foster-parents and adoptive parents did not deliberately 'destroy' our children," Dyer wrote. "They did not understand the importance of reinforcing a positive identity in their culturally different child." Dyer saw foster and adoptive parents as "'victims' of a system over which they had little control." The ACPA and its successor organization regularly sponsored outings "where the families are able to interact socially with other Aboriginal people."[85]

Dyer acted as an important mediator between the Aboriginal self-determination movement and the white liberals she encountered through her child welfare work. White adoptive families asked her why Aboriginal people were now questioning the removal of their children. "I stated that prior to 20 years ago, we were heading fast towards assimilation," she recounted. "During the past 20 years, Aboriginal people have developed a stronger voice and are openly resenting programs and policies based on white criteria because that is not what we want. I said we felt it was to the advantage of white people to accept us as an important part of Australian history and culture—we were proud of that and had no intention of losing what little was left of our culture and in fact were in the process of learning more from our elders to enable us to bring back to life the culture we had almost lost." Dyer possessed an ability to express her views forcefully while still reaching out to non-Indigenous people.[86]

As Dyer worked with white liberals, she developed an analysis that challenged many of their assumptions. First she sought to humanize Indigenous people, whose lives were so often reduced to numerical data. In reference to Northern Territory statistics on Aboriginal child welfare, she wrote, "The figures supplied are in themselves horrific even on an objective or sterile statistical level. But for those of us who know the individuals behind those statistics, the experience is shattering."[87] It was important to Dyer and others to provide the crucial context for the litany of grim statistics so that non-Indigenous liberals would understand the true gravity of the situation Aboriginal people faced. She sought to counter liberal "plight" narratives through proposing a film "to highlight and analyse the situation and problems of Aboriginal children and their families in Victoria." She planned to film the children as they visited more traditional Aboriginal communities in the Northern Territory. Their visit to Alice Springs would include interviews with Aboriginal leaders and visits to Aboriginal communities but also depictions of the appalling conditions under which some Aboriginal people in the Northern Territory lived. Dyer wrote, "The film will show the difficulties of the Aboriginal people but also their strengths and dignity in the face of this, the positive aspects of their culture and lifestyle, and the growing trend toward Aboriginal identification and self-determination."[88] Non-Indigenous observers rarely portrayed the dignity and resilience that were the flip side of "plight."

Dyer also challenged the liberal notion that fostering and adopting Indigenous children was an act that benefited Indigenous people. A group of seven white families who had adopted Indigenous children in Melbourne told her, "We were concerned about the raw deal that Aboriginal people are getting so we decided to adopt an Aboriginal child to make sure that child would get a better deal." The group read Dyer's submission to the first Conference on Adoption and met with her personally. This changed their minds. "It seems now that what we considered with good intention can only create further problems for our child," they told Dyer.[89]

Activists such as Dyer were deeply committed to Indigenous child welfare, but they lacked funding to turn their ideals and commitments into a reality. Like the Saskatchewan Native Women's Movement that struggled to gain government support, Dyer found that the government of Victoria was largely indifferent to her funding applications, even as the Social Welfare Department continued to ask for her help in dealing with adoption breakdowns. She decided to apply for an Aboriginal Overseas

Study Award in 1976 so that she could learn from Canadian and American organizations about how to obtain greater financial backing for her child welfare work.

Through her trip to North America in 1976, Dyer set in motion transnational connections that became key to strengthening the Australian self-determination movement and its commitment to Aboriginal child welfare.[90] Dyer began her trans-Pacific tour in Ontario, Canada, where she visited a children's home near Kenora, met with the director of the Children's Aid Society, and consulted with the chiefs at the White Dog and White Fish reservations. She flew on to Saskatoon, where she enrolled in a three-week course of study on behavioral modification and "reality therapy" at Saskatchewan Indian Federated College's branch campus in Prince Albert. The other participants in the course, which was "designed by Indians for Indians," were at first suspicious of Dyer. They asked her to speak about her background and her purpose. A man in the audience then "came to the platform" after her explanation and "suggested that the students give a sister they never knew they had a warm Indian welcome."[91]

Dyer found many such kin in Saskatchewan: like-minded Indigenous activists and carers who were seeking ways to prevent their children from being institutionalized, fostered, and adopted. Dyer spent three weeks in Prince Albert and each day during lunch, a different group of students would invite her to sit with them. "We would discuss and compare what was happening in our communities," she recalled. Since many participants "were unaware of" Indigenous people in Australia, Dyer raised awareness among Canadian Indigneous people and also learned of the parallels between Aboriginal and First Nations and Métis child welfare.[92] "When asked to make a comparison between the situation amongst the Indian people here in Canada to that of the Aboriginees [sic] in Australia," a reporter wrote, she said, "The similarities are many, with the Treaty Status of the Indian people as the only difference."[93] After attending the course Dyer wrote to the Federation of Saskatchewan Indians' journal, the *Saskatchewan Indian*, "Through your circulation, I would appreciate very much if you would convey to all the students and teachers at the Prince Albert Student Residence, my sincere gratitude for their friendliness and acceptance of one 'homesick' Australian Aboriginal and a special message to any of them who may visit

Victoria in future to please contact me personally and I will guarantee to give them the same hospitality."[94]

Dyer flew to the United States from Saskatchewan and met first with various governmental and private non-Indian authorities, who offered her the official position on Indian child welfare. Dyer started at BIA headquarters in Washington DC and then traveled to New York City, where she initially met with several judges who were involved in child welfare issues and then visited the North American Center on Adoption, the Child Welfare League of America, and the New York Society for the Prevention of Cruelty to Children, all pro-adoption groups.

Finally Dyer met with Steve Unger and Bert Hirsch of the AAIA, just two days before journeying further on her American tour. This meeting would have an enduring impact. Unger and Hirsch took Dyer sightseeing, from Greenwich Village and China Town to Little Italy and the Jewish sector. "Everywhere," she wrote, "people greeted Steve and Bert warmly. We sampled so much ethnic food that day, I could hardly walk." Traveling around the city all day by subway, Dyer wrote that "the deafening noise, speed and dust . . . along with the musty smell stuck with me for several days." Dyer proclaimed, "It was an experience I will never forget." In addition to treating Dyer to a whirlwind tour of New York City, Unger and Hirsch tutored Dyer in American Indian politics. "Steve pointed out that virtually all of the places I had visited were government-funded and controlled," she wrote in her memoir. He had arranged for the rest of her trip to "visit reservations where the programs were largely managed and controlled by Indian people." This meeting cemented an alliance that would lead to further transnational exchanges.[95]

Dyer continued from New York City on a back-breaking journey across the country, first to Mississippi, where she met with Choctaws on the Pearl River Reservation, spoke at a black church, and learned of the Foster Grandmothers program, a group of women who spent three hours every Saturday with institutionalized Indian youth. From there she traveled to Arizona, where she toured the Navajo Reservation; the Inter-mountain Youth Center in Tucson, "an alternative to incarceration for troubled and delinquent Indian adolescents"; the White Mountain Apache reservation; and the Jewish Adoption Agency in Phoenix. She then flew to Michigan, Ohio, and Illinois, visiting various agencies concerned with either Indian or black children in care. These experiences proved useful to Dyer and probably quite eye-opening to her hosts, but she had not quite found what she was looking for and had grown quite exhausted.[96]

She fulfilled her purpose on the last leg of her journey, in Yakima, Washington. Dyer stayed with Maxine Robbins, "a fully qualified social worker" with a master's degree in social work. "I felt comfortable with her right from the start. She was about my age. . . . She was like our own elders who, with patience and perseverance, constantly chipped away at problems and made consistent gains until they achieved the final result." Of greatest interest to Dyer, Robbins had founded and directed a program called Ku-Nak-We-Sha, meaning "the caring place" in Yakima (see chapter 4). "After my long journey, it was here, at the end of it, that I would find the program that I had been searching for," wrote Dyer. Robbins' program provided preventative services to Yakima families, offered short-term emergency facilities for children who had to be removed from their homes, and recruited and compensated Yakima foster families.[97]

The meeting between Dyer and Robbins was not only of great professional import but also of personal significance. Dyer stayed with Robbins in downtown Yakima with Robbins's eighty-nine-year-old mother. "I spent many happy hours with them," wrote Dyer. "Although I had been treated with great consideration and care everywhere I went on my trip, Maxine and her mother were different. They were like sister and mother to me. In the short time I knew them, I grew to love them both very much." Dyer and Robbins mixed personal connection with professional acumen. Robbins helped Dyer "draft notes for a submission for funds to establish a similar agency in Australia." The bond between Dyer and Robbins led to a powerful transnational connection.[98]

Dyer returned home to Fitzroy after visiting Robbins. She soon convened a group of Aboriginal community workers and told them about her experiences. She recommended that they model their newly established ACPA on Robbins's Ku-Nak-We-Sha. The group decided to change their name from the Aboriginal Child *Placement* Agency to the Aboriginal Child *Care* Agency (ACCA). This signaled an important shift from an emphasis on removal and placement to a new focus on caring. Dyer later explained to the DAA that the new title "emphasises the retention of the Aboriginal child within his family." She and a colleague used Dyer's notes from Robbins to draw up a "sophisticated submission" as their funding request to the government of Victoria, which to Dyer's great anger rejected her for the second time.[99] Dyer continued to strengthen the transnational connections she had made. Her ACCA colleague Graham Atkinson traveled in June 1978 with another Aboriginal activist, Ted Lovett, to visit Robbins's program at Yakima, the Warm Springs Reservation in Oregon, and other American Indian communities that were developing innovative child welfare programs.[100]

Dyer activated the transnational circuits she and Atkinson had sparked in order to build support for her work back home. She arranged for Robbins to come to Australia for a conference for Australia's celebration of Children's Week in October 1978. Robbins brought her now ninety-year-old mother along. Dyer strategically deployed her transnational colleague during the conference and subsequent visits with government agencies to help push for greater Aboriginal control over Aboriginal child welfare. Robbins questioned Australian government authorities as to why there were no provisions made for Aboriginal people to attend or speak at the conference. They told her the conference was to educate whites, but she "countered this by saying that this education should come from Australian Aborigines rather than a Native American Indian." In response, conference organizers welcomed Aboriginal people to attend their meeting in Morwell, a small city in eastern Victoria. They "turned up in force." At the meeting, according to Dyer, "Maxine's skill rose like cream to the top. She had Aborigines join in their own afternoon workshops. She put everyone in a circle . . . [and] would draw out the quiet folk to have their say. . . . She asked each Aborigine to talk about the struggles they had experienced in a community dominated by white culture."[101] Robbins was perhaps able to gain the attention of government administrators in ways that Dyer had been unable to accomplish.

After the conference Dyer sent Robbins to meet directly with government officials. Her meeting with the federal government's coordinator of Aboriginal Legal Services led to an invitation for an appointment for her and Dyer with the minister for Aboriginal affairs in Canberra. Robbins detailed at length the crisis center she had developed for Yakima children, and "described the opposition of Indians to adoption as the same as Aborigines." She "stressed the importance that funding for ACCA not be placed under any [state] government agency." The minister admitted that "he had been misinformed" about Dyer's proposed program. Robbins also helped to strategize with Aboriginal activists, spending two weeks after the Children's Week conference with the staff of ACCA. Dyer used Robbins, in part, to pressure the government to support her efforts with ACCA, which proved to be a successful tactic. Shortly after Robbins's visit, the Office of Child Care for the state of Victoria made its first substantial grant to ACCA.[102]

To build on the momentum of Robbins's visit, Dyer and her compatriots decided to organize a one-day local meeting called If Everyone Cared—Aboriginal Child Survival, the title of Dyer's mother's newly published book. Very quickly the meeting grew into a three-day national seminar tied to the United Nations International Year of the Child.[103] Dyer invited Robbins to attend again, as well as Lenora Mundt, another social worker in Washington State. She also wrote to Unger, asking him if "there is any way you can beg, borrow, steal or cajole enough funds to come over to our Seminar in April this year. . . . You may not be fully aware, but you are indirectly responsible for our success in that you arranged a major proportion of my itinerary during my overseas visit, and introduced me to Maxine Robbins." Dyer added, "I am sure your trip would be worth while, and give you much material for your publication—it just may be that this is the first time in history that another country has modelled a program (which is successful, too) along the lines of a Native American program."[104] Through applying to a number of foundations for funding, Unger was able to make the trip in 1979.

Robbins's and Unger's contributions to the If Everyone Cared seminar resonated with Aboriginal participants. Robbins spoke about her child welfare program at Yakima and Unger discussed the years of activism leading up to ICWA. Aboriginal participants found profound parallels with and inspiration from the American experience. This experience stunned Unger, who wrote to the AAIA's director Bill Byler, "My reception here by the Aboriginal people has been of a kindness, generosity, acceptance and warmth beyond my wildest dreams. After my speech at the seminar . . . I was invited absolutely all over Australia. . . . Quite a number of people came up to me afterwards and said, 'You gave us hope.'" After his speech, a "young Aboriginal man, now in law school but only recently a drop-out with severe alcoholism/drug problems and apparently bitter, frustrated, and very angry, got up and in front of the whole audience" of two to three hundred people, and told Unger, "You made me feel more free." Unger was overcome. "Try to imagine how I felt," he wrote to Byler.[105] Unger was elated that the AAIA's work in the United States had not only benefited American Indian communities but was also rippling out far from its origins to embolden Aboriginal people as well.

This transnational exchange influenced seminar participants in generating resolutions. These included a recommendation to establish a National Committee of ACCAs to be convened by Mollie Dyer and a demand that all states enact Aboriginal child welfare legislation similar to ICWA.[106] Unger believed that the group would have proposed such resolutions whether he had been there or not. Dyer had distributed *Indian Family Defense* and other AAIA publications, and "the AAIA has had an influence on Australia, especially the Aboriginal community, regardless of me or any of us actually being here," Unger wrote to Byler.[107] Surely, though, Unger's presence helped participants to understand the intricacies and significance of ICWA.

The presence of international visitors seemed to propel the group to consider further international action: "This Conference instruct[s] [Aboriginal] Legal Services to put a case before the International Court of Justice seeking an injunction and conscionable damages against State Governments whose policies and practices in the past and at present amount to social, cultural and physical genocide of Aboriginal families, especially with regard to wholesale removal of Aboriginal children from their natural family and kin group."[108] The seminar enabled Aboriginal and American Indian activists and their allies not only to share common stories of child removal but also to exchange strategies. The pain of shared trauma profoundly moved many participants, and the possibility of greater control moving into the hands of Indigenous people deeply stirred them as well. Dyer believed the international guests gave many Aboriginal people "something concrete to work on and a ray of hope for the future."[109]

Just as she had utilized Robbins during her earlier visit to meet with government ministers, Dyer had arranged for Unger to visit the Australian Law Reform Commission in New South Wales and the DAA in Canberra after the seminar.[110] As with Robbins, this proved a winning strat-

Fig. 14. Mollie Dyer and Steven Unger at the seminar If Everyone Cared, Melbourne, Australia, April 1979. From Denise Robin, "Putting Family First," *Aboriginal News* 3, no. 7 (1979): 9.

egy. Dyer received a phone call from the DAA after Unger's meeting with them. They wanted him to stop over there again before returning to the United States. "It seems that you created quite a 'stir' there," Dyer wrote to Unger. The agency would get department heads together "to get your observations on the deficiencies in the system throughout Australia." Dyer was clearly grateful, but also annoyed, that government authorities would listen to a white American man but not local Aboriginal people. Dyer wrote to Unger: "This is the first time I have ever known the 'bureaucrats' to show a sign of life and also the first time something more than a polite but disinterested hearing has been achieved."[111]

Dyer and Atkinson accompanied their international guests to Aboriginal communities in every state of Australia after the seminar and on Unger's governmental visits. Robbins and Mundt only had time to visit Adelaide, Alice Springs, and Darwin, but Unger stayed on.[112] "At the invitation [and expense of local] Aboriginal groups and organizations," by June 1979 Unger had traveled to Melbourne, Adelaide, Alice Springs, Darwin, Canberra,

Sydney, Brisbane, and Perth as well as locations in Tasmania.[113] Dyer considered it unprecedented that these groups had both invited and raised money for Unger to visit them.[114] Aboriginal activists took inspiration from what they learned. Heather Shearer observed, "We met Maxine Robbins and Steve Unger . . . way back in 1979, and heard of the achievements of the Indigenous people in America. They have their own courts, they have their own judicial system. What is to stop us from being able to implement those kind of structures[?]"[115] Aboriginal activists were hungry for the information Unger provided, and the experience of American Indians that he conveyed resonated with them strongly. Writing to Byler, Unger noted, "I find that I can make virtually any comment I want on Australia without mentioning Aboriginal people at all, but by referring to American Indians & leaving it to the Australians to make the connection."[116]

Unger's extended trip with Aboriginal activists helped to nurture the Australian national movement. Graham Atkinson of ACCA asserted that his national tour with Unger "enabled me to link up with other committees or groups that were operating, or trying to establish similar structures in other States. That experience, I suppose, led us into thinking about a more formal national structure or network of Aboriginal child care agencies."[117] Just as Dyer had knit together diverse communities in North America as she traveled from one to the other, Unger strengthened the web of Aboriginal activists and their allies.

Unger was deeply moved by his work in Australia and came to see the American Indian child welfare crisis as part of a larger global pattern of injustice against Indigenous peoples. As he traveled to the Northern Territory he learned that "the wholesale theft of Aboriginal children has been going on here for decades, and on our trip north up through the center of the country it seemed to be the rare Aboriginal family that did *not* have a story to tell of child-stealing," he wrote to Byler. "The stories would tear your heart out. After the first trip up north, . . . I just felt emotionally and psychologically devastated by what we learned. In fact, had I spent a month travelling [there] first, I doubt I would have had the strength to address the conference at all. In a sense, my ignorance made it possible for me to talk about wounds and hopes almost too deep to be recalled in tranquility."[118] Unger was especially moved by Dyer, writing, "I think that people like Mollie are the unacknowledged heroes of the world."[119]

This transnational exchange led to substantive change in Australia. After her international visitors returned home, Dyer informed them that Aboriginal groups in Darwin, Western Australia, and Tasmania had all applied for funding to support child welfare groups, and "I don't think any of this would have happened if you three had not come to Australia and spoken so strongly in support of an issue rather than what is happening in Australia."[120] Even before this continental tour, the American example had been helpful, as conveyed through Dyer. South Australian Aboriginal activist Brian Butler remembered that "Mollie Dyer invited me to come across to Melbourne from Adelaide and it was . . . learning how they had done things in America that spurred me on. She encouraged me to take what I had learned back to South Australia and see if we couldn't develop a similar agency there."[121] As Aboriginal child care agencies formed in other Australian states, Dyer's organization became the Victorian ACCA (VACCA). Gradually these organizations came to include Torres Strait Islanders, and some became Aboriginal and Islander child care agencies (AICCAs).[122]

VACCA developed a positive relationship with the state government, but ACCAs in other states struggled to gain support. Activists in NSW organized sit-ins in the minister's office in an attempt to enable grandparents and other extended family members to receive payment for taking in children. In Queensland, too, Aboriginal organizers had an adversarial relationship with the state administration. According to Mary Graham, white workers with the Family Services Department actually met with her and other Aboriginal activists clandestinely; they wanted to work with them but were "absolutely hamstrung by their own legislation, by their own policy of their Department."[123] By the 1980s many Aboriginal groups had succeeded in getting state funding for Aboriginal and Islander child care agencies despite initial opposition. With VACCA taking the lead, they formed a nationwide network called the Secretariat of National Aboriginal and Islander Child Care (SNAICC).[124]

Activists in these programs and other Aboriginal groups proved ingenious in the programs they developed. The Aboriginal Medical Service in Perth played off the iconic Australian flying doctors to develop a new Emergency Child Care Service called the "Flying Grandmother Scheme." It offered temporary short-term care for Aboriginal children in the Perth area. "When one or both parents are unable to provide care for the children because of a crisis situation (particularly when a mother has to have hospitalisation) and there are no other means of help," the group explained, "an older Aboriginal woman will go into the home or take the children into her home whilst the mother is hospitalised."[125] This program fulfilled an important need, as the hospitalization of an Indigenous mother had proven a prime time for removals of older children. This innovative program combined respect for Aboriginal traditions of caring with a modern symbol of the Australian nation.

Dyer and other activists hoped to apply what she had learned from American activists in one other way as well. "Ideally," she wrote, "Aboriginal child welfare legislation should be enacted along the lines of the American Indian Child Welfare Act that was recently passed by Congress."[126] Activists looked to ICWA as a model and circulated it at SNAICC meetings. The Australian federal government, however, never enacted such legislation. Instead ACCAs negotiated agreements with state governments to adopt the Aboriginal Child Placement Principle, modeled on ICWA's priority of placement and developed by Dyer and others through the Aboriginal Legal Service. Activists first articulated the principle at the 1976 Conference on Adoption. In 1980 they succeeded in getting the DAA at the federal level to adopt it. SNAICC and AICCAs lobbied in the 1980s to have the principle enacted legislatively in all jurisdictions, and they were eventually successful.[127]

Activists recognized a common problem regarding the welfare of Indigenous children that transcended national boundaries and a vast ocean. They exchanged information about the practice in their respective countries and took inspiration from one another's efforts to develop Indigenous organizations and work toward changing government policy and practice. Their mutual discoveries prompt us to examine the Indigenous welfare crises in the United States, Canada, and Australia from a different angle. A transnational perspective enables us to see that they were not only distinct crises, each operating in its own national context, but were also part of a global phenomenon. Three settler colonial nations had precipitated these crises in their ongoing efforts to solve the "problem" of Indigenous peoples in their modern nation-states. Social welfare officials often conceptualized this problem as one of irreparably dysfunctional families who lived in "dead end" Indigenous communities. A transnational perspective, however, reveals that the "problem" derived instead from the very policies that these nations had enacted against their Indigenous peoples. Past policies of family breakup and child removal had left a bitter inheritance, and current policies only exacerbated the problem. As Unger wrote in 1979, "The similarity of the breakup of Native families in the two countries, though half a world apart, offers indirect evidence that it is the conflict of cultures, and not pathology in the Indian or Aboriginal communities, that must be overcome if Indian and Aboriginal families are to be able to raise their children in an atmosphere free from unwarranted governmental interference and coercion."[128]

Adoption proponents in the United States, Canada, and Australia all imagined that the transfer of Indigenous children to white, middle-class families would lead to better outcomes for individual children as well as to racial reconciliation, albeit through the elimination of Indigenous peoples as distinct cultures and nations. But the placement of Indigenous children in white families did not go as planned. It generated unforeseen consequences that still trouble many Indigenous families and haunt our societies today.

It can be an uncanny experience when you discover that you share a birthday with someone, a bit like discovering a long-lost twin. I was poring over old newspapers in the bustling, not-so-quiet State Library of Victoria, in Melbourne, Australia, in March 2013, when I came across one of my birthday twins: Russell Moore, also known as James Savage. Moore and I had both been born on January 31, 1963.

He and I had recently turned fifty, an achievement that often leads people to reflect on how they got to this point. Looking back, you imagine how thousands of little events and decisions—many of them entirely beyond your control and often made before you were born—twisted your life in a particular direction. I was a tenured full professor of history on sabbatical for a year. I had traveled from snowy Nebraska to sunny Melbourne. Moore, however, was serving a life sentence in the Okaloosa prison in Florida, convicted in 1988 of the heinous rape and murder of Barbara Ann Barber, a white businesswoman.

From our births on the same day, Moore and I started from disparate positions. I was the child of a career army non-commissioned officer and a college-educated stay-at-home mother. I had been born at an army hospital in Southern California. An ocean away, Moore had been born to a fourteen-year-old Wamba Wamba mother, Beverley Moore, at a hostel in North Fitzroy, a suburb of Melbourne. Fifty years later I was staying in a hotel just a few blocks from where Moore was born.

Moore's path and my own converged to an extent during our childhoods. My father died when I was five, but I grew up in a middle-class home. I had my own room and more than enough toys and books. I was never hungry. Authorities removed Moore from his mother and placed him for adoption with a white middle-class couple, Reverend Graeme Savage and his wife, Nesta, who renamed him James Savage. The Savages moved around a lot, eventually immigrating to the United States. They, too, it seems, brought up their adopted son with all the material comforts he needed.

The fulfillment of basic material needs alone, however, does not guarantee a happy childhood. We have other, often more inchoate, longings to feel connected with and accepted by those around us. This was where Savage and I parted ways. I spent most of my childhood in a small community about twenty miles west of Colorado Springs. Almost everyone with whom I attended school was white, like me. I grew up with an unconscious sense of belonging. Behind the walls of his middle-class home, however, all was not well for Savage. He later told an Aboriginal community worker that his adoptive father called him "Nigger" and treated him differently than his siblings. Savage also experienced racism whenever he ventured out of his home in Florida. Like many other Indigenous adoptees, Savage struggled to understand his identity beginning in early adolescence.

Savage began drinking and getting into trouble with the law. He went in and out of juvenile detention centers and then jail as an adult. His adoptive parents eventually lost touch with him and moved back to Australia. He had been released from prison just a month before that evening in 1988 when he took the life of Barbara Ann Barber. We can never know what possessed Savage to commit this crime. We can only wonder what kind of directions his life might have taken if James Savage had remained Russell Moore, growing up with his Wamba Wamba mother in Victoria, Australia. We can only imagine what might have been if Moore and I had shared not only a birthday but all the basic necessities, familial connections, and sense of belonging that a child needs to thrive.

# CHAPTER 8

# Historical Reckoning with Indigenous Child Removal in Settler Colonial Nations

Residents of the small city of Melbourne, Florida, woke on Thanksgiving Day 1988 to discover that a grisly murder had occurred in their midst. An assailant had brutally raped and strangled Barbara Ann Barber, a successful interior decorator, in a back alley. Three days later police captured her alleged killer, James Savage, a twenty-six-year-old Australian Aboriginal homeless man who had spent nine out of the last ten years in American juvenile detention centers and jails for crimes ranging from armed robbery to sexual assault to car theft.[1] The crime horrified the central Florida town as well as the Australians who learned of Savage's background in August 1989.

Savage had been born to fourteen-year-old Beverley Moore, an Aboriginal woman who had grown up in Deniliquin on the New South Wales border with Victoria, not far from the homeplace of Margaret Tucker and her family. Beverley Moore was part of a community of about one hundred Aboriginal people who had fled the government-controlled mission near town and built a village of tin huts on the Edward River. She and the other children called themselves "river rats." When she was just thirteen, Moore had become lovers with Frank Whyman, another river rat, and soon she was pregnant. Her grandmother, from Swan Hill, Victoria, insisted that she have the child at a Salvation Army hostel for unwed mothers in North Fitzroy, an inner-city suburb of Melbourne, near where Mollie Dyer and other activists would start the Aboriginal Child Care Agency a little more than a decade later.

Moore named her son Russell and hoped to raise him herself, but the Aborigines Welfare Board removed Russell just four days after his birth and placed him with Reverend Graeme and Nesta Savage, a white missionary couple. Board authorities then applied unrelenting pressure on Moore to give her son up for adoption. She finally signed adoption consent forms about two weeks after Russell's birth. Within two more weeks, however, she regretted her decision and took steps to revoke her consent, which adoption laws permitted. The board, however, threatened "that if she persisted she might, as a minor, face police action because she was in a sexual relationship" with Russell's father. They warned her that they might take her four brothers and sisters from their family and place them for adoption if she insisted on keeping her son. "Blackmailed" by authorities, as she put it, Moore reluctantly withdrew her revocation of the adoption consent. She later had four more children with Whyman, and the couple legally married in 1971.[2]

The Savages formally adopted Russell, renamed him James Hudson (after a nineteenth-century English missionary in China), and moved on to a variety of missionary postings, from Western Australia to California and then to Florida. Up to his adolescence, the Savages regarded their adopted son as a "perfectly normal child." But Savage experienced intense problems soon after the family moved to Florida when he was eleven. He longed to know about his heritage and birth family at the same time as he experienced acute racial prejudice at school, in church, and even, allegedly, within his own home from his adopted father. At fifteen Savage started drinking and committing crimes, landing him in various institutions for the next ten years of his life. By his late teens, Savage "had no place to call home. He lived under bridges, in deserted buildings and houses and would break into other houses just to find food, clothing and any money that would help him to 'survive.'" By the time he was twenty his adoptive parents had returned to Australia without him.[3]

Authorities wrote up a dozen disciplinary reports against Savage while he was incarcerated, and when he became an adult they transferred him to a maximum-security prison, where he spent several months under twenty-four-hour lockdown in solitary confinement. In 1988 he attempted suicide in prison and landed in the psychiatric wing for four months. There he told a doctor "he was rejected all his life. His adoptive parents rejected him. . . . He never had a satisfactory relationship with a single human being."[4] Later that year the state of Florida reduced Savage's sentence by 233 days and released him as part of an effort to reduce overcrowding in the state's prisons.

Savage showed up at the Christ Is the Answer mission in Melbourne, Florida, soon after his release. He told a minister there that he wanted to "go right" and not go back to prison. He stayed at the mission for half of the month and then set up camp with another ex-con under a causeway. He sought work at the Labor Force work center in Melbourne at 6:30 a.m. on the day before Thanksgiving, but there were no jobs available. He spent several hours in a bookstore that afternoon and then loitered around Barbara Ann Barber's nearby interior design shop. Barber stayed late that evening to work. She loaded several items from the shop in her car, which she had parked in a back alley. Savage supposedly intended to steal her car, but when Barber left her shop at 9:00 p.m., Savage beat her with his fists, strangled her with a lamp cord, and raped her. Police found Barber's body the day after Thanksgiving and took Savage in for questioning and arrested him later that day. Three days later they charged him with first-degree murder, sexual battery, and robbery.[5]

A Florida white woman befriended Savage while he was imprisoned and awaiting trial, and she contacted Aboriginal Legal Services in Australia. They located his birth mother in August 1989, and activists arranged a reunion between Beverley Moore Whyman and her son in the Florida prison.[6] Whyman had been looking for her son since she had turned eighteen and when she learned of his situation, she declared, "I'm just going to devote myself to him. . . . I will eat, breathe, and sleep Russell."[7] She reunited with him on September 23, 1989, in a one-hour visit. Although his ankles and hands were in chains, they "just grabbed each other." They discussed his childhood, how he was taken from her and from his native country. Whyman brought her son a book, *Australian Dreaming: 40,000 Years of Aboriginal History*, which she had had inscribed by Mollie Dyer: "To Russell We know who you are. We know where you came from. We have trust you will return to us. We all care about you." Whyman visited her son three times a week and attended every day of his trial. The Savages, too, had returned to Florida since learning of their adoptive son's murder charge, and they visited him in prison. At the trial, which began on November 13, 1989, Nesta Savage sat just two rows behind Whyman.[8]

As observers struggled to understand what might have led Savage to commit these ghastly crimes, the case took on significant but divergent meanings in Melbourne, Florida, versus Melbourne, Australia. In Florida Savage's crimes became emblematic of problems in the state's criminal justice system. Two reporters for the *Orlando Sentinel* conducted a four-part investigative series on Savage's early release, dramatically titled "The Savage Story." Asserting that if he were guilty, the state was his "silent accomplice," the reporters indicted Florida's policies at the same time as they disclosed Savage's violent past.[9] To these reporters and many Floridians, the James Savage case highlighted the need for the state to get tough on crime and build more prisons.

Many Australians derived a different lesson from the Savage case and identified a different accomplice: the Australian government. Beverley Whyman "blamed her son's problems on an Australian government policy that forced her to give her son up for adoption at birth. . . . 'He's paying for his crime, yet who's going to pay for Australia's?'" she asked.[10] For Aboriginal Australians, the Savage/Moore case exposed the damage that state policies had done to their children. Arguing that the state was partly culpable for his crimes, they lobbied hard for the Australian government to provide legal representation for Savage. The minister of justice refused.[11]

After a jury found Savage guilty on November 20, 1989, of murder, rape, and robbery, Aboriginal activists with the Victorian Aboriginal Legal Service finally convinced the Australian government to send a delegation of eight expert witnesses—including Whyman, Mollie Dyer, former New South Wales judge Hal Wooten, historian Peter Read, and a former member of the Savages' church congregation—to testify at the penalty phase of Savage's trial. They hoped to convince the jury and judge that Savage should be spared the death penalty and that he should be transferred to a prison in Australia where he could be closer to kin.[12] The judge ruled the expert witness testimony of Wooten irrelevant, and the defense withdrew Read and one other expert witness. Dyer took the stand and testified powerfully that "based on her conversations with Savage, she found similarities between the children she has assisted [through the Victorian ACCA] and Savage's situation, specifically a lack of confidence, lack of identity, frustration at not knowing where he fitted into one family or where he did not fit in at all, frustration and acting out behavior, which she stated is very common in these situations."[13]

The defense successfully persuaded the jury that Australian state policies had contributed to Savage's crime, and the jury voted 11 to 1 for a life sentence rather than execution. However, a few months later, the judge ignored the jury's recommendation and sentenced the troubled young man to the electric chair. Aboriginal activists and death penalty opponents organized petition and letter-writing campaigns to protest Savage's sentence. The Florida Supreme Court overturned the death sentence in 1991, and Moore—who has officially reclaimed his birth name—still resides in a Florida prison, serving out three consecutive life terms, far from home and kin.[14]

The Russell Moore tragedy challenges us to examine government programs that promoted the placement of Indigenous children in non-Indigenous homes not just in Australia but also in the United States and Canada. Advocates championed these programs as a means of taking care of "forgotten" Indigenous children, but they functioned as social experiments that undermined Indigenous families and communities and often had dire consequences for the individual children involved. These assimilation efforts exacerbated the very problems they were supposedly meant to solve and left complicated legacies in their wake. Indigenous activists and their allies in Australia and Canada have generated a vigorous public debate about Indigenous child removal. Both nations have confronted their Indigenous child welfare policies and practices, issued formal apologies to Indigenous people, and taken steps toward reconciliation. By contrast, the United States has avoided any wholesale evaluation of its history of Indian child removal, let alone any public recognition of or compensation for the wrongfulness of those policies.

A comparative and transnational approach to studying the Indigenous child welfare crises of the late twentieth century leads to a valuable perspective. When we examine the removal of one Indigenous child in a particular place and at a specific time, it is easy to get caught up in clashing notions of what constitutes proper care and what is in the best interests of one individual child. When we zoom out and take a global view, we see parallel Indigenous child welfare crises as part of a pattern among settler colonial nations. The ubiquity of Indigenous child removal, fostering, and adoption in the United States, Canada, and Australia in the post–

World War II era profoundly challenges the pronouncements of many local authorities who claimed they were simply acting in the best interests of Indigenous children.

The Indigenous child welfare crises of the late twentieth century represented both a legacy of earlier settler colonial policies and the latest manifestation of them. Australia, the United States, and Canada had all originated as distinctive British settler colonial projects that rested on the displacement of Indigenous peoples from their lands and their replacement with a settler population through what Patrick Wolfe so evocatively calls "the logic of elimination."[15] Once the United States gained its independence and Australia and Canada became nations in their own right, they continued to act on settler colonial logic. Yet none of these settler colonial ventures ever resulted in the complete elimination of Indigenous people or the transfer of all their lands into settler hands, despite the use of brute violence, legal maneuvers, and sometimes treaty making. British humanitarianism and homegrown reform movements gained ascendance in the mid to late nineteenth century, and outright massacres of Indigenous people or blatant land grabs became increasingly indefensible. Instead, all three settler colonial societies turned to assimilation efforts by the late nineteenth century, to eviscerate cultural differences and undermine vestiges of communal landholding. Officials focused these assimilation efforts on Indigenous children. Authorities claimed to be intervening in Indigenous families as a gesture of benevolence, but their policies served the same settler colonial aims and continued to inflict great trauma on Indigenous peoples.

Through the forcible removal of children to institutions from the late nineteenth century onward, state and church authorities intentionally weakened Indigenous families and communities, making it difficult for them to sustain Indigenous ways of caring for and raising children. At the same time, paternalistic policies and the ongoing dispossession of Indigenous people of their lands undermined Indigenous livelihoods and impoverished generations of Indigenous people.[16] Such policies had undermined some Indigenous families to such an extent by the second half of the twentieth century that it became difficult to care for their own children. This was a bitter legacy of earlier settler colonial policies.

The Indigenous child welfare crises of the late twentieth century cannot be attributed merely to past policies and their disastrous consequences for Indigenous families, however. Authorities in the post–World War II era often removed Indigenous children from their families without good reason. Indigenous child welfare crises also derived from specific post-war policies based on a relentless drive to eliminate Indigenous peoples' distinctive status and their claims to land and sovereignty. Each of these settler colonial nations continued to wrestle with their Indigenous "problem," as officials referred to the persistence of Indigenous people, and the removal, fostering, and adoption of Indigenous children constituted a primary means of managing Indigenous populations in the post–World War II era. New bureaucratic imperatives to rid federal governments in the United States and Canada and state governments in Australia of their longstanding obligations to Indigenous peoples dovetailed with purportedly color-blind liberalism in all three of these nations to make the adoption of Indigenous children a particularly appealing solution to the Indigenous problem.

Authorities claimed to be acting on the laudable notion of extending universal human rights to Indigenous minorities, but their policies and practices actually divested Indigenous people of their sovereignty and group rights. They required that Indigenous people assimilate or integrate into the larger population and cease to affiliate with their prior group identity. As in earlier eras, authorities deemed children the best hope for enacting their vision. Indigenous children would become indistinguishable from the rest of the population if they could be separated from their communities and raised in modern white families, and Indigeneity would eventually disappear. Authorities in all three nations were hell bent on assimilating Indigenous people rather than providing for their real needs. They failed to muster the resources—adequate jobs, sufficient public assistance, useful social services—that would truly have helped Indigenous families, and they undermined Indigenous people's efforts to take control of their own destinies. Instead government authorities demonized and then penalized poor Indian families. Claiming to have the best interest of their children at heart, they robbed Indigenous people again, this time of their most precious resource.

These postwar policies had many unanticipated results. Proponents of Indigenous adoption, who claimed to be blind to color, did not foresee the troubles that many Indigenous adoptees would face as they grew up in decidedly color-aware societies. Most adoptees lived in predominantly white communities with few Indigenous people, and they often suffered from a sense of alienation. Donna Micklos, of Edmonton, Alberta, remembers that when she walked anywhere, people would stare and gawk at her and her family.[17] School proved particularly painful. Joanne Nimik, of the Swan Lake First Nation in Manitoba, was the only Indian in her class, and she felt singled out and embarrassed because her textbook depicted the Indian way of life as degraded. Similarly, Denise Roulette remembered, "When questioned by the teacher in front of the class to explain my family history, all I knew was I was a dirty, lazy Indian."[18]

James Savage experienced a similar sense of dislocation as well as blatant racism. According to his adoptive sister Glenise, the communities of Starke and Salem, Florida, "were the worst places the family lived in terms of the way Savage was treated," especially at church, where the other children, including his siblings, sought to exclude him from activities. Florida may have been a particularly difficult environment for Savage as de facto segregation still prevailed. When Reverend Savage sought to integrate the board of the small Bible college where he was president, his family "suffered incredible persecution" and received death threats.[19] Although treated as a black by whites, Savage did not fit in with the black community either, and thus he endured "absolute cultural isolation" in Florida. As Aboriginal activists put it, "To be a minority of one is to be the object of perpetual discrimination." Unlike Aboriginal adoptees in Australia, "shorn from his cultural heritage, Russell Moore had nobody there when he encountered harassment from people who viewed him as 'different.'"[20]

Even if adoptive families were loving and caring, many adoptees grew up confused and troubled by their identities. Cameron Longo, of Duck Bay and Waterhen, Manitoba, remembers, "For many years . . . I hated being Indian. I wanted to be White. There was that constant struggle within me that wanted to be White so badly. I hated my dark skin, dark hair, and dark eyes. I wished that I could be blond, blue-eyed, and have white skin."[21] Such low self-worth led many adoptees to abuse alcohol and drugs beginning in their teens. Evidence suggests that adult adoptees have elevated levels of suicide, incarceration, depression, and addiction.[22]

Authorities constantly justified their programs as efforts to rescue forgotten children and give them a better life, but much evidence suggests that out-of-home placements for Indigenous children were often trau-matic. Anthropologist Susan Devan Harness located and studied twenty-five adult American Indian adoptees. Although a small sample, her study provides some of the only quantitative data on long-term Indian adop-tion "outcomes." She found that 44 percent (eleven individuals) endured some form of abuse in their adoptive families; of these 70 percent expe-rienced sexual abuse, 73 percent physical abuse. She noted, too, that 48 percent struggled with mental health issues; of these nine of twelve felt their adoption had contributed to the problem. She found that 32 percent (eight) suffered from substance abuse; six of them felt their adoption had contributed to the problem.[23]

Many adoptees unfortunately reported widespread abuse within their adoptive non-Indigenous families, the very families that were supposedly rescuing them from lives of neglect and deprivation. Russell Moore told a psychiatrist that he had been "beat with a belt" and "reprimanded ver-bally and physically by his father at a frequency and intensity different from his siblings."[24] When testifying for the prosecution in his adopted son's trial, Graeme Savage claimed not to "remember striking Savage in the face and calling him a nigger, though he understands Savage said it and he cannot say he was wrong."[25] Tellingly, he did not deny the abuse.

Many other fostered children and adoptees suffered sexual molesta-tion by parents or siblings within their new families. Such abuse has led many adoptees to reflect that even when their Indigenous homes were less than ideal, they were still better than the adoptive homes. Canadian Sandra Kakeeway asserts, "The neglect and abandonment I experienced when my mom was drinking did not have nearly the devastating effects that the sexual abuse did when I supposedly was in care of the Children's Aid Society [a Canadian placement agency]."[26] The frequency with which adoptees and fostered children recall physical and sexual abuse suggests that child welfare authorities did not properly vet prospective adoptive or foster families, nor follow up to ensure that Indigenous children were truly protected. Based on stereotypes of dysfunctional Indian families, they seem to have assumed that *any* non-Indigenous family would pro-vide better care for a child than would an Indigenous family.

Sometimes, too, children suffered emotional abuse from their adop-tive parents, often rooted in racism. Sandy Whitehawk, who was adopted from the Rosebud Reservation by a missionary family, remembered that her adoptive mother would tell her "ugly stories about what it meant to be Indian" and told her she was "lucky to be brought where you are."[27] Russell Moore told an Aboriginal community worker that while "Mrs. Savage always treated him kindly," "his pet name was 'Nigger' by his adoptive father."[28] A family friend of the Savages confirmed Moore's sense that he was treated differently than his siblings. Laurel Oglethorpe had attended the same church as the Savages from 1966 to 1968, had been the Sunday School teacher, and had helped with the Savage children at their home because Mrs. Savage was often sick. Oglethorpe "wrote a powerful letter to Moore's lawyers when she learnt he was facing the death penalty" and traveled as part of the Australian delegation of eight witnesses for the penalty phase of the trial, testifying that she observed that the Savage parents "were not as strict with [their two other children] as they were with Savage, and he always was the odd man out and got the blame for everything."[29] Many other adoptees have reported similar emotional abuse within their families.

Even adoptees who developed close and loving relationships with their adopted parents often felt they did not fit in, and they longed to know more about their heritage. As Diane Tells His Name (Oglala Lakota) put it, "I grew up in blissful suburbia [in Southern California] with a nice big house, a swimming pool in the backyard, and at my doorstep the morning of my sixteenth birthday, a new Mustang. I had the promise of an education at any college I wanted. . . . Yet, something was missing from my life."[30] Like Diane, many adoptees, even content ones, had a vague unease. Susan Smith (Grand Portage/White Earth Ojibwe) asserted, "My childhood was happy and stable. It's not that I wanted to replace my parents. I just wanted to know where I came from and who I looked like."[31]

Most fostered and adopted children had intense curiosity about their backgrounds, but many adoptive families believed that it was inadvisable to discuss their heritage with them. Of the twelve Indian adoptees that Jeffrey Peterson studied, only three had adoptive families who told them of their Indigenous heritage, and only two families made an effort to expose them to their cultures. This led to bitterness and frustration. One adoptee observed, "I feel like I have been robbed of that part of my life." Another felt her "rights were taken away, the rights to heritage, rights to knowledge of parentage," while another felt he was "stripped of everything."[32] In James Savage's case, from the age of eight "he had constantly badgered his parents about the identity of his natural mother. 'I just couldn't get anything from them,' he said. 'I always thought I had been just given away and it made me feel mad.'" Reverend Savage discouraged James from developing any contact with Aboriginal culture. Even when the Savages lived in Western Australia, where their adopted son attended school with eighty other Aboriginal pupils, the six-year-old Savage did not fit in with his peers, who regarded him as "well-dressed Nyoongah [Aboriginal] boy with white parents."[33] Savage and other adoptees were deeply interested in their Indigenous backgrounds, but their adoptive parents rarely helped them to learn about or take part in Indigenous communities and activities.

Adoption schemes did not lead, as expected, to the seamless assimilation of Indigenous adoptees into mainstream life. Instead they created a defining feature of modern Indigenous life in all three of these nations: removal and displacement. In the worst-case scenario this led to a profound sense of alienation from both Indigenous and non-Indigenous communities, as in Russell Moore's case. It would be a mistake, however, to assume that Russell Moore's case epitomizes the adoptee experience, or to characterize all Indigenous adoptees and fostered children as tragic victims. In some circumstances their experiences could lead to what one adoptee, "John," characterized as living in the best of both worlds. John told me that through his adoptive family, he had a "world of prospect" opened to him, while his extended Indian family offered him the place that "became home." Many adoptees experienced great trauma, but as the scholar Raven Sinclair puts it, "There are those who persevere and extract the best they can from their experiences." She concluded that the participants in her study were "resilient and insightful."[34] My own experience of meeting many adoptees and former foster children, as well as reading countless accounts, confirms this portrait of adaptive survivors.

Authorities did not envision that many adoptees would seek to reunite with their communities (84 percent in Harness's study of twenty-five American Indian adoptees). Many have embarked on recovery and healing through reconnecting with their Indigenous families and communities. Sandy Whitehawk, who followed a trajectory of self-hate and self-abuse, eventually reclaimed her life through reuniting with family members from the Rosebud Sioux reservation. Since then she has established the First Nations Orphans Association and the First Nations Repatriation Institute and has developed a powerful welcoming home ceremony to help adoptees or those who have been in foster care. The ceremony includes an honor song for adoptees and family members who have lost children and a Lakota ceremony known as "wiping away the tears" or Wanblecheya.[35] Sinclair remarks that repatriation of adoptees to their Indigenous communities and cultures is often "concurrent with a sense of healing."[36] Although the promotion of fostering and adoption did rupture many Indigenous families and led to serious trauma for many Indigenous children, it did not result in the hoped-for disappearance of Indigeneity.

In yet another way authorities failed to foresee the consequences of Indigenous child removal in the late twentieth century. They never imagined the strength of the resistance that would form among Indigenous people to government schemes. While policy and practice followed similar patterns in all three nations, opposition among Indigenous people also developed along parallel lines. Women took leading roles in the Indigenous child welfare movement in all three countries. Their efforts to organize themselves as Indigenous women coalesced with their campaign to address the Indigenous child welfare crisis. Indigenous women's movements made family and child welfare a centerpiece. They asserted that their traditional caring roles had been highly valued in Indigenous societies, and they articulated a distinctive type of Indigenous feminism that was at odds with both the mainstream feminist and some of the Indigenous self-determination movements of the time.

By the late 1970s and early 1980s, Indigenous struggles to reclaim the care of children had paid off in the 1978 Indian Child Welfare Act in the United States, the ascendancy of the Aboriginal Child Placement Principle among state governments in Australia, and with myriad tripartite agreements in Canada. Tribes and Indigenous groups also formed independent child welfare agencies to care for children within their own communities. Attempts by authorities to obliterate Indigeneity through removing children thus backfired, leading instead to greater self-determination among Indigenous communities.

Resistance to Indigenous child removal eventually built into social movements that questioned the very foundations of settler colonial society, at least in Australia and Canada. The James Savage/Russell Moore case played an important role in exposing the experience of the Stolen Generations and leading to a government inquiry in Australia. As Russell's aunt Nellie Moore explained, "For the first time the white Australian people are getting to know what really happened to our kids. This has really happened and this is the end result. Some people can survive their experiences and some can't." Rather than giving in to despair over Russell's fate, the Moore family hoped Australians would take steps to ensure that his experience would not be repeated. As Nellie Moore put it, "Our hearts are broken but our spirits will never give in. My heart aches for Russell. . . . He was a young Aboriginal man brought up in another country, unsure of what or who he was. Whatever happened to him happened to hundreds of our children who, as teenagers began to return back to us to live with their own families, unsure, because they had lost their years of belonging."[37]

Moore's murder trial coincided with an Australian government inquiry into the large numbers of deaths of Aboriginal prisoners. Prime Minister Bob Hawke established a Royal Commission into Aboriginal Deaths in Custody in 1987; it filed an interim report in 1988 and its final report in 1991. Among its findings, the commission reported a strong correlation between separation from family and incarceration. Of the ninety-nine deaths it investigated in the 1980s, forty-three were of Aboriginal people who had been separated from their families as children.[38] This alarming statistic helped to build momentum for a separate inquiry into what Australians call the Stolen Generations. In 1995 the government established a National Inquiry into the Separation of Aboriginal and Torres Strait Islander Children from Their Families, and the inquiry released its findings in the *Bringing Them Home* report in 1997. The report recommended that the federal government respond with an official apology and monetary compensation for members of the Stolen Generations, but the conservative John Howard government refused on both accounts.[39]

The Howard government did establish the Council for Aboriginal Reconciliation, however, which focused on public education and created community-based tool kits to assist communities in planning local reconciliation activities. When this organization ended, a nonprofit called Reconciliation Australia took up where it left off. Lack of official national action led to grassroots reconciliation efforts, such as National Sorry Day and the Sorry Book Campaign, started in 1998, in which organizers circulated more than a thousand books that everyday Australians could sign in churches, schools, and libraries. On February 13, 2008, as his first official act, new prime minister Kevin Rudd issued a formal apology. However, like his predecessor, he refused to make money available for individual victims or communities at large.[40] Individual Aboriginal people who were removed as children or had children apprehended from them have brought some legal proceedings against government authorities, but so far only one case has been successful.[41]

Indigenous outcry in Canada had also led to official inquiries over the removal of Indigenous children to residential schools. The Canadian government, churches, and the Assembly of First Nations negotiated the Indian Residential School Settlement Agreement in 2006 in response to more than twelve thousand individual claims and several class action lawsuits filed on behalf of approximately seventy thousand former students against the federal government and churches, which shared responsibility for the schools. In 2007 courts in every province and territory approved the agreement. The settlement provides monetary reparation to all former students based on simple verification of school attendance. It also includes a separate process that "adjudicates physical and sexual abuse claims and awards financial compensation," a health support program for survivors, a commemoration program for memorial projects, and the creation of the Truth and Reconciliation Commission (TRC).[42] Prime Minister Stephen Harper made a formal apology for the Indian residential schools, as a stipulation of the settlement, in June 2008, just a few months after Australia's apology.[43]

Canada and Australia have taken different paths toward a historical reckoning with Indigenous child removal. Canadian scholar Paulette Regan points out that Australia's approach was unusual in that it promoted grassroots activity in contrast to that of Canada, which manifested as a top-down legal effort. Canada's TRC is "of interest to the international community as a potential model for addressing historical injustices affecting Indigenous peoples across the globe," according to Regan. It is the first TRC to be established as part of a judicially supervised negotiated agreement rather than by legislative or executive order, and it is the only national TRC so far to focus on Indigenous peoples. The TRC aims to gather diverse stories of former students, staff and administrators, and government and church officials for its first five years, from 2009 to 2014. Then it is to produce a report and make recommendations based on its findings.[44]

Many Indigenous activists and their allies, however, have critiqued these processes. In Canada critics worry that settlers will listen to Indigenous people's testimonies as "consumers of, not witnesses to, historical accounts of injustice and trauma" and that the TRC will make a spectacle of Indigenous people's trauma and grief.[45] Those Indigenous people affected by the Indigenous child welfare crisis of the 1950s through the 1970s criticize the process for failing to include them. Now they, too, have organized a class action lawsuit against the Canadian government, on behalf of sixteen thousand survivors of the child welfare system.[46]

Australia's Stolen Generations inquiry has included children who were adopted, but as historian Shurlee Swain points out, "Indigenous adoptees have been marginalized . . . in the story of the Stolen Generations" because their experiences are "difficult to retrieve," and are "more complex and contested than that of the children subject to cruelty and abuse in institutions and mission dormitories." In Australia, too, a series of subsequent public apologies in 2009 and 2013 to Lost Innocents and Forgotten Australians (non-Indigenous British child migrants as well as institutionalized children and wards of the states) and to non-Indigenous unwed mothers who were forced to give up their children for adoption may have diluted the power of the Stolen Generations apology.[47] These processes of national reckoning in Canada and Australia are not perfect. Yet they represent a public acknowledgment that governments were culpable in the unjust removal of Indigenous children.

No such national effort at truth and reconciliation around Indian child welfare has occurred in the United States. One could regard the congressional hearings of the 1970s on Indian child welfare as a kind of truth and reconciliation process, and some scholars consider ICWA as a gesture of partial reparation for past historical wrongs.[48] ICWA provided Indian people with legal support for their efforts to keep their children, but it did not spark a national public conversation about the meaning of Indian child removal.

This dialogue instead has taken place between Indians and some officials far from the public's scrutiny. As part of his keynote speech to the

National Indian Child Welfare Association conference in 2001, Shay Bilchik, the president of the Child Welfare League of America, delivered a heartfelt apology for the league's role in the Indian Adoption Project. Bilchik noted that "while adoption was not as wholesale as the infamous Indian schools, in terms of lost heritage, it was even more absolute." He acknowledged that "no matter how well intentioned and how squarely in the mainstream this was at the time, it was wrong; it was hurtful," and he stated unequivocally, "I deeply regret the fact that CWLA's active participation gave credibility to such a hurtful, biased, and disgraceful course of action."[49] Bilchik seemed well aware of events in other countries to heal historical injustices. "The spirit in which I stand before you today, as a representative of CWLA and as an individual, is the spirit of truth and reconciliation," he declared. And he continued:

> In recent years, many countries have dealt with the aftermath of a period of great injustice by creating national truth commissions. This approach was based in the belief that while the past could not be undone, it could be faced squarely, and in a highly public forum—and that a full accounting of the truth was the best possible basis for moving forward to build the future. When the truth had been told as fully as possible, those who had been offended could have at least the knowledge that denial was at an end, and that the world knew what they had suffered. The perpetrators shared that knowledge. Reparations and reconciliation could proceed, on the foundation of truth.[50]

Bilchik's gesture could not take the place of a comprehensive national truth and reconciliation process, but the CWLA did commit to developing meaningful responses to the continued overrepresentation of Indian children within the child welfare system.

Some Indian activists, in concert with child welfare workers, have initiated grassroots campaigns to uncover the historical injustice of Indigenous child removal and to work toward healing rather than waiting for a national response. In Maine, Denise Altvater, a Passamaquoddy who had been removed from Pleasant Point as a child, developed a truth and reconciliation process in the state through her work with the American Friends Service Committee, an organization that had long supported Indian self-determination. In 2000 the Muskie School of Public Service contacted Altvater about videotaping her story "as part of an effort to help state workers in Maine understand the significance of the Indian Child Welfare Act." Altvater went public with her very painful story. When she was seven, she recounted, "state workers came onto the reservation. My five sisters and I were home. My mother was not home. They took all of our belongings and they put them in garbage bags. They herded us into station wagons and . . . took us to a state foster home . . . and left us there for four years. During those four years, our foster parents sexually assaulted us. They starved us. They did some horrific things to us." After breaking the silence about her own story, Altvater "helped train over 500 state workers" before "experienc[ing] a period of deep depression. She had told her story, but she didn't have the supports that she needed to cope with the post traumatic stress it invoked." After working for seven to eight years with tribal child welfare workers, the Muskie School, and state social workers, Altvater initiated a formal process to aid other Indians in coming forward with their stories and beginning to heal.[51]

Representatives of the five Wabanaki tribes and the governor of Maine signed a declaration of intent in 2011 to establish a statewide TRC to take testimony from other Maine Indians who had experienced the trauma of separation from their families. The Declaration of Intent noted that "important progress has been made with the passage of the ICWA and the work of the Maine ICWA Workgroup." However, the declaration asserted, "we have come to realize that we must unearth the story of Wabanaki people's experiences in order to fully uphold the spirit, letter and intent of the ICWA in a way that is consistent and sustainable."[52] The commission aims "to make recommendations for structural changes that will improve the way Wabanaki children and families are treated in the future" and "to give Wabanaki people a place where their voices will be heard, a place where they can heal, where they can be believed."[53] Altvater's grassroots campaign blossomed into a statewide effort to recognize Indigenous grievances publicly.

Despite these important developments, by and large, the American nation as a whole has ignored the issue. The Stolen Generations and the Indian residential schools garnered headlines and engendered public debate in Australia and Canada, but the American federal government and most American media are virtually silent about American Indian child removal. The Supreme Court issued a landmark ruling on the *Adoptive Couple v. Baby Girl* case in 2013 that weakened ICWA, but the media focused primarily on the court's rulings on the Defense of Marriage Act and provisions of the Voting Rights Act. American Indians are a small minority who have little impact in national elections, so they are at pains to make their grievances known and have them taken seriously. It is doubtful, however, that American Indian communities can achieve full self-determination as well as economic and social equality within American society, or that the United States can transcend its settler colonial past and present, without a full historical reckoning of the devastation wrought by Indigenous child removal policies and practices.

Indigenous people have gained a greater voice in deciding the destinies of their children, but rates of child removal and fostering are still elevated within their communities. According to attorney Robert McEwen, in 2013 American Indian children "represent[ed] .9 percent of all children but represent[ed] 2 percent of the total number of children in the foster care system in the United States. . . . They are twice as likely to be investigated, as compared to the general population, by the child welfare system. They are twice as likely to be substantiated, as compared to the general population. And they are three times as likely to be placed outside of their home, as compared with the general population." Some states have a higher overrepresentation of Indian children. Native American youth comprised 1.8 percent of that population but made up 7.1 percent of out-of-home placements in Nebraska in 2013.[54] Aboriginal and Torres Strait Islander children comprised 4.6 percent of Australian children in 2011–12 but 34 percent of all children living in out-of-home care. Indigenous children in Australia are ten times more likely than non-Indigenous children to be removed from their homes. Due to the Aboriginal Child Placement Principle, however, 68.8 percent of all Indigenous children were placed within their extended families, with other Indigenous carers, or in Indigenous residential care.[55] In Canada the rate of investigations for child maltreatment was 4.2 times higher for Aboriginal children than non-Aboriginal children in 2008.[56] Indigenous child welfare crises have proven much more intractable than Indigenous activists foresaw in the heady days of the late 1970s and early 1980s when ICWA gave Indigenous communities so much hope in the United States and abroad.

This persistence of Indigenous child welfare problems has many causes. Governments did not follow through with promises to provide adequate financial support to make Indigenous-run preventative and rehabilitative services a reality. The U.S. Congress, for example, did not consistently appropriate adequate funds for the implementation of ICWA, especially for the preventative social services called for in Title II of the act.[57] Efforts to slash budgets for *all* welfare and public assistance programs among these three nations throughout the last several decades have also made it difficult for Indigenous communities to develop and sustain viable programs.[58]

The crises persist, too, because Indigenous child removal has been a multigenerational, cyclical phenomenon that is difficult to reverse. Authorities had been carrying out Indigenous child removal for about a century when Congress passed ICWA in 1978. By then multiple generations had been affected by this damaging practice. It may take longer than a few decades to repair the damage. Justice Murray Sinclair, head of Canada's TRC, explained in a presentation in November 2013 that seven generations went through the residential schools in Canada. "Families were lost through disruption and breakdown. Communities lost leaders. Tribes lost status and authority," Sinclair points out. He believes that it may take seven generations to fix the damaged relationships within families and between Indigenous people and other Canadians.[59]

At base, the Indigenous child welfare crises persist because Indigenous people lack full self-determination and true justice. Justice will prove elusive until non-Indigenous people become fully aware of and properly acknowledge just what transpired. It will remain out of reach until the citizens in each nation make a genuine reckoning with past policies and practices of Indigenous child removal. Many Americans, Canadians, and Australians regard the persistence of problems in Indigenous communities as proof of their dysfunction and prefer to ignore the long history of government policies and practices that have inflicted great trauma on Indigenous families. But Justice Sinclair reminds us: "This is not an Aboriginal problem; it belongs to all of us."[60]

Canadians and Australians, no matter how imperfectly, have begun to grapple with the long history of interfering in Indigenous families. Canada is even making financial restitution for these damaging policies. The United States has moved in the opposite direction. The Supreme Court's 5-4 ruling in the Baby Veronica case represents an erasure of the long history of Indigenous child removal that led to the passage of ICWA. Justice for American Indians remains a distant dream.

# Afterword

Much of this book has been concerned with recovering an important truth about the egregious violation of Indigenous people's rights in the United States, Canada, and Australia in the recent past. In the righting of such historical wrongs, the companion to truth is reconciliation. But it may be premature to talk about reconciliation when there is still so much more truth to tell. And Indigenous people have other priorities than reconciliation: justice, sovereignty, self-determination, economic development, healing, and recovery—of their land and resources, of their families, of their languages and cultures. Decolonization is more pressing for Indigenous people than a rush to reconcile with their colonizers.

Reconciliation, too, can have dangerous implications. Many of the non-Indigenous people discussed in this book had a vision of reconciliation. They looked with alarm at the "plight" of Indigenous people and wanted to take part in an effort to right historical wrongs. They cared about the Indigenous children they fostered and adopted, and they imagined their blended families as harbingers of a new era of reconciliation between themselves and the descendants of the first peoples who lived on their continents. They rarely realized that such adoptions undermined rather than promoted possibilities for reconciliation. That is because their mode of reconciliation required that Indigenous people cease to be Indigenous. They believed that Indigenous people would only ever escape their plight of chronic unemployment, impoverishment, and poor health if they abandoned their cultures and erased their histories. Indigenous people were to reconcile themselves to their own elimination. I worry that talk of reconciliation today may similarly devolve into a call for Indigenous people to forgive and forget, to move on, to get over it.

While researching this book, however, I came across an intriguing photograph in the pages of *Indian Affairs*, the monthly newsletter of the Association on American Indian Affairs, which offers an alternative vision of reconciliation. The photo shows a gathering of people in a courtroom in the state of Michigan sometime in 1978 or 1979. Richard and Judith Nelson, a white couple, stand on the left with Edward Walksnice, a Northern Cheyenne boy they have just adopted through a special session of the Northern Cheyenne Tribal Court held in Escanaba, Michigan. Edward Walksnice holds the hand of his mother, Loretta Walksnice, who sits in a chair in the center of the picture. Terence Wallace Nelson, an older adopted Indian child, and Blake Walksnice, Edward's older brother, stand together on the other side of Ms. Walksnice. Northern Cheyenne social service providers and courtroom officials stand in the back behind the adoptee and his two families. The camera has frozen each participant in the moment, and we are left to wonder at their feelings. Edward, aged eight, smiles broadly, and his adoptive parents look relieved. Edward's brother Blake grins, but his new adoptive brother stares unflinchingly at the photographer. Is he thinking about his own path from his Indian family to the Nelsons, and how it differed from this unusual day in court? Ms. Walksnice clutches Edward's hand with both of hers. Her tentative smile conveys a deep sorrow but a resigned acceptance. Marie Sanchez, the chief judge of the tribal court, smiles warmly in the background, but the other tribal officials look on somberly.

The accompanying article explains that the Montana Department of Social Services had removed Edward and placed him with the Nelsons at their home in Michigan. The Nelsons filed to adopt Edward in a Michigan court, and the Northern Cheyennes challenged the jurisdiction of the state court, as the recently enacted ICWA now allowed them to do. The white adoptive couple then did something unexpected; they "voluntarily agreed that the Tribal Court was the proper forum for deciding the issue." A Michigan state court judge allowed the Northern Cheyenne Tribal Court the use of the courtroom for this special session. The Tribal Court heard testimony from all involved as well as from a child psychiatrist who examined the child and the adoptive family. "The Tribal Court decided," according to the article, "that the adoption should be allowed in accordance with Northern Cheyenne traditional custom and practice. Thus the adoption was granted, but there was no termination of parental

Fig. 15. The Northern Cheyenne Tribal Court approves the adoption of Edward Walk-snice, Escanaba, Michigan, ca. 1979. (Front, left to right): Richard Nelson, Judith Nelson, Edward Walksnice, Loretta Walksnice, Terence Wallace Nelson, and Blake Walksnice. (Back, left to right): Mike Bear Comes Out, probation counselor of the tribal court; Dolores Underwood, family counselor of the Cheyenne Home; Marie Sanches, chief judge of the tribal court; and Margaret Shoulderblade, juvenile clerk. From "Tribal Adoption Granted in Unique Court Session," *Indian Affairs* 98 (Fall–Winter 1978–79): 3. Courtesy and permission of the Association on American Indian Affairs.

rights of the natural family, as is done in non-Indian adoptions, and the Walksnice family will continue to have a relationship with Edward."[1] In a sense, the Northern Cheyennes adopted the Nelsons as part of Edward's extended family as much as the Nelsons adopted Edward.

Here was an American Indian vision of reconciliation. It was built on respect, not contempt, for Indian ways of life. It rested on recognition of Indian rights, not their abrogation. It sought to sustain rather than sever family connections. It furthered the survival and persistence of Indian peoples rather than their elimination. It was based on mutuality, not just the interests of white adoptive couples or a state power that wished to terminate Indians.

This photograph offers a vision of genuine reconciliation. The Indian Child Welfare Act, and the years of activism that led to its enactment, made this vision possible. But ultimately it took the actions of everyday people—the Nelsons, the Walksnice family, the community servants among the Northern Cheyenne and the state of Michigan—to arrive at this moment of reconciliation. They challenge us all to take our own tentative steps down the path toward a respectful and genuine reconciliation.

# Notes

ABBREVIATIONS USED IN NOTES

**AAIA papers**
Association on American Indian Affairs papers, Princeton, New Jersey

**AFSC records**
American Friends Service Committee records, Swarthmore, Pennsylvania

**AM**
Archives of Manitoba, Winnipeg, Canada

**BIA Social Service Records**
Bureau of Indian Affairs records, Washington DC

**CAR papers**
Council for Aboriginal Rights papers, Melbourne, Australia

**CWLA papers**
Child Welfare League of America papers, Minneapolis

**HRDA papers**
Human Resources Development Agency papers, Regina, Canada

**SAB**
Saskatchewan Archives Board, Regina and Saskatoon, Canada

**SPC fonds**
Social Planning Council fonds (papers), Winnipeg, Canada

### INTRODUCTION

1. "Adoption Controversy" (video), *Dr. Phil* web site; this clip is also available at http://www.youtube.com/watch?v=hdWzeOzdhaw.
2. *Adoptive Couple v. Baby Girl.* For an overview of the case, including all trial transcripts see "Adoptive Couple v. Baby Girl," Supreme Court blog. In essence, the court majority ruled that "a non-custodial Indian father invoking the

statute to counter the voluntary adoption initiated by a non-Indian mother seemed to the majority to be outside of the law's scope." See Rolnick, "Adoptive Couple v. Baby Girl (1 of 4)." See also "Adoptive Couple v. Baby Girl," Radio Lab transcript.

3. Hall, "A Sioux Mother Battles White In-Laws"; *Brokenleg v. Butts*.
4. *Brokenleg v. Butts*, 853, 855.
5. *Brokenleg v. Butts*, 853, 855, 857.
6. *Brokenleg v. Butts*, 853, 857. See also Indian Child Welfare Program, Second Report, July 1976–October 1976, 42, box 365, folder 2, Association on American Indian Affairs Records, 1851–2010, Public Policy Papers, Department of Rare Books and Manuscripts, Princeton University Library, Princeton, New Jersey.
7. Hall, "A Sioux Mother Battles White In-Laws"; Bertram Hirsch, interview by author, September 30, 2011.
8. Appendix G, "Indian Child Welfare Statistical Survey, July 1976, Association of American Indian Affairs," in U.S. Senate, Select Committee on Indian Affairs, *Indian Child Welfare Act of 1977: Hearing before the United States Senate Select Committee on Indian Affairs, 95th Congress, First Session on S. 1214,* August 4, 1977, 538–603 (hereafter cited as U.S. Senate, *ICWA Congressional Hearing 1977*).
9. "Adoptive Couple v. Baby Girl," Radio Lab transcript.
10. *Indian Country Today* has provided thorough coverage of the case. See http://indiancountrytodaymedianetwork.com/story/baby-veronica.
11. U.S. Senate, *ICWA Congressional Hearing 1977*, 493.
12. Human Rights and Equal Opportunity Commission, *Bringing Them Home*; Regan, *Unsettling the Settler Within*; Nobles, *Politics of Official Apologies*.

PROLOGUE

1. Adams, *Education for Extinction*; Jacobs, *White Mother*, 1–86.
2. Miller, *Shingwauk's Vision*; Milloy, *A National Crime*; Haebich, *Broken Circles*.
3. Ortiz, *from Sand Creek*.
4. Graybill, *The Red and the White*.
5. Bauer, *We Were All Like Migrant Workers*, 49; Madley, "Patterns of Frontier Genocide," 178.
6. Jackson, *A Century of Dishonor*.
7. Wolfe, "Land, Labor, and Difference."
8. Jacobs, *White Mother*, 149–92, 229–80.
9. Anderson, *A Recognition of Being*, 83, 170, 171. See also Krosenbrink-Gelissen, "Caring Is Indian Women's Business," 108–9; Stremlau, *Sustaining the Cherokee Family*.

10. Gertrude Bonnin took on her Nakota name, Zitkala-Ša, later in life. Her serialized memoir has been reprinted as *American Indian Stories*, with a new introduction by Susan Rose Dominguez.
11. Hertzberg, *Search for an American Indian Identity*.
12. Meriam, *The Problem of Indian Administration*, 11, 15.
13. Fixico, *Indian Resilience and Rebuilding*, 70–95; Marsha Weisiger's *Dreaming of Sheep in Navajo Country* offers a complex and nuanced view of Collier's administration.

MODERN INDIAN LIFE

1. Figure 3.2: Current, Binge, and Heavy Alcohol Use among Persons Aged 12 or Older, by Race/Ethnicity: 2010, in U.S. Department of Health and Human Services, *Results from the 2010 National Survey*. Some studies have found somewhat higher rates of alcohol use and abuse among Native populations, but nothing approaching 90 percent. For an overview of mental health studies of American Indians and Alaska Natives, including alcohol abuse and dependence, see Gone and Trimble, "American Indian and Alaska Native Mental Health."
2. ABC's 20/20, "A Hidden America." For another example, also from Pine Ridge—a media favorite—see Fuller, "In the Shadow of Wounded Knee."

1. BUREAUCRACY OF CARING FOR INDIAN CHILDREN

1. Fortunate Eagle, *Pipestone*. See also Child, *Boarding School Seasons*, for more on how Indian families used the boarding schools in the early twentieth century as part of their economic strategies.
2. Adams, *Education for Extinction*; Jacobs, *White Mother*.
3. Minnesota Legislative Interim Committee on Indian Affairs, "Statement prepared for Senate Committee on Organization for Department of Interior," March 1957, box 120, folder: Indian Committee, 1957–1964, Child Welfare Services–Indian Children, United Way of Minnesota papers SW 070, Social Welfare History Archives, Special Collections, University of Minnesota Libraries, Minneapolis (hereafter cited as United Way papers).
4. Minnesota Legislative Committee, "Statement," March 1957, United Way papers.
5. Quoted in Bremmer, *Children and Youth in America*, 1324–25, 1328–29. See also Lee, *Diagnosis and Treatment*, 183.
6. Rosier, "'They Are Ancestral Homelands,'" 1301; Ulrich, *American Indian Nations*; Wilkinson, *Blood Struggle*, 57–86; Fixico, *Termination and Relocation*, 91–110.

7. Fixico, *Termination and Relocation*, 183, 103.

8. Wilkinson, *Blood Struggle*, 81.

9. AAIA report, "The American Indian Relocation Program," December 1956, box 120, folder: Indian Committee, January 1956–April 1956, United Way papers; Fixico, *Termination and Relocation*, 134–57.

10. AAIA report, "The American Indian Relocation Program," United Way papers.

11. Goldberg-Ambrose, *Planting Tail Feathers*. Congress allegedly made exceptions for Red Lake in Minnesota and Warm Springs in Oregon because they deemed these reservations to have sufficiently developed and well-functioning legal systems (49). PL-280 complicated jurisdiction considerably. For the enormously varied responsibilities states adopted as a result of it, see Task Force Four, *Report on Federal, State, and Tribal Jurisdiction*, 4–33, especially the chart, 8–9. See also Fixico, *Termination and Relocation*, 111–33.

12. Goldberg-Ambrose, *Planting Tail Feathers*, 2, 244. Idaho and North Dakota stipulated that tribes consent to their assumption of jurisdiction under PL-280.

13. Goldberg-Ambrose, *Planting Tail Feathers*, 10–12, 56, 37.

14. Memo from Beasley to Assistant Commissioner, March 16, 1954, box 1, folder: General, July 1954–June 1955; Memo from Hastings to Chief, Branch of Budget and Finance, February 16, 1960, box 1, folder: General, January 1960–December 1961; both in Miscellaneous Subject Files, 1929–68, Division of Social Services, Records of the Bureau of Indian Affairs, Record Group 75, National Archives and Records Administration, Washington DC (hereafter cited as BIA Social Service Records).

15. Letter from Rovin to Dr. Peter Dorner, Department of Economics, Harvard University, October 2, 1958, box 3, folder: General, July 1957–December, 1959, BIA Social Service Records.

16. Letter from Beasley to Chief, Branch of Personnel, April 4, 1955, box 1, folder: General, July 1954–June 1955, BIA Social Service Records.

17. Letter from Beasley to Assistant Commissioner, June 24, 1955, box 1, folder: General, July 1954–June 1955, BIA Social Service Records.

18. Minutes of Branch of Welfare Conference, Washington DC, December 1–9, 1955, dated March 21, 1955, 4, box 5, folder: Conference, BIA Social Service Records.

19. Register, Aleta Brownlee Papers, 1945–1950, Hoover Institution Archives, Stanford University, available in the Online Archive of California, http://www.oac.cdlib.org/findaid/ark:/13030/tf4t1nb0jj/admin/#bioghist-1.7.4, accessed July 17, 2013.

20. For more on Lucile Hastings and her family, see "Annual Meeting, Oklahoma Historical Society," *Chronicles of Oklahoma*.

21. Letter from Vinita Lewis to Harold Tascher, April 15, 1954, box 1, folder: General, July 1954–June 1955; Personnel Notes of Vinita Lewis, Welfare Specialist, March 21, 1955, box 5, folder: Conference, both in BIA Social Service Records.

22. U.S. Department of the Interior, *Annual Report of the Commissioner of Indian Affairs*, 1954, 241 (hereafter cited as *Annual Report of Indian Affairs*).

23. Brownlee, "American Indian Child," 59.

24. Fuchs and Havighurst, *To Live on This Earth*, 228–29; Reyhner and Eder, *American Indian Education*, 237–41.

25. Unger, "Indian Child Welfare Act of 1978," 164.

26. Memo from Jerdone to Butler, October 17, 1968, box 2, folder: General Program Admin., January–December 1968, BIA Social Service Records.

27. Jacobs, *White Mother*, 229–327.

28. *Annual Report of Indian Affairs*, 1954, 239; 1955, 245; 1957, 251.

29. Memo from Brownlee to Gifford, July 29, 1953, box 1, folder: General, July 1954–June 1955, BIA Social Service Records.

30. *Annual Report of Indian Affairs*, 1954, 241; 1955, 246; 1956, 213; 1957, 252. See also Fuchs and Havighurst, *To Live on This Earth*, 14–15, 227; Reyhner and Eder, *American Indian Education*, 244, 248–49.

31. Letter from Brownlee to Chief, Welfare Branch, April 8, 1955, box 1, folder: General, July 1954–June 1955, BIA Social Service Records.

32. Remarks of Clare Golden at Conference of South Dakota Health, Welfare, and Rehabilitation, September 21, 1961, box 1, folder: General, January 1960–December 1961, BIA Social Service Records.

33. Memo from Jerdone to Chief, Branch of Social Services, January 23, 1968, box 2, folder: General Program Admin., January–December 1968, BIA Social Service Records.

34. *Annual Report of Indian Affairs*, 1952, 399. The BIA made the same transfer of child welfare services to Nevada in 1955. See *Annual Report of Indian Affairs*, 1955, 213.

35. *Annual Report of Indian Affairs*, 1958, 209–10; 1959, 238; 1960, 204.

36. Letter from Beasley to Chief, Branch of Relocation, April 5, 1955, box 1, folder: General, July 1954–June 1955, BIA Social Service Records.

37. Letter from Beasley to Assistant Commissioner, April 11, 1955, box 1, folder: General, July 1954–June 1955, BIA Social Service Records.

38. Minnesota Legislative Committee, "Statement," March 1957, United Way papers.

39. *Annual Report of Indian Affairs*, 1954, 241; 1955, 246; 1958, 209.

40. In 1909, at the prestigious White House Conference on Dependent Children convened by President Theodore Roosevelt, reformers resolved that depen-

dent children should not be placed in institutions and that every effort should be made to keep families intact. In particular, participants emphasized that children should not be removed for reasons of poverty. See Ashby, *Saving the Waifs*, 31, 34, 54, 58, 65; Tiffin, *In Whose Best Interest?*, 110.

41. Department of Public Welfare, "Child Welfare Services–Indian Children," March 15, 1957, box 120, folder: Indian Committee, 1957–1964, 3, United Way papers.

42. Letter from Brownlee to Chief, Welfare Branch, April 8, 1955, box 1, folder: General, July 1954–June 1955, BIA Social Service Records.

43. Memo from Brownlee to Miss Bloodworth, June 15, 1960, box 1, folder: General, January 1960–December 1961, BIA Social Service Records.

44. Letter from Mrs. Ira Mikesell, Monticello, Indiana, to "Dear Sir," August 23, 1954, box 2, folder: General, 1953–June 1955, BIA Social Service Records.

45. Greenwood to Sen. Russell, March 15, 1954 with letter attached from J. R. Bryant, February 14, 1954, box 2, folder: General, 1953–June 1955, BIA Social Service Records.

46. Minutes of Branch of Welfare Conference, Washington DC, December 1–9, 1955, dated March 21, 1955, 24, 35, box 5, folder: Conference, BIA Social Service Records.

47. *Annual Report of Indian Affairs*, 1958, 208; 1959, 238; Memo from Rovin to Commissioner, July 22, 1958, box 3, folder: General, July 1957–December, 1959, BIA Social Service Records; Lyslo, "Adoptive Placement of American Indian Children with Non-Indian Families, Part I: The Indian Project," *Child Welfare* 40, no. 5 (May 1961): 4; Brownlee, "American Indian Child," 55–60. See memo from Reid to CWLA Member Agencies, April 1, 1959, box 17, folder 3, and Arnold Lyslo, "Progress Report of the IAP," May 14, 1963, box 17, folder 4, both in Child Welfare League of America papers, Social Welfare History Archives, Special Collections, University of Minnesota Libraries, Minneapolis (hereafter cited as CWLA papers).

48. Letter from Rovin to Rev. Arnold Purdie, Philadelphia, January 5, 1968, box 2, folder: General Program Admin., January–December 1968, BIA Social Service Records; University of Minnesota, Class of 1945, yearbook, http://www .eyearbook.com/yearbooks/University_Minnesota_Gopher_Yearbook/1945 /Page_188.html, accessed on April 4, 2011.

49. Memo from Rovin to Commissioner, July 22, 1958, box 3, folder: General, July 1957–December, 1959, BIA Social Service Records.

50. Fanshel, *Far From the Reservation*, 340.

51. "Indian Adoption Project," April 1960 report, a 7-page document describing the project, probably written by Arnold Lyslo, 1–2, box 17, folder 3: Indian Adoption Project, 1959–1962, CWLA papers. See also Lyslo, "Adoptive Place-

ment, of American Indian Children with Non-Indian Families, Part I: The Indian Project," *Child Welfare* 40, no. 5 (May 1961): 4.

52. Arnold Lyslo, "The Indian Adoption Project, 1958–1967," Report, April 1, 1968, 7, box 17, folder 4, CWLA papers.

53. Barbara Lewis Roberts, "Indian Adoption Project Annual Report 1972," box 17, folder 4; box 89, folders: ARENA News, 1968–1975, ARENA News 1977–1979, CWLA papers.

54. Description of position for Director, Special Project III (Indian Adoption Project), in CWLA Position Descriptions, 1965, 28, box 8, folder 9, CWLA papers.

55. Memo from Reid to CWLA Member Agencies, April 1, 1959, box 17, folder 3, CWLA papers.

56. Lyslo, "The Indian Adoption Project, 1958–1967," 1–5, box 17, folder 4, CWLA papers.

57. Collmeyer, "From 'Operation Brown Baby' to 'Opportunity,'" 255.

58. "Indian Adoption Project," April 1960 report, 3–4, box 17, folder 3, CWLA papers, emphasis added.

59. "Indian Adoption Project," April 1960 report, 1.

60. Joseph Reid to Philleo Nash, CIA, October 19, 1962, Quarterly report on IAP, box 17, folder 3, CWLA papers.

61. Arnold Lyslo, "Progress Report of the IAP," May 14, 1963, box 17, folder 4, CWLA papers.

62. Arnold Lyslo, Report to Agencies who participated in the CWLA Questionnaire concerning the adoptive placement of Indian children in 1965, October 11, 1966, 1, box 17, folder 4, CWLA papers.

63. Lyslo, "The Indian Adoption Project, 1958–1967," 6, 7, box 17, folder 4, CWLA papers.

64. Lyslo, "The Indian Adoption Project, 1958–1967," 7.

65. Reid to Philleo Nash, October 19, 1962, Quarterly report on IAP, box 17, folder 3, CWLA papers.

66. Lyslo, "The Indian Adoption Project, 1958–1967," 9.

67. Reid to Philleo Nash, October 19, 1962, Quarterly report on IAP.

68. Lyslo, "The Indian Adoption Project, 1958–1967," 9.

69. Lyslo, Report to Agencies who participated in the CWLA Questionnaire, 2–3.

70. Reid to Nash, May 7, 1963, 1, box 17, folder 4, CWLA papers, emphasis added.

71. "Indian Adoption Project," April 1960 report, 2, box 17, folder 3, CWLA papers.

72. "Indian Adoption Project," April 1960 report, 2.

73. See Hostbjor, "Social Services," 7, 8.

74. Hostbjor, "Social Services," 8.

75. Hostbjor, "Social Services," 8.

76. Hostbjor, "Social Services," 8, 9.

77. "Indian Adoption Project," April 1960 report.

78. Lyslo, "The Indian Adoption Project, 1958–1967," 10, box 17, folder 4, CWLA papers.

79. Brownlee, "American Indian Child," 57.

80. Hostbjor, "Social Services," 7.

81. May, *Homeward Bound.*

82. "Indian Adoption Project," April 1960 report, 2.

83. Lyslo, "The Indian Adoption Project, 1958–1967," 9, box 17, folder 4, CWLA papers.

84. Reid to Nash, October 19, 1962, Quarterly report on IAP.

85. Reid to Philleo Nash, July 29, 1963, 3, box 17, folder 4, CWLA papers.

86. Quintana, *Ordeal of Change,* 125–26.

87. Lyslo, "The Indian Adoption Project, 1958–1967," 6.

88. Lyslo, "The Indian Adoption Project, 1958–1967," 6.

89. Lyslo, "Adoption for American Indian Children," *Child Welfare* 39, no. 6 (June 1960): 32.

90. Lyslo, "Adoptive Placement of American Indian Children with Non-Indian Families, Part I: The Indian Project," *Child Welfare* 40, no. 5 (May 1961): 6.

91. Memo from Joseph Reid to CWLA Member Agencies, April 1, 1959, box 17, folder 3, CWLA papers.

92. "Content of Child Welfare," Report prepared by Bernice Scroggie and Annie Lee David, May 1953, box 12, folder 11, CWLA papers.

93. Booklet, "Child Welfare League of America Standards for Child Protective Service" (New York: CWLA, 1960), 12, box 14, folder 5, CWLA papers.

94. Arnold Lyslo, "Progress Report of the IAP," May 14, 1963, box 17, folder 4, CWLA papers, emphasis added.

95. "Social Work Practice in Child Welfare," manual, May 1958, 8, 25, box 12, folder 11, CWLA papers.

96. Lyslo, "The Indian Adoption Project, 1958–1967," 9, box 17, folder 4, CWLA papers.

97. Brownlee, "American Indian Child," 60.

98. "Indian Adoption Project," April 1960 report, 4, box 17, folder 3, CWLA papers.

99. Quoted in Unger, "Indian Child Welfare Act of 1978," 240.

## 2. CARING ABOUT INDIAN CHILDREN IN A LIBERAL AGE

1. Doss, *Family Nobody Wanted,* 6, 30.

2. Doss, *Family Nobody Wanted,* 222.

3. Doss, *Family Nobody Wanted,* 140–41, 142, 176.

4. The adoption of Indian children prior to World War II was much less common, though not unheard of. See Jacobs, "Breaking and Remaking Families"; and Jagodinsky, "'In a Family Way.'"

5. Doss, *Family Nobody Wanted*, 31, 188.

6. For example, see Kilpatrick, *Celluloid Indians*; Marubbio, *Killing the Indian Maiden*; Aleiss *Making the White Man's Indian*.

7. Harvey and Goff, *Columbia Documentary History of Religion*, 4. For more on the relationship between religion and the nuclear arms race and the Cold War, see Wuthnow, *Restructuring of American Religion*, 39–45.

8. Allitt, *Religion in America since 1945*, 22–25, 43–55.

9. For the widespread coverage of the Navajo crisis, and the letters Americans wrote to the president regarding it, see Rosier, *Serving Their Country*, 123–30.

10. Fey, "Most Indians Are Poor," 592–93.

11. Jenkins, *Dream Catchers*, 65–153; quote on La Farge, 121. Although Jenkins identifies a "wave of radical cultural and religious experimentation in the late 1940s" that similarly lionized Indian religious cultures, he notes that these "currents of thought . . . went underground" in the 1950s and "returned to full view in the mid-1960s" (138). Jenkins notes, too, that public interest in Indian religion and culture declined in the 1950s (151–53.)

12. Jacobs, *Engendered Encounters*.

13. Mathews, *Wah'kon-tah* and *Sundown*; Standing Bear, *Land of the Spotted Eagle*; McNickle, *The Surrounded*; Neihardt, *Black Elk Speaks*; Jenkins, *Dream Catchers*, 120–22.

14. Weston, *Native Americans in the News*, 105.

15. Day, "Methodism and the Navajos," 4, 5.

16. In *Hippies, Indians, and the Fight for Red Power* Sherry Smith shows how involved Christian progressives were in supporting the Red Power movement in the 1960s and 1970s. See especially 8–9, 34–51, 152–56, 195–200, and 208–11.

17. Harold Fey obituaries, *New York Times*, February 2, 1990; *Chicago Tribune*, January 1990; *Los Angeles Times*, February 1, 1990, all accessed June 21, 2012: http://www.nytimes.com/1990/02/02/obituaries/harold-e-fey-91-a-writer-and -editor-on-religious-topics.html; http://articles.chicagotribune.com/1990–01–31 /news/9001090201_1_christian-church-professor-of-christian-ethics-current -editor; http://articles.latimes.com/1990–02–01/news/mn-1298_1_ecumenical -magazine.

18. Fey and McNickle, *Indians and Other Americans*.

19. Fey, "Most Indians Are Poor," 592.

20. Fey, "Most Indians Are Poor," 592.

21. Fey, "Our Neighbor the Indian," 361, 362.

22. Fey, "Indian Winter," 265.

23. Fey, "Our Neighbor the Indian," 361.

24. Fey, "Our National Indian Policy."

25. Fey, "The Indian and the Law," 299.

26. Fey, "The Church and the Indian," 728.

27. Secular urban groups—including Travelers Aid Societies, which contracted with the BIA to give emergency assistance to relocated Indians; the National Urban League; and local groups such as the Elliot Park Neighborhood House in Minneapolis—also provided services to Indian families, and Indian-run Indian centers developed in urban areas to support Indian communities. See AAIA report, "The American Indian Relocation Program," December 1956, 16, box 120, folder: Indian Committee, January 1956–April 1956, United Way of Minnesota papers SW 070, Social Welfare History Archives, Special Collections, University of Minnesota Libraries, Minneapolis (hereafter cited as United Way papers).

28. Rev. David Clark, United Church Committee on Indian Work, Report, September 1953–October 1954, box 120, folder: Indian Affairs, 1948–1955, United Way papers.

29. "The Indian Center," Los Angeles, brochure, 1952–53, American Friends Service Committee records, Swarthmore College Peace Collection, Swarthmore, Pennsylvania (hereafter cited as AFSC records).

30. AFSC, Pacific Southwest Regional Office, Pasadena, California, "How . . . Can We Close the Gap of Misunderstanding?" brochure, ca. 1950, AFSC records.

31. AFSC, "How . . . Can We Close the Gap of Misunderstanding?"

32. AAIA report, "The American Indian Relocation Program," 16, United Way papers.

33. Garrett, "Mormons, Indians and Lamanites," 9, 229, 230.

34. Garrett, "Mormons, Indians and Lamanites," 101, 102. The LDS Church eventually expanded this program. For its work in Canada, see Wright, "Negotiating Home."

35. Quoted in Garrett, "Mormons, Indians and Lamanites," 417.

36. Lyslo, "Adoption for American Indian Children," *Child Welfare* 39, no. 6 (June 1960): 32–33; Lyslo, "Adoptive Placement of American Indian Children with Non-Indian Families, Part I: The Indian Project," *Child Welfare* 40, no. 5 (May 1961): 4–6.

37. Arnold Lyslo, "1966 Year End Summary of the IAP," March 15, 1967, box 17, folder 4: Indian Adoption Project, 1963–1972, CWLA papers. See Silberman, "When Noel Came Home," 80, 171.

38. Lyslo, "1966 Year End Summary of the IAP," CWLA papers.

39. *ARENA News*, Supplement no. 13, August, 1970, box 89, folder: *ARENA News* Supplement, CWLA papers. See also *ARENA News* issues no. 13 (September 1980), no. 17 (March 1971), and no. 24 (January–February 1972), box 89, folder: *ARENA News*, 1968–1975, CWLA papers.

40. Position description for director of ARENA, 1972, 11, box 8, folder 11, CWLA papers.

41. "Indian Adoption Project," April 1960 report, 3, box 17, folder 3, CWLA papers.

42. Reid to Philleo Nash, October 19, 1962, box 17, folder 3: Indian Adoption Project, 1959–1962; Reid to Nash, January 29, 1963; Reid to Nash, May 7, 1963; Reid to Nash, July 29, 1963; and Arnold Lyslo, "1966 Year End Summary of the IAP," all in box 17, folder 4: Indian Adoption Project, 1963–1972, CWLA papers; Lyslo, "The Indian Adoption Project: An Appeal to Catholic Agencies to Participate," *Catholic Charities Review* 48, no. 5 (May 1964): 12–16; Lyslo, "Adoptive Placement of American Indian Children," *Catholic Charities Review* 51, no. 2 (February 1967): 23–25.

43. Rosene, "A Follow-up Study of Indian Children Adopted by White Families," vi, 19.

44. Reid to Joseph Bobbitt, November 6, 1968, box 118, folder 11, Association on American Indian Affairs Records, 1851–2010, Public Policy Papers, Department of Rare Books and Manuscripts, Princeton University Library, Princeton, New Jersey.

45. I detail this denigration of Indian family life in my book, *White Mother to a Dark Race*.

46. Horton, *Race and the Making of American Liberalism*, 121.

47. Pascoe, *What Comes Naturally*, 313. See also Bonilla-Silva, *Racism without Racists*.

48. "Babies without Homes," *Saturday Evening Post*, February 16, 1963, 16, in box 16, folder 1, CWLA papers.

49. Article clipping, "The ARENA: Where Hard-to-Place Children and Selective Families Meet," (my emphasis), *Family Planner*, November 18, 1970, 14, box 16, folder 3, CWLA papers.

50. Doss, *Family Nobody Wanted*, 30.

51. Lyndon B. Johnson later used the same term to describe Native Americans in general in a well-known 1968 speech to Congress; see Johnson, "Special Message."

52. "Indian Adoption Project," April 1960 report, box 17, folder 3, CWLA papers.

53. Some of the material in this section has been published in Jacobs, "Remembering the 'Forgotten Child.'"

54. Pascoe, *What Comes Naturally*, 313; Bonilla-Silva, *Racism without Racists*, 57.

55. "Research Schedule on Indian Adoption Project," ca. 1960, 7, 8, box 17, folder 3, CWLA papers.

56. Fanshel, *Far from the Reservation*, 62, 65, 66.

57. Virginia Shake, United Charities, Family Service, Chicago, "Case Work Service to Unmarried Mothers Who Keep Their Babies," paper presented at National Association on Service to Unmarried Parents at National Conference of Social Work, p. 1, May 21, 1957, Philadelphia, Pennsylvania, in box 4, folder 32, Beatrice Bernhagen papers SW 134, Social Welfare History Archives, Special Collections, University of Minnesota Libraries, Minneapolis. For more on the widespread belief in the post–World War II era that unwed pregnancy in white women was a "result of deep-seated neurosis in the pregnant woman, a psychological state that made her, by definition, an unfit mother," see Balcom, *Traffic in Babies*, 29.

58. Hostbjor, "Social Services," 7–8.

59. Reid to Philleo Nash, CIA, July 29, 1963, 6, based on Lyslo's meeting with Colorado State Department of Public Welfare, box 17, folder 4, CWLA papers.

60. Brownlee, "American Indian Child," 56.

61. See Hostbjor, "Social Services," 8, 9.

62. "Indian Adoption Project," April 1960, 2, box 17, folder 3, CWLA papers.

63. May, *Homeward Bound*.

64. Davis, "One Agency's Approach," 15.

65. Weston, *Native Americans in the News*, 106–7.

66. Lyslo, "The Indian Adoption Project: An Appeal to Catholic Agencies to Participate," *Catholic Charities Review* 48, no. 5 (May 1964): 13.

67. Changes in American religious life due to anti-communism and the Cold War may have undermined the more radical critique of the 1950s. Churches that took progressive stands in favor of civil rights and social justice, including the United Methodist Church, the Presbyterians, the United Church of Christ, and the Episcopal Church, all saw declines in membership during this era. See Harvey and Goff, *Columbia Documentary History of Religion*, 7.

68. For more on Collier's administration, including his turn to the use of anthropologists, see Kelly, *Assault on Assimilation*, and Philp, *John Collier's Crusade*.

69. For detailed background on the history of anthropology in this era, see Darnell, *Invisible Geneaologies*. Darnell traces the rise of "culture and personality" studies in anthropology.

70. MacGregor, *Warriors without Weapons*.

71. MacGregor, *Warriors without Weapons*, 52–53.

72. MacGregor, *Warriors without Weapons*, 56, 93, 127–28, 205.

73. MacGregor, *Warriors without Weapons*, 121, 191, 209.

74. MacGregor, *Warriors without Weapons*, 118, 58.

75. MacGregor, *Warriors without Weapons*, 57, 118–19.

76. Moynihan, "The Negro Family."

77. Lewis, "The Culture of Poverty," 19.

78. Lewis, "The Culture of Poverty," 23, 25.

79. Hostbjor, "Social Services," 7.

80. Fanshel, *Far from the Reservation*, 339.

81. Davis, "One Agency's Approach," 15.

82. Davis, "One Agency's Approach," 12.

83. Letter from Mrs. Winifred Kromholtz to Senator Warren Magnuson, in U.S. Senate, ICWA *Congressional Hearing 1977*, 493.

84. "Proposed Agenda, Joint Conference of Indian Adoption Project," September 15, 1960, New York City, 2; and "Indian Adoption Project," April 1960 report, 3; both in box 17, folder 3, CWLA papers.

85. Trip Report from Jerdone, May 20, 1968, box 2, folder: General Program Admin., January–December 1968, Miscellaneous Subject Files, 1929–68, Division of Social Services, Records of the Bureau of Indian Affairs, Record Group 75, National Archives and Records Administration, Washington DC.

86. *ARENA News*, no. 20, August 1971, 1–2, box 89, folder: *ARENA News*, 1968–1975, CWLA papers.

87. *ARENA News*, no. 5, April 1969, 2, 3; no. 9, November 1969, 3; box 89, folder: *ARENA News*, 1968–1975, CWLA papers.

88. Fanshel, *Far from the Reservation*, 337; Roherty, *Exploratory Project on Outcome of Adoption*, 9.

89. Herman, *Kinship by Design*, 197. Similar trends were evident in the other three nations with which this book is concerned. In Canada, for example, the baby boom peaked in 1959 with a concomitant rise in illegitimate birth and divorces. The number of children in care doubled from 1959 to 1969 to 100,000. However, in 1969, therapeutic abortions were legalized and the prohibition on the sale and advertising of birth control was lifted, leading to a decline in the numbers of "white" children available for adoption. See Hepworth, *Foster Care and Adoption in Canada*, 1, 19–28.

90. Fanshel, *Far from the Reservation*, 92–93.

91. Box 12, folder 8, CWLA papers. For more on racial matching, see Herman, *Kinship by Design*, 121–54; Melosh, *Strangers and Kin*, 51–104; Simon and Altstein, *Adoption, Race, and Identity*, 1–14.

92. Booklet, "Child Welfare League of America Standards for Adoption Service" (New York: CWLA, revised 1968), 34, box 13, folder 8, CWLA papers. In response to criticism from both American Indian groups and the National

Association of Black Social Workers in the early 1970s, the CWLA shifted its position on transracial adoption again.

93. Mary Battenfeld, "Introduction," in Doss, *The Family Nobody Wanted*, xiv–xxvi, quotes at xviii and xx.

94. Fanshel, *Far from the Reservation*, 71, 87, 93–94.

95. Fanshel, *Far from the Reservation*, 141, 148, 195.

96. Fanshel, *Far from the Reservation*, 141, 198.

97. Fanshel, *Far from the Reservation*, 374, 322.

98. Fanshel, *Far from the Reservation*, 88, 84, emphasis added.

99. Roherty, *Exploratory Project on the Outcome of Adoption*, 9.

100. Fanshel, *Far from the Reservation*, 21, 121, 128, 179.

101. Fanshel, *Far from the Reservation*, 85, 88.

102. Fanshel, *Far from the Reservation*, 92.

### 3. LOSING CHILDREN

1. "AAIA Reunited Five Indian Families," *Indian Family Defense*, a bulletin of the American Association on American Indian Affairs, no. 3 (May 1975): 7; Bertram Hirsch, interview by author, September 30, 2011.

2. Roherty, *Exploratory Project on Outcome of Adoption*, 34, 35.

3. Lyslo, "The Indian Adoption Project: An Appeal to Catholic Agencies to Participate," *Catholic Charities Review* 48, no. 5 (May 1964): 13–14.

4. "The Mother and Child Reunion," transcript of *Native America Calling* radio show, September 9, 2011, http://www.nativeamericacalling.com/nac_past .shtml, accessed November 16, 2011.

5. Testimony of Cheryl DeCoteau, U.S. Senate, Committee on Interior and Insular Affairs, Subcommittee on Indian Affairs, 93rd Congress, 2nd Session, *Hearing on Problems that American Indian Families Face in Raising their Children and How these Problems are Affected by Federal Action or Inaction*, April 8 and 9, 1974, 65–68 (hereafter cited as U.S. Senate, *ICWA Congressional Hearing 1974*). After taking her baby, the state—the South Dakota Division of Social Welfare—initiated proceedings to have her older child, Herbert, placed in foster care on the basis of neglect, because DeCoteau regularly left him with her great-grandmother. AAIA attorney Bertram Hirsch was successful in having DeCoteau's two children returned to her. This case, however, went all the way to the Supreme Court over jurisdictional and treaty issues, and on these issues, the tribe lost. Robert Leach, program administrator of the South Dakota Department of Social Services, Division of Social Welfare, contested the AAIA's version of events, asserting that the great-grandmother sought foster care for the child left in her care and that DeCoteau voluntarily gave up her child for adoption. See Leach to William Byler,

AAIA, March 11, 1974, box 78, folder 2, Association on American Indian Affairs Records, 1851–2010, Public Policy Papers, Department of Rare Books and Manuscripts, Princeton University Library, Princeton, New Jersey (hereafter cited as AAIA papers). For more on the DeCoteau case, see "Cheryl De Coteau," *Indian Family Defense* 1 (Winter 1974), 6; *DeCoteau v. District County Court for the Tenth Judicial District*, 420 U.S. 425, 95 S. Ct. 1082 (1975).

6. The form is included with a series of Office Memoranda from 1959, including Memo from Winifred Nash, Public Health Division to Mr. Robert Hollinger, Legislative Legal Liaison Officer re. Indian Health—Adoption Procedure—Authorization for Discharge of infant child . . . ," September 9, 1959, box 78, folder 4: Child Welfare, 1975, AAIA papers.

7. Flood, *Lost Bird of Wounded Knee*, 10–11.

8. Fessler, *The Girls Who Went Away*, 8; Solinger, *Wake Up Little Susie*. At this time, however, social workers did not encourage black women to give their babies up for adoption. See Solinger, "Race and Value."

9. Fanshel, *Far from the Reservation*, 60. Ages: 25 percent were between 20 and 24; 20.9 percent between 25 and 29, 15.6 percent between 30 and 34, and 10.4 percent over 35 years of age.

10. Fanshel, *Far from the Reservation*, 61.

11. Briggs, *Somebody's Children*, 178–93, 201–22.

12. Fanshel, *Far from the Reservation*, 64.

13. Fanshel, *Far from the Reservation*, 64.

14. Minnesota Legislative Interim Committee on Indian Affairs, "Statement prepared for Senate Committee on Organization for Department of Interior," March 1957, 6, box 120, folder: Indian Committee, 1957–1964, Child Welfare Services—Indian Children," United Way papers.

15. "Indian Child Welfare Reform First Report," March 1976–June 1976, 34, box 365, folder 1, AAIA papers.

16. AAIA, "Indian Family Defense Legal Services Program," Proposal to the Lilly Endowment, n.d., ca. 1975, 2, box 365, folder 1, AAIA papers.

17. Booklet, "Child Welfare League of America Standards for Child Protective Service" (New York: CWLA, 1960), 10, box 14, folder 5: Standards—Protective Services, 1937, 1957–60, CWLA papers.

18. George Keller, superintendent of Rosebud, to Dr. Orval Westby, Department of Social Services, South Dakota, October 15, 1976, and "Case #4, October 1976 referrals," 2, both in box 88, folder 14, AAIA papers. The Social Security Act of 1935 established Aid to Dependent Children for single mothers. In 1962 the government changed the name to Aid to Families with Dependent Children. Keller was using the earlier name.

19. Smithson to Hirsch, May 12, 1972; Resolution from [North Dakota State Attorney General's office], October 19, 1971; United Tribes Welfare Board, Proposal for Implementation of AFDC-FC in North Dakota, Working Draft, ca. 1971 or 1972; all in box 225, folder 1, AAIA papers.

20. AAIA report, "The American Indian Relocation Program," December 1956, 9, United Way papers. This report recommended elimination of these "local laws which set up residence requirements for public welfare assistance" (22). The report is critical of the relocation program because "although it does not itself exert evil pressure upon Indians," it "is carried out in a total Indian situation in which enormous force is being brought to bear upon the Indian people" (18). The report recommends repeal of House Concurrent Resolution 108, termination policy, and genuine efforts to promote economic development on reservations to obviate the need for Indians to relocate to urban areas to find employment (18–21).

21. Westermeyer, "Ravage of Indian Families in Crisis," 47–52.

22. Proceedings, Indian Child Welfare and Family Services Conference, AAIA, January 20 [26], 1974, Biltmore Hotel, New York, 69, box 365, folder 4, AAIA papers.

23. Fanshel, *Far from the Reservation*, 63.

24. Fanshel, *Far from the Reservation*, 61–62.

25. Fanshel, *Far from the Reservation*, 61.

26. Fanshel, *Far from the Reservation*, 61.

27. Fanshel, *Far from the Reservation*, 64, 60.

28. Melosh, *Strangers and Kin*, 114.

29. Morey and Gilliam, *Respect for Life*, 85, 89, 83.

30. Robert Olmos, "State, Grandparents Battle in Court," *Oregonian*, ca. April 1977, and Abe Weisburd, "Grandparents Fight for Their Children," *Guardian*, June 1, 1977, box 79, folder 1; "Indian Child Welfare Reform First Report," March 1976–June 1976, 28, box 365, folder 1, AAIA papers.

31. Olmos, "State, Grandparents Battle in Court," and Weisburd, "Grandparents Fight for Their Children"; "Indian Child Welfare Reform First Report," March 1976–June 1976, 28. Despite this court ruling, Hirsch contacted the Oregon state director of adoptions, who was receptive to placing the children with their grandparents. Hirsch suggested the BIA do a home study of the grandparents. The adoption director forwarded a request to the BIA, who asked Jewish Social Services in Phoenix to conduct the home study. Although they found the grandparents fit to take care of the children, Oregon's adoption director refused to follow the recommendations made in the home study. See "Indian Child Welfare Reform First Report," March 1976–June 1976, 28, 29, box 365,

folder 1; Indian Child Welfare Program, Second Report, July 1976–October 1976, 36, box 365, folder 2; both in AAIA papers.

32. Booklet, "Child Welfare League of America Standards for Adoption Service" (New York: CWLA, revised 1968), 8, box 13, folder 8, CWLA papers.

33. "Research Schedule on Indian Adoption Project," ca. 1960, 7, 8, box 17, folder 3, CWLA papers.

34. Garrett, quoted in Janet Ades, "American Indian Child Welfare," 11–12, box 78, folder 2: Child Welfare, 1974, AAIA papers, emphasis added.

35. Shurlee Swain argues that this post–World War II view has its roots in the British child welfare movement that extended sympathy to children but not their parents. See Swain, "Child Rescue," 105.

36. James Molley, social worker, LDS Church, to "[Navajo] parents," December 10, 1969, box 282, folder 12, AAIA papers.

37. Martin Topper, "Mormon Placement," in Swenson, *Supportive Care,* 50, 49.

38. "Navajo Children Removed Without Right Authority," *Navajo Times* 5, no. 11 (March 12, 1964): 15; "Placement on Adoption," *Navajo Times* 7, no. 11 (March 17, 1966): 28. The *Navajo Times* also included articles and letters to the editors that showed support for the program among its readers. See, for example, "Indian Students Become Leaders While Learning in 'Mormon' Plan," *Navajo Times* 5, no. 19 (May 7, 1964): 10, 23; and "Letter to the Editor," *Navajo Times* 6, no. 27 (July 8, 1965): 4–5.

39. Minutes of Adoption Meeting, held at Branch of Social Services [BIA], Window Rock, Arizona, May 15, 1975, 1, box 209, folder 7, AAIA papers.

40. Handwritten letter from Tim [illegible] to Hirsch, April 20, 1974, box 282, folder 12, AAIA papers. Alaska Natives faced a similar situation. In 1976 the AAIA became involved in *Tobeluk v. Lind,* a case in which parents of Alaska Native middle and high school–age children sued the state to provide local secondary education in their communities. Students had been forced to leave home for ten months of the year to get a secondary education hundreds of miles away or forgo education altogether. The governor of Alaska agreed to an out-of-court settlement that phased out boarding schools over the subsequent three years and gradually offered local village education. See Indian Child Welfare Program, Second Report, July 1976–October 1976, 55, box 35, folder 3, AAIA papers.

41. Garrett, "Mormons, Indians and Lamanites."

42. Yvette Hall to Hirsh, January 22, 1973, box 288, folder 11, AAIA papers.

43. Andy Lindstrom, "City Woman Fighting Battle to Keep Indian Children," *State Journal Register,* Springfield, Illinois, May 22, 1977, box 79, folder 1: Child Welfare, 1976–1977, AAIA papers.

44. Lindstrom, "City Woman." The mothers denied that guardianship papers they signed were for permanent transfer. Hirsch said they were for one year.

45. Lindstrom, "City Woman."

46. Proceedings, Indian Child Welfare and Family Services Conference, AAIA, January 20 [26], 1974, Biltmore Hotel, New York, 78, box 365, folder 4, AAIA papers.

47. William Lamb, First Quarterly Report to Lilly Foundation, 7, box 365, folder 2, AAIA papers.

48. Lamb, First Quarterly Report, 4; Indian Child Welfare Program, Second Report, July 1976–October 1976, 34, both in box 365, folder 2, AAIA papers.

49. "Norma Jean Serena: A Conspiracy to Destroy a Family," 4-page pamphlet/ newsletter from Council of Three Rivers American Indian Center in Pittsburgh, ca. 1975, box 80, folder 1: Child Welfare, undated, AAIA papers; Kluchin, *Fit to Be Tied*, 110–11.

50. Torpy, "Native American Women and Coerced Sterilization." See also Lawrence, "The Indian Health Service and the Sterilization"; Kluchin, *Fit to Be Tied*, 108–9.

51. David Jordan, "Indians Battle to Keep Foster Children on Reservation," *Minneapolis Tribune*, July 28, 1968, clipping, box 390, folder 2, AAIA papers.

52. Appendix G, "Indian Child Welfare Statistical Survey, July 1976, Association of American Indian Affairs," in U.S. Senate, *ICWA Congressional Hearing 1977*, 538.

53. Westermeyer, "Ravage of Indian Families in Crisis," 54.

4. RECLAIMING CARE

1. Testimony of Mrs. Alex Fournier, U.S. Senate, *ICWA Congressional Hearing 1974*, 51–54, quotes at 52, 53, 51; List of Devil's Lake Delegation at AAIA Press conference, July 16, 1968, box 77, folder 7, AAIA papers; Report, "Child Neglect Proceedings in North Dakota," no author or date, but probably written by Gabe Kamiewitz, Columbia Center on Social Welfare Policy and Law, ca. September 1968, 10, 11, box 77, folder 7, AAIA papers.

2. This chapter does not pretend to be the definitive and comprehensive story of Indian activism for Indian child welfare but only one part of the story. Other organizations, including the American Indian Movement (AIM) and the National Indian Youth Council (NIYC), were somewhat involved in child welfare. For information on the NIYC's protest against adoption in the early 1970s, see "The Latest in the Social Genocide Field: Adoption of Indian Children by White Families," *Akwesasne Notes* 4, no. 4 (Summer 1972): 10–11. For AIM's involvement, see Davis, *Survival Schools*.

3. William Byler, Statement, "American Indian Child Custody Problems—II,"
   n.d., ca. July 1968; letter from Lewis Goodhouse to Mr. Leslie Ovre, Director of
   Public Welfare Board of North Dakota, n.d., ca. September 1968; Report, "Child
   Neglect Proceedings in North Dakota," 2, 3; all in box 77, folder 7, AAIA papers;
   Janet Ades, "American Indian Child Welfare," 9, box 78, folder 2, AAIA papers.
4. Report, "Child Neglect Proceedings in North Dakota," 5, 6, 8.
5. David Jordan, "Indians Battle to Keep Foster Children on Reservation," *Minneapolis Tribune*, July 28, 1968, clipping, box 390, folder 2, AAIA papers.
6. Jordan, "Indians Battle."
7. List of Devils Lake Delegation at AAIA Press conference, July 16, 1968, box 77,
   folder 7, AAIA papers.
8. Telegram from William Byler to 100 media representatives, July 11, 1968, box
   77, folder 7, AAIA papers.
9. AAIA press release and fact sheet, July 12, 1968. In a separate statement,
   "American Indian Child Custody Problems—I," July 9, 1968, Byler noted that
   at Devils Lake, "out of a population of approximately 1000 children, 107 are in
   foster homes, 93 in BIA boarding schools, and 64 in adoptive homes."
10. Murray Kempton, "Devils Lake," *New York Post*, July 17, 1968, clipping, box 390,
    folder 2, AAIA papers.
11. Bertram Hirsch, video of presentation on ICWA to Alaska Native group on
    Kodiak Island, July 18, 1989, in possession of the author. For the BIA response,
    see the following items in the BIA Social Service Records: Letter from Act-
    ing Assistant Commissioner Ralph Reeser to Miss Rhoda Ruff, November 29,
    1968, box 4, folder: General Information, July–December 1968; Report from
    Clare Jerdone, October 21, 1968; Report on field trip from Jerdone, October 16,
    1968; Memo from Jerdone to Chief, Branch of Social Services, September 13,
    1968; Clare Jerdone, Notes, August 12, 1968; Jerdone notes, August 11, 1968;
    Jerdone, notes, August 9, 1968; Memo from Jerdone to Asst. Chief, Branch of
    Social Services, 26–28, April 25, 1968; all in box 2, folder: General Program
    Admin., January–December 1968, Miscellaneous Subject Files, 1929–68, Divi-
    sion of Social Services, Records of the Bureau of Indian Affairs, Record Group
    75, National Archives and Records Administration, Washington DC.
12. Letter from Florence Kinley, Marietta, Washington, to Byler, October 3, 1968,
    box 390, folder 2, AAIA papers.
13. Hirsch, video presentation, and letter from Hirsch [to state agencies], n.d.
    [1968], seeking information on numbers of Indian children in foster care or
    placed for adoption, box 77, folder 7, AAIA papers.
14. Proceedings, Indian Child Welfare and Family Services Conference, AAIA,
    January 20 [26], 1974, Biltmore Hotel, New York, 207, box 365, folder 4, AAIA

papers (hereafter cited as Proceedings, AAIA Indian Child Welfare Conference, 1974).

15. Letter from AAIA [Bertram Hirsch] to Charles Rovin, Division of Community Services, Welfare Branch, BIA, April 25, 1968; Statement re. telephone conversation between Bertram Hirsch, AAIA Research Asst. and Charles Rovin, BIA, April 25, 1968; BIA in Arizona to Hirsch, AAIA, December 6, 1968; Letter from Wayne Morse, Chair of Senate's Special Subcommittee on Indian Education to Stewart Udall, Secretary of Interior, November 29, 1968; Robert Bennett, BIA, to Wayne Morse, December 18, 1968; all in box 77, folder 7, Child Welfare, 1968–1969, AAIA papers. See also Letter from Rovin to Hirsch, May 21, 1968, box 4, folder: General Information, January–June 1968, BIA Social Service Records.

16. Letter from Hirsch [to state agencies], n.d. [1968]; Idaho Department of Public Assistance, January 28, 1969; Ned Thompson letter to Byler, November 29, 1968; State of Iowa Department of Social Services, January 27, 1969; State of Wyoming Department of Public Welfare to Hirsch, December 18, 1968; all in box 77, folder 7: Child Welfare, 1968–1969, AAIA papers.

17. Byler to Mrs. C. G. DeSantis, Minneapolis, January 15, 1974, box 78, folder 3: Child Welfare, 1974, AAIA papers.

18. The AAIA started collecting its statistics in the late 1960s, but in the mid-1970s, under contract from the American Indian Policy Review Commission, established by Congress, the AAIA conducted a comprehensive survey of Indian child placements in nineteen states with large Indian populations (Alabama, Arizona, California, Idaho, Maine, Michigan, Minnesota, Montana, Nebraska, New Mexico, New York, North Dakota, Oklahoma, Oregon, South Dakota, Utah, Washington, Wisconsin, and Wyoming). See Unger, "Indian Child Welfare Act of 1978," 75–76. These statistics were eventually included in Appendix G, "Indian Child Welfare Statistical Survey," July 1976, in U.S. Senate, ICWA Congressional Hearing 1977.

19. Bertram Hirsch, interview by author, September 30, 2011.

20. Proceedings, AAIA Indian Child Welfare Conference, 1974, 38.

21. Evelyn Blanchard, interview by author, September 22, 2011.

22. U.S. Senate, ICWA Congressional Hearing 1974, 44.

23. Bertram Hirsch, interview by author, September 23, 2011. California Indian Legal Services, for example, took on some Indian child welfare cases. See *California Indian Legal Services Newsletter* 6, no. 2 (May 1, 1974); 6, no. 3 (October 15, 1974); 8, no. 1 (January 15, 1976); and 8, no. 4 (October 1976). A Navajo Legal Services group, Dinebeiina Nahiilna Be Agaditahe (DNA) also helped many Indian families get their children back. See "DNA Helps a Navajo Family," *DNA*

*in Action* 2, no. 1 (August 31, 1969); "DNA Reunites Mother and Child," *DNA in Action* 4, no. 5 (August 30, 1972).

24. "American Indian Family Defense Project: A Three Year Program," n.d., ca. 1972; " Report on Great Plains Family Defense Project," May 1, 1972–January 2, 1973; "Indian Family Defense Legal Services Program," Proposal to the Lilly Endowment, n.d., ca. 1975; "Indian Child Welfare Reform First Report," March 1976–June 1976; all in box 365, folder 1, AAIA papers.

25. "Indian Family Defense Legal Services Program," Proposal to Lilly Endowment, 2.

26. Letter from Barbara Alovia and Anita Kobre (both from Spring Valley, New York) to Senator Edward Kennedy, January 15, 1973, box 78, folder 1: Child Welfare, 1973, AAIA papers.

27. Letter from Eloise Lahr Doan, Senior Vice Chairman, National Association of Blackfeet Indians, Browning, Montana, to Hirsch, June 29, 1976, box 365, folder 1, AAIA papers.

28. Mary Lou Byler, interview by author, September 1, 2011.

29. Proposal for American Indian Youth and Family Program, n.d., ca. 1973, list of board of directors of AICPDP, box 288, folder 11, AAIA papers. Testimony of Mike Chosa, U.S. Senate, *ICWA Congressional Hearing 1974*, 167.

30. "NW Women Organizing," *Yakima Nation Review* 8, no. 15 (March 3 1978): 6.

31. Letter from Janet McCloud, "Out of Our Mailbag," "NIWC Formally Organized," *Yakima Nation Review* 10, no. 12 (December 31, 1979): 10.

32. Bennett, "The Puyallup Tribe Rose from the Ashes," 157–58.

33. Evelyn Blanchard, interview by author, September 22, 2011.

34. Jerry Bergsman, "Indian Family Program Wins Honor for Founder," *Seattle Times*, March 22, 1980, box 67, folder 1, AAIA papers. See also Proceedings, AAIA Indian Child Welfare Conference, 1974, 98; Swenson, *Supportive Care*, 42; Dyer, *Room for One More*, 117–18, quotes at 117; "From the Office of Child Development," *Yakima Nation Review* 4, no. 7 (August 11, 1975): 1. In the early 1980s the *Yakima Nation Review* referred to the program more commonly as Nak-Nu-We-Sha, which they defined as "we care." See "Nak Nu We Sha Strives to Keep Families Intact," *Yakima Nation Review* 19, no. 16 (April 25, 1988): 2; "Superman Had Foster Parents," *Yakima Nation Review* 20, no 3 (June 20, 1988): 5. Pat Bellanger, an activist in Minneapolis, mentioned in the 1978 congressional hearings that she had visited Ku Nak We Sha and was impressed with how it worked. See "Indian Child Welfare Act of 1978," U.S. House, *ICWA Congressional Hearing 1978*, 132. Many other Washington state Indian women were active in child welfare issues, including Goldie Denny (Quinault), who became a close friend of Blanchard's, and

Ramona Bennett. See U.S. Senate, *ICWA Congressional Hearing 1977*, 79, 80, 82, 102–3, 164.

35. Anderson, *A Recognition of Being*, 158, 159.

36. Anderson, *A Recognition of Being*, 83, 170, 171. See also Krosenbrink-Gelissen, "Caring Is Indian Women's Business," 108–9.

37. Jacobs, *White Mother*; Udel, "Revision and Resistance"; Anderson, *A Recognition of Being*.

38. Swenson, *Supportive Care*, 39.

39. Evelyn Blanchard, Statement regarding Goldie Denny, August 23, 2012, in possession of the author; Swenson, *Supportive Care*, 40.

40. Evelyn Blanchard, interview by author, September 22, 2011.

41. U.S. Senate, *ICWA Congressional Hearing 1974*, 165, 166, 167. For more on Jack, see box 288, folder 11, AAIA papers.

42. Swenson, *Supportive Care*, 39.

43. Proceedings, AAIA Indian Child Welfare Conference, 1974, 6.

44. Swenson, *Supportive Care*, 7, 42, 58.

45. Swenson, *Supportive Care*, 11, 57.

46. Announcement from Boston Indian Council re. Association of American Indian and Alaskan Native Social Workers, ca. 1978, 3, box 144, folder 9, AAIA papers.

47. "Working with Abusive/Neglectful Indian Parents," spring 1979 (revised spring 1980), 1, 2, box 77, folder 2: Child Abuse, 1976–1986, AAIA papers. This document was funded by a grant from the National Conference on Child Abuse and Neglect in the Children's Bureau and developed and distributed by the Native American Coalition in Tulsa.

48. "Working with Abusive/Neglectful Indian Parents," 2.

49. "Working with Abusive/Neglectful Indian Parents," 3.

50. "Working with Abusive/Neglectful Indian Parents," 1.

51. "Working with Abusive/Neglectful Indian Parents," 3.

52. "Working with Abusive/Neglectful Indian Parents," 3.

53. Proposal for American Indian Youth and Family Program, n.d., ca 1973, box 288, folder 11, AAIA papers.

54. "Indian Family Defense Legal Services Program," Proposal to Lilly Endowment, 2.

55. Morey and Gilliam, *Respect for Life*, 20.

56. Swenson, *Supportive Care*, 18.

57. Swenson, *Supportive Care*, 59, repeated on 61 as last recommendation.

58. Proceedings, AAIA Indian Child Welfare Conference, 1974, 6.

59. Memo from Services for Children and Youth, Social Service Board of North Dakota to Directors, County Welfare Boards, November 4, 1971 re. "Resolutions

Relating to Indian Children Living on Federal Indian Reservations," box 77, folder 2, AAIA papers.

60. "Choctaw Children Get Bill of Rights," box 77, folder 1: Child Abuse, 1976, AAIA papers. This document was modeled on the Bill of Rights for Foster Children; see box 78, folder 1.

61. Parts of the resolution of the Navajo Tribal Council, "Regulations for the Care, Custody, and Control of Abandoned, Neglected and Delinquent Navajo Children," adopted March 21, 1957, and Resolution of the Navajo Tribal Council, "Tribal Policy on Adoption of Navajo Orphans or Neglected and Abandoned Children," November 18, 1960, enclosed with Letter from Area Director, Navajo Area Office (Arizona), BIA, to Bertram Hirsch, rec'd October 31, 1968, box 209, folder 7, AAIA papers. See also "Welfare Program Offers Assistance," *Navajo Times* 1, no. 2 (September 1960): 2.

62. "Tribal Policy on Adoption," November 18, 1960, is included in Excerpt from Navajo Tribal Code on Adoption, n.d., ca. 1960, 87, box 209, folder 7, AAIA papers.

63. July 29, 1963 Report on IAP, Reid to Nash, box 17, folder 4: Indian Adoption Project, 1963–1972, CWLA papers.

64. "Indian Family Defense Legal Services Program," Proposal to Lilly Endowment, appendix: "Brief Overview of Community-Based Indian Family Defense and Child-Welfare Programs, 1–2. For more on the Devils Lake project, see also Thomas Smithson, Native American Rights Fund, "Protection of the Family Rights of Native American Children," Working Paper, March 27, 1972, 4–5, box 77, folder 8, AAIA papers.

65. Swenson, *Supportive Care,* 22, 23, 24.

66. Minutes of September 25, 1973 meeting, box 78, folder 2: Child Welfare, 1974, AAIA papers.

67. Minutes of August 26, 1973 meeting, box 78, folder 2: Child Welfare, 1974, AAIA papers.

68. Alan Gurwitt MD, Carl Mindell MD, Report to the AAIA, January 1974, box 78, folder 3: Child Welfare, 1974, AAIA papers.

69. Swenson, *Supportive Care,* 79–80.

70. Memorandum of Law in Support of the Confirmation of Native Custom Adoptions from Alan G. Sherry, Attorney for Alaska Legal Services Corporation, to Judge E. Moody of Superior Court, 1971, box 77, folder 8: Child Welfare, 1970–1972, AAIA papers.

71. Letter from Charlotte Goodluck, MSW, Indian Child Advocate, Lupton and Phoenix, to BIA Branch of Social Services, Window Rock, Arizona, rec'd May 21, 1979, box 209, folder 7, AAIA papers.

72. Swenson, *Supportive Care,* 30–32.

1. Proceedings, AAIA Indian Child Welfare Conference, 1974, 7. See also Blanchard, "To Prevent the Breakup of the Indian Family," 334, note 20.

2. Shreve, *Red Power Rising*; Cobb, *Native Activism in Cold War America*; Wilkinson, *Blood Struggle*; Smith and Warrior, *Like a Hurricane*.

3. Wilkinson, *Blood Struggle*, 191, quote at 193.

4. Wilkinson, *Blood Struggle*, 194–96. Gerard and Ducheneaux served as staff for the Senate and House Interior Committees, respectively, beginning in 1971 and 1973.

5. Quoted in Swenson, *Supportive Care*, 62.

6. AAIA press release, July 12, 1968; letter from Byler to Wilbur Cohen, Secretary of Department of Health, Education and Welfare, July 12, 1968; Byler sent a similar letter to Stewart Udall, Secretary of the Interior, on the same day; all in box 77, folder 7, AAIA papers.

7. Bertram Hirsch, interviews by author, September 23 and 30, 2011; Bertram Hirsch, video of presentation on ICWA to Alaskan Native group on Kodiak Island, July 18, 1989, in possession of the author.

8. Indian Child Welfare Program, Second Report, July 1976–October 1976, 4, box 365, folder 2, AAIA papers.

9. Indian Child Welfare Program, Second Report, 1976, 6. See this entire folder for more on the AAIA's work with states.

10. Evelyn Blanchard, interview by author, September 22, 2011; Indian Child Welfare Program, Second Report, 1976, 7.

11. "Second Quarter Report" to Lilly Foundation, n.d., ca. November 1976, 1, box 365, folder 2, AAIA papers; Hirsch interview, September 30, 2011.

12. Hirsch interview, September 30, 2011.

13. Indian Child Welfare Program, Second Report, 1976, 16.

14. For the New Mexico case, see Echo Hawk, *In the Courts of the Conquerors*, 217–32.

15. Indian Child Welfare Program, Second Report, 1976, 12.

16. Biltmore conference participants (partial list), Proceedings, AAIA Indian Child Welfare Conference, 1974. Hillary Rodham had graduated from Yale Law School in 1973, after which she worked for a year with the Yale Child Study Center on children's rights and served as staff attorney for the Children's Defense Fund in Cambridge, Massachusetts. See "Biography: Hillary Rodham Clinton," *American Experience*, PBS.org, http://www.pbs.org/wgbh/american experience/features/biography/clinton-hillary/, accessed March 1, 2014.

17. Proceedings, AAIA Indian Child Welfare Conference, 1974, 64.

18. Proceedings, AAIA Indian Child Welfare Conference, 1974, 6.
19. Proceedings, AAIA Indian Child Welfare Conference, 1974, 12.
20. Proceedings, AAIA Indian Child Welfare Conference, 1974, 15.
21. Proceedings, AAIA Indian Child Welfare Conference, 1974, 129–39, 144–45.
22. Proceedings, AAIA Indian Child Welfare Conference, 1974, 44.
23. Proceedings, AAIA Indian Child Welfare Conference, 1974, 36.
24. Proceedings, AAIA Indian Child Welfare Conference, 1974, 49, 51, 52, 57 (Gurwitt quote).
25. Proceedings, AAIA Indian Child Welfare Conference, 1974, 24.
26. To get a sense of just how thorny jurisdictional issues were, see the chart showing what each state has jurisdiction over in regard to Indian tribes in Task Force Four, *Report on Federal, State, and Tribal Jurisdiction*, 8–9.
27. Proceedings, AAIA Indian Child Welfare Conference, 1974, 98, 153. For more on the discussion of PL-280, see 7, 82–84, 140, 150–57, 161.
28. Proceedings, AAIA Indian Child Welfare Conference, 1974, 39.
29. Proceedings, AAIA Indian Child Welfare Conference, 1974, 219–21. McDowell published "The Indian Adoption Problem" in the *Wall Street journal* on July 12, 1974; see clipping in box 78, folder 3, AAIA papers. At least one Indian newspaper, *Yakima Nation Review*, reprinted McDowell's article.
30. Proceedings, AAIA Indian Child Welfare Conference, 1974, 228.
31. Proceedings, AAIA Indian Child Welfare Conference, 1974, 215–16.
32. The statement is available in Swenson, *Supportive Care*, 5, 81–86. See also Swenson and Rosenthal, *Warm Springs*, ii.
33. Evelyn Blanchard, interview by author, September 22, 2011.
34. Swenson, *Supportive Care*, 9, quote at 3.
35. Hirsch interview, September 30, 2011; Hirsch, video of presentation on ICWA to Alaska Native group on Kodiak Island, July 18, 1989, in possession of the author; Unger, "Indian Child Welfare Act of 1978," 231.
36. U.S. Senate, *ICWA Congressional Hearing 1977*, 220. See also Abourezk, *Advise and Dissent*, 219.
37. Hirsch, video presentation.
38. Blanchard interview, September 22, 2011.
39. Testimony of William Byler, U.S. Senate, *ICWA Congressional Hearing 1974*, 21.
40. U.S. Senate, *ICWA Congressional Hearing 1974*, 165, 166. For more on Jack, see box 288, folder 11, AAIA papers.
41. U.S. Senate, *ICWA Congressional Hearing 1974*, 68. For more on Hirsch's assessment of the DeCoteau case, see Proceedings, AAIA Indian Child Welfare Conference, 1974, 66.

42. Bertram Hirsch, "BIA Child Welfare Services," Draft, June 1, 1972, 7–8, 9, box 77, folder 8, AAIA papers.

43. U.S. Senate, *ICWA Congressional Hearing 1974*, 45–51, quotes at 46, 47.

44. U.S. Senate, *ICWA Congressional Hearing 1974*, oral testimony 54–60; formal statement 61–64.

45. U.S. Senate, *ICWA Congressional Hearing 1974*, 334.

46. Fanshel, *Far from the Reservation*, 129, table V-10 at 136.

47. Roherty, *Exploratory Project on Outcome of Adoption*, 19, 20, 21.

48. Fanshel, *Far from the Reservation*, 133, 208, 237.

49. U.S. Senate, *ICWA Congressional Hearing 1974*, oral testimony 54–60; formal statement 61–64; quotes at 55, 62.

50. U.S. Senate, *ICWA Congressional Hearing 1974*, 45–51, quotes at 46, 47.

51. U.S. Senate, *ICWA Congressional Hearing 1974*, oral testimony 54–60; formal statement 61–64; quotes at 55, 62.

52. U.S. Senate, *ICWA Congressional Hearing 1974*, oral testimony 54–60; formal statement 61–64; quotes at 55, 62.

53. U.S. Senate, *ICWA Congressional Hearing 1974*, 45–51, 54–64, quotes at 46, 47.

54. U.S. Senate, *ICWA Congressional Hearing 1974*, 157.

55. Letter from Justine Wise Polier, Director, Juvenile Justice Project of Children's Defense Fund to Hirsch, January 29, 1974, box 78, folder 2: Child Welfare, 1974, AAIA papers; *Clampett v. Madigan* US District Court for the District of SD, Southern Division (Civ. No. 73–4018).

56. Janet Ades, "American Indian Child Welfare," 10, box 78, folder 2: Child Welfare, 1974, AAIA papers; Proceedings, AAIA Indian Child Welfare Conference, 1974, 19.

57. U.S. Senate, *ICWA Congressional Hearing 1974*, 214.

58. U.S. Senate, *ICWA Congressional Hearing 1974*, 169.

59. U.S. Senate, *ICWA Congressional Hearing 1974*, 169.

60. Bertram Hirsch, video of presentation on ICWA to Alaska Native group on Kodiak Island, July 18, 1989, in possession of the author.

61. Task Force Four, *Report on Federal, State, and Tribal Jurisdiction*, 2, 78–88, 177–242.

62. Bertram Hirsch, interview by author, September 23, 2011; email from Bert Hirsch to the author, February 18, 2014; *Indian Family Defense* no. 8 (November 1977): 2. The AAIA's *Indian Family Defense* publication printed its legislative recommendations in its first issue of Winter 1974 and the first draft of the bill in its February 1978 issue, with a section-by-section analysis (3–6).

63. U.S. Senate, *ICWA Congressional Hearing 1977*, 50–51.

64. U.S. Senate, *ICWA Congressional Hearing 1977*, 76.

65. U.S. Senate, *ICWA Congressional Hearing 1977*, 55.

66. U.S. Senate, *ICWA Congressional Hearing 1977*, 73.

67. U.S. Senate, *ICWA Congressional Hearing 1977*, 502.

68. U.S. Senate, *ICWA Congressional Hearing 1977*, 74.

69. U.S. Senate, *ICWA Congressional Hearing 1977*, 74.

70. U.S. Senate, *ICWA Congressional Hearing 1977*, 75.

71. U.S. Senate, *ICWA Congressional Hearing 1977*, 392, 393, 396. See also "Summary" of CWLA Statement on Indian Child Welfare Act in box 71, folder: Minorities Project, 1979–80, CWLA papers.

72. U.S. Senate, *ICWA Congressional Hearing 1977*, 192–216; Garrett, "Mormons, Indians and Lamanites," 361, 369. The LDS Church later excommunicated George Lee for apostasy. See "Mormons Excommunicate Navajo Elder for 'Apostasy'; Lee Says 'Racism,'" and "Author Sees 'Spiritual Chasm' Between Mormon Church, Navajo People," *Yakima Nation Review* 21, no. 10 (September 15, 1989): 10.

73. U.S. Senate, *ICWA Congressional Hearing 1977*, 171, 172–73.

74. U.S. Senate, *ICWA Congressional Hearing 1977*, 193–216, NCAI resolution 218–19. The AAIA had been involved in efforts to determine that the LDS program should have to abide by the Interstate Compact on the Placement of Children as well as in efforts to ensure that tribal governing bodies, not just state agencies, should receive notification when Indian children were taken out of their communities. See letter from Brendan Callanan, Project Director, American Public Welfare Association, to "colleague," November 10, 1976, box 282, folder 12, AAIA papers. See also Garrett, "Mormons, Indians and Lamanites," 367.

75. U.S. Senate, *ICWA Congressional Hearing 1977*, 480, 479.

76. U.S. Senate, *ICWA Congressional Hearing 1977*, 495.

77. U.S. Senate, *ICWA Congressional Hearing 1977*, 487, 491.

78. U.S. Senate, *ICWA Congressional Hearing 1977*, 260.

79. U.S. Senate, *ICWA Congressional Hearing 1977*, 167.

80. U.S. Senate, *ICWA Congressional Hearing 1977*, 222, 223. The Reeveses had moved to Washington DC, where Don Reeves worked for the Friends Committee on National Legislation.

81. U.S. Senate, *ICWA Congressional Hearing 1977*, 220.

82. U.S. Senate, *ICWA Congressional Hearing 1977*, 538, 540. For the entire appendix, see 537–603.

83. Copy of S. 1214 as passed by the Senate, in U.S. House, *ICWA Congressional Hearing 1978*, 2–28.

84. *ICWA Congressional Hearing, 1978*, 151.

85. *ICWA Congressional Hearing, 1978*, 144, 251.

86. *ICWA Congressional Hearing, 1978*, 139; Ramirez, *Native Hubs*.

87. *ICWA Congressional Hearing, 1978*, 78.

88. *ICWA Congressional Hearing, 1978*, 159–172.

89. *ICWA Congressional Hearing, 1978*, 79. The LDS church dropped its opposition to ICWA once it was clear that it would not impinge on the Indian Student Placement Program.

90. *ICWA Congressional Hearing, 1978*, 87–88.

91. *ICWA Congressional Hearing, 1978*, 193.

92. Unger, "Indian Child Welfare Act of 1978," 303–34; Bertram Hirsch, interview by author, September 23, 2011.

93. *Indian Child Welfare Act of 1978*, U.S. Code, vol. 25 (1978). Available online at http://www.tribal-institute.org/lists/chapter21_icwa.htm, author's emphasis, accessed July 29, 2013. Bertram Hirsch, interview by author, September 30, 2011.

94. Letter from Steven Unger to Mario Vallejos, December 26, 1979, box 67, folder 1, AAIA papers. In this letter Unger mentions that Congress appropriated these funds in November 1979.

95. Ada Deer, President's Message, Newsletter of Association of American Indian and Alaska Native Social Workers (Fall 1979), box 71, folder: "Minorities Project—Indian," CWLA papers.

96. Swenson and Rosenthal, *Warm Springs*, 1, ii.

97. Swenson and Rosenthal, *Warm Springs*, iv.

98. Swenson and Rosenthal, *Warm Springs*, 6, 9, 28, 29.

99. Swenson and Rosenthal, *Warm Springs*, 37, 39, 41, 43.

100. Swenson and Rosenthal, *Warm Springs*, 35.

6. INDIGENOUS CHILD WELFARE CRISIS IN CANADA

1. "Children Sent to Mich. to Stay with Foster Parents," *Moose Jaw Times Herald*, August 2, [1975], III.H.15 (a), R-1298, Alex Taylor fonds; letter from Doucettes to Rolfes, received March 1, 1976, I.46d-55–1a, R-1100, Herman Rolfes fonds; Press Release Re. "Mr. and Mrs. Doucette—Prince Albert" from E. C. Boychuk, Ombudsman, August 1, 1975, 22, III.H.15 (d), Taylor fonds; all in Saskatchewan Archives Board, Regina (hereafter cited as SAB; *fonds* is commonly used in Canada for archival collections of the papers of individuals and nongovernment organizations).

2. Letter from Doucettes to Rolfes, received March 1, 1976; "Doucettes File for Adoption," *Regina Leader-Post*, September 12, 1975, III.H.15 (a), Taylor fonds, SAB.

3. "Snyder's Mind Made Up Before Meeting Couple," *Moose Jaw Times Herald*, July 23 [1975], and John Drabble, "'Raised Since Babies' Foster Children

Taken," *Prince Albert Herald*, July 11 [1975]; Deifenbacker, quoted in "Dief Says Action 'Unjust, Cruel,'" *Prince Albert Herald*, July 15 [1975], III.H.15 (a), Taylor fonds, SAB.

4. "U.S. Couple Blames Media for Failure of Adoption," *Saskatoon Star Phoenix*, September 27 [1975]; Fred Harrison, "The Adoption that Backfired at Ann Arbor," *Regina Leader-Post*, September 27, 1975; both in III.H.15 (a), Clippings File, Taylor fonds, SAB; "Minister Responds to Advisory Committee Report," press release, October 17, 1975, with Memo to Herman Rolfes, from Jim Oxman, Director, Information and Public Relations, July 8, 1976, I.46d-55–1a, Rolfes fonds, SAB.

5. Letter from Herman Rolfes to Mr. E. Robert Stromberg (attorney), June 24, 1976; "Rolfes Reviews State of Children," news release, n.d., ca. June 1976; and Margaret Lipman, National Adoption Desk, to Gerald E. Jacob, Director, REACH, May 19, 1976, I.46d-55–1a, Rolfes fonds, SAB.

6. Letter from Doucettes to Rolfes, received March 2, 1976, I.46d-55–1a, Rolfes fonds, SAB.

7. Johnston, *Native Children and the Child Welfare System*, xvii, xviii; Armitage, *Comparing the Policy of Aboriginal Assimilation*, 83–87. For more on the many permutations of the Indian Act, see Miller, *Skyscrapers Hide the Heavens*, 137–38, 198, 254, 260–61, 275, 281, 325–26, 357–59.

8. Milloy, *A National Crime*; Miller, *Shingwauk's Vision*.

9. Miller, *Skyscrapers Hide the Heavens*, 325–26; Shewell, *"Enough to Keep them Alive,"* 171–205.

10. Letter from J.P.B. Ostrander to BIA, March 22, 1955, box 1, folder: General, July 1954–June 1955, Miscellaneous Subject Files, 1929–68, BIA Social Service Records.

11. Report quoted in Timpson, "Four Decades of Child Welfare," 276.

12. This trend continued well after this era. As late as 1985, 57 percent of Indian migrants to cities were women. See Winnipeg Coalition on Native Child Welfare, Aboriginal Community Development Planning Network pamphlet, 1985, box P5052, file 5, Social Planning Council fonds, Archives of Manitoba, Winnipeg (hereafter cited as SPC fonds, AM).

13. Minutes, Housing for Girls of Indian Descent Committee, box 647, folder 5; Lloyd Lenton to Missionaries serving Indians and Metis in Manitoba, February 1954, box 723, folder 12; box 721, folder 2, all in SPC fonds, AM. This group had much in common with nineteenth-century white women's groups in the United States, such as the Women's National Indian Association, that were concerned with Indian affairs. See Jacobs, *White Mother*, 87–148.

14. Minutes, Housing for Girls of Indian Descent Committee.

15. For founding of conference, see box 7014, folder 2, SPC fonds, AM. For the establishment of the Friendship Centre and its initial board membership, see box 721, folder 2, and box 2367, folder 20, in the same collection. For attempts by the largely non-Indian committee to mobilize Indians to attend the annual conference, see Minutes, Programme Committee, Indian and Metis Conference, January 12, 1960, box 2367, folder 18, SPC fonds, AM.

16. White women were particularly active among the "friends of the Indian." See Jacobs, *White Mother to a Dark Race*, especially 87–148.

17. See news clippings in box 6829, folder 2, Beatrice Brigden fonds, Archives of Manitoba, Winnipeg (hereafter cited as Beatrice Brigden fonds, AM), and box 721, folder 2, SPC fonds, AM.

18. Minutes of Meeting of Indian and Metis Committee, June 10, 1960, box 2367, folder 18, SPC papers, AM.

19. IEA pamplet, n.d., ca. 1966, box P2392, folder 5, SPC fonds, AM. See also McEwen, *Community Development Services for Canadian Indian and Metis Communities*. As in the United States, what I call "plight stories" regarding Indigenous people were ubiquitous in the media in this period. For another example from Canada, see G. A. Dafoe, "Let's Not Hide Those Poverty Pockets," news clipping, ca. 1967–1968, box 6829, folder 2, Beatrice Brigden fonds, AM.

20. Shewell, *"Enough to Keep them Alive,"* 207–27, quotes 208, 227; Strong-Boag, *Finding Families*, 148.

21. Miller, *Skyscrapers Hide the Heavens*, 328–339, quote at 331; Johnston, *Native Children and the Child Welfare System*, 6; Armitage, *Comparing the Policy of Aboriginal Assimilation*, 80.

22. Shaun Herron, "The Herron Folk," column, emphasis added, *Winnipeg Free Press*, May 4, 1968, clipping in box 2395, folder 15, SPC fonds, AM.

23. Strong-Boag, *Finding Families*, 143. See also Shewell, *"Enough to Keep them Alive,"* 189–90.

24. Saskatchewan Department of Welfare, *Annual Report* (1967–1968), 30; Saskatchewan Department of Welfare, *Annual Report* (1968–1969), 20. Reports available at SAB.

25. Hepworth, *Foster Care and Adoption in Canada*, 115, 118, 119.

26. Quoted in Strong-Boag, *Finding Families*, 152–53.

27. W. W. Struthers to Sihvon, March 30, 1967, folder I.49, Deputy Minister Records, R-935, SAB.

28. Nancy Gelber, "Under the Dome," March 26, 1970, *Regina Leader-Post*, news clipping, folder 5.1, Department of Social Services, R-1721, SAB.

29. Nancy Gelber, "Adoption Program Planned," *Regina Leader-Post*, April 10, 1967, news clipping, folder I.49, Deputy Minister Records, SAB.

30. Department of Welfare, Province of Saskatchewan, "Adopt Indian-Metis Project," Report 1967–69, 4, 5, file 8.6.23, folder 1, Department of Social Services, R-1655, SAB.

31. News clipping, op-ed, "Families of their Own," *Regina Leader-Post*, March 21, 1968, folder I. 49, Deputy Minister Records, SAB. In *Babies without Borders: Adoption and Migration across the Americas*, Karen Dubinsky argues that color-blind liberalism played a prominent role in the Open Door Society's promotion of the adoption of mixed-race children in Montreal in the 1950s. In regard to Native adoption she finds instead that "the public conversation about Aboriginal adoption begins and ends . . . with a static, essential notion of 'Native identity,' irrevocably 'lost' in adoption" (80). This may have been true by the late 1970s or 1980s, but in earlier decades, a similar liberal narrative pervaded the discussion.

32. "The AIM Program," news release, Department of Welfare, Regina, September 4, 1967, folder I.49, Deputy Minister Records, SAB.

33. Regional Office of the Department of Welfare, Government of Saskatchewan, Ad, January 14, 1967, in *Prince Albert Herald*, Robert Doucette fonds #1035, file 618, SAB, Saskatoon.

34. Department of Welfare, Province of Saskatchewan, "Adopt Indian-Métis Project," Report 1967–69, 8, file 8.6.23, folder 1, Department of Social Services, SAB. For more on cross-border adoptions of Canadian Indigenous children in the United States, see Balcom, *Traffic in Babies*, especially 195–231.

35. "Adopt Indian Metis Report for Minister," March 20, 1972, and "Adopt Indian Metis Program," report, January 21, 1970, both in folder I.49, Deputy Minister Records, SAB.

36. Memos from G. E. Jacob, REACH Director, to L. Dunsmore, February 13, 1976, and Cameron, August 9, 1976, file III.21.a, Deputy Minister Records, SAB.

37. Balcom, *Traffic in Babies*, 210–11. See also Ward, *Adoption of Native Canadian Children*, 9.

38. Strong-Boag, *Finding Families*, 153; Joseph Reid to Philleo Nash, July 29, 1963, box 17, folder 4: Indian Adoption Project, 1963–1972, CWLA papers.

39. Strong-Boag, *Finding Families*, 109.

40. "Summary of Discussion Regarding AIM," March 2, 1970, Memo from C. A. Westcott, Deputy Minister, to C. P. MacDonald, Minister, December 7, 1967, folder I.49, Deputy Minister Records, SAB. See also Memo from Cameron to F. J. Bogdasavich, Deputy Minister, October 4, 1976, file III.18.a, folder I.49, in the same collection.

41. Balcom, *Traffic in Babies*, 210, chart on 212. See also Strong-Boag, *Finding Families*, 152. Interestingly, when questioned by the AAIA, Betty Graham of

the Ontario Ministry of Community and Social Services was reluctant to admit that her agency placed Native children across the border, but she did mention that they worked with ARENA. See Graham to Byler, December 3, 1973, box 75, folder 3, AAIA papers. A representative from the Yukon Territory's social welfare branch also informed Byler that they worked with ARENA to place a few Indian children in the United States. See June Miller to Byler, January 7, 1974, box 75, folder 3, AAIA papers.

42. Figure 1–2, Donald S. Schaeffer et. al., "Native and Non-Native Clients of the C.A.S.: An Evaluation of the Native Urban Adjustment Program Evaluation, Part I," n.d., ca. 1975–76, box P5041, folder 15: Native Urban Adjustment Program, SPC fonds, AM.

43. Miller, *Skyscrapers Hide the Heavens*, 328–39.

44. Brochure of Manitoba Metis Federation, ca. 1968, box 2395, folder 15, SPC fonds, AM. Louis Riel, a Métis, was the founder of Manitoba. For more on his fascinating life and his mythic status in Canada, see Reid, *Louis Riel.*

45. For board composition of the center in 1968, see box 2396, folder 2. For the new role of the center in 1969, see box 2398, folder 13; both in SPC fonds, AM.

46. See box 2449, folders 5, 6, and 7, SPC fonds, AM.

47. Richard to Mount Carmel Clinic, November 27, 1975, box 2445, folder 4, SPC fonds, AM.

48. "Child Welfare Services," Federation of Saskatchewan Indians *Outlook,* November 1967, Regina, Saskatchewan, 2–3, Federation of Saskatchewan Indians, Collection #2098, SAB, Saskatoon.

49. "Child Welfare Services," *Outlook,* November 1967, 2–3. Unlike later activists, at this point Lavallee and Ewack wanted jurisdiction to be transferred from the federal government to the provinces so that they could access social services.

50. "Proposal to Federal Government for Funding from 1972–1974," from the Saskatchewan Native Women's Movement, August 25, 1972, and "Application for Incorporation," by the SNWM Society, June 1972, folder I.C.19a, Human Resources Development Agency papers, R-921, SAB (hereafter cited as HRDA papers, SAB).

51. "A Proposal to Establish a Native Women's Half-Way House—'We Care Home,'" submitted by Saskatchewan Native Women's Association, ca. 1975, folder I.C.19c, HRDA papers, SAB.

52. "First Indian Women's Conference, Manitoba, October 14–16, 1969, Winnipeg, box 2398, folder 10, SPC fonds, AM. See also feature on Mary Ann Lavallee, clipping, "Canadian Indians, 1968" by Barbara Frum, *Chatelaine,* November 1968, box 6829, folder 2, Beatrice Brigden fonds, AM.

53. For the early years of the Indian Homemakers' Clubs, see Harris and McCallum, "'Assaulting the Ears of Government," 225–39.

54. Tom Williams, "Indian Women Speak Up," *Winnipeg Free Press*, June 15, 1961, news clipping, box 6829, folder 3, Beatrice Brigden fonds, AM. For more on Indian Homemakers Clubs as "initiatives designed to encourage imitation of settler-family models," see Strong-Boag, *Finding Families*, 145.

55. Terry French, "Indian Women Call for Prompt Action," and "Prime Minister Urged to Aid Indian Women, *Native Voice*, Vancouver, July–August 1968, news clippings, box 6829, folder 2, Beatrice Brigden fonds, AM.

56. See Stevenson, "Vibrations across a Continent," especially 226–28; Krosenbrink-Gelissen, "Caring Is Indian Women's Business."

57. French, "Indian Women call for Prompt Action," with subtitle: "Men Don't Understand." For more on a Métis woman's difficulties with Native men, see Campbell, *Halfbreed*, 151, 155.

58. Janovicek, "'Assisting Our Own.'"

59. "Proposal to Federal Government for Funding from 1972–1974," from the Saskatchewan Native Women's Movement, August 25, 1972, and "Application for Incorporation," by the SNWM Society, June 1972, folder I.C.19a, HRDA papers, SAB.

60. Isabel Conn, Acting Executive Director of HRDA to Beth Paul, SNWM Conference Coordinator, September 20, 1972, folder I.C.19a, HRDA papers, SAB.

61. SNWM Board Meeting, April 10, 1973, folder I.C.19a, HRDA papers, SAB.

62. Letter from Herman Rolfes, Minister, Department of Social Services, to Mr. and Mrs. Gordon Fairburn, February 4, 1977, file III.73, Deputy Minister Records, SAB.

63. "Historical Perspective on the Saskatchewan Native Women's Movement Society," prepared by Josefowicz, March 15, 1976, I.C.19b, HRDA papers, SAB. Folder I.C.25 on the Native Women's Counselling and Referral Centre in Prince Albert, in the same collection, shows the bureaucratic hoops the group had to go through—including showing support from men's organizations—to get funding. And two years later, in 1978, the group was still gaining the praise of officials while struggling to fund its important work. See "Community Services Division, Attendance Memo," November 1978, file 1.64, Office of Deputy Minister, R-1428, SAB.

64. Memo from Cameron to A.W. Sihvon, Deputy Minister, January 31, 1972, folder I.49, Deputy Minister Records, SAB. For more on Howard Adams, see his *Prison of Grass: Canada from the Native Point of View*. A few non-Indian social workers also raised red flags about AIM's approach. The regional welfare director at Meadow Lake complained to the AIM director in 1972, "My first

impression [of AIM's new posters] was that they looked like 'Wanted Posters.'" He talked it over with his supervisor and they agreed that they should not post these in their waiting area. Since the majority of their clients are Native, this employee asserted, "I feel sure they would object to children of their race being advertised in this way." See L. W. Boyd to Jacob, March 28, 1972, folder 5.70, Department of Social Services, R-1721, SAB.

65. Statement from Métis Society, included in Memo from Sinclair to Sihvon, December 3, 1971, folder I.49, Deputy Minister Records, SAB.

66. Metis Society, Statement "Opposed to AIM Ads," included in Memo from Sinclair to Sihvon, December 3, 1971, folder I.49, Deputy Minister Records, SAB.

67. Sihvon to Snyder, March 29, 1972, folder I.49, Deputy Minister Records, SAB.

68. Memo from Cameron to Regional Welfare Directors, May 9, 1972, re. change of focus for Aim Centres, folder I.49, Deputy Minister Records, SAB. See also Letter from Snyder to Adams, February 29, 1972, and Adams to Snyder, March 9, 1972; memo from Cameron to Regional Welfare Directors, February 28, 1972, all in the same folder.

69. Memo from Sihvon to Sinclair, December 14, 1971, "Adopt Indian Metis Report for Minister," March 20, 1972, folder I.49, Deputy Minister Records, SAB.

70. SNWM Board Meeting, April 10, 1973, folder I.C.19a, HRDA papers, SAB.

71. Letter from SNWM, February 28, 1973, folder I.49, Deputy Minister Records, SAB. This letter also ran in the April edition of an Indigenous publication, *New Breed*, with a petition, and was included with a letter from Jacob to Joice, April 9, 1973, in the same folder.

72. "Native Women's Assoc. protests adoption program," *Western Producer*, April 5, 1973, news clipping in folder 5.1, Department of Social Services, R-1721, SAB.

73. "A Proposal to Establish a Native Home for Native Children in Saskatoon," submitted by SNWM, June 18, 1973, folder I.C.19a, HRDA papers, SAB.

74. Application for "Native Homes Project," June 21, 1974, from MSS [Métis Society of Saskatchewan], Local #9, Regina, folder, I.C.34, HRDA papers, SAB. For provincial resistance to their work, see Memos from Joe Dufour, Gov't of Province of Saskatchewan, July 19 and July 23, 1974, in the same folder.

75. See Cameron to All Regional Directors, May 22, 1973 re. Native Foster Homes, and a number of responses from regional directors, folder I.49; and REACH Resources for Adoption of Children Proposal, September 23, 1974, file II.68, Deputy Minister Records, SAB.

76. Memo from Jacob to Dunsmore, February 13, 1976, re. "Newspaper Column–'A Child Is Waiting,'" file III.21.a, Deputy Minister Records, SAB.

77. REACH advertisement, Department of Social Services, n.d., ca. 1975, file 8–6.23, Department of Social Services records, R-1655, SAB.

78. Memo from Cameron to Bogdasavich, June 22, 1976, file III.18.a, Deputy Minister Records, SAB.

79. Mary Graves, Welcome House, to Hirsch, September 19, 1973 and November 20, 1973, box 75, folder 3, AAIA papers.

80. Letter from Byler to Ketzler, October 22, 1973; letters from Ketzler to Manual [sic] and Wah-Shee, October 30, 1973; and letter from Byler to Ketzler, November 12, 1973, box 75, folder 3, AAIA papers. George Manuel (1921–89) was not only an important leader but also a writer. See his *The Fourth World: An Indian Reality*, co-written with Michael Posluns. The National Indian Brotherhood, which Manuel headed from 1970 to 1976, is now known as the Assembly of First Nations. See "Chronology of National Chiefs," Assembly of First Nations website, http://www.afn.ca/index.php/en/about-afn/chronology-of -national-chiefs, accessed July 31, 2013.

81. Wah-Shee to Byler, December 18, 1973, box 75, folder 3, AAIA papers.

82. Horn-Pichovich to Byler, n.d., ca. July 1974, and Unger to Horn-Pichovich, July 17, 1974, box 75, folder 3, AAIA papers.

83. Memo from Jacquie to Marie, January 10, 1974, box 75, folder 3, AAIA papers.

84. Lazarus to Byler, December 10, 1973, box 75, folder 3, AAIA papers.

85. Robert Doucette, interview by author, June 14, 2013.

86. Doucette interview, June 14, 2013.

87. Adams, *Prison of Grass*, 141, 143. While earning a PhD at UC Berkeley and participating in the civil rights struggle in the 1960s, Adams fully embraced his native heritage and came to see the position of Indians and Métis in Canada as that of colonized peoples (176–77).

88. Doucette interview, June 14, 2013.

89. John Drabble, "Doucettes Going to Ann Arbor to See Children," *Prince Albert Daily Herald*, July 17, 1975, Robert Doucette fonds, SAB, Saskatoon; Geoff White, "P.A. Couple Plans Trip in Hopes of Retrieving Three Foster Children," *Saskatoon Star Phoenix*, July 17 [1975], III.H.15 (a), Taylor fonds, SAB. Warned that their participation in the caravan could ruin their chances of getting the children back, the Doucettes did not take part in it. It appears, too, that after traveling to Regina, the organizers called off the remainder of the caravan trip.

90. Drabble, "Doucettes Going to Ann Arbor."

91. Geoff White, "P.A. Foster Parents Protest Adoption," *Saskatoon Star Phoenix*, July 11 [1975]; "Centre Wants Moratorium," *Prince Albert Herald*, July 18 [1975]; John Drabble, "Doucettes Go to Regina; Plan to Meet with Snyder," *Prince Albert Herald*, July 22 [1975], Taylor fonds, SAB.

92. "Children to Remain in Mich. Despite Ombudsman Report," *Saskatoon Star Phoenix*, August 2 [1975], III.H.15 (a), Taylor fonds, SAB.

93. Press Release Re. "Mr. and Mrs. Doucette—Prince Albert" from E. C. Boychuk, Ombudsman, August 1, 1975, 7–10, 16, quote, p. 10, III.H.15 (d), Taylor fonds, SAB.

94. Quoted in "P.A. Couple Disappointed with Adoption Decision," *Moose Jaw Times Herald*, August 5, [1975], III.H.15 (a), Taylor fonds, SAB.

95. Peter Hawley, "Decision Remains Firm in Doucette Case Handling," *Regina Leader-Post*, July 23, 1975; Steuart quoted in Tim Naumetz, "Steuart Questions Adoption by Americans," *Regina Leader-Post*, July 11, 1975, III.H.15 (a), Taylor fonds, SAB; Press Release Re. "Mr. and Mrs. Doucette—Prince Albert" from E. C. Boychuk, Ombudsman, August 1, 1975, 9, III.H.15 (d), Taylor fonds, SAB.

96. Press Release Re. "Mr. and Mrs. Doucette—Prince Albert" from E. C. Boychuk, 10, 6.

97. Fred Harrison, "The Adoption that Backfired at Ann Arbor," *Regina Leader-Post*, September 27, 1975, III.H.15 (a), Taylor fonds, SAB.

98. See, for example, Adoption Desk Bulletin 1, no. 1 (Ottawa: Health and Welfare, May 1976), I.46d-55–1a, Rolfes fonds, SAB.

99. Ogata, *Designing the Creative Child*, 6–7.

100. Press Release Re. "Mr. and Mrs. Doucette—Prince Albert" from E. C. Boychuk, 11–12.

101. Quoted in Press Release Re. "Mr. and Mrs. Doucette—Prince Albert" from E. C. Boychuk, 17.

102. Doucette interview, June 14, 2013; Letter from Doucettes to Rolfes, received March 2, 1976, I.46d-55–1a, Rolfes fonds, SAB.

103. Geoff White, "Number of Children in Home Led to Decision," *Saskatoon Star Phoenix*, October 18 [1975], III.H.15 (a) Clippings File, Taylor fonds, SAB.

104. Press Release Re. "Mr. and Mrs. Doucette—Prince Albert" from E. C. Boychuk, 20.

105. White, "Number of Children in Home Led to Decision."

106. "U.S. Couple Blames Media for Failure of Adoption," *Saskatoon Star Phoenix*, September 27 [1975], III.H.15 (a) Clippings File, Taylor fonds, SAB.

107. Geoff White, "P.A. Foster Parents Protest Adoption," *Saskatoon Star Phoenix*, July 11 [1975]; "Family Isn't Giving Up," *Regina Leader-Post*, July 23, 1975; Tim Naumetz, "Steuart Questions Adoption by Americans," *Regina Leader-Post*, July 11, 1975; III.H.15 (a) Clippings File, Taylor fonds, SAB; Press Release Re. "Mr. and Mrs. Doucette—Prince Albert" from E. C. Boychuk, 6, 7, 13, 22, 29.

108. Letter from Doucettes to Rolfes, received March 2, 1976.

109. Letter from Doucettes to Rolfes, received March 2, 1976.

110. Letter from Doucettes to Rolfes, received March 2, 1976.

111. Letter from Doucettes to Rolfes, received March 2, 1976.

112. Letter from Doucettes to Rolfes, received March 2, 1976.

113. Letter from Rolfes to the Doucettes, May 13, 1976, I.46d-55–1a, Rolfes fonds, SAB.

114. Quoted in John Drabble, "Snyder Still Convinced Adoption Was Correct," *Prince Albert Herald*, July 23 [1975]; see also "Snyder's Mind Made Up Before Meeting Couple," *Moose Jaw Times Herald*, July 23 [1975], III.H.15 (a) Clippings File, Taylor fonds, SAB.

115. Mrs. R[ita] Doucette to Editor, "Outraged by REACH Publicity Format," n.d., ca. February 1976, and Letter to editor of *Prince Albert Herald* from B. Delorme, "REACH Tactic Criticized," January 30, 1976, I.46d-55–1a, Rolfes fonds, SAB.

116. Margaret Lipman, National Adoption Desk, to Jacob, May 19, 1976, I.46d-55–1a, Rolfes fonds, SAB.

117. White, "Number of Children in Home Led to Decision."

118. Press Release Re. "Mr. and Mrs. Doucette—Prince Albert" from E. C. Boychuk, 26.

119. Letter from E. R. Stromberg, lawyer, to Herman Rolfes, June 4, 1976, "Laliberte Children Summary—September 9/75 to June 8/76," June 10, 1976, and REACH Bulletin, June 1976, I.46d-55–1a, Rolfes fonds, SAB.

120. Letter from Herman Rolfes, Minister of Social Services, to the Doucettes, June 2, 1976, and Letter from Herman Rolfes to Mr. E. Robert Stromberg (attorney), June 24, 1976, I.46d-55–1a, Rolfes fonds, SAB. Rolfes's letter to the Doucettes was returned "unclaimed."

121. Garnet Wipf, Member of Legislative Assembly, to Herman Rolfes, Minister of Social Services, October 11, 1977, and Wipf to Mr. and Mrs. Doucette, December 2, 1977, I.46d-55–1a, Rolfes fonds, SAB.

122. Doucette interview, June 14, 2013.

123. Geoff White, "Doucettes Intend to Continue Case," *Saskatoon Star Phoenix*, August 2 [1975], III.H.15 (a) Clippings File, Taylor fonds, SAB.

124. Ruth Warick, "Adoption Protests: Native Persons Occupy Office of Deputy Minister," *Regina Leader-Post*, March 24, 1976, news clipping, file 5.2, Department of Social Services records, R-1721, SAB. See also Memo from Cameron to F. J. Bogdasavich, Deputy Minister, October 4, 1976, file III.18.a, folder I.49, Deputy Minister Records, SAB; and memo from Cameron to Regional Directors and DNS, October 23, 1975, file 58.9, Department of Social Services, R-1406, SAB.

125. "Adoption Review Committee Begins Work," news release, May 26, 1977, file 5.5, Department of Social Services, R-1721, SAB.

126. Warick, "Adoption Protests."

127. Draft of speech for minister to SASW, April 4, 1976, folder 5.8, Department of Social Services, R-1721, SAB.

128. Memo from Jim Oxman to Fran Bogdasavich, October 12, 1976, file III.21.a, Deputy Minister Records, SAB.

129. Petition enclosed with letter from Wipf to Herman Rolfes, Minister of Social Services, October 11, 1977, I.46d-55–1a, Rolfes fonds, SAB.

130. "Indian Children Taken Illegally," *Saskatchewan Indian* 7, no. 11 (January 1977), accessed at http://www.sicc.sk.ca/archive/saskindian/a77jan11.htm, December 6, 2012.

131. Lawrence Fuchs to Unger, April 22, 1980, box 75, folder 3, AAIA papers.

132. Unger statement at Select Commission on Immigration and Refugee Policy, Albany, New York, May 5, 1980, summary, 5, 6; Unger to Jessica Mahkewa, National Indian Brotherhood, Ottawa, May 6, 1980, box 75, folder 3, AAIA papers.

133. Chartier to Unger, December 19, 1980; Unger to Chartier, January 12, 1981; Chartier to Unger, February 5, 1981, box 75, folder 3, AAIA papers.

134. Canadian Indian Lawyers Association, Indian Child Welfare Rights Workshop Agenda, March 18–20, 1981, held in Regina, Saskatchewan, box 75, folder 3, AAIA papers.

135. Unger to Barbara Murphy, April 30, 1981, Richard Schifter, P.C., Washington DC, to Unger, July 22, 1982, box 75, folder 3, AAIA papers.

136. Evelyn Blanchard, "Canada: Keeping Our Children Home," *The Association*, Association of American Indian and Alaskan Native Social Workers Newsletter (Phoenix), June 1982, 1, box 144, folder 9, AAIA papers.

137. Kimelman, *Transcripts*.

138. Kimelman, *Transcripts*, 334, 160, 161, 196, emphasis in original.

139. Kimelman, *Transcripts*, 73, 49, 45, emphasis in original.

140. Kimelman, *Transcripts*, 276, 328–29, 330, emphases in original.

141. Kimelman, *No Quiet Place*, 36, 338–40.

142. Kimelman, *Transcripts*, 126; G. McRae, "Summary of the Position Paper on the Proposed Child and Family Services Act," 1984, box 5055, file 29, SPC fonds, AM.

143. Johnston, *Native Children and the Child Welfare System*, xix–xx, 106–7. See also "A By-law for the Care of our Indian Children: Spallumcheen Indian Band By-Law #3," 1980, and Handwritten agreement between Spallumcheen Band and British Columbia Minister of Human Resources, 1980, in box 75, folder 3, AAIA papers.

144. Armitage, *Comparing the Policy of Aboriginal Assimilation*, xi.

145. "Canada-Manitoba-Indian Child Welfare Agreement," February 22, 1982, and "Manitoba Indian Child Welfare Subsidiary Agreement," April 1, 1983, box 5048, folder 4, SPC fonds, AM. See also Esther Seidl, "The Development of Manitoba Indian Child Welfare," in same folder, and West Region Child and Family Services, "Proposal for the Delivery of Off-Reserve Child Welfare Services to Band Members," June 1984, box 5055, file 27, SPC fonds, AM.

146. G. McRae, "Summary of the Position Paper on the Proposed Child and Family Services Act," 1984, box 5055, file 29, SPC fonds, AM.

147. "Indian Adoption Program—Interim Agreement," March 30, 1984, between Federation of Saskatchewan Indian Nations and Her Majesty the Queen, file 54.85, Department of Social Services, R-1406, SAB.

148. Michael Downey, "Canada's Genocide: Thousands Taken from Their Homes Need Help," *Macleans*, April 26, 1999, news clipping, Robert Doucette fonds, SAB, Saskatoon.

149. G. McRae, "Summary of Proposed Child and Family Services Act." For more on the longstanding tradition of custom adoptions within Native communities, which were at odds with the closed adoptions carried out by state agencies, see Johnston, *Native Children and the Child Welfare System*, 71–72; Strong-Boag, *Finding Families*, 16–18, 35, 135–36, 139.

MEETING AUNTY DI

1. "It's her 22nd School," *Herald*, Melbourne, April 2, 1962; Allan Nicholls, "Aborigine," *Age*, Melbourne, March 31, 1962; both in MS 12913 box 14/8 Children, 1960–62, Press Cuttings, Council for Aboriginal Rights MS 12913, State Library of Victoria, Melbourne, Australia (hereafter cited as CAR papers).

7. CRISIS IN AUSTRALIA AND TRANSNATIONAL ACTIVISM

1. Brenda Nicholls, "Award for Services to Aborigines," *Courier*, June 23, 1979, news clipping, box 67, folder 1, AAIA papers.

2. Letter from Mollie Dyer to American Indian Law Center, University of New Mexico, October 29, 1975; letter from B. V. Brown, Office of Australian Consulate-General, to Steven Unger, July 22, 1976; both in box 66, folder 7, AAIA papers.

3. Letter to the Editor from Mollie Dyer, *Indian Family Defense*, no. 5 (July 1976): 7–8.

4. Letters from Dyer to AAIA, November 10, 1975, and to Unger, March 7, 1976; both in box 66, folder 7, AAIA papers.

5. Dyer, *Room for One More*, 118.

6. Unger to Byler, April 30, 1979, box 67, folder 1, AAIA papers. Unger also got a lot of press coverage that drew out the parallels between American Indian and Aboriginal experience. See for example, "Black Adoption Plan Winds Down," *National Times*, June 2, 1979, clipping in box 67, folder 1, AAIA papers.

7. There is much evidence that Maori families in New Zealand also suffered from a child welfare crisis in the 1960s and 1970s. The experience of Maori families is different from that of Indigenous peoples in the United States, Canada, and Australia, however, for a number of reasons. First, the New Zealand government did not have a history of forcibly removing large numbers of Maori children

to boarding schools or other institutions. Second, the government hired Maori women as welfare workers in the decades after World War II, and these women made every attempt to keep Maori children in Maori families. The Maori Land Court, too, which colonial authorities had established in 1865, not only adjudicated land claims but formalized Maori custom adoptions up until 1962. Increasing numbers of Maori children did enter the child welfare system and became fostered or adopted by non-Maori families after 1955, when the New Zealand government passed a new Adoption Act, which established strict secrecy in regard to adoption proceedings. In 1962 the government transferred all adoption proceedings to magistrate's courts, including those of Maori children in the Land Court. As increasing numbers of Maori people moved to urban areas, more of their children fell under the power of the government's child welfare authorities. The exact numbers of children remain hidden from view because of strict confidentiality and racial categorizations that treated people of less than one-half Maori as Pakeha, or white. For more on this complex situation, see Newman, "'A Right to be Maori?'" and Newman, "History of Transracial Adoption."

8. Haebich, *Broken Circles*.
9. Jacobs, *White Mother*, 31–39.
10. Quoted in Haebich, *Spinning the Dream*, 195–96.
11. Armitage, *Comparing the Policy of Aboriginal Assimilation*, 46; Haebich, *Spinning the Dream*, 367.
12. "Homes Wanted for 150 Young Aborigines: Policy to Assimilate," *Sun-Herald* (Sydney), November 20, 1955, box 13/5: Press Cuttings, Children 1952–58, CAR papers.
13. Armitage, *Comparing the Policy of Aboriginal Assimilation*, 60, 61–62.
14. Haebich, *Spinning the Dream*, 251, 366.
15. Armitage, *Comparing the Policy of Aboriginal Assimilation*, 47.
16. Armitage, *Comparing the Policy of Aboriginal Assimilation*, 51–52.
17. Armitage, *Comparing the Policy of Aboriginal Assimilation*, 47.
18. Armitage, *Comparing the Policy of Aboriginal Assimilation*, 54.
19. Haebich, *Spinning the Dream*, 222.
20. "They Adopt Their Family 'At Home,'" *Daily Telegraph* (Sydney), July 29, 1963, box 16/3: Press Cuttings, Children, Council for Aboriginal Rights papers, MS 12913, CAR papers.
21. "Their Aim—To Help Others," *Advertiser* (Adelaide), January 26, 1961, box 14/8: Children, 1960–62, Press Cuttings, CAR papers.
22. Jay Spencer, "Foster-Family to Aborigine Children," ca. 1965, no publication, Scrapbook: "Aboriginal Children, 1965, 1966, 1967," box 21/2: Scrapbooks, vols. 19–21, CAR papers.

23. South Australia ACCA Report, ca. 1980, 3, box 67, folder 1, AAIA papers.

24. South Australia ACCA Report, ca. 1980.

25. "Aboriginal Girl's Good Start," no publication, September 1, 1965; Margaret Walsh, "Aboriginal Wins a Bright Future," no publication, n.d., ca. 1965; "Miranda's New Life, February 5, 1966, *Times Courier* (Lae, New Guinea), all in Scrapbook: "Aboriginal Children, 1965, 1966, 1967," box 21/2: Scrapbooks, vols. 19–21, CAR papers. See also "Black Boy in the House: Dutch Family Sets a Fine Example," *Sun* (Sydney), January 27, 1961, and "Their Aim—To Help Others," *Advertiser* (Adelaide), January 26, 1961; both in box 14/8: Children, 1960–62, Press Cuttings, CAR papers.

26. Thanks to scholar Lorenzo Veracini for this insight over a cup of coffee at the State Library of Victoria in March 2013.

27. "Harold Blair Talks on Assimilation of Aborigines," April 13, 1966, *Leader Budget* (Northcote, Victoria), Scrapbook: "Aboriginal Children, 1965, 1966, 1967," box 21/2: Scrapbooks, vols. 19–21, CAR papers; Haebich, *Spinning the Dream*, 368–69.

28. "Your Help Needed," *Examiner* (Launceton, Tasmania), August 9, 1965; Claudia Wright, "'My Son Is No Symbol,'" *Herald*, Melbourne, April 22, 1967, both in Scrapbook: "Aboriginal Children, 1965, 1966, 1967," box 21/2: Scrapbooks, vols. 19–21, CAR papers.

29. "The New Arrival," *Sun* (Melbourne), April 1, 1966, Scrapbook: "Aboriginal Children, 1965, 1966, 1967," box 21/2: Scrapbooks, vols. 19–21, CAR papers.

30. Wright, "'My Son Is No Symbol.'"

31. "Ten Eyes a Poppin'!: Waifs Find Love, Care," *Sun* (Sydney) January 26, 1956; box 13/5: Press Cuttings, Children 1952–58, CAR papers.

32. "Adoption of Aborigines," letter to the editor, *Advertiser*, Adelaide, March 10, 1966, Scrapbook: "Aboriginal Children, 1965, 1966, 1967," box 21/2: Scrapbooks, vols. 19–21, CAR papers.

33. Fay Patience, "It's Not the Color That Counts," *Woman's Weekly*, Melbourne, April 2, 1956; box 13/5: Press Cuttings, Children 1952–58, CAR papers.

34. "Happiness—in Black and White: A Story for Your Heart!" *Mirror* (Sydney), October 2, 1962, box 14/8: Children, 1960–62, Press Cuttings, CAR papers.

35. Isabel Carter, "The Aboriginal Cinderella," *Woman's Day* (Sydney), September 8, 1958, and "Joyce Wakes to a Glittering World: From Lean-to to Luxury," no publication, August 16, 1958, box 13/5: Press Cuttings, Children 1952–58; Erica Parker, "Rosy Life for Young Aboriginal," *Telegraph* (Brisbane), September 4, 1962, box 14/8: Children, 1960–62, Press Cuttings, all in CAR papers.

36. Fay Patience, "It's Not the Color That Counts."

37. Letter to the editor from Mrs. I Schulz, secretary of Integration League of South Australia, "No Problem," *News*, Adelaide, June 7, 1967; see also letter

to editor, "Aborigines Adopted," *Advertiser* (Adelaide), April 15, 1966; Sean Hanrahan, "Adopted Native Girl Vanishes," *Herald* (Melbourne), December 2, 1967; all in Scrapbook: "Aboriginal Children, 1965, 1966, 1967," box 21/2: Scrapbooks, vols. 19–21, CAR papers.

38. Margaret Walsh, "Aboriginal Wins a Bright Future," no publication, n.d., ca. 1965; Alan Dearn, "Problems of Adopting a Native Child," *Herald* (Melbourne), December 18, 1967; both in Scrapbook: "Aboriginal Children, 1965, 1966, 1967," box 21/2: Scrapbooks, vols. 19–21, CAR papers.

39. Haebich, *Spinning the Dream*, 207, 248, Middleton quoted at 248.

40. Haebich, *Spinning the Dream*, 252.

41. Haebich, *Spinning the Dream*, 248.

42. Fay Patience, "It's Not the Color That Counts."

43. "Adoption Is the 'Only Way,'" March 16, 1966, *News* (Adelaide), Scrapbook: "Aboriginal Children, 1965, 1966, 1967," box 21/2: Scrapbooks, vols. 19–21, CAR papers.

44. Gabrielle Schneeman, "A Pilot Study Exploring and Where Possible Describing the Position of a Sample of Aboriginal Wards of the State of Victoria Known to Be in Residential Care at the Time of the Study, in Regard to their Background, Present Situation and Expected Future," November 28, 1978, 12, in box 66, folder 8, AAIA papers.

45. Attwood, *Rights for Aborigines*, 31–35, 54–78.

46. Attwood, *Rights for Aborigines*, 35–53.

47. Attwood, *Rights for Aborigines*, 131–60. The Council became the Federal Council for the Advancement of Aborigines and Torres Strait Islanders in 1964 in order to include the Indigenous people living in the islands to the north of Australia.

48. Attwood, *Rights for Aborigines*, x, 163. For the full story of the referendum, see 161–80.

49. Attwood, *Rights for Aborigines*, 307–49.

50. Armitage, *Comparing the Policy of Aboriginal Assimilation*, 62–64.

51. Letter from Dyer to Unger, May 20, 1977, box 66, folder 7, AAIA papers.

52. Brenda Nicholls, "Award for Services to Aborigines," *Courier*, June 23, 1979, news clipping, box 67, folder 1, AAIA papers.

53. Nicholls, "Award for Services to Aborigines."

54. On Dyer's first foster child, Diane Singh (née Day), see "It's her 22nd School," *Herald* (Melbourne), April 2, 1962; Allan Nicholls, "Aborigine," *Age* (Melbourne), March 31, 1962, box 14/8: Children, 1960–62, Press Cuttings, both in CAR papers.

55. Quoted in Briskman, *Black Grapevine*, 27–28.

56. Letter from Dyer to American Indian Law Center, University of New Mexico, October 29, 1975; see also letter from B. V. Brown, Office of Australian Consulate-General, to Steven Unger, July 22, 1976, both in box 66, folder 7, AAIA papers.

57. Letter from Dyer to Unger, May 20, 1977, box 66, folder 7, AAIA papers.

58. Barbara Rowlands, "Caring for Kids Ended in Triumph," *Aboriginal News* 3, no. 7 (1979): 6–8, quote at 6.

59. "Let Aboriginal Children Stay with Families," March 15, 1966, *Journal* (Traralgon, Victoria), Scrapbook: "Aboriginal Children, 1965, 1966, 1967," box 21/2: Scrapbooks, vols. 19–21, CAR papers.

60. Letter to editor form Stan Davey, director Aborigines Advancement League, Victoria, "Better Way to Care," no publication, December 5, 1967, box 21/2: Scrapbooks, vols. 19–21, CAR papers.

61. Research Study by Christine Watson, Department of Aboriginal Affairs, Canberra, "Aboriginal Children and the Care of the State in Victoria," November 1976, 1, 2, included in box 66, folder 7, AAIA papers.

62. Schneeman, "A Pilot Study," 7, box 66, folder 8, AAIA papers.

63. Armitage, *Comparing the Policy of Aboriginal Assimilation*, 52.

64. Quoted from *Nunga News* in "ACCA News, Views, Etc.," ca. 1979, 6, box 67, folder 1, AAIA papers.

65. Robert Ball, "Child Care and the Aboriginal Family," *Advertiser*, October 24, 1978, clipping in box 66, folder 7, AAIA papers.

66. Research Study by Christine Watson, 7.

67. Dyer, quoted in Schneeman, "A Pilot Study," 23.

68. "Custody Wrangle: Native Children to Be Returned to Parents," no publication, September 1965; "Order for Children to Leave Catholic Mission," no publication, October 1, 1965; "'I Want my Children Back,'" *News* (Darwin), November 1, 1965; "Aboriginal Paternity Case: Father Wanted Payment for Daughter," November 2, 1965; "Native Children Custody Case: The First in Legal History," no publication, November 3, 1965; "Parents Wait on Custody Verdict," no publication, November 4, 1965; Douglas Lockwood, "Parents Fail to Get Back 3 Children," no publication, November 16, 1965; "Parents Plan Custody Appeal," no publication, December 1965; "Natives' Bid for Children," *News* (Adelaide), December 3, 1965; all clippings in Scrapbook: "Aboriginal Children, 1965, 1966, 1967," box 21/2: Scrapbooks, vols. 19–21, CAR papers.

69. Tonie Blackie, "Missing Richard Returns Home," *The Age* (September 5, 1978): 1. In another article, Thomas is identified as Jeannette, not Jennifer. See Lindsay Murdoch, "Countdown for a Happy Reunion," *The Age* (September 6, 1978): 3.

70. Tonie Blackie, "Bid to Trace Missing Mothers," *The Age* (September 6, 1978): 3.

71. "Aboriginal Child Care Agency History and First Six Months' Operation," November 15, 1978, 15, 16; "Aboriginal Child Care Agency History and First Twelve Months' Operation," November 15, 1978, Appendix F, both in box 66, folder 7, AAIA papers.

72. Bob Lenton, "A Young Mother Gives up Hope," *Daily News* (Perth), March 10, 1965, Scrapbook: "Aboriginal Children, 1965, 1966, 1967," box 21/2: Scrapbooks, vols. 19–21, CAR papers.

73. Bob Lenton, "Report: Barry in Cuba," no publication, ca. March 1965, Scrapbook: "Aboriginal Children, 1965, 1966, 1967," box 21/2: Scrapbooks, vols. 19–21, CAR papers.

74. Research Study by Christine Watson, 17, 21.

75. News clipping, *National Times*, ca. 1979, box 67, folder 1, AAIA papers.

76. "Aboriginal Child Care Agency History and First Six Months' Operation," November 15, 1978, 6, box 66, folder 7, AAIA papers.

77. Jo Gorman, "Why Black Bugsie Thinks He's White," *The Age*, February 25, 197[6?], box 66, folder 7, AAIA papers; Research Study by Christine Watson, 4.

78. "Aboriginal Child Care Agency History and First Six Months' Operation," November 15, 1978, 3, box 66, folder 7, AAIA papers.

79. Tomlinson, *Is Band-Aid Social Work Enough?*, 259–68, 279–89; White, *True Stories of the Top End*, 66–71, quote at 70; Schneeman, "A Pilot Study," 9, box 66, folder 8, AAIA papers.

80. Sommerlad, "Aboriginal Children Belong in the Aboriginal Community: 172, 173, 168, 174.

81. Department of Aboriginal Affairs, "Aboriginal Adoption and Fostering—Policy Guidelines," January 1977, box 66, folder 7, AAIA papers.

82. Anna Glover, "Our Troubled Children, *Aboriginal News* (Canberra)3, no. 7 (1979): 4–5; "Aboriginal Child Care Agency History and First Twelve Months' Operation," November 15, 1978, 2, box 66, folder 7, AAIA papers.

83. "Aboriginal Child Care Agency History and First Six Months' Operation," 5, 6.

84. "Aboriginal Child Care Agency History and First Six Months' Operation," 3; "Aboriginal Child Care Agency History and First Twelve Months' Operation."

85. "Aboriginal Child Care Agency History and First Twelve Months' Operation," appendix F; "Aboriginal Child Care Agency History and First Six Months' Operation," 11.

86. Report from Mollie Dyer, April 28, 1976, 2, box 66, folder 7, AAIA papers. Judith Collard, a faculty member in art history at the University of Otago, Dunedin, New Zealand, attended a presentation I gave at that university on March 1, 2013, and shared her memories as a child of a progressive Christian family who was acquainted with Dyer in the 1970s.

87. Paper by Mollie Dyer to Department of Aboriginal Affairs for seminar on Aboriginal juvenile delinquency, included in G. Harwood to Dyer, March 30, 1977, box 66, folder 7, AAIA papers.

88. ACCA proposal to make a documentary film, n.d., ca. 1979, 1, 4, box 67, folder 1, AAIA papers.

89. Report from Mollie Dyer, April 28, 1976, 1, box 66, folder 7, AAIA papers.

90. A few scholars have written about Indigenous transnational and/or international activism, but most of this has centered on activities at the UN. See De Costa, *A Higher Authority*.

91. Dyer, *Room for One More*, 98.

92. Dyer, *Room for One More*, 99.

93. "Australian Aboriginee Guest at Course," *Saskatchewan Indian* 6, no. 7 (July 1976): 34.

94. "Australian View," letter to editor from Mollie Dyer, *Saskatchewan Indian* 6, no. 7 (July 1976): 4.

95. Dyer, *Room for One More*, 100–1, quotes at 101.

96. Dyer, *Room for One More*, 101–3, 113–17.

97. Dyer, *Room for One More*, 117–18, quotes at 117. See chapter 4 for a detailed discussion of Robbins's program.

98. Dyer, *Room for One More*, 118. See also *Yakima Nation Review* 6, no. 12 (November 23, 1976): 13.

99. Dyer, *Room for One More*, 119–21; Department of Aboriginal Affairs, "Children's Services for Indigenous Peoples," summary of talks given by Mrs. Maxine Robbins and Mrs. Mollie Dyer by Sue Ingram, November 16, 1977, 3, P6811, Australian Institute of Aboriginal and Torres Strait Islander Studies Library, Canberra, Australia.

100. Carol Craig, "Australians Visit Ka-Nuk-We-Sha," *Yakima Nation Review* 9, no. 6 (August 21, 1978): 14.

101. Dyer, *Room for One More*, 121–22.

102. Dyer, *Room for One More*, 122; "Aboriginal Child Care Agency History and First Six Months' Operation," November 15, 1978, inside cover; Department of Aboriginal Affairs, "Children's Services for Indigenous Peoples."

103. Letter from Dyer to Unger, February 12, 1979, box 67, folder 1, AAIA papers.

104. Letter from Dyer to Unger, February 12, 1979, box 67, folder 1, AAIA papers. See also Dyer, *Room for One More*, 131; Letter from Unger to Dyer, February 23, 1979, box 67, folder 1, AAIA papers. Unger raised most of his funds from the Australian Consulate in New York; see, for example, Unger to Burton, Australian Consulate General, March 20, 1979, box 67, folder 1, AAIA papers.

105. Letter from Unger to Byler, April 30, 1979, box 67, folder 1, AAIA papers.

106. "ACCA News, Views, Etc.," ca. 1979, 9, box 67, folder 1, AAIA papers. See also VACCA International Year of the Child, 1979, International Conference, "If Everyone Cared—Aboriginal Child Survival," April 23–25, 1979, Resolutions, 5, 6, in the same folder.

107. Letter from Unger to Byler, April 30, 1979, box 67, folder 1, AAIA papers.

108. "ACCA News, Views, Etc." ca. 1979, 9.

109. "ACCA News, Views, Etc." ca. 1979, 10.

110. "International Year of the Child Seminar"—funding proposal, n.d., ca. January 1979, 1, box 67, folder 1, AAIA papers.

111. Letter from Dyer to Unger, May 23, 1979, box 67, folder 1, AAIA papers.

112. "ACCA News, Views, Etc.," ca. 1979, 10.

113. Letter from Unger to Byler, May 25, 1979, box 67, folder 1, AAIA papers.

114. Letter from Unger to Byler, May 26, 1979, box 67, folder 1, AAIA papers.

115. Quoted in Briskman, *Black Grapevine*, 173.

116. Letter from Unger to Byler, May 25, 1979, box 67, folder 1, AAIA papers.

117. Quoted in Briskman, *Black Grapevine*, 41.

118. Letter from Unger to Byler, May 26, 1979, box 67, folder 1, AAIA papers.

119. Letter from Unger to John Morieson, August 3, 1979, box 67, folder 1, AAIA papers.

120. Dyer to Unger, Maxine, and LeNora, August 14, 1979, box 67, folder 1, AAIA papers.

121. Quoted in Briskman, *Black Grapevine*, 53–54.

122. "Aboriginal Child Care Agency History and First Twelve Months' Operation."

123. Briskman, *Black Grapevine*, 46, quote at 52. Activists in the Northern Territory, such as Barbara Cummings and Betty Pearce, also struggled for support from both the territorial administration and male Aboriginal organizations. See 48–49.

124. Briskman, *Black Grapevine*, 59–71; Armitage, *Comparing the Policy of Aboriginal Assimilation*, 54–55, 65–67.

125. Document from Jean Collins, Social Worker, Aboriginal Medical Service in Perth, January 1, 1979, box 67, folder 1, AAIA papers.

126. "ACCA News, Views, Etc." ca. 1979, 7.

127. Briskman, *Black Grapevine*, 110, 84; Armitage, *Comparing the Policy of Aboriginal Assimilation*, 54–55, 65–67.

128. "International Year of the Child Seminar"—funding proposal, n.d., ca. January 1979, 2, box 67, folder 1, AAIA papers.

8. HISTORICAL RECKONING WITH
INDIGENOUS CHILD REMOVAL

1. Tony Hewett, "Savage Indictment," *Sydney Morning Herald*, September 15, 1989. In the coverage of Savage's case, many of the details of Savage's back-

ground vary (for example, his mother's age at his birth). Hewett's in-depth story seems to be the best researched and most accurate.

2. Hewett, "Savage Indictment"; Anne Groer, "Aborigine Fights to Save the Son She Never Knew," *Orlando Sentinel,* September 10, 1989. Tragically, just three weeks after the couple married, Frank Whyman was killed in a car accident.

3. "Support Russell Moore—Stop Genocide," *Koorier* 3 (December 1989): 3. Sources differ as to why James Savage became homeless. Aboriginal activists in the *Koorier* asserted that his parents had moved and did not let him know where they were, but the Savages testified that he refused to return home when he was released from one of his terms of detention, and they simply did not know where he was. See Hewett, "Savage Indictment."

4. Sean Holton and Mark Vosburgh, "The Savage Story: Explosions of Violence and Deviant Behavior, 'He Never Had a Satisfactory Relationship with a Single Human Being,'" *Orlando Sentinel,* August 15, 1989.

5. Sean Holton and Mark Vosburgh, "The Savage Story: Is the State a Silent Accomplice in Gruesome Rape-Strangling?" *Orlando Sentinel,* August 13, 1989; "The Savage Story: This Time a Murder Charge," *Orlando Sentinel,* August 16, 1989.

6. Lynne Bumpus-Hooper, "She Helped 'Teddy Bear' Find His Mom," *Orlando Sentinel,* September 10, 1989.

7. Hewett, "Savage Indictment."

8. See Lynne Bumpus-Hooper's 1989 series in the *Orlando Sentinel:* "Savage, Mother Will Meet Today for 1st Time," September 23; "Savage, Mom finally Meet after 26 Years," September 24; "Aborigines Put Blame on Australia in Savage Case," September 26; "Savage's Adoption Could Figure in Trial," November 13. And see "Man Is Guilty of Murdering Florida Decorator," *New York Times,* November 23, 1989.

9. See Sean Holton and Mark Vosburgh's 1989 series "The Savage Story" in the *Orlando Sentinel:* "Is the State a Silent Accomplice?" August 13; "Out of Control and Back in Brevard," August 14; "Explosions of Violence and Deviant Behavior" August 15; "This Time a Murder Charge" August 16.

10. "Support Russell Moore—Stop Genocide," *Koorier* 3 (December 1989): 3; Lynne Bumpus-Hooper, "Judge Sentences Savage to Death," *Orlando Sentinel,* January 24, 1990. Savage's appeal provides more on Aboriginal activists' contention that the Australian state was at fault: see National Aboriginal and Islander Legal Services Secretariat Inc., "Brief of Amicus Curiae, in Support of the Appellant," *James Hudson Savage, Appellant v. State of Florida, Appellee,* Case No. 75-494, in the Supreme Court of Florida, filed October 12, 1990.

11. "Support Russell Moore—Stop Genocide," 3.

12. "Australia to Send Experts for Savage," *Orlando Sentinel,* November 29, 1989.

13. State of Florida, "Answer Brief of Appellee," *James Hudson Savage, Appellant v. State of Florida, Appellee,* Case No. 75, 494, in the Supreme Court of Florida, filed January 10, 1991, 17–18.

14. "Support Russell Moore—Stop Genocide," 4; "To All Community Organisations," *Koorier* 3 (June 1990): 25. See Lynne Bumpus-Hooper's follow-up coverage in the *Orlando Sentinel:* "Australia Rejects Calls for Savage's Return," December 13, 1989; "Savage Jury Asks Judge to Allow Murderer to Live," December 15, 1989; "Judge Sentences Savage to Death," January 24, 1990; "State Supreme Court Saves Savage from Chair," October 4, 1991; "Judge Orders 3 Life Terms, Ensures Brevard Killer Never Goes Free," March 5, 1992. See also "Murderer James Hudson Savage Wants to Serve Life Sentence in Aussie Jail, *Daily Telegraph* (Sydney), November 16, 2009; Bernard Lagan, "Bring Me Home: Killer's Plea," *Sydney Morning Herald,* November 29, 2010. For more on the judge's decision to bar testimony from Judge Hal Wooten and for the withdrawal of two other expert witnesses, see National Aboriginal and Islander Legal Services Secretariat, "Brief of Amicus Curiae," 5; and State of Florida, "Answer Brief of Appellee," 16; Peter Read, "In the Courts: 'In the Middle of the Ocean, Drowning,'" in his *A Rape of the Soul So Profound,* 188–210; Read, "The Stolen Generations," 51–61. Read's accounts contain some inaccuracies, including the assertion that Dyer was withdrawn as a witness.

15. Wolfe, "Land, Labor, and Difference."

16. Jacobs, *White Mother.*

17. *Book of Voices,* 140.

18. *Book of Voices,* 157, 171.

19. State of Florida, "Answer Brief of Appellee," 21, 30.

20. National Aboriginal and Islander Legal Services Secretariat, "Brief of Amicus Curiae," 9.

21. *Book of Voices,* 106, 163.

22. *Book of Voices,* 260. Such statistics are difficult to verify as no comprehensive data have been gathered, pointing to the need for increased research on the subject.

23. Devan Harness, *Mixing Cultural Identities,* 103, 104, 98.

24. National Aboriginal and Islander Legal Services Secretariat, "Brief of Amicus Curiae," 5, 48.

25. State of Florida, "Answer Brief of Appellee," 30.

26. *Book of Voices,* 88.

27. *Book of Voices,* 258.

28. State of Florida, "Answer Brief of Appellee," 19. See also "Support Russell Moore—Stop Genocide," *Koorier* 3 (December 1989): 3.

29. Bernard Lagan, "Bring Me Home: Killer's Plea," *Sydney Morning Herald*, November 29, 2010; State of Florida, "Answer Brief of Appellee," 17.

30. Quoted in DeMeyer and Cotter-Busbee, *Two Worlds*, 12.

31. Quoted in DeMeyer and Cotter-Busbee, *Two Worlds*, 162–63.

32. Peterson, "Lostbirds," 65–66, 68, 69.

33. Tony Hewett, "Savage Indictment," *Sydney Morning Herald*, September 15, 1989.

34. Sinclair, "All My Relations," 250, 253.

35. Kreisher, "Coming Home"; *Book of Voices*, 260–61; Mary Annette Pember, "To Dry the Eyes of Indian Adoptees," originally published in *Daily Yonder*, March 16, 2010, reprinted in DeMeyer and Cotter-Busbee, *Two Worlds*, 247–53.

36. Sinclair, "All My Relations," 239.

37. "Nellie Moore's Story," *Koorier* 3 (June 1990): 25.

38. Australian Human Rights Commission, "Timeline: History of Separation." For the full report of the Royal Commission, see http://www.austlii.edu.au/au /other/IndigLRes/rciadic/.

39. Human Rights and Equal Opportunity Commission, *Bringing Them Home*.

40. Regan, *Unsettling the Settler Within*, 58–59.

41. For the only successful case, *Trevorrow v South Australia* (2007), see Antonio Buti, "The Stolen Generations and Litigation Revisited," *Melbourne University Law Review* 32 (2008), 382–421, http://www.mulr.com.au/issues/32_2/32_2_2 .pdf, accessed March 12, 2014. For an earlier case brought by Lorna Cubillo and Peter Gunner, two members of the Stolen Generations, see Robert Van Krieken, "Is Assimilation Justiciable? Lorna Cubillo and Peter Gunner v Commonwealth," *Sydney Law Review* 239 (June 2001), http://www-personal.usyd .edu.au/~robertvk/CivOz/papers/cubillo.htm, accessed January 5, 2014. For a recent unsuccessful case, see "WA Court dismisses Stolen Generation compensation claim launched by Collard family," *ABC News*, December 20, 2013, http://www.abc.net.au/news/2013-12-20/stolen-generations-test-case -dismissed-in-wa-court/5169640, accessed January 5, 2014.

42. Regan, *Unsettling the Settler Within*, 6.

43. For an insightful comparative analysis of these and other apologies, see Nobles, *Politics of Official Apologies*.

44. Regan, *Unsettling the Settler Within*, 8.

45. Regan, *Unsettling the Settler Within*, 50, 10.

46. Marcia Brown and Robert Commanda brought this class action lawsuit to an Ontario court in 2010. The court did not find in their favor, but they have appealed. See "Sixties Scoop Class Action Lawsuit," website, http://sixties scoopclaim.com/.

47. Swain, "'Homes Are Sought for These Children'"; Cuthbert and Quartly, "Forced Child Removals." For the most recent apology to unwed mothers, see "Julia Gillard Apologises to Australian Mothers for Forced Adoptions," *Guardian*, March 20, 2013, http://www.theguardian.com/world/2013/mar/21/julia -gillard-apologises-forced-adoptions, accessed July 31, 2013.

48. Lorie Graham, "Reparations, Self-Determination."

49. Judith Graham, "Adoption Apology Too Late for Indians."

50. Bilchik, "Working Together."

51. American Friends Service Committee, "Conversation with Denise Altvater," and "Preparing the Way for Truth and Reconciliation in Maine."

52. LePage and Native officials, "Declaration of Intent"; Altvater, Comments, Truth and Reconciliation signing ceremony.

53. American Friends Service Committee, "Conversation with Denise Altvater." See also the website of the Maine Wabanaki–State Child Welfare Truth and Reconciliation Commission, http://www.mainewabanakitrc.org/#&panel1–1, accessed January 5, 2014.

54. State of Nebraska, Senate, Transcript, Health and Human Services Committee Meeting on Nebraska Indian Child Welfare Act, 9–10. See also testimony of Liz Neeley, member of the Foster Care Review Office, 35. Thank you to attorney Robert McEwen for sharing this document with me.

55. Australian Institute of Family Studies "Child Protection" fact sheet. A majority of Indigenous children removed from their families in the Northern Territory and Tasmania are living in non-Indigenous families.

56. Sinha et al., *Kiskisik Awasisak: Remember the Children*, x–xii.

57. Blanchard, "To Prevent the Breakup," 307.

58. Strong-Boag, *Finding Families, Finding Ourselves*, 46; Briggs, *Somebody's Children*, 9.

59. Sinclair, "Indian Residential School System of Canada."

60. Sinclair, "Indian Residential School System of Canada."

AFTERWORD

1. "Tribal Adoption Granted in Unique Court Session," *Indian Affairs* 98 (Fall–Winter 1978–79): 3.

# Bibliography

MANUSCRIPT COLLECTIONS

### Australia

Council for Aboriginal Rights (CAR) papers, MS 12913. State Library of Victoria, Melbourne.

Summary of talks given by Mrs. Maxine Robbins and Mrs. Mollie Dyer by Sue Ingram, November 16, 1977, P6811. Australian Institute of Aboriginal and Torres Strait Islander Studies Library, Canberra.

### Canada

Archives of Manitoba (AM), Winnipeg.

    Beatrice Brigden fonds.

    Social Planning Council (SPC) fonds.

Saskatchewan Archives Board (SAB), Regina.

    Alex Taylor fonds, R-1298.

    Department of Social Services records, R-1406.

    Department of Social Services records, R-1655.

    Department of Social Services records, R-1721.

    Deputy Minister records, R-935.

    Herman Rolfes fonds, R-1100.

    Human Resources Development Agency (HRDA) papers, R-921.

    Office of Deputy Minister records, R-1428.

Saskatchewan Archives Board (SAB), Saskatoon.

    Federation of Saskatchewan Indians, Collection #2098.

    Robert Doucette fonds, #1035.

### United States

Aleta Brownlee Papers, 1945–1950, register. Hoover Institution Archives, Stanford University.

American Friends Service Committee (AFSC) records. Swarthmore College Peace
Collection, Swarthmore, Pennsylvania.

Association on American Indian Affairs Records (AAIA), 1851–2010. Public Policy
Papers, Department of Rare Books and Manuscripts, Princeton University
Library, Princeton, New Jersey.

National Archives and Records Administration, Washington DC.
Division of Social Services, Miscellaneous Subject Files, 1929–1968, Records of
the Bureau of Indian Affairs (BIA), Record Group 75.

Social Welfare History Archives, Special Collections, University of Minnesota
Libraries, Minneapolis.
Beatrice Bernhagen papers, SW 134.
Child Welfare League of America (CWLA) papers.
United Way of Minnesota papers, SW 070.

### INTERVIEWS BY AND ITEMS IN POSSESSION OF THE AUTHOR

Blanchard, Evelyn. Phone interviews, September 22 and 29, 2011. Recording and
transcript in possession of the author.
————. Statement regarding Goldie Denny, August 23, 2012. In possession of the
author.

Byler, Mary Lou. Phone interview, September 1, 2011. Notes in possession of the
author.

Doucette, Robert. Interview, June 14, 2013, Saskatoon, Canada. Notes in possession
of the author.

Hirsch, Bertram. Phone interviews, September 23 and 30, 2011. Recordings and
transcripts in possession of the author.
————. Presentation on Indian Child Welfare Act to Alaskan Native group on
Kodiak Island, videotaped July 18, 1989. In possession of the author.

Sinclair, Justice Murray. "The Indian Residential School System of Canada: The
Search for Truth—the Need for Reconciliation." Presentation to the Indigenous Enslavement and Incarceration in North American History conference,
November 15, 2013, Gilder Lehrman Center for the Study of Slavery, Resistance, and Abolition, Yale University, New Haven, Connecticut.

Singh, Diane. Interview, March 18, 2013, Melbourne, Australia. Notes in possession
of the author.

### PERIODICALS

*Aboriginal News* (Department of Aboriginal Affairs, Canberra, Australia), 1979.
*California Indian Legal Services Newsletter* (Escondido CA), 1974, 1976.
*Catholic Charities Review* (Baltimore MD), 1964, 1967.

*Child Welfare* (Washington DC), 1960–61.

*Christian Century* (Chicago IL), 1955.

*DNA in Action* (Dinebeiina Nahiilna Be Agaditahe, Window Rock AZ; initially called *Law in Action*), 1969, 1972 .

*Indian Affairs* (New York), 1968–1979.

*Indian Family Defense* (New York), 1974–78.

*Koorier* (Sydney, Australia), 1989–90.

*Navajo Times* (Window Rock AZ), 1960, 1964–66.

*Saskatchewan Indian* (Prince Albert, Saskatchewan), 1976–77.

*Yakima Nation Review* (Toppenish WA), 1975–79, 1988–89.

### PUBLISHED SOURCES

ABC's 20/20. "A Hidden America: Children of the Plains" (video). Broadcast October 14, 2011. http://abcnews.go.com/2020/video/hidden-america-children-plains -robert-crumbling-trailer-dreams-2020–14742304 (accessed July 29, 2013).

Abourezk, James G. *Advise and Dissent: Memoirs of South Dakota and the U.S. Senate.* Chicago: Lawrence Hill Books, 1989.

Adams, David Wallace. *Education for Extinction: American Indians and the Boarding School Experience, 1875–1928.* Lawrence: University Press of Kansas, 1995.

Adams, Howard. *Prison of Grass: Canada from the Native Point of View.* Toronto: New Press, 1975.

"Adoption Controversy: Battle Over Baby Veronica" (video). *Dr. Phil* website, originally aired October 18, 2012. http://www.drphil.com/shows/show/1895 (accessed December 10, 2013).

*Adoptive Couple v. Baby Girl,* 570 U.S. ___ 133 S. Ct. 2552, 186 L. Ed. 2d 729 (2013).

"Adoptive Couple v. Baby Girl," Supreme Court of the United States blog. http:// www.scotusblog.com/case-files/cases/adoptive-couple-v-baby-girl/ (accessed December 8, 2013).

"Adoptive Couple v. Baby Girl," transcript of radio program, May 30, 2013, Radio Lab. http://www.radiolab.org/blogs/radiolab-blog/2013/may/30/adoptive -couple-v-baby-girl/ (accessed July 15, 2013).

Aleiss, Angela. *Making the White Man's Indian: Native Americans and Hollywood Movies.* Westport CT: Praeger, 2005.

Allitt, Patrick. *Religion in America since 1945.* New York: Columbia University Press, 2003.

Altvater, Denise. Comments. Truth and Reconciliation signing ceremony, June 6, 2011. http://afsc.org/document/denise-altvaters-comments-truth-and -reconciliation-signing-ceremony (accessed May 20, 2013).

American Friends Service Committee. "Conversation with Denise Altvater on Truth and Reconciliation in Maine." N.d., ca. 2011. https://afsc.org/resource/conversation -denise-altvater-truth- and-reconciliation-maine (accessed May 20, 2013).

———. "Preparing the Way for Truth and Reconciliation in Maine." N.d., ca. 2011. https://afsc.org/story/preparing-way-truth- and-reconciliation-maine (accessed May 20, 2013).

Anderson, Kim. *A Recognition of Being: Reconstructing Native Womanhood.* Toronto: Second Story Press, 2000.

Anaya, James, special rapporteur on the situation of human rights and fundamental freedoms of Indigenous people. "Observations on the Northern Territory Emergency Response in Australia." Human Rights Council, 15th session, United Nations General Assembly, February 23, 2010. Available at http://unsr .jamesanaya.org/special-reports/observations-on-the-northern-territory -emergency-response-in-australia-2010 (accessed July 15, 2013).

"Annual Meeting, Oklahoma Historical Society." *Chronicles of Oklahoma* 16, no. 2 (June 1938). http://digital.library.okstate.edu/chronicles/v016/v016p250.html (accessed June 20, 2013).

Armitage, Andrew. *Comparing the Policy of Aboriginal Assimilation—Australia, Canada, and New Zealand.* Vancouver: University of British Columbia Press, 1995.

Ashby, LeRoy. *Saving the Waifs: Reformers and Dependent Children, 1890–1917.* Philadelphia: Temple University Press, 1984.

Attwood, Bain. *Rights for Aborigines.* Crows Nest, New South Wales: Allen and Unwin, 2003.

Australian Human Rights Commission. "Timeline: History of Separation of Aboriginal and Torres Strait Islander Children from their Families." http://www .humanrights.gov.au/timeline-history-separation-aboriginal- and- torres-strait -islander-children-their-families-text (accessed July 10, 2013).

Australian Institute of Family Studies. "Child Protection and Aboriginal and Torres Strait Islander Children." Fact sheet, June 2013. http://www.aifs.gov.au/cfca /pubs/factsheets/a142117/ (accessed July 13, 2013).

Balcom, Karen. *The Traffic in Babies: Cross-Border Adoption and Baby-Selling between the United States and Canada, 1930–1972.* Toronto: University of Toronto Press, 2011.

Bauer, William. *We Were All Like Migrant Workers Here: Work, Community, and Memory on California's Round Valley Reservation, 1850–1941.* Chapel Hill: University of North Carolina Press, 2012.

Bennett, Ramona. "The Puyallup Tribe Rose from the Ashes." In *Messengers of the Wind: Native American Women Tell Their Life Stories*, ed. Jane Katz, 147–65. New York: Ballantine Books, 1995.

Bilchik, Shay. "Working Together to Strengthen Supports for Indian Children and Families: A National Perspective." Keynote speech, National Indian Child Welfare Association conference, Anchorage, Alaska, April 24, 2001. http://www.cwla.org/execdir/edremarks010424.htm (accessed May 20, 2013).

Blanchard, Evelyn. "To Prevent the Breakup of the Indian Family: The Development of the Indian Child Welfare Act of 1978." PhD diss., University of New Mexico, 2010.

Bonilla-Silva, Eduardo. *Racism without Racists: Color-Blind Racism and the Persistence of Racial Inequality in the United States.* New York: Rowman and Littlefield, 2003.

Bonnin, Gertrude. *American Indian Stories.* Introduction by Susan Rose Dominguez. Lincoln: University of Nebraska Press, 2003.

*Book of Voices: Voices of Aboriginal Adoptees and Foster Children.* Winnipeg: Stolen Generations, 2000.

Bremner, Robert H., ed. *Children and Youth in America: A Documentary History,* vol. 3, 1933–1973. Cambridge MA: Harvard University Press, 1974.

Briggs, Laura. *Somebody's Children: The Politics of Transracial and Transnational Adoption.* Durham NC: Duke University Press, 2012.

Briskman, Linda. *The Black Grapevine: Aboriginal Activism and the Stolen Generations.* Leichhardt, New South Wales, Australia: Federation Press, 2003.

*Brokenleg v. Butts,* 559 S.W. 2d 853, 855, 857 (Tex. Civ. App. 1977), *rev'd in part and aff'd in part.*

Brownlee, Aleta. "The American Indian Child." *Children* 5, no. 2 (March–April 1958): 55–60.

Buti, Antonio. "The Stolen Generations and Litigation Revisited." *Melbourne University Law Review* 32 (2008), 382–421, http://www.mulr.com.au/issues/32_2/32_2_2.pdf, (accessed March 12, 2014).

Campbell, Maria. *Halfbreed.* Lincoln: University of Nebraska Press, 1973.

Child, Brenda. *Boarding School Seasons: American Indian Families, 1900–1940.* Lincoln: University of Nebraska Press, 1998.

*Clampett v. Madigan,* U.S. District Court for the District of South Dakota, Southern Division (Civ. No. 73–4018).

Cobb, Daniel. *Native Activism in Cold War America: The Struggle for Sovereignty.* Lawrence: University Press of Kansas, 2008.

Collier, John. *From Every Zenith: A Memoir.* Denver: Sage Books, 1963.

Collmeyer, Patricia. "From 'Operation Brown Baby' to 'Opportunity': The Placement of Children of Color at the Boys and Girls Aid Society of Oregon." *Child Welfare* 74, no. 1 (January–February 1995): 242–63.

Cuthbert, Denise, and Marian Quartly. "Forced Child Removals and the Politics of National Apologies in Australia." *American Indian Quarterly* 37, nos. 1–2 (Winter–Spring 2013): 178–202.

Darnell, Regna. *Invisible Geneaologies: A History of Americanist Anthropology.* Lincoln: University of Nebraska Press, 2001.

Davis, Julie. *Survival Schools: The American Indian Movement and Community Education in the Twin Cities.* Minneapolis: University of Minnesota Press, 2013.

Davis, Mary. "One Agency's Approach to the Indian Adoption Project." *Child Welfare* (June 1961): 12–15.

Day, Muriel. "Methodism and the Navajos." *Christian Advocate* 125, no. 20 (May 18, 1950): 4–5, 27.

De Costa, Ravi. *A Higher Authority: Indigenous Transnationalism and Australia.* Sydney: University of New South Wales Press, 2006.

*DeCoteau v. District County Court for the Tenth Judicial District,* 420 U.S. 425, 95 S. Ct. 1082 (1975).

DeMeyer, Trace A., and Patricia Cotter-Busbee. *Two Worlds: Lost Children of the Indian Adoption Projects.* Greenfield MA: Blue Hand Books, 2012.

Devan Harness, Susan. *Mixing Cultural Identities through Transracial Adoption: Outcomes of the Indian Adoption Project (1958–1967).* Lewiston NY: Edwin Mellen Press, 2008.

Doss, Helen Grigsby. *The Family Nobody Wanted.* New York: Little, Brown, 1954; Boston: Northeastern University Press, 2001.

———. "We Adopt an International Family," *Christian Advocate* (July 7, 1949): 4, 23, 29.

Dubinsky, Karen. *Babies without Borders: Adoption and Migration across the Americas.* Washington Square: New York University Press, 2010.

Dyer, Mollie. *Room for One More: The Life of Mollie Dyer.* East Melbourne, Victoria: Aboriginal Affairs Victoria, 2003.

Echo Hawk, Walter. *In the Courts of the Conquerors: The Ten Worst Indian Law Cases Ever Decided.* Golden CO: Fulcrum, 2010.

Fanshel, David. *Far from the Reservation: The Transracial Adoption of American Indian Children.* Metuchen NJ: Scarecrow Press, 1972.

Fessler, Ann. *The Girls Who Went Away: The Hidden History of Women Who Surrendered Children for Adoption in the Decades before* Roe v. Wade. New York: Penguin Press, 2006.

Fey, Harold E. "The Church and the Indian." *Christian Century* 72 (June 22, 1955): 728–30.

———. "The Indian and the Law." *Christian Century* 72 (March 9, 1955): 297–99.

———. "Indian Winter." *Christian Century* 72 (March 2, 1955): 265–67.

———. "Most Indians Are Poor." *Christian Century* (May 18, 1955): 592–94.

———. "Our National Indian Policy," *Christian Century* 72 (March 30, 1955): 395–97.

————. "Our Neighbor the Indian." *Christian Century* 72 (March 23, 1955): 361–64.

Fey, Harold, and D'Arcy McNickle. *Indians and Other Americans: Two Ways of Life Meet.* New York: Harper, 1959.

Fixico, Donald L. *Indian Resilience and Rebuilding: Indigenous Nations in the Modern American West.* Tucson: University of Arizona Press, 2013.

————. *Termination and Relocation: Federal Indian Policy, 1945–1960.* Albuquerque: University of New Mexico Press, 1986.

Flood, Renée Samson. *Lost Bird of Wounded Knee: Spirit of the Lakota.* New York: Scribner, 1995.

Fortunate Eagle, Adam. *Pipestone: My Life in an Indian Boarding School.* Norman: University of Oklahoma Press, 2010.

Fuchs, Estelle, and Robert J. Havighurst. *To Live on This Earth: American Indian Education.* Albuquerque: University of New Mexico Press, 1972.

Fuller, Alexandra. "In the Shadow of Wounded Knee." *National Geographic* 222, no. 2 (August 2012): 30–67.

Garrett, Matthew R. "Mormons, Indians and Lamanites: The Indian Student Placement Program, 1947–2000." PhD diss., Arizona State University, 2010.

Goldberg-Ambrose, Carole. *Planting Tail Feathers: Tribal Survival and Public Law 280.* Los Angeles: American Indian Studies Center, University of California—Los Angeles, 1997.

Gone, Joseph P., and Joseph E. Trimble. "American Indian and Alaska Native Mental Health: Diverse Perspectives on Enduring Disparities." *Annual Review of Clinical Psychology* 8 (2012): 131–60.

Graham, Judith. "Adoption Apology Too Late for Indians." *Chicago Tribune,* May 7, 2001. http://articles.chicagotribune.com/2001–05–07/news/0105070184_1 _indian-child-welfare-act-adoptive-bureau-of-indian-affairs/2 (accessed March 20, 2012).

Graham, Lorie. "Reparations, Self-Determination, and the Seventh Generation." In *Facing the Future: The Indian Child Welfare Act at 30,* ed. Matthew L. M. Fletcher, Wenona T. Singel, and Kathryn E. Fort, 50–110. East Lansing: Michigan State University Press, 2009.

Graybill, Andrew. *The Red and the White: A Family Saga of the American West.* New York: W. W. Norton, 2013.

Haebich, Anna. *Broken Circles: Fragmenting Indigenous Families, 1800–2000.* Fremantle, Western Australia: Fremantle Arts Centre Press, 2000.

————. *Spinning the Dream: Assimilation in Australia, 1950–1970.* Fremantle, Western Australia: Fremantle Press, 2008.

Hall, Sarah Moore. "A Sioux Mother Battles White In-Laws for her Child in the Bitter Case of Brokenleg v. Butts." *People* 11, no. 25 (June 25, 1979). http://www

.people.com/people/archive/article/0,,20073976,00.html (accessed July 20, 2013).

Harris, Aroha, and Mary Jane Logan McCallum, "'Assaulting the Ears of Government': The Indian Homemakers' Clubs and the Maori Women's Welfare League in Their Formative Years." In *Indigenous Women and Work: From Labor to Activism*, ed. Carol Williams, 225–39. Urbana: University of Illinois Press, 2012.

Harvey, Paul, and Philip Goff, eds. *The Columbia Documentary History of Religion in America since 1945*. New York: Columbia University Press, 2005.

Hepworth, H. Philip. *Foster Care and Adoption in Canada*. Ottawa, Ontario: Canadian Council on Social Development, 1980.

Herman, Ellen. *Kinship by Design: A History of Adoption in the Modern United States*. Chicago IL: University of Chicago Press, 2008.

Hertzberg, Hazel. *The Search for an American Indian Identity: Modern Pan-Indian Movements*. Syracuse NY: Syracuse University Press, 1982.

Horton, Carol A. *Race and the Making of American Liberalism*. New York: Oxford University Press, 2005.

Hostbjor, Stella. "Social Services to the Indian Unmarried Mother." *Child Welfare* 40, no. 5 (May 1961): 7–9.

Human Rights and Equal Opportunity Commission. *Bringing Them Home: Report of the National Inquiry into the Separation of Aboriginal and Torres Strait Islander Children from their Families*. Canberra: Commonwealth of Australia, 1997.

Indian Child Welfare Act of 1978, U.S. Code, vol. 25 (1978). Available online at http://www.tribal-institute.org/lists/chapter21_icwa.htm (accessed July 29, 2013).

"Indigenous Life Expectancy." Australian Institute of Health and Welfare, http://www.aihw.gov.au/indigenous-life-expectancy/ (accessed July 15, 2013).

Jackson, Helen Hunt. *A Century of Dishonor: A Sketch of the United States Government's Dealings with Some of the Indian Tribes*. Foreword by Valerie Sherer Mathes. Norman: University of Oklahoma Press, 1995.

Jacobs, Margaret D. "Breaking and Remaking Families: The Fostering and Adoption of Native American Children in Non-Native Families in the American West, 1880–1940." In *On the Borders of Love and Power: Families and Kinship in the Intercultural West*, ed. David Wallace Adams and Christa De Luzio, 19–46. Berkeley: University of California Press, 2012.

———. *Engendered Encounters: Feminism and Pueblo Cultures, 1879–1934*. Lincoln: University of Nebraska Press, 1999.

———. "Remembering the 'Forgotten Child': The American Indian Child Welfare Crisis of the 1960s and 1970s." *American Indian Quarterly* 37, nos. 1–2 (Winter–Spring 2013): 136–59.

————. *White Mother to a Dark Race: Settler Colonialism, Maternalism, and the Removal of Indigenous Children in the American West and Australia, 1880–1940*. Lincoln: University of Nebraska, Press, 2009.

Jagodinsky, Katrina. "'In a Family Way': Guarding Indigenous Women's Children in Washington Territory." *American Indian Quarterly* 37, nos. 1–2 (Winter–Spring 2013): 160–177.

Janovicek, Nancy. "'Assisting Our Own': Urban Migration, Self-Governance, and Native Women's Organizing in Thunder Bay Ontario, 1972–1989." In *Keeping the Campfires Going: Native Women's Activism in Urban Communities*, ed. Susan Applegate Krouse and Heather Howard, 56–75. Lincoln: University of Nebraska Press, 2009.

Jenkins, Philip. *Dream Catchers: How Mainstream America Discovered Native Spirituality*. New York: Oxford University Press, 2004.

Johnson, Lyndon Baines, U.S. President. "Special Message to Congress on the Problems of the American Indian: 'The Forgotten American.'" March 6, 1968. http://www.presidency.ucsb.edu/ws/index.php?pid=28709#axzz1tg4zchrR (accessed April 27, 2012).

Johnston, Elliott. *Royal Commission into Aboriginal Deaths in Custody: National Report*. Canberra: Australian Government Publishing Service, 1991. http://www.austlii.edu.au/au/other/IndigLRes/rciadic/ (accessed July 10, 2013).

Johnston, Patrick. *Native Children and the Child Welfare System*. Toronto: Canadian Council on Social Development–James Lorimer and Company, 1983.

Kelly, Lawrence. *The Assault on Assimilation: John Collier and the Origins of Indian Policy Reform*. Albuquerque: University of New Mexico Press, 1983.

Kilpatrick, Jacquelyn. *Celluloid Indians: Native Americans and Film*. Lincoln: University of Nebraska Press, 1999.

Kimelman, Edwin C., Associate Chief Judge and Chairman, Review Committee on Indian and Metis Adoptions and Placements. *No Quiet Place: Final Report to the Honourable Muriel Smith, Minister of Community Services, Manitoba*. Manitoba Community Services, 1985.

————. *Transcripts and Briefs*. Manitoba Community Services, 1985. Available at Legislative Library, Winnipeg.

Kluchin, Rebecca. *Fit to Be Tied: Sterilization and Reproductive Rights in America, 1950–1980*. New Brunswick NJ: Rutgers University Press, 2009.

Kreisher, Kristen. "Coming Home: The Lingering Effects of the Indian Adoption Project. *Children's Voice* (March 2002). http://www.cwla.org/articles/cv0203 indianadopt.htm (accessed June 12, 2012).

Krosenbrink-Gelissen, Lilianne E. "Caring Is Indian Women's Business, but Who Takes Care of Them? Canada's Indian Women, the Renewed Indian Act, and Its Implications for Women's Family Responsibilities, Roles, and Rights." In

*Law & Anthropology: International Yearbook for Legal Anthropology,* vol. 7, ed. René Kuppe and Richard Potz, 107–30. Dordrecht, Netherlands: Martinus Nijhoff Publishers, 1994.

Lawrence, Jane. "The Indian Health Service and the Sterilization of Native American Women." *American Indian Quarterly* 24, no. 3 (Summer 2000): 400–19.

"The Latest in the Social Genocide Field: Adoption of Indian Children by White Families." *Akwesasne Notes* 4, no. 4 (Summer 1972): 10–11.

Lee, Melvin. *Diagnosis and Treatment of Prevalent Diseases among North American Indian Populations.* Manchester NH: Irvington Publications, 1974.

LePage, Paul, Governor (Maine) and Native officials from Maine's five tribes. "Declaration of Intent" to begin a Truth and Reconciliation process, May 31, 2011. http://afsc.org/document/tribal-state-declaration (accessed May 20, 2013).

Lewis, Oscar. "The Culture of Poverty." *American* 215, no. 4 (October 1966): 19–25.

Lyslo, Arnold. "Adoption for American Indian Children," *Child Welfare* 39, no. 6 (June 1960): 32–33.

———. "Adoptive Placement of American Indian Children." *Catholic Charities Review* 51, no. 2 (February 1967): 23–25.

———. "Adoptive Placement of American Indian Children with Non-Indian Families, Part I: The Indian Project." *Child Welfare* 40, no. 5 (May 1961): 4–6.

———. "The Indian Adoption Project: An Appeal to Catholic Agencies to Participate." *Catholic Charities Review* 48, no. 5 (May 1964): 12–16.

Madley, Benjamin. "Patterns of Frontier Genocide, 1803–1910: The Aboriginal Tasmanians, the Yuki of California, and the Herero of Namibia." *Journal of Genocide Research* 6, no. 2 (June 2004): 167–92.

Manuel, George, and Michael Posluns. *The Fourth World: An Indian Reality.* New York: Free Press, 1974.

Marubbio, M. Elise. *Killing the Indian Maiden: Images of Native American Women in Film.* Lexington: University Press of Kentucky, 2006.

Mathews, John Joseph. *Sundown.* Norman: University of Oklahoma Press, 1981.

———. *Wah'kon-tah: The Osage and the White Man's Road.* 3rd ed. Norman: University of Oklahoma Press, 1981.

May, Elaine Tyler. *Homeward Bound: American Families in the Cold War Era.* New York: Basic Books, 1988.

MacGregor, Gordon. *Warriors without Weapons: A Study of the Society and Personality Development of the Pine Ridge Sioux.* Chicago IL: University of Chicago Press, 1946.

McEwen, E. R. *Community Development Services for Canadian Indian and Metis Communities.* Pamphlet of the Indian-Eskimo Association (IEA) of Canada. Toronto: IEA, 1968.

McNickle, D'Arcy. *The Surrounded*. 1936; Albuquerque: University of New Mexico Press, 1978.

Melosh, Barbara. *Strangers and Kin: The American Way of Adoption*. Cambridge MA: Harvard University Press, 2002.

Meriam, Lewis. *The Problem of Indian Administration: Report of a Survey Made at the Request of Hubert Work, Secretary of the Interior, and Submitted to Him, February 21, 1928*. Baltimore: Johns Hopkins Press, 1928.

Miller, J. R. *Shingwauk's Vision: A History of Native Residential Schools*. Toronto: University of Toronto Press, 1996.

———. *Skyscrapers Hide the Heavens: A History of Indian-White Relations in Canada*. 3rd ed. Toronto: University of Toronto Press, 2000.

Milloy, John S. *A National Crime: The Canadian Government and the Residential School System, 1879–1986*. Winnipeg: University of Manitoba Press, 1999.

Morey, Sylvester M., and Olivia L. Gilliam, eds. *Respect for Life: Report of a Conference at Harper's Ferry, West Virginia, on the Traditional Upbringing of American Indian Children*. Garden City NJ: Waldorf Press, 1974.

"The Mother and Child Reunion." *Native America Calling*, transcript of radio program, September 9, 2011. http://www.nativeamericacalling.com/nac_past.shtml (accessed November 16, 2011).

Moynihan, Daniel Patrick. "The Negro Family: The Case for National Action." March 1965. http://www.dol.gov/oasam/programs/history/webid-meynihan.htm (accessed June 26, 2012).

National Aboriginal and Islander Legal Services Secretariat Inc. "Brief of Amicus Curiae, in Support of the Appellant." *James Hudson Savage, Appellant vs. State of Florida, Appellee*, Case No. 75–494, in the Supreme Court of Florida. Filed October 12, 1990.

Neihardt, John. *Black Elk Speaks: Being the Life Story of a Holy Man of the Oglala Sioux*. William Morrow and Company, 1932; repr. Albany: State University of New York Press, 2008.

Newman, Erica. "'A Right to be Maori'? Identity Formation of Maori Adoptees." MA thesis, University of Otago, Dunedin, New Zealand, 2011.

———. "History of Transracial Adoption: A New Zealand Perspective," *American Indian Quarterly* 37, no. 2 (spring 2013): 237–57.

Nobles, Melissa. *The Politics of Official Apologies*. Cambridge UK: Cambridge University Press, 2008.

Ogata, Amy F. *Designing the Creative Child: Playthings and Places in Midcentury America*. Minneapolis: University of Minnesota Press, 2013.

Ortiz, Simon. *from Sand Creek*. Tucson: University of Arizona Press, 2000.

Pascoe, Peggy. *What Comes Naturally: Miscegenation Law and the Making of Race in America*. New York: Oxford University Press, 2009.

Peterson, Jeffrey. "Lostbirds: An Exploration of the Phenomenological Experience of Transracially Adopted Native Americans." PhD diss., University of Wisconsin, Madison, 2002.

Philp, Kenneth. *John Collier's Crusade for Indian Reform*. Tucson: University of Arizona Press, 1977.

Quintana, Frances Leon. *Ordeal of Change: The Southern Utes and Their Neighbors*. New York: AltaMira Press, 2004.

Ramirez, Renya. *Native Hubs: Culture, Community, and Belonging in Silicon Valley and Beyond*. Durham NC: Duke University Press, 2007.

Read, Peter. *A Rape of the Soul So Profound: The Return of the Stolen Generations*. St Leonards, New South Wales: Allen and Unwin, 1999.

———. "The Stolen Generations, the Historian, and the Court Room." *Aboriginal History* 26 (2002): 51–61.

Regan, Paulette. *Unsettling the Settler Within: Indian Residential Schools, Truth Telling, and Reconciliation in Canada*. Vancouver: University of British Columbia Press, 2010.

Reid, Jennifer. *Louis Riel and the Creation of Modern Canada: Mythic Discourse and the Postcolonial State*. Albuquerque: University of New Mexico Press, 2008.

Reyhner, John, and Jeanne Eder. *American Indian Education: A History*. Norman: University of Oklahoma Press, 2004.

Roherty, Catherine. *Exploratory Project on Outcome of Adoption of Indian Children by Caucasian Families*. Report to Division of Family Services. Madison WI: State Department of Health and Human Services, 1968.

Rolnick, Addie. "Adoptive Couple v. Baby Girl (1 of 4): Why the Court's ICWA Ruling Matters." Prawfsblog, June 29, 2013. http://prawfsblawg.blogs.com/prawfsblawg/2013/06/adoptive-couple-v-baby-girl-1-of-4-why-the-courts-icwa-ruling-matters-.html (accessed July 15, 2013).

Rosene, Linda Roberts. "A Follow-up Study of Indian Children Adopted by White Families." PhD diss., Fielding Institute, 1985.

Rosier, Paul. *Serving Their Country: American Indian Politics and Patriotism in the Twentieth Century*. Cambridge MA: Harvard University Press, 2009.

———. "'They Are Ancestral Homelands': Race, Place, and Politics in Cold War Native America, 1945–1961." *Journal of American History* (March 2006): 1300–26.

Saskatchewan Department of Welfare, *Annual Reports*, 1967–69.

State of Florida. "Answer Brief of Appellee." *James Hudson Savage, Appellant vs. State of Florida, Appellee*, Case No. 75, 494, in the Supreme Court of Florida. Filed January 10, 1991.

Shewell, Hugh. *"Enough to Keep Them Alive": Indian Welfare in Canada, 1873–1965.* Toronto: University of Toronto Press, 2004.

Shoemaker, Nancy. *American Indian Population Recovery in the Twentieth Century.* Albuquerque: University of New Mexico Press, 2000.

Shreve, Bradley. *Red Power Rising: The National Indian Youth Council and the Origins of Native American Activism.* Norman: University of Oklahoma Press, 2011.

Silberman, Arlene. "When Noel Came Home." *Good Housekeeping* 161 (1965), 80, 171.

Simon, Rita J., and Howard Alstein. *Adoption, Race, and Identity: From Infancy through Adolescence.* Westport CT: Praeger, 1992.

Sinclair, Raven. "All My Relations—Native Transracial Adoption: A Critical Case Study of Cultural Identity." PhD diss., University of Calgary, 2007.

Sinha, Vandha, Nico Trocmé, Barbara Fallon, Bruce MacLaurin, Elizabeth Fast, Shelly Thomas Prokop, et al. *Kiskisik Awasisak: Remember the Children—Understanding the Overrepresentation of First Nations Children in the Child Welfare System.* Ontario: Assembly of First Nations, 2011. Available at http://cwrp.ca/publications/2280 (accessed July 29, 2013).

"Sixties Scoop Class Action Lawsuit." http://sixtiesscoopclaim.com/ (accessed July 29, 2013).

Smith, Paul Chaat, and Robert Allen Warrior. *Like a Hurricane: The Indian Movement from Alcatraz to Wounded Knee.* New York: New Press, 1996.

Smith, Sherry. *Hippies, Indians, and the Fight for Red Power.* New York: Oxford University Press, 2012.

Solinger, Rickie. "Race and Value: Black and White Illegitimate Babies, 1945–1965." In *Mothering: Ideology, Experience, and Agency,* ed. Evelyn Nakano Glenn, G. Chang, and L. R. Forcey, 287–310. London: Routledge, 1994.

———. *Wake Up Little Susie: Single Pregnancy and Race before* Roe v. Wade. New York: Routledge, 1994.

Sommerlad, Elizabeth A. "Aboriginal Children Belong in the Aboriginal Community: Changing Practices in Adoption." *Australian Journal of Social Issues* 12, no. 3 (1977): 167–77.

Standing Bear, Luther. *Land of the Spotted Eagle.* 1933; repr. Lincoln: University of Nebraska Press, 2006.

State of Nebraska, Senate. Transcript, Health and Human Services Committee Meeting on Nebraska Indian Child Welfare Act. September 25, 2012.

Stremlau, Rose. *Sustaining the Cherokee Family: Kinship and the Allotment of an Indigenous Nation.* Chapel Hill: University of North Carolina Press, 2011.

Strong-Boag, Veronica. *Finding Families, Finding Ourselves: English Canada Encounters Adoption from the Nineteenth Century to the 1990s.* Don Mills, Ontario: Oxford University Press, 2006.

Stevenson, Allyson. "Vibrations across a Continent: The 1978 Indian Child Welfare Act and the Politicization of First Nations Leaders in Saskatchewan." *American Indian Quarterly* 37, nos. 1–2 (Winter–Spring 2013): 218–36.

Sullivan, Laura, and Amy Waters. "Native Foster Care: Lost Children, Shattered Families." Transcript of radio program, National Public Radio, October 25, 2011. http://www.npr.org/2011/10/25/141672992/native-foster-care-lost-children-shattered-families (accessed December 19, 2011).

Swain, Shurlee. "Child Rescue: The Emigration of an Idea." In *Child Welfare and Social Action in the Nineteenth and Twentieth Centuries*, ed. Jon Lawrence and Pat Starkey, 101–20. Liverpool, England: Liverpool University Press, 2001.

——. "'Homes Are Sought for These Children': Locating Adoption within the Australian Stolen Generations Narrative." *American Indian Quarterly* 37, nos. 1–2 (Winter–Spring 2013): 203–17.

Swenson, Janet P., ed. *Supportive Care, Custody, Placement and Adoption of American Indian Children*. Report from a National Conference sponsored by the American Academy of Child Psychiatry, April 19–22, 1977, Bottle Hollow, Utah. Washington DC: American Academy of Child Psychiatry, 1977.

Swenson, Janet P., and Gail Rosenthal, eds. *Warm Springs: A Case Study Approach to Recognizing the Strengths of American Indian and Alaska Native Families*. Washington DC: Academy of Child Psychiatry, 1980.

Task Force Four. *Report on Federal, State, and Tribal Jurisdiction*. Final report to American Indian Policy Review Commission. Washington DC: U.S. Government Printing Office, 1976.

Tiffin, Susan. *In Whose Best Interest? Child Welfare Reform in the Progressive Era*. Westport CT: Greenwood Press, 1982.

Timpson, Barbara. "Four Decades of Child Welfare Services to Native Indians in Ontario: A Contemporary Attempt to Understand the 'Sixties Scoop' in Historical, Socioeconomic and Political Perspective." PhD diss., Wilfrid Laurier University, 1993.

Tomlinson, John. *Is Band-Aid Social Work Enough?* Darwin, Australia: Wobbly Press, 1977.

Torpy, Sally J. "Native American Women and Coerced Sterilization: On the Trail of Tears in the 1970s." *American Indian Culture and Research Journal* 24, no. 2 (2000): 1–22.

Tucker, Margaret. *If Everyone Cared*. Sydney, Australia: Ure Smith, 1977.

Udel, Lisa J. "Revision and Resistance: The Politics of Native Women's Motherwork." *Frontiers* 22, no. 2 (2001): 43–62.

Ulrich, Roberta. *American Indian Nations from Termination to Restoration, 1953–2006*. Lincoln: University of Nebraska Press, 2010.

Unger, Steven. "The Indian Child Welfare Act of 1978: A Case Study." PhD diss., University of Southern California, 2004.

U.S. Department of Health and Human Services. *Results from the 2010 National Survey on Drug Use and Health: Summary of National Findings.* http://www .samhsa.gov/data/nsduh/2k1onSDUH/2k1oresults.htm#Fig3–2 (accessed July 10, 2013).

U.S. Department of the Interior. *Annual Report of the Commissioner of Indian Affairs.* Washington DC: Government Printing Office, 1952, 1954–60.

U.S. House of Representatives, Committee on Interior and Insular Affairs, Subcommittee on Indian Affairs and Public Lands, 95th Congress, 2nd Session. *Hearing on Indian Child Welfare Act of 1978 (S. 1214),* February 9 and March 9, 1978 (Serial No. 96–42). Washington DC: U.S. Government Printing Office, 1981.

U.S. Senate, Committee on Interior and Insular Affairs, Subcommittee on Indian Affairs, 93rd Congress, 2nd Session. *Hearing on Problems that American Indian Families Face in Raising their Children and How these Problems are Affected by Federal Action or Inaction,* April 8 and 9, 1974. Washington DC: U.S. Government Printing Office, 1975.

U.S. Senate, Select Committee on Indian Affairs, 95th Congress, 1st Session. *Indian Child Welfare Act of 1977: Hearing before the United States Select Committee on Indian Affairs, 95th Congress, First Session on S. 1214,* August 4, 1977. Washington DC: U.S. Government Printing Office, 1977.

Ward, Margaret. *The Adoption of Native Canadian Children.* Cobalt, Ontario: Highway Book Shop, 1984.

Weisiger, Marsha. *Dreaming of Sheep in Navajo Country.* Seattle: University of Washington Press, 2009.

Westermeyer, Joseph. "The Ravage of Indian Families in Crisis." In *The Destruction of American Indian Families,* ed. Steven Unger , 47–56. New York: Association on American Indian Affairs, 1977.

Weston, Mary Ann. *Native Americans in the News: Images of Indians in the Twentieth Century Press.* Westport CT: Greenwood Press, 1996.

White, Ken. *True Stories of the Top End.* Melbourne, Australia: Indra Publishing, 2005.

Williams, Carol, ed. *Indigenous Women and Work: From Labor to Activism.* Urbana: University of Illinois Press, 2012.

Wilkinson, Charles. *Blood Struggle: The Rise of Modern Indian Nations.* New York: Norton, 2005.

Wolfe, Patrick. "Land, Labor, and Difference: Elementary Structures of Race." *American Historical Review* 106, no. 3 (June 2001): 866–905.

Wright, Darrell Ian. "Negotiating Home: Four Children's Experiences in the Mormon Indian Student Placement Program." MA thesis, University of British Columbia, 2002.

Wuthnow, Robert. *The Restructuring of American Religion: Society and Faith since World War II*. Princeton NJ: Princeton University Press, 1988.

# Index

*Page numbers in italic indicate illustrations.*

assimilation policies: in Australia, 216, 222, 225; boarding schools and, 5–7; in Canada, 172; family models and, 26; resistance to, xxxiv–xxxv; settler colonial focus, xxxii–xxxiii, 258–59; through adoption, 19. *See also* relocation programs; termination policies

Association of American Indian and Alaskan Native Social Workers, 114

Association on American Indian Affairs (AAIA): Biltmore conference (1974), 133–37; Brokenleg case, xxv–xxvi; confronting the crisis, 98, 102–4, 105–6, 128; congressional hearings, 138–42; drafting child welfare legislation, 148–49; Lake Traverse Welfare Committee and, 122; on the LDS program, 303n74; legal work for families, 78, 104–5, 130–33; statistics supportive of ICWA, 155; strategies, 130; transnational exchanges, 205–6, 240, 244; work with Devils Lake Sioux mothers' delegation, 100–102

Atkinson, Graham, 242, 246

Attwood, Bain, 225

Aunty Di, 211–12

Australian Aborigines' League (AAL), 223–24

Australian Children's Week conference, 242

Australian Conference on Adoption (1976), 235

Balcom, Karen, 182

Bambiaga, Nola, 234

Barber, Barbara Ann, 251, 253, 255–56

Barrett, Robert, 97–100

Bear Comes Out, Mike, *275*

Beasley, Robert, 11

Bellanger, Pat, 297n34

"Beloved Child" concept, 118

Beltrami County (MN) Courts, 24

Bennett, Ramona, 108, 139, 154, 297n34

Benson County (ND) Welfare Board, 97, 98–100

Bergman, Robert "Bob," 137, 142

Berkshire Conference on the History of Women (2011), 95–96

BIA. *See* Bureau of Indian Affairs (BIA)

Big Boy, Marla Jean, xxvi

Bilchik, Shay, 268

Biltmore conference (1974), 133–37

Blackburn, Doris, 228

*Black Elk Speaks* (Neihardt), 41

Blair, Harold, 219

Blair Project, 219–20

Blanchard, Evelyn: author's visit with, 125–26; at the congressional hearings, 139, 146; on the government's power, 104; images of, *112, 113*; personal experience with removal, 111–12; as social worker, 108–9; transnational exchanges, 205–6; work with AAIA, 131, 137

blue-ribbon babies, 60–61, 218, 289n89

boarding schools: addressed in ICWA, 155; for Alaska Natives, 293n40; changing perspectives on, 16–17; closing of, 12–14; effects of on families, xxxiii–xxxiv, 115–16; origins of, xxxi

Bonilla-Silva, Eduardo, 51–52

Bonnin, Gertrude (Zitkala-Ša), xxxiv, 279n10

Bottle Hollow (UT) conference, 114–15, 118–19, 129–30, 138

Boychuk, Ernest, 194–95, 198–99, 202

*Bringing Them Home* (report), 265

child welfare reform movement (Canadian Indigenous): agreements reached with provincial governments, 208–10; Kimelman's inquiry into, 206–8; results of, 264; transnational exchange in, 204–6; women's role in, 264

child welfare services: in America, 6; in Australia, 215, 217–18; Australian Aboriginal-run, 235–37, 247–48; in Canada, 176; for non-Indigenous people, 29–30

Chivington, John, xxi

Choctaw Children's Bill of Rights, 119–20

Chosa, Mike, 139, 146

Christian, Wayne, 208–9

*The Christian Century* (magazine), 40–41

Christian religious groups: IAP's work with, 49; progressive views, 39, 42–46; Quakers, 46–47; role in relocation efforts, 45–46; social justice advocacy, 40; views on the "Indian problem," 42–48. *See also* LDS church

Chuck (Indian foster child), 16–17

churches. *See* Christian religious groups

Church of Jesus Christ Latter Day Saints. *See* LDS church

*Clampett v. Madigan*, 145

Clark, David, 45

Clements, Theresa, 224

Clinton, Hillary Rodham. *See* Rodham, Hillary

Cohen, Felix, 148

Cohen, Wilbur, 101–2

Collard, Judith, 320n86

Collier, John, xxxiv–xxxv, 7, 56

Colorado state welfare agency, 27

color-blind racial ideologies, 49–51, 61–62, 63, 173, 176–79, 307n31

Committee on Human Development (University of Chicago), 56

communities (American Indian): cultural life of, 3–4, 41; economic conditions in, 7; effects of child removal on, 31, 93; effects of termination on, 8–9, 10; genuine reconciliation with, 273–76; jurisdiction issues, 9–10; recovery and reunification in, 263–64; traditional structures of, 56–58; unwed motherhood in, 24–26; women's role in, 108, 110

communities (Australian Aboriginal): effects of child removal on, 232–34; portrayals of, 219, 220

communities (Canadian Indigenous): agreements reached with provincial governments, 208–10; governmental categorization of, 171–72; loss of cultural identity through child removal, 198–99; stereotypes of, 199–200

Congress, 8–10, 12, 13, 159. *See also* government (United States)

congressional hearings (1974), 138–47

congressional hearings (1977), 149–55

congressional hearings (1978), 155–57

consent forms (adoption), 73, 74–75, 294n44

Cook, Leon "Lee," 31, 127, 134, 135, 139

Cooper, William, 223

Council for Aboriginal Rights (CAR), 224

courts. *See* legal systems

cross-border adoptions. *See* transnational adoption

cultural assimilation. *See* assimilation policies

"The Culture of Poverty" (Lewis), 58

cultures (Indigenous): effects of child removal on, xxxiii–xxxiv, 77, 110,

258–59; loss of identity in, 93, 143–44, 198–99, 262–63; non-Indigenous interest in, 41, 285n11; survival of, 157

Cumeroogunga Aboriginal community, 223–24

custom marriages, 25, 53, 83

CWLA. *See* Child Welfare League of America (CWLA)

DAA (Department of Aboriginal Affairs), 235, 244–45

Dana (white adoptive mother), 33–35

Davey, Stan, 228–29

Davis, Mary, 54, 59

Day, Dianne, 211–12

Day, Muriel, 42

Day of Mourning (Australia), 223

"deadbeat Indian father" stereotype, 40, 53

DeCoteau, Cheryl Spider, *72*, 72–73, 140–41, *141*, 290n5

DeLaCruz, Joe, 108

Deloria, Sam, 90, 134, 160

Delorme, Mrs. B., 201

Denny, Goldie, 111, *112*, 114, 139, 150, 297n34

Department of Aboriginal Affairs (DAA), 235, 244–45

Department of Indian Affairs (DIA), 186

*The Destruction of American Indian Families* (Unger), 95

Devils Lake Sioux Indian tribe, 85–86, 97, 98–102, 121, 295n9

DIA (Department of Indian Affairs), 186

Diefenbacker, John, 170

dispersal policy (Australia), 223

Doan, Eloise Lahr, 105–6

Doss, Carl, 37–39, *38*

Doss, Donny, 37, *38*

Doss, Gregory, 37

Doss, Helen Grigsby, 37–39, *38*, 50–51, 61–62

Doss, Laurie, *38*

Doss, Richard, 37

Doss, Rita, *38*

Doss, Susan, *38*

Doss, Ted, *38*

Doucette, Marcien, 165–67, 169–70, 192–203, 204, 311n89

Doucette, Rita, 165–67, 169–70, 192–203, 204, 311n89

Doucette, Robert, 166–67, 192–93, 197–98, 202–3

Douglas, Mrs. Albert, 186

*Dr. Phil* (TV talk show), xxiii–xxiv

Dubinsky, Karen, 307n31

DuBois, Ben, 99–100

DuBois, Mary, 99–100

Ducheneaux, Frank, 129, 148

Durocher, Rod, 203

Dyer, Mollie, 211–12; activist work, 236–47; identifying child welfare crisis, 229–34; images of, *245*; personal experiences with removal, 225–28; Russell Moore case, 255, 256; transnational exchanges, 213–15, 239–41, 248

EchoHawk, Marlene, 129–30, 138

economics, 134, 145–47. *See also* poverty

education, 81, 88–89, 293n40

Eel River Massacre (1859), xxxii

elimination policies, xxxi–xxxiii

Elk family (adoptive grandparents), 84

Eskimo Indians, 171–72

Ewack, Rose, 184–85

extended family networks: breakdown of, 116; child-raising practices in, 53–54, 127; legal cases involving, 131–32;

Munro, Jenny, 226
Murawina program (Australia), 228

NAIWA (North American Indian Women's Association), 106–7
*National Survey on Drug Use and Health* (2010), 3
National Tribal Chairmen's Association, 108
Navajo Indian tribe, 13, 82, 87–88, 120–21, 152–53
*Navajo Times* (newspaper), 87–88
neglect: criteria for determining, 78–79, 81–82; defined, 29; discussed at Biltmore conference, 135; as justification for child removal, 77–79; misuse of criteria in child removal, 69–70, 230
"The Negro Family" (Moynihan), 58
Neihardt, John, 41
Nelson, Judith, 274–76
Nelson, Richard, 274–76
Nelson, Terence Wallace, 274–76
Nevada Readjustment Bill (HR 3239), 15–16
New Zealand's Maori people, 315n7
Nicholls, Doug, 223, 224, 226
Nimik, Joanne, 260
Nixon, Richard, 129
non-Aboriginal activists, 228–29, 234–35
non-Indian unwed mothers, 76
non-Indigenous people: genuine reconciliation requirements, 273–76; ICWA passage and changing perceptions of, 128, 154–55; interest in Indian culture, 285n11; postwar era perceptions of Indians, 3–4, 40–48
non-status Indians (Canadian Indigenous), 171–72
North American Indian Women's Association (NAIWA), 106–7

North Dakota social services, 23, 80, 98–102
Northwest Indian Women's Council, 108
NSW Aborigines Welfare Board, 216
nuclear family ideal, 26, 54, 85, 222
Nuwman, Alexine, 203

OEO (Office of Economic Opportunity), 129
Office of Economic Opportunity (OEO), 129
Ogata, Amy, 196
Oglethorpe, Laurel, 262
Ontario Ministry of Community and Social Services, 307n41
Ontario Select Committee on Civil Liberties, 173
Operation Relocation (BIA), 9, 45–46, 46–47, 80–81
Ortiz, Alfonso, 106
Ortiz, Simon, xxi–xxii

parental rights, 29–30, 73, *74, 75,* 140
Pascoe, Peggy, 50
pathology, 54, 56, 207, 249
Pennsylvania Child Welfare Services, 92
permanency of adoption, 54, 151, 202
Peterson, Jeffrey, 262
Pettit, Mrs., 219, 220
Pima reservation (AZ), 43–44
Pine Ridge (SD) Sioux, 3–4, 56–58
Pipestone Indian Boarding School (MN), 5, 6, 16
PL-280, 9–10, 136, 280n11
plight narratives, 40–42, 114, 157, 238. *See also* stereotypes
Polier, Justine Wise, 133
poverty, 39, 41, 42, 43, 58, 79–81
prejudice. *See* racism

press coverage. *See* media coverage

*The Problem of Indian Administration*
(report), xxxiv

progressive Christianity, 39, 42–46, 61–
62, 288n67

protests. *See* activism

public assistance. *See* welfare services

publicity campaigns. *See* advertising
campaigns

Public Law 280 (PL-280), 9–10, 136, 280n11

Public Law 587, 44


Quaker groups, 46, 268–69

Quetone, Allen, 84


Racette, Vicki, 188

racism: in adoption practices, 61–62, 63–
64; in Australia, 221–23; in Canada,
192–93; experienced by removed
children, 142–44, 214, 221, 222, 261–
62; liberalism's stand against, 38–39,
49–51; as opposition argument to
ICWA, 150–51; Russell Moore case,
252, 254

Ramirez, Renya, 156

Rappaport, Lawrence, 105, 130

REACH (Resources for Adoption of Children) program, 190, 204. *See also* AIM
(Adopt Indian Métis) program

Read, Peter, 256

reconciliation, 273–76

Red Lake (MN) Indian Reservation, 24,
280n11

Red Power activism, 128

Reeves, Barbara, 154

Reeves, Don, 154

Regan, Paulette, 266

Regina Native Women's Movement, 203

Regina SNWM women's center, 187

Reid, Joseph, 21, 23, 29, 49, 53

Reifel, Ben, 53

religion, 62, 218–19

religious groups: IAP's work with, 49;
Jewish Indian Adoption Program,
123–24, 292n31; progressive views, 39,
42–46; Quakers, 46–47; role in relocation efforts, 45–46; social justice
advocacy, 40; views on the "Indian
problem," 42–48. *See also* LDS church

relocation programs, 46–47; churches'
role in, 45–46; effect on Indian
families, 80–81; effects of on Indian
families, 116; following termination
policies, 8–9; opposition to, 292n20;
secular-run programs, 286n27

Rendon, David, 69–70

Rendon, Jason, 69–70

Rendon, Louisa, 69–70

reservations (American Indians). *See*
communities (American Indian)

residential schools (Canada), 172, 183–84,
266–67, 271

Richard, Mary, 183–84

Robbins, Maxine: at the Biltmore conference, 133–34, 136; extended family
history, 114; Ku-nak-we-sha project,
109–10; on reclaiming traditions,
118–19; transnational exchanges, 214,
241, 242–43, 245

Rockefeller, Nelson, 105

Rodham, Hillary, 144, 300n16

Roherty, Catherine, 63, 71, 143

Rolfes, Herman, 165, 166, 200–201

*Room for One More* (Dyer), 228

Roosevelt, Franklin D., xxxiv

Roosevelt, Theodore, 281n40

Rosebud Sioux tribe, 145

Rosier, Paul, 8

Roulette, Denise, 260
Rovin, Charles, 11
Rudd, Kevin, 266
Russell, Lynette, 211–12

Sanchez, Marie, 274–75
Sand Creek massacre, xxi
Sarracino, Victor, 117–18
Saskatchewan Conference of Indian Women, 184
Saskatchewan Department of Social Services, 194–203
Saskatchewan Native Women's Movement (SNWM), 185, 187–88, 189, 204, 309n63
Savage, Glenise, 260
Savage, Graeme, 252, 253–57, 260, 261, 262, 263, 323n3
Savage, James. *See* Moore, Russell
Savage, Nesta, 252, 253–57, 323n3
Sawyer, Diane, 3–4
Saxby, H., 216, 220
Schneeman, Gabrielle, 229
Schulz, Mrs., 221
Scooter, Nessie, 231
Secretariat of National Aboriginal and Islander Child Care (SNAICC), 247–48
Section 204 (ICWA), 153–54, 155
self-determination movement (American Indians): AAIA's work in, 106; AFSC's belief in, 46; Biltmore conference discussion of, 135; Collier's support of, xxxiv–xxxv; embodied in ICWA, 158; impact of child welfare reform movement on, 128–29; as solution to child welfare crisis, 160–61
self-determination movement (Australian Aboriginal): child welfare in, 225, 227–28, 229; effects of activism on,

224–25; historical roots of, 223–24; non-Aboriginal supporters of, 234–35; reclaiming care, 235–38; results of, 264; transnational exchanges in, 241–48
self-determination movement (Canadian Indigenous), 182–84
Senate hearings on ICWA, 59–60, 72, 138–47, 149–55
Senate Resolution 133, 147
Senate Select Committee on Indian Affairs, 149–55
Serena, Norma Jean, 92–93
settler colonial policies, xxxii, 31, 258–59
sexual abuse, 91, 261
Shearer, Heather, 246
Shewell, Hugh, 175
Shoulderblade, Margaret, *275*
Sinclair, Agnes, 203
Sinclair, Murray, 271
Sinclair, Raven, 263, 264
Singh, Diane, 211–12
Sisseton-Wahpeton Sioux tribe, 121–22
Smith, Susan, 262
Smithson, Thomas, 80
SNAICC (Secretariat of National Aboriginal and Islander Child Care), 247–48
SNWM. *See* Saskatchewan Native Women's Movement (SNWM)
social justice, 39, 43–44
social science field, 56–59
Social Security Act, 146, 291n18
social services. *See* welfare services
social workers: American Indian workers, 98, 108–10, 111, 114–19; biases against Indigenous families, 70, 144; critiqued in the Kimelman inquiry, 206–7; legal influence of, 142; standards for child removal, 70, 84–85; use of coercion, 72–77, 140